SPECTACLES
GREEK PHILOSOPHY

In fourth-century Greece (BCE), the debate over the nature of philosophy generated a novel claim: that the highest form of wisdom is *theoria*, the rational "vision" of metaphysical truths (the "spectator theory of knowledge"). This book offers an original analysis of the construction of "theoretical" philosophy in fourth-century Greece. In the effort to conceptualize and legitimize theoretical philosophy, the philosophers turned to a venerable cultural practice: *theoria* (state pilgrimage). In this traditional practice, an individual journeyed abroad to officially witness sacralized spectacles. This book examines the philosophic appropriations and transformations of the practice of *theoria*. It offers a detailed analysis of fourth-century conceptions of "theoretical" wisdom, using an approach which combines philosophy and new historicism. By examining the link between traditional and philosophic *theoria*, this book locates the creation of theoretical philosophy in its historical context and analyzes *theoria* as a cultural and an intellectual practice.

ANDREA WILSON NIGHTINGALE is an Associate Professor of Classics and Comparative Literature at Stanford University. She is the author of *Genres in Dialogue: Plato and the Construct of Philosophy* (Cambridge University Press, 1995), and has written numerous essays on Greek philosophy and culture. She is a recent recipient of Guggenheim and American Council of Learned Societies Fellowships.

SPECTACLES OF TRUTH IN CLASSICAL GREEK PHILOSOPHY

Theoria in its Cultural Context

ANDREA WILSON NIGHTINGALE

Stanford University

CAMBRIDGE
UNIVERSITY PRESS

CAMBRIDGE UNIVERSITY PRESS
Cambridge, New York, Melbourne, Madrid, Cape Town, Singapore, São Paulo, Delhi

Cambridge University Press
The Edinburgh Building, Cambridge CB2 8RU, UK

Published in the United States of America by Cambridge University Press, New York

www.cambridge.org
Information on this title: www.cambridge.org/9780521117791

© Cambridge University Press 2004

First published 2004
Third printing 2006
This digitally printed version 2009

A catalogue record for this publication is available from the British Library

ISBN 978-0-521-83825-2 hardback
ISBN 978-0-521-11779-1 paperback

For Carlo

Contents

Acknowledgments

First, I want to thank my magnificent mentor, Tony Long, who read this book twice in manuscript and offered invaluable comments and criticisms; words cannot express my gratitude to this brilliant teacher and generous friend. I am deeply grateful to my father, Douglas Wilson, who read the entire manuscript of this book in an early draft – this labor of love will always be remembered. Many thanks also to my dear friend Rush Rehm for his tireless work on this project and his courageous work as a political activist.

I would like to thank a number of scholars who have helped me think through the ideas in this book: Joseph Dunne, Bob Gregg, Sepp Gumbrecht, Robert Harrison, Michael Hendrickson, Peter Hawkins, Rachel Jacoff, Josh Landy, Richard Martin, Reviel Netz, and Natasha Peponi. In addition, I want to extend my thanks to Shadi Bartch, for sharing chapters from the manuscript of her forthcoming book; to Jas' Elsner, for sending me his spendid book and essays on pilgrimage; and to Ian Rutherford, for sharing his unpublished work with me, and for answering questions that I could not have answered myself.

I am especially grateful to Kathryn Morgan for her superb expertise and deep generosity. Also, heartfelt thanks to Alexander Nehamas, who offered vital support at the early stages of this project. Finally, I owe a lifelong debt to Oliver Taplin, who has generously supported this (and all) my projects.

I am, as always, grateful to my colleagues and students in Classics and Comparative Literature at Stanford (and especially to my superb research assistants, James Collins and Bill Gladhill).

I would like to thank my editor, Michael Sharp, for his insight and support. I am also grateful to my superb copy-editor, Linda Woodward. Finally, I want to thank the anonymous readers, who offered excellent advice and criticisms.

Eternal thanks to my beloved mother and father, Douglas and Diana Wilson; to my luminous sister, Fiona Theodoredis (and her children, Molly and Kai); to the everpresent Spook Nightingale; and to the Diablerets Massif in the Swiss Alps, on whose slopes this book was brought into the world, step by rocky step.

I am profoundly grateful to Charles Griswold for the great gift of his mind and heart. This book is lovingly dedicated to him.

I was honored to receive fellowships from the Guggenheim Foundation and the American Council of Learned Societies for the completion of this book. I am deeply grateful for their generous support.

Material from several portions of this book have appeared in print: "On Wondering and Wandering: *Theoria* in Greek Philosophy and Culture," *Arion* vol. IX (2001), 111–46, and "Aristotle on the 'Liberal' and 'Illiberal' Arts," in *Proceedings of the Boston Area Colloquium in Ancient Philosophy* 12 (1996) 29–58. Permission to reprint is gratefully acknowledged. An extract from the following published translation has been used in this work: ARISTOPHANES: VOL. II: PEACE. BIRDS. FROGS, Loeb Classical Library Vol. 179, translated by B. B. Rogers, Cambridge MA: Harvard University Press, 1924. The Loeb Classical Library ® is a registered trademark of the President and Fellows of Harvard College.

Introduction

Think of the long trip home./ Should we have stayed home and
thought of here? Where should we be today?/ Is it right to be watching
strangers in a play/ in this strangest of theatres?/ What childishness is
it that while there's a breath of life/ in our bodies, we are determined
to rush/to see the sun the other way around?

Elizabeth Bishop, "Questions of Travel"

Questioning attains its own ground by leaping.

Heidegger, Introduction to Metaphysics

Italo Calvino's dazzling book, *Mr. Palomar*, offers a portrait of postmodern
ways of seeing. Its hero, Mr. Palomar – named after a famous telescope –
spends his time conducting experiments in viewing and contemplating
the world around him.[1] In a chapter entitled "The Contemplation of the
Stars," Palomar ventures out to look at the heavens "in order to detach
himself from the earth." In this endeavor, Palomar deliberately follows the
example of the ancient Greeks who, he believes, achieved knowledge and
tranquillity from this exercise. He goes to the darkness of a nearby beach
and, after spending half an hour perusing his astronomical charts, settles
down to study the stars.

This activity, however, turns out to be quite complicated: "to decipher
a chart in the darkness he must also bring along a flashlight. The frequent
checking of sky against chart requires him to turn the light on and off, and
in the passages from light to darkness he remains almost blinded and has to
readjust his vision every time" (43). In addition, Palomar wears eyeglasses
to read, which means that he must put them on to study the charts and
remove them to look at the sky:

In other words, to locate a star involves the checking of various maps against the
vault of the sky, with all the related actions: putting on and taking off eyeglasses,

---

[1] Calvino 1985, 37–48 ("The Eye and the Planets" and "The Contemplation of the Stars").

turning the flashlight on and off, unfolding and folding the large chart, losing and finding again the reference points.

Instead of discovering the "exact geometry of the sidereal spaces" that the ancients found, Palomar sees a complicated and confused picture in which "everything seems to escape him." The heavens look unstable and contradictory, and he ends up distrusting what he knows: "oppressed, insecure, he becomes nervous over the celestial charts, as over railroad timetables when he flips through them in search of a connection" (47). Contemplating the stars leads to anguish rather than tranquillity, and Palomar's effort to emulate the ancients is thus thwarted. After spending several hours in this vain endeavor, Palomar stops and looks around: he now sees that a group of people have gathered around him to watch his frenzied activities, "observing his movements like the convulsions of a madman" (48).

In this vignette, Calvino performs a postmodern reading of an ancient tale: Plato's Analogy of the Cave, the foundational story of enlightenment. In books 5–7 of the *Republic*, Plato introduced a new kind of sage – a philosophic theorist "in love with the spectacle of truth." Plato describes in lavish detail how the philosopher detaches himself from the earthly world and journeys into the radiant realm of "reality." When he enters this region, the philosopher is at first blinded by the light of the sun that shines there. His eyes slowly adjust to this light, and eventually he can gaze directly upon the beings in the metaphysical realm, including the sun-like Form of the Good. He now sees that the shadow-figures in the cave were (at best) copies of the true beings in this realm, and that this region is the locus of true reality. With reluctance, he goes back into the cave and is initially blinded by its darkness. When he returns, the people who dwell there say that the journey has destroyed his vision; they mock him and think that he has lost his mind.

Calvino captures some central aspects of this famous story of philosophical theorizing. First, he reveals that Plato's tale is as much about blindness as it is about insight. For, like Plato's theorist, Calvino's Palomar experiences intermittent periods of blindness in his efforts to see and study the heavens. And he also blinds himself on a larger level, since he turns away from the human world to search for fixed truths (deliberately emulating the detachment of the ancients). Here, Palomar closely resembles his model, for the Platonic philosopher detaches from society in his quest for knowledge, and suffers from bouts of blindness as he journeys out of, and back into, the cave. Finally, like his Platonic predecessor, Palomar appears to the ordinary person as a mad fool. In both stories, the theorist is himself the object of public perception: other people see his blindness (but not, as it seems, his insight). In the Analogy of the Cave, the philosopher is not of course practicing astronomy. But the philosopher's effort to turn his gaze from darkness to light, from images to real beings, is wonderfully refigured in Palomar's move from star charts to stars, from artificial to heavenly light. Calvino also reminds us that Plato's Analogy is about heat as well as light – about passion and yearning as well as seeing. Palomar longs for the tranquillity that accompanies stable knowledge: he longs for the absence of longing, the end of wonder. He seeks *sophia* rather than *philosophia* – wisdom without its love. But Palomar ends in frustration and failure, whereas the Greek theorist transcends *aporia*, *eros*, and wonder. Or does he?

The Greek thinkers of the fourth century BCE were the first to call themselves philosophers, the first to define philosophy as a specialized discipline and a unique cultural practice. Creating the professional discipline of philosophy required an extraordinary effort of self-definition and legitimation. In addition to developing ideas and arguments, these philosophers had to stake out the boundaries of their discipline and articulate the ways that it differed from other modes of wisdom. Plato, Aristotle, and other fourth-century thinkers all matched themselves against traditional "masters of truth" even as they developed different conceptions of philosophy in competition with one another. In this period, the debate over the true nature of philosophy – and thus the highest form of knowledge – was lively and contentious. This foundational debate generated (among other things) a novel and subversive claim: that the supreme form of wisdom is *theoria*, the rational "vision" of metaphysical truths.

In the effort to conceptualize and legitimize theoretical philosophy, the fourth-century thinkers invoked a specific civic institution: that which the ancients called "*theoria*." In the traditional practice of *theoria*, an individual (called the *theoros*) made a journey or pilgrimage abroad for the purpose of witnessing certain events and spectacles.[2] In the classical period, *theoria* took the form of pilgrimages to oracles and religious festivals. In many cases, the *theoros* was sent by his city as an official ambassador: this "civic" *theoros* journeyed to an oracular center or festival, viewed the events and spectacles there, and returned home with an official eyewitness report. An individual could also make a theoric journey in a private capacity: the "private" *theoros*, however, was answerable only to himself and did not need to publicize his findings when he returned to the city. Whether civic or private, the practice

---

[2] I analyze the cultural practice of *theoria* in chapter 1. I use the masculine pronoun throughout this book when referring to the *theoros*, since *theoria* (both traditional and philosophical) was predominantly – though not exclusively – practiced by males.

of *theoria* encompassed the entire journey, including the detachment from home, the spectating, and the final reentry. But at its center was the act of seeing, generally focused on a sacred object or spectacle.[3] Indeed, the *theoros* at a religious festival or sanctuary witnessed objects and events that were sacralized by way of rituals: the viewer entered into a "ritualized visuality" in which secular modes of viewing were screened out by religious rites and practices.[4] This sacralized mode of spectating was a central element of traditional *theoria*, and offered a powerful model for the philosophic notion of "seeing" divine truths.

The comparison of philosophical activity to *theoria* at religious festivals was not a casual rhetorical trope: this move had powerful ideological associations. For, by linking philosophical theorizing to an institution that was at once social, political, and religious, the fourth-century thinkers identified theoretical philosophy as a specific kind of cultural practice. By aligning their discipline with the traditional practice of *theoria*, the fourth-century thinkers attempted to ground theoretical philosophy in the social and political world. The philosophers claimed a specific place for theoretical activity in the polis, even though metaphysical contemplation *per se* detaches the theorist for a time from the social world. Indeed they explicitly raised the question of the role of the intellectual in civic and political affairs (a question that is still very much with us today). As I will suggest, all of the fourth-century philosophers located the contemplative activities of the theorist within the context of political life (albeit in very different ways). The detached activity of theoretical contemplation is, they claim, central to the life of a flourishing polis.[5]

Plato – who was the first to conceptualize philosophic "theorizing" – made full use of the model of traditional *theoria*, with its journey abroad, viewing of a spectacle, and subsequent return home. In the *Republic* 5–7 – the most detailed account of *theoria* in the Platonic corpus – Plato models philosophic *theoria* on the traditional practice of civic *theoria*.[6] In this kind of *theoria*, the *theoros* journeys forth as an official witness to a spectacle, and then returns as a messenger or reporter: at the end of the journey, he gives a verbal account of a visual, spectacular event. The journey as a whole, including the final report, is located in a civic context. In Plato's

---

[3] The Greek word *theoria* means, in its most literal sense, "witnessing a spectacle."

[4] As Elsner (2000) argues. I will discuss the notion of "ritualized visuality" in chapter 1.

[5] This does not mean that the people of the fourth century actually accepted the philosophers' claims (though some politicians did study with these men). See Humphreys 1978, ch. 9 for an analysis of the changing role of the intellectual in archaic and classical Greece.

[6] As we will see, in other texts Plato describes the theorist as living a private, nonpolitical life. I discuss Plato's different accounts of *theoria* in chapters 2–4.

*in which sense ÷ O. a philosophy altered
by his primacy of theoria ?.*

account of philosophic *theoria* in the *Republic*, theoretical activity is not confined to the rational contemplation of the Forms; rather, it encompasses the entire journey, from departure to contemplation to reentry and reportage. The intellectual "seeing" at the center of the journey – which I call "contemplation" – is thus nested in a larger context which is both social and political. As Plato claims, the philosophic theorist will, when he returns, "give an account" of his vision which is open to inspection and to questioning. In addition, he will translate his contemplative wisdom into practical and (under certain conditions) political activities: his theoretical wisdom provides the basis for action. In the good city, moreover, the theoretical philosophers will rule the polis: here, Plato places the philosophic theorist at the very center of political life.

According to Plato, the philosopher is altered and transformed by the journey of *theoria* and the activity of contemplation. He thus "returns" as a sort of stranger to his own kind, bringing a radical alterity into the city. When the philosopher goes back to the social realm, he remains detached from worldly goods and values even when he is acting in the world. Even in the ideal city, the philosopher is marked by detachment and alterity – he possesses a divine perspective that is foreign to the ordinary man. This peculiar combination of detachment and engagement allows the Platonic theorist to perform on the social stage in a fashion that is impartial, just, and virtuous.

Philip of Opus (a member of Plato's Academy) offers a quite different account of philosophic *theoria*: his philosophic theorist contemplates the stars. As he argues, the true philosopher engages in the activity of astronomical *theoria*, in which he beholds and apprehends "visible gods" in the heavens. This activity cultivates the virtue of piety, which has a direct impact on practical and political action. Paradoxically, viewing and studying the heavens makes the philosopher a supremely good and virtuous man on earth. Like Plato, Philip claims that *theoria* provides the only proper grounding for political *praxis*: the theoretical philosopher can and should govern the city. But Philip diverges from Plato by directing the theoretical gaze to the physical heavens rather than the metaphysical Forms.

To these fourth-century theorists, Aristotle responds with a bold new claim: *theoria* does not lead to *praxis*. Narrowing the scope of theoretical philosophy, Aristotle identifies *theoria* as an exclusively contemplative activity. In fact, he even separates the processes of learning and demonstration from the activity of *theoria*. To be sure, the theorist will attempt to argue and account for his findings, but this is not considered part of the *theoria*.

Rather, *theoria* is a distinct activity that is an end in itself, completely cut off from the social and political realm.

In his accounts of *theoria*, Aristotle retains the traditional notion of sacralized spectating, but he does not link this activity to the world of politics or *praxis*. Aristotle's theorist, in short, does not bring his wisdom into practical or political life. Indeed, as Aristotle claims, theoretical knowledge is completely "useless" (*achreston*) in the practical sphere: the philosopher engages in *theoria* for its own sake, as an end in itself.[7] Where, then, does Aristotle locate the theorist within the polis? He certainly does not believe that the philosopher should rule or lead a political life. Rather, as he claims in the *Politics* (books VII–VIII), the polis as a whole should orient itself towards the education and leisure that allows the wisest men to engage in theoretical activity.[8] Since business and politics are directed towards the higher goal of leisure, the good constitution should aim to promote noble leisure activities for citizens in the polis. According to Aristotle, the best and most proper leisure activity is that of philosophic *theoria*, since the perfection of intellectual virtue is the ultimate *telos* of the human being. Ultimately, practical and political activities should serve the higher purpose of creating the conditions for philosophic *theoria*, which is the best form of human activity. The good polis, then, must strive to bring about the full actualization of human capacities, even if only a few men can achieve this goal (i.e. the theoretical philosophers). Theoretical activity is thus given a unique and privileged place in the life of the city.

The fourth-century proponents of theoretical philosophy turned to the traditional practice of *theoria* in their efforts to conceptualize and artic-ulate a new mode of wisdom. In aligning themselves with a venerable cultural practice, the philosophers claimed legitimacy and authority for philosophic *theoria*. They appropriated the traditional practice of *theoria* by translating the physical journey to a sanctuary into a metaphysical quest for truth: wandering was reconceived as wondering, physical seeing as intel-lectual "gazing." Fourth-century thinkers such as Plato, Philip of Opus, and Aristotle claimed that the philosophic theorist (*theoros*) gazes with the "eye of reason" upon divine and eternal verities.

---

[7] See chapter 5. In this book, I focus on Aristotle's explicit discussions of *theoria* in the *Protrepticus*, *NE*, and *Metaphysics* (and his analysis of *nous* in the *De Anima*). Aristotle often uses the verb *theorein* to signify "seeing" or "observing" in the most general sense, and occasionally uses the noun *theoria* to identify any sort of observation or investigation. I will confine my study to his explicit discussions of contemplative *theoria*.

[8] As Yack (1991, 23) rightly argues, "although the polis is prior to the individual, according to Aristotle, it still exists for the sake of the good life led by individuals; individuals do not exist for the sake of the perfection of the polis."

The fourth-century philosophers differed quite strongly in their epistemological, psychological, ethical, and political theories. Yet all believed that wisdom takes the form of "seeing" truth. In this book, I will examine the Greek conception of the philosopher as a "spectator" – an idea that has had a profound impact on Western thinking. How did the fourth-century philosophers articulate and defend this new conception of knowledge? What is at stake, philosophically and politically, in identifying the philosopher as a sort of seer, detached from the physical and social world while he contemplates the verities? How and what does the philosophic theorist see? How (if at all) can the disembodied apprehension of truth be embodied and enacted in the practical realm? Where does the theoretical philosopher position himself vis-à-vis the political life of the city? In this study, I am not attempting to offer a philosophic analysis of fourth-century epistemology. Rather, I will investigate the foundational construction of theoretical philosophy in its intellectual and its cultural context, and explore the philosophical and historical ramifications of this momentous development.

There were of course many cultural factors and conditions involved in this radical reconception of wisdom in the fourth century: the implementation and impact of the technology of writing; aristocratic self-fashioning in democratic Athens and its opposition to democratic "wisdom"; the professionalization of numerous disciplines and occupations in fourth-century Greece; the creation of schools of higher education; and the decline of the city-state and the rise of imperial politics (which placed elites and intellectuals in a new position vis-à-vis the systems of power). In addition to analyzing the different philosophical constructions of *theoria* in the fourth century, then, we need to attend to the cultural and historical context in which this development occurred.

THEORIZING THE ANCIENT THEORISTS

In the modern and postmodern periods, philosophers and scholars have analyzed and attacked "the spectator theory of knowledge" from many different angles; in general, they identify Platonic and Aristotelian epistemology (and Cartesian dualism) as the primary culprits in this philosophic enterprise. Most twentieth-century thinkers, of course, view Greek metaphysical philosophy with suspicion if not scorn. The conception of knowledge as *theoria* is, for some, a cowardly flight from the world of action and, for others, a pernicious power-grab posing as disinterested speculation. Modern attacks on the "spectator theory of knowledge" and its claims to objectivity have been numerous and diverse, ranging from

phenomenologists such as Husserl, Heidegger, and Merleau-Ponty to pragmatists such as Dewey and Rorty, to poststructural and psychoanalytic
theorists such as Foucault, Derrida, Lacan, and Irigaray. Nonetheless, the
nature and scope of "visual thinking" – and various forms of "the gaze" –
continue to be analyzed in many different disciplines.[9]

Nietzsche articulates, concisely and trenchantly, some of the key claims in
the modern (and postmodern) attack on the spectator theory of knowledge:

> Let us be on guard against the dangerous old conceptual fiction that posited a
> "pure, will-less, painless, timeless knowing subject"; let us guard against the snares
> of such contradictory concepts as "pure reason," "absolute spirituality," "knowledge
> in itself": these always demand that we should think of an eye that is completely
> unthinkable, an eye turned in no particular direction, in which the active and
> interpreting forces, through which alone seeing becomes seeing *something*, are
> supposed to be lacking; these always demand of the eye an absurdity and a nonsense.
> There is *only* a perspective seeing, *only* a perspective "knowing" . . . But to eliminate
> the will altogether, to suspect each and every affect, supposing we were capable of
> this – what would that mean but to *castrate* the intellect?[10]

Here, Nietzsche rejects (1) the notion of the disembodied intellect, (2)
the conception of a non-perspectival viewpoint, (3) the claim that we can
apprehend objective truths not constructed or affected by the human mind,
and (4) the belief in a mode of cognition separated from will, desire, and
the emotions.

This is powerful rhetoric, but it hardly does justice to the Greek theorists.
In Plato's conception of *theoria*, theoretical knowledge is a sort of "hot
cognition" (to borrow Damasio's term) in which eros and the affect of
wonder play a key role in the activity of contemplation.[11] Plato hardly
"castrates" the intellect: on the contrary, *theoria* is fueled and sustained by
erotic desire. In addition, Plato believes that theoretical philosophers can,
at best, achieve only a partial view of the Forms – a view that is distorted (in
differing degrees) by the ontological and ethical limitations of their souls.
In order to "see" reality, in fact, the philosopher must become blind to
the human world: theoretical vision is by no means panoptic. While Plato
does not, of course, argue for a perspectival or constructivist conception

---

[9] See, e.g., Rorty 1979, Jonas 1966, Levin 1988 (and the essays in his 1993a volume), Foster 1988, Jay
   1993, Goldhill 1996, 1999a, Crary 1999. For a discussion of the gaze in Roman culture, see Bartch
   forthcoming (she analyzes the gaze in connection with eroticism and self-knowledge).
[10] *Genealogy of Morals* III, 12 (trans. Kaufmann).
[11] The neurologist Damasio (2000) offers a powerful demonstration of the role that emotions play
   in the rational activities of the human brain. Opposing himself to Descartes and other Western
   philosophers who have detached reason from desire and the emotions, Damasio argues that cognition
   and ratiocination are invariably dependent on and accompanied by emotional processes (hence the
   phrase "hot cognition").

of knowledge, his human philosopher never achieves a perfect, "frontal" view of the Forms.[12] Finally, side by side with Plato's "official" account of theoretical contemplation as a disembodied activity focusing exclusively on metaphysical objects, we find another account that does not exclude the body from philosophic theorizing. For, in some dialogues, Plato argues that the visual perception of beautiful bodies – both human and celestial – plays a vital role in the activity of *theoria*. We are far, indeed, from Nietzsche's "will-less" subject with an "eye turned in no particular direction."

Most modern and postmodern critics of Greek *theoria* also emphasize the "spectatorial distance" that allows the subject to stand over against the object and apprehend it in a neutral and undistorted fashion: "objective truth" is achieved by reifying the object and keeping it separate from the viewing subject. As Hans Jonas claims, because of the spectatorial distance involved in seeing, the subject avoids direct engagement with the object; this separation of the subject from the object, in fact, produces

the very concept of objectivity, of the thing as it is in itself as distinct from the thing as it affects me, and from this distinction arises the whole idea of *theoria* and theoretical truth.[13]

Building on this notion of the subject gaining an "objective" (neutral, undistorted) grasp of its object, many thinkers have made the additional claim that theoretical "vision" *objectifies* the things it sees – it views the things in the world as objects available for the viewer's use and control. Thus Levin (a neo-Heideggerian) claims that vision is "the most reifying of all our perceptual modalities"; this reification, he adds, encourages the subject to control and dominate the object:

to the extent that the will to power captures our capacity for vision, there is a strong inveterate tendency in our vision to fixate whatever our eyes behold, to "bring it to a stand," a standstill, in our grasp and hold . . . Since the characer of our everyday vision is such that we tend to reify, to substantialize, and to totalize, philosophical thinking, increasingly under the sway of a vision-based and vision-centered paradigm, represents itself as standing positioned in a relation of *opposition* to being.[14]

---

[12] And, when he "returns" (again and again) to the human world, he does engage in a constructivist project, for he must then attempt to create verbal and practical "imitations" of the Forms in the earthly realm – to represent truth in words and deeds. For the notion of the "frontal" view, see Levin (1988, *passim* and 1993a, esp. 202–3), who follows Heidegger in his criticism of ancient conceptions of truth and knowledge.

[13] Jonas 1966, 147.

[14] Levin 1988, 65; 1993a, 202. Heidegger's meditations on seeing and theorizing are in fact far more complex than Levin's (and they evolved as his philosophy matured). For an excellent account of Heidegger's discussions of the Greek conceptions of *theoria*, see McNeill 1999.

Not surprisingly, once one brings in the will to power, it is but a short step to Derrida's assertion of "the ancient clandestine friendship between light and power, the ancient complicity between theoretical objectivity and technico-political possession."[15]

I do not want to discuss the many and incisive attacks on the enterprise of Western metaphysics. Let me simply point out that these critiques of "ocularcentrism" are more pertinent to Cartesian thinking (and, correlatively, to modern science) than to Greek theorizing. In stark contrast to the Cartesian tradition, the Greek theoretical philosophers sought to change themselves rather than the world around them. Indeed, the theoretical understanding of metaphysical objects was far from a neutral, scientific apprehension achieved at a distance: rather, the Greek theorist *distanced himself from the world* in order to achieve a *proximity to metaphysical objects*. Greek theorizing was based on the kinship – rather than the distance – between subject and object. Because of this kinship, the theorizing mind could grasp and even identify with metaphysical objects. In this activity (which was itself driven by a "desire to know") the theorist experienced a powerful *pathos*: a transformation of self and soul.

What, then, is the nature of this pathology? Let us look briefly at the fourth-century theories of physical vision that provided the analogue for theoretical "vision."[16] In the *Timaeus*, Plato claims that human beings possess "light-bearing eyes" (φωσφόρα . . . ὄμματα) – eyes that contain a "pure fire which is akin (ἀδελφόν) to the light of day" (45b). This internal light

flows through the eyes (διὰ τῶν ὀμμάτων ῥεῖν) in a smooth and dense stream . . . and whenever the stream of vision is surrounded by daylight, it flows out like unto like, and by coalescing with this it forms a single body (σῶμα) along the eyes' visual path, wherever the fire which streams out from within makes contact with that which meets it from without. (45c–d)

The human perceiver, then, sends forth the light contained in the eye beyond the boundaries of his body out into the world: the eye's "light" flows forth like a tentacle and meets with the "light of day," which is akin to it.[17] Because of this kinship, the eye's light is able to coalesce with sunlight to form a "single body" of light. When this chain of light comes into contact with things in the world, it "distributes the motions of every object" to the

---

[15] Derrida 1978, 91.
[16] For discussions of ancient optical theories, including those of Plato and Aristotle, see Beare 1906, Ronchi 1957, Lindberg 1976, 6–9, Burnyeat 1976, and Simon 1988.
[17] It is "similar in its properties because of its similar nature" (45d).

body and soul of the perceiver.[18] Seeing, then, is not the passive reception of external impressions or effluences but a participatory activity in which the human being interacts with its object in the medium of light. In fact, vision occurs when the subject reaches out and, in some sense, "touches" the object. The perceiver's visual faculty does not, however, become identical with either the light or the object of vision. Rather, the kinship between the "light-bearing eyes" and the external light allows for the perception of the quite different essence of the object.

While Plato's theory combines extramission and intromission, Aristotle rejects both of these alternatives. In the *De Anima*, Aristotle claims that vision takes place through the transparent medium of light, which stretches from the object to the interior of the human eye. The sense faculty itself must not touch the object – for if one puts an object right up against the eye, the person will not be able to see. Sight can only take place through the medium of light: the object affects the light and, through this medium, the form of the object reaches the sense faculty.[19] According to Aristotle, in perception, an alteration takes place in the perceiver: the sense faculty is acted upon by the object and becomes what that object is "in actuality."[20] Or, to be more precise, this faculty becomes identical with the *form* of the object, for the sense-organ receives sensible forms without their matter (424a–425b, 435a). As Aristotle suggests, "during the process of being acted upon the sentient faculty is unlike, but when it has been acted upon it is assimilated to that object and shares its quality" (418a5–6).[21] According to this theory, the perceiver does not send forth emanations but rather receives the form of the sense-object through the transparent medium of light. The sense faculty, then, becomes identical to the forms of things in the world:

---

[18] Plato does not say what the "motions" of the object are, but he suggests in the *Theaetetus* (156d) that the object, as well as the eyes, sends forth emissions: the eyes emit light and the object emits corpuscles (both of which emissions "are carried around in the space between" viewer and viewed).

[19] *De Sensu* 11.438a–b, *De Anima* 418a–419a, 432a, 435a. Aristotle offers a different account of vision in the *Meteorology*, where he subscribes to the theory of the extramission of visual rays (2.9.370a–3.4.374b; cf. *De Insomniis*, 11.459b–460a). On Aristotle's theory of vision, see Sorabji 1974 and 1992, Lear 1988, 101–16, Silverman 1989, Burnyeat 1992, Nussbaum and Putnam 1992, Everson 1997, 24–5, 115–16 and *passim*.

[20] *DA* 416b33–5, 417a6–20, 418a3–4. According to Aristotle, that which is capable of perception (*to aisthetikon*) is potentially what the sense-object (*to aistheton*) is in actuality (*DA* 418a3–4).

[21] Whether the alteration in the perceiver is material or nonmaterial (or both) is a matter of debate: Aristotle never quite explains how the human mind becomes aware of a sensible perception. Burnyeat (1992) argues for a nonmaterial account of vision (perceiving requires no concomitant material change): all that is involved in the sense faculty's taking on the sensible form is the person's becoming aware of its object; cf. Sorabji 1974 and 1992, Nussbaum and Putnam 1992. Lear (1988, 110–11) argues that neither a purely material account nor a purely mental account is adequate. I favor Nussbaum and Putnam's position.

this is not a matter of touching or intermingling (as in Plato) but rather of actual identification.

Both Plato's and Aristotle's theories of physical vision illuminate their conceptions of rational or mental "vision" (though Aristotle pushes the analogy between the operation of physical and mental vision further than Plato). In Plato, the light of the Form of the Good makes metaphysical "seeing" possible. Illuminated by this light, the human soul contemplates the Forms, which are ontologically distinct from it: while metaphysical beings are "akin" to *nous* and for that reason intelligible, they are not identical to the rational part of the soul. The living, moving soul seeks to apprehend unitary and unchanging beings that differ from it in kind; yet this apprehension is made possible by a basic kinship between reason and metaphysical realities. Aristotle, by contrast, claims that the mind has the potentiality to become what its objects are in actuality. Here, there is no "spectatorial distance" at all: in the activity of *theoria*, the philosopher's noetic faculty becomes identical with its object.

In philosophic *theoria*, as I have suggested, wandering is translated into wondering. Philosophy originates in wonder and *aporia* and aims for certainty and knowledge. How does the human mind relate and respond to the reality it apprehends? In Plato, the philosopher contemplates divine realities that are "kindred" to the soul but are nonetheless different in kind. When the soul encounters the Forms, it grasps both its kinship to and difference from "reality." By virtue of this kinship, the mind is able to apprehend the Forms, but it also recognizes the ontological uniqueness of these divine beings and thus experiences a powerful sense of awe and wonder. Plato's foundational conception of *theoria*, then, is grounded in a peculiar paradox: when the philosophical theorist achieves a vision of true being, he experiences knowledge and wonder simultaneously. In "seeing" and apprehending metaphysical reality, the Platonic theorist develops a sort of reverential knowledge: wisdom accompanied by wonder and awe.[22] In addition, the soul's encounter with "Being" also leads to an understanding of the soul's own nature, boundaries, and capacities. In its ongoing attempts to "see" the Forms, the soul grasps its own nature and limitations by apprehending both its kinship to and difference from these timeless, changeless beings.

For Aristotle, the activity of *theoria* is separate from that of inquiring, learning, and wondering: we may identify it as *sophia* rather than *philosophia*. According to Aristotle, the philosopher "escapes" from wonder

---

[22] See chapter 6 for a full discussion of this issue.

and perplexity when he "theorizes the cause" (τεθηωρηκόσι τὴν αἰτίαν, *Met.* 983a14–15). When the philosopher "theorizes" or "sees" the cause, he moves from perplexity to knowledge and his wonder comes to an end. Philosophy, then, begins in wonder and culminates in *theoria*. What sort of knowledge does the Aristotelian theorist achieve? Aristotle claims that *theoria* is characterized by the activity and actualization of *nous*, the divine faculty in man. The ultimate object of the theorizing mind is divine *nous* (the primary substance and cause in the universe).[23] In theorizing the first cause, then, the theorist's noetic faculty becomes identical (for a time) with divine being. By engaging in *theoria*, the theorist actualizes his highest and most divine faculty – the part of man that is, as Aristotle claims, his true self.[24]

It may seem paradoxical to suggest that *theoria* – the rational apprehension of objective truth – has anything to do with the human "self." In fact, theoretical contemplation is an activity that transcends the individual's personal perspective and interests. As Gadamer observes:

Greek metaphysics conceives the essence of *theoria* and of *nous* as being purely present to what is truly real, and for us too the ability to act theoretically is defined by the fact that in attending to something one is able to forget one's own purposes . . . *Theoria* is a true participation, not something active but something passive (*pathos*), namely being totally involved in and carried away by what one sees . . . Considered as a subjective accomplishment in human conduct, being present has the character of being outside oneself . . . this kind of being present is a self-forgetfulness, and to be a spectator consists in giving oneself in self-forgetfulness to what one is watching.[25]

How can we attribute selfhood to the "self-forgetful" soul? How can the theorist – who is blind to the world as he contemplates eternal beings – achieve any sort of self-understanding? The fourth-century philosophers went in search of new kinds of selves.[26] In particular, they reexamined the boundaries between the human and the divine, positing a kinship between human *nous* and divine and metaphysical beings. Departing from traditional Greek views, these philosophers introduced the notion of a theorizing

---

[23] I will discuss this in detail in chapter 5.

[24] In *NE* x, 1178a2–4, Aristotle claims that *nous* is the true self; in choosing the life of *theoria*, he says, a man chooses the life that belongs "to himself rather than to another." See also *NE* ix, 1166a16–17.

[25] Gadamer 1960/1990, 126–7.

[26] Heraclitus – who "went in search of [him]self" (fr. 101 DK) – was the first thinker to explicitly address the question of the "limits" of the soul (fr. 45) and to reconceive the human self as coextensive with a world that transcends the human individual. For an excellent discussion of Heraclitus' conception of the "self," see Long 1992, 266–75 (see also Annas 1985, 127–9). The fourth-century philosophers articulated a similar idea, but their theorizing "selves" were completely metaphysical.

self, which they defined in relation to metaphysical and divine beings and to the rationally organized cosmos. In placing the human being in this (new) relation to the divine, these philosophers developed a conception of human identity that was not socially or environmentally defined. Of course Plato and Aristotle fully understood that we are composite creatures that live in the terrestrial realm: their constructions of the theorizing "self" did not blind them to the fact that the embodied human being is defined in relation to the social and natural world. But, by identifying the human self with the best that is in him – the rational faculty – the ancient philosophers invited people to conceive of themselves (and the world) in a whole new way.

THEORIA IN ITS CULTURAL CONTEXT

In his portrait of Palomar contemplating the stars, Calvino makes fun of the nostalgic contemplative and affirms the contemporary understanding of human perception that so radically separates us from the Greek philosophers. Indeed, throughout *Mr. Palomar*, Calvino repeatedly reminds us that the human' viewpoint is subjective and perspectival – that the viewer "constructs" what he sees and thus can never achieve the objectivity and truth to which the Greeks laid claim (and which Palomar vainly seeks). Calvino's comic tale might seem to suggest that the Greek philosophers were rather simple and naive. The very opposite is true: these thinkers grappled with sophisticated arguments for skepticism, relativism, and cultural pluralism; and, in the city of Athens, they confronted the aims and claims of "democratic wisdom," with its consensualist and egalitarian ideology.[27]

The ancient conceptions of philosophic *theoria* are much more complex and sophisticated than modern and postmodern interpreters have allowed. In fact, the philosophers of the fourth century set forth a number of different conceptions of *theoria* (responding, among other things, to pragmatist attacks on the theoretical enterprise): our modern and postmodern contestations of ancient *theoria* overlook the fact that this idea was contested from the very beginning. Rather than grouping these theories together under the heading of "ocularcentrism" or "the spectator theory of knowledge," we need to analyze the different versions of *theoria* offered in the fourth century and to locate these first theories of "theory" in their intellectual and sociopolitical context. From its inception, theoretical philosophy was a discipline characterized by an ongoing dialogue with voices

---

[27] For an excellent discussion of "democratic wisdom," see Ober 1998.

both inside and outside the academy: the theorists picked a quarrel with traditional ideologies and practices even as they fought energetically for cultural capital.[28] From the very beginning, then, theoretical philosophy was a dialogical enterprise: its discourse was multivocal, even when it dreamed of univocity.

In attempting to understand the construction of "theoretical wisdom" in its historical context, we must remember that the fourth-century philosophers were (among other things) powerful polemicists making a serious bid for cultural capital. They claimed legitimacy, authority, and status in the culture at large and instituted the first schools of higher education as centers of "knowledge." If one looks at intellectual life in the fourth century as a whole, one can see that the philosophers were participating in a broad-scale effort to create a new, cosmopolitan elite identified by culture and education. This effort of elite self-fashioning was, at least in part, directed against democratic ideology and practice. In the fourth-century Athenian democracy, power and money were no longer the markers of elite superiority; indeed it was possible for any citizen to acquire wealth and political influence. Since the aristocrats did not have an exclusive claim to property or political power in this period, many looked for other ways to distinguish themselves from their inferiors (especially the upwardly mobile).[29] The possession of a liberal or philosophical education served this purpose, since it identified the elite by recourse to criteria other than wealth or power.[30]

In addition to being great thinkers, Plato, Aristotle, and their associates were also great rhetoricians: against tremendous odds, they sought to persuade people that the theoretical philosopher is the most free, noble, and happy human being. This individual is a new kind of *aristos*, and is identified and defined by traditional aristocratic markers. In particular, the claim that *theoria* is nonproductive, leisured, and fully free directly reflects the aristocratic ideology of classical Greece. All of the fourth-century philosophers define *theoria* in opposition to "banausic" activities and manual forms of labor (though each philosopher uses this rhetoric in a different way). And all identify theoretical philosophy as the only truly "free" activity, contrasting it with the "servile" pursuits of lesser individuals. Aristotle goes even further, arguing that theoretical activity is completely impractical and

---

[28] On Plato's "dialogical" definition and practice of philosophy, see Nightingale 1995.

[29] See, e.g., Aristotle *NE* II, 1107b16–20, IV, 1122a28–33, and especially IV, 1123a18–27 (on these and related passages, see Von Reden 1995, 85 and Nightingale 1996b, 32–3).

[30] As Raaflaub (1983, 534) has shown, the rhetoric of "illiberal" and "liberal" arts and activities (which included those of "philosophy") was part of a larger ideology constructed by aristocrats hostile to democracy.

nonproductive. To be sure, these philosophers deploy aristocratic rhetoric in order to elevate themselves above traditional aristocrats; they do not simply pay lip-service to aristocratic ideology. But their use of this rhetoric reveals the elitist, antidemocratic aspect of theoretical philosophy in its foundational constructions.

Of course there were other important factors that contributed to the construction of the discipline of theoretical philosophy in the fourth century.[31] One should note, in particular, the institution of philosophical schools and the increasing use and dissemination of written texts. These new forms of promulgating wisdom introduced a system of intellectual and cultural exchange quite different from that operating in the sixth or fifth centuries. In founding the first school of "philosophy" (*circa* 393 BCE), Isocrates created an educational institution permanently settled in one place which, offered a lengthy and systematic course of study.[32] This new institutional form offered the possibility of extensive intellectual interchange in a private and leisured environment. Soon after Isocrates, Plato founded the Academy, using the Pythagorean *thiasos* or religious brotherhood as a model; refusing to take fees, Plato created an organization devoted to the cult of the Muses. Finally, in the 330s, Aristotle established his own philosophical school in the Lyceum.[33] People from all over the Greek world – including many powerful and influential men – came to study at these schools, many of whom were attracted by the written works of these philosophers. These institutions of learning conferred on the philosophers an established position and great prestige in the Greek world, thus rendering it unnecessary for them to travel abroad or perform in public to attract students.

In addition, because of the spread of literacy in the fourth century, the dissemination of written texts could take the place of verbal displays of wisdom.[34] The need for public performances of wisdom was thus reduced if not eliminated. Clearly, a written text could travel the Greek world far

---

[31] In the fourth century, a different kind of elite began to emerge, one defined by (higher, specialized) education rather than by aristocratic lineage, wealth, or power.

[32] Like the sophists, Isocrates charged a fee for his teaching (1,000 drachmas for a 3–4 year course of study), but he was neither a traveler nor a performer: students came to Athens from all over Greece to enroll in his school.

[33] Initially the Lyceum was housed in public buildings (since Aristotle, as a metic, could not own property in Athens), but Theophrastus (Aristotle's successor as the head of the Lyceum) bought property near the grove and created a permanent place for the school. For a detailed discussion of Aristotle's school, see Lynch 1972.

[34] On the extent of literacy in classical Athens and the ways in which writing was used in this period, see Harris 1989, ch. 4, Thomas 1989, ch. 1 and 1992, ch. 7. Of course many philosophers who disseminated ideas in writing felt anxiety about the efficacy of this new technology (see, e.g., Alcidamas "On the Sophists," Plato, *Phaedrus* 275d–e, Isocrates *To Philip* 25–7).

more easily than its author. The disembodied word had the advantage of communicating across great distances and creating a community of readers that transcended civic politics. At the same time, writing facilitated the presentation of long and technical arguments and gave readers a chance to study and respond to difficult ideas.[35] The fact that Plato and Aristotle attracted pupils from all over Greece would suggest that their writings were widely disseminated.[36] By reaching beyond the boundaries of their own cities, these philosophers communicated with like-minded, educated Greeks, thus contributing to the formation of an elite community of cultured intellectuals.

THE CREATION OF THE PHILOSOPHIC THEORIST

How did the fourth-century philosophers conceptualize "theoretical" wisdom and define it as an intellectual practice? The central metaphor used in the philosophic literature of this period was that of spectating at a religious festival. We find an excellent example of the philosophic use of this metaphor in a fragment of Heraclides of Pontus (a member of Plato's Academy), which is summarized by Cicero. In this passage, Heraclides draws an explicit parallel between the *theoros* at the Olympic games and the philosophic theorist, who contemplates "the nature of things":[37]

The life of man resembles the festival [at Olympia] celebrated with the most magnificent games before a gathering collected from all of Greece. For at this festival some men trained their bodies and sought to win the glorious distinction of a crown, and others came to make a profit by buying or selling. But there was also a certain class, made up of the noblest men, who sought neither applause nor gain, but came for the sake of spectating and closely watched the event and how it was done.[38]

---

[35] Though Goody and Watt (1968) go too far in claiming that the technology of writing caused the conceptual shift that made philosophic thinking possible (see also Havelock 1963). Lloyd (1987, 70–83) offers a compelling response to Goody and Watt's thesis.

[36] For a discussion of the readership of Plato and Isocrates in the fourth century, see Usener 1994, 74–119, 174–230.

[37] Heraclides puts this idea in the mouth of Pythagoras, thus retrojecting this fourth-century conception of wisdom back onto the ancients and investing it with a venerable pedigree (as Jaeger 1923/1948, Appendix, Burkert 1960 and Gottschalk 1980, 29–33 have demonstrated; cf. Joly 1956, 22 and *passim*). I will discuss this revisionist move in more detail below.

[38] Cicero, *Tusculan Disputations* v.3: *esset autem quoddam genus eorum idque vel maxime ingenuum, qui nec plausum nec lucrum quaererent, sed visendi causa venirent studioseque perspicerent quid ageretur et quo modo.* A similar account is found in Iamblichus' *Life of Pythagoras* 58 (though this does not mention Heraclides as the author). Gottschalk (1980) offers a complete study of the extant fragments of Heraclides; he discusses Heraclides' "Image of the Festival" (and the dialogue in which it was included) in ch. 2.

Here, Heraclides depicts three groups of individuals gathered at the Olympian festival: the competitors, who seek glory and honor; the businessmen, who pursue wealth; and the *theoroi*, who go to the festival simply "for the sake of spectating." This latter group provides the model for the theoretical philosophers. For, as Heraclides claims, the philosopher resembles "the most liberal man at the Olympic festival, who spectates without seeking anything for himself" (*liberalissimum esset spectare nihil sibi acquirentem*). The "noble" philosophers, Heraclides says, are "a special few who, counting all else as nothing, studiously contemplate (*intuerentur*) the nature of things." In this passage, then, Heraclides claims that the activity of contemplative "spectating" is disinterested, noble, and liberal: the philosophical theorist engages in the contemplation of metaphysical realities as an end in itself.

Aristotle uses this same "festival image" in his popularizing dialogue, the *Protrepticus*:

Wisdom is not useful or advantageous (χρησίμη . . . μηδ' ὠφέλιμος), for we call it not advantageous but good, and it should be chosen not for the sake of any other thing, but for itself. For just as we go to the Olympian festival for the sake of the spectacle (θέας), even if nothing more should come of it – for the *theoria* (θεωρία) itself is more precious than money; and just as we go to theorize (θεωροῦμεν) at the Festival of Dionysus not so that we will gain anything from the actors (indeed we pay to see them) . . . so too the *theoria* (θεωρία) of the universe must be honored above all things that are considered to be useful (χρησίμων). For surely we should not go to such trouble to see men imitating women and slaves, or athletes fighting and running, and not consider it right to theorize without payment (θεωρεῖν ἀμισθί) the nature and truth of reality. (B44)[39]

Here, Aristotle compares the philosophic "theorist" to the *theoros* who goes to a festival to see dramatic, musical, or athletic competitions. Aristotle emphasizes that both do this "for the sake of the spectacle" rather than for profit or gain, though he clearly elevates the philosophic theorist above the ordinary *theoros* (who views the inferior spectacles of drama and athletics). The philosophic *theoros* contemplates "the nature of truth and reality," pursuing this as an end in itself rather than for goal-oriented, utilitarian purposes. For this reason, philosophic *theoria* is not "useful or advantageous" and does not offer any "payment" or wage in the external world – rather, it is a completely free and leisured activity. Like Heraclides, Aristotle claims that the theorist does not seek personal profit but engages in an activity that is noble, impractical, and disinterested.[40]

---

[39] In this book, I will use Düring's edition of the *Protrepticus*, with his numeration of the fragments.
[40] I will discuss Aristotle's *Protrepticus* in detail in chapter 5.

As these passages reveal, Heraclides and Aristotle defined *theoria* in opposition to practical activities: contemplation was starkly contrasted with economic transactions or political affairs. The theoretical philosopher, when
he engages in contemplation, is disembedded from the social and political
systems of exchange in the city and engages in transactions in a completely
different sphere. The construction of this opposition between contemplation and action led, in turn, to the distinction between the theoretical and
the practical (or political) life, and the question whether *theoria* had any
purchase in the practical realm.[41] Numerous philosophers in the fourth
century discussed and debated these issues. As we will see, some thinkers
in this period, cleaving to traditional notions of wisdom, championed the
life of practical and political "virtue"; others extolled a life that combines
contemplative and political activities; and yet others valorized the purely
contemplative life.

Aristotle provides evidence of the fourth-century debate over this issue
in the *Politics*. In book VII, he outlines a contemporary controversy over
the question whether one should choose

the life of politics and action (ὁ πολιτικὸς καὶ πρακτικὸς βίος) or rather a life
detached from all external affairs, for example a theoretical life (θεωρητικός),
which some say is the only life for the philosopher (τινές φασιν εἶναι φιλοσόφου).
(VII.2, 1324a25–9)

Here, Aristotle links together politics and moral *praxis* – the man living this
kind of life displays his practical virtue in the political arena.[42] Aristotle sets
this in opposition to the "theoretical life," which has little if any involvement
in "external affairs" but aims, instead, at contemplative wisdom. He also
reports that some thinkers consider that the purely contemplative life is
the *only* one for philosophers; we may infer that other advocates of *theoria*
consider intellectual contemplation the principle but not the exclusive aim
of the philosophical life. Note that the distinction between the two kinds
of life hinges on the participation in or detachment from political affairs –
the practical life involves "active citizenship and participation in politics,"
whereas the theoretical life is "that of a foreigner, detached from political
participation" (ὁ διὰ τοῦ συμπολιτεύεσθαι καὶ κοινωνεῖν πόλεως . . . ὁ

---

[41] Note that some fifth-century texts (e.g. Euripides' *Antiope, Ion*, and *Hippolytus*) set forth the idea
that a quietist life is superior to the life of politics. In this period, quietism was associated with
"musical" or religious activity rather than philosophy (indeed, as I have argued, "philosophy" had
not yet been constructed as a specialized discipline). See, e.g., Joly 1956, Carter 1986 (I discuss the
debate over the political and "musical" life in the *Antiope* in Nightingale 1995, ch. 2).

[42] See also *NE* x.7–8.

ξενικὸς καὶ τῆς πολιτικῆς κοινωνίας ἀπολελυμένος).[43] The contemplative philosopher, according to this account, lives as a *"xenikos"* – a (virtual) foreigner who is a sort of stranger in the polis.

Having set forth this debate in general terms, Aristotle examines the arguments used to bolster these positions:

> Some reject the idea of holding political offices in the city, believing that the life of the free man is different from that of the political man and the most choiceworthy of all; others consider the political life superior on the grounds that a man who does nothing cannot do well, and doing well and happiness are the same thing.[44]

The proponents of the theoretical life, then, use "freedom" as the marker of the good and happy life; by "freedom" they mean leisure and detachment from external exigencies and constraints (rather than mere political freedom). Advocates of the practical life, on the other hand, identify "action" as the marker of the good life; the theorists, they say, are "doing nothing" and thus can't be said to live well. Aristotle admits that both sides have some claim to truth; in the end, however, he argues for the superiority of the theoretical life:

> The active life is not necessarily active in relation to other people, as some men think, nor are only those thoughts active that are pursued for the sake of the things that result from action, but far more [active] are those theoretical ideas and thoughts that are ends in themselves and pursued for their own sake.[45]

Here, Aristotle rejects the pragmatists' argument by claiming that *theoria* is eminently "active" even though it does not aim at external results or goals and is done "for its own sake."[46]

Aristotle does not refer to the participants in this debate by name, but we can certainly identify some of the major players. Of the extant fourth-century authors, Isocrates champions practical and political over theoretical philosophy, Plato and Philip argue that the philosophic life combines

---

[43] *Politics* VII.2, 1324a15–17.
[44] οἱ μὲν γὰρ ἀποδοκιμάζουσι τὰς πολιτικὰς ἀρχάς, νομίζοντες τόν τε τοῦ ἐλευθέρου βίον ἕτερόν τινα εἶναι τοῦ πολιτικοῦ καὶ πάντων αἱρετώτατον, οἱ δὲ τοῦτον ἄριστον, ἀδύνατον γὰρ τὸν μηδὲν πράττοντα πράττειν εὖ, τὴν δ'εὐπραγίαν καὶ τὴν εὐδαιμονίαν ταὐτόν (VII.3, 1325a18–23).
[45] ἀλλὰ τὸν πρακτικὸν οὐκ ἀναγκαῖον εἶναι πρὸς ἑτέρους, καθάπερ οἴονταί τινες, οὐδὲ τὰς διανοίας εἶναι μόνας ταύτας πρακτικάς, τὰς τῶν ἀποβαινόντων χάριν γιγνομένας ἐκ τοῦ πράττειν, ἀλλὰ πολὺ μᾶλλον τὰς αὐτοτελεῖς καὶ τὰς αὐτῶν ἕνεκεν θεωρίας καὶ διανοήσεις (VII.3, 1325b16–21).
[46] Aristotle adds that cities are "active" even when isolationist; and god is active even though he has no external activities.

contemplation and virtuous action (which is based on theoretical wisdom), and Aristotle detaches *theoria* from *praxis*, ranking the theoretical life as the best and happiest.[47] As fragmentary evidence attests, Heraclides of Pontus, Theophrastus, and Dicaearchus also weighed in on this issue, and no doubt many other figures participated in the debate whose names have been lost (e.g. the author of the *Magna Moralia*). Cicero, for example, tells us that Dicaearchus and Theophrastus (both members of Aristotle's Lyceum) took opposite sides in the controversy, the former championing the practical life and the latter the theoretical life.[48]

As I have suggested, some men participating in this debate advocated a pragmatist programme that was diametrically opposed to the claims of the "theorists." These thinkers aligned themselves with traditional Greek notions of wisdom, explicitly opposing the newly invented discipline of theoretical philosophy. One of the most influential proponents of pragmatism was Isocrates, who offered a direct response to the arguments for *theoria* issuing from the Academy and Lyceum. In the *Antidosis*, for example, Isocrates reports that most men believe that philosophers who are "skilled in disputation or in astronomy, geometry, and things of that sort" are doing nothing but "prattling and splitting hairs, since none of these things is useful (χρήσιμον) either in private or in public life" (261–2). Isocrates goes on to agree that these studies are useless (μηδὲν χρησίμην . . . τὴν παιδείαν ταύτην, 263), and claims that the name "philosopher" should not be given to these abstract thinkers "who ignore the things that are necessary" (τοὺς δὲ τῶν μὲν ἀναγκαίων ἀμελοῦντας, 284–5). In fact, he argues, one should only give this title to "those who learn and practice the studies which will enable them to manage wisely their private households and the commonwealth of the city, since it is for the sake of these things that one should work, philosophize, and act" (285). Isocrates thus champions a pragmatic, antitheoretical brand of philosophy explicitly designated as "useful" and geared towards the "necessary" aspects of human life: he exalts his own wisdom precisely by reference to its relevance for practical and political life.[49]

---

47 Though the theorist will of course engage in practical activities insofar as he is a human being – a "composite" of body and soul.
48 *Letters to Atticus*, 11.16: *tanta controversia est Dicaearcho, familiari tuo, cum Theophrasto, amico meo, ut ille tuus* τὸν πρακτικὸν βίον *longe omnibus anteponat, hic autem* τὸν θεωρητικόν . . .
49 According to Einarson (1936, 272–8), Aristotle's *Protrepticus* was a direct response to Isocrates' arguments in the *Antidosis*; the fact that both authors use the same terminology of "useful/useless," "necessary/unnecessary" is indeed striking (see also Eucken 1983 for a more detailed discussion of Isocrates' response to the positions adopted in the Academy and the Lyceum).

FOURTH-CENTURY "REVISIONINGS" OF THE EARLY GREEK THINKERS

The development of *theoria* in the fourth century marked a significant departure from previous theories and intellectual practices. Scholars have not fully acknowledged this shift, in part because the fourth-century philosophers themselves represented theoretical philosophy as an ancient, time-honored practice. In making this revisionist move, they claimed that early thinkers such as Thales, Pythagoras, and Anaxagoras were engaging in *theoria* and living the "theoretical" life – i.e. the life of detached, non-political contemplatives. But, as earlier sources attest, these (and other) preplatonic thinkers were highly political and pragmatic *sophoi*. As I will argue, the fourth-century philosophers retrojected their own conception of theoretical wisdom back onto the ancients and thus invested it with a venerable pedigree.[50] This projection of fourth-century conceptions of philosophy onto earlier Greek thinkers has the effect of concealing the radical paradigm shift that occurred in this period.

We find an excellent example of this revisionist move in Aristotle's *Protrepticus*. According to Aristotle, Pythagoras and Anaxagoras were philosophers whose sole purpose was to contemplate and, indeed, to "theorize" the heavens:

For what end did nature and god bring us into being? Pythagoras, when asked this question, said, "to behold the heaven" (θεάσασθαι . . . τὸν οὐρανόν) and he also claimed that he was a *theoros* of nature (θεωρόν . . . τῆς φύσεως) and that he had come into being for this purpose. And when someone asked Anaxagoras for what end he would choose to exist and live, he said "for the sake of beholding (θεάσασθαι) the heaven and the stars and the moon and sun," since all other things were worth nothing (τῶν ἄλλων γε πάντων οὐδενὸς ἀξίων ὄντων) . . . Whether the cosmos is the object of this knowledge or some other nature, we must inquire later; but this is sufficient as a beginning. (B18–20)

These early Greek thinkers, Aristotle asserts, practiced theoretical philosophy and considered this the highest form of wisdom. Note, however, the slight qualification in the last line: Pythagoras and Anaxagoras contemplated the physical cosmos rather than metaphysical objects (which, from Aristotle's perspective, is a primitive form of *theoria*).

---

[50] As Jaeger 1923/1948, Appendix, Burkert 1960, and Gottschalk 1980, 29–33 have demonstrated; cf. Joly 1956, 22 and *passim*.

Aristotle expresses a similar idea in the *Nicomachean Ethics* book VI:

People say that men such as Anaxagoras and Thales are wise (*sophoi*) but not prudent (*phronimoi*) when they see them displaying their ignorance of things that are advantageous to themselves; they believe that these men possess a knowledge that is rare, marvellous, difficult, and divine, but that it is useless because they do not seek things that are good for human beings. (VI.7, 1141b)

Here, Aristotle draws a stark contrast between the wise (*sophos*) and the prudent (*phronimos*) man in order to illustrate the differences between theoretical and practical wisdom.[51] In this passage, Aristotle claims that Thales and Anaxagoras pursued the theoretical life of "useless" contemplation and paid no attention to earthly affairs. Aristotle thus portrays his predecessors – all of whom were famous for their practical and political activities – as proto-theorists who turned their back on the human world to contemplate higher realities.

Plato makes a similar move in the "digression" in the *Theaetetus*, where he draws a stark contrast between the contemplative philosopher and the politician (172c–176d). In this passage, Socrates reports that Thales fell into a well while gazing at the stars because he didn't see what was at his feet (174a–b). Once again, we find a fourth-century text representing an ancient sage as a philosophic contemplative.[52] Here, Thales is stargazing rather than engaging in metaphysical *theoria* (though his practice of astronomy was no doubt based on expertise in mathematics). Although Socrates does not explicitly identify him as a "theorizer" (by using the terminology of *theoria*), he clearly represents Thales as living an exclusively contemplative life. In fact, this passage depicts, for the first and only time in Plato, an impractical philosopher who is completely ignorant of human affairs: he doesn't know his neighbors, doesn't notice what he is doing, and "scarcely knows whether he is a man or some other kind of creature" (174b).[53] Indeed, this philosopher experiences complete *aporia* in the human world, since

---

[51] Although Aristotle credits some unnamed "people" with this view, he appears to agree with their basic position.

[52] One might think that the *Hippias Major* 281c offers a similar account of earlier thinkers. Here, Socrates says that most of the early wise men down to Anaxagoras kept clear of politics. But he is almost certainly being ironic, for he has just mentioned Pittacus, Bias, and Thales, who were famous for their political activities.

[53] Even the otherworldly *Phaedo* does not suggest that the philosopher, while on earth, is or should be impractical and ignorant of human affairs. We must remember that, in the *Phaedo*, the ideal of "practicing death" is set forth by Socrates – a philosopher who pursues a practical form of wisdom and who has extensive interactions with the city and people of Athens. Note also the claim at the opening of the *Sophist* that the true philosopher comes in many guises, including that of the sophist and statesman (216c–d).

"only his body lives and sleeps in the city" while his mind wings its way up into the heavens (173e–174a).

I do not believe that Plato endorsed this extreme form of contemplative philosophy. Rather, he includes in his dialogue a conception of philosophy – no doubt embraced by some contemporary thinkers – that conflicts, in important ways, with his depiction of the philosopher in the dialogues dealing with *theoria*.[54] In particular, the fact that he puts this extreme view in the mouth of Socrates should certainly give us pause. For Socrates pursued a form of wisdom that was ethical and practical; in addition, he was intimately connected with numerous people and seriously engaged with the political issues of the day.[55] But, regardless of whether Plato espoused this conception of the philosopher (here represented by the contemplative Thales), the very existence of this story about Thales is revealing. For it reminds us that philosophers of the fourth century were refiguring certain archaic thinkers as contemplative "theorists."

Heraclides also engages in this revisionist project. For example, he put the "festival-image" (quoted above) in the mouth of Pythagoras: it was Pythagoras, he suggests, who was the first to call himself a philosopher, the first to practice *theoria*. Scholars have rejected this attribution, since before the fourth century the word *philosophia* signified "intellectual cultivation" in the broadest sense and did not pick out a specific discipline or intellectual practice.[56] In asserting that Pythagoras identified himself not only as a "philosopher" but a philosopher engaged in *theoria*, Heraclides clearly retrojects the fourth-century conception of theoretical philosophy back onto the ancients. In another fragment of a dialogue of Heraclides, moreover, we find Thales claiming that he always lived in solitude as a private individual and kept aloof from state affairs.[57] In stark contrast to earlier sources, who describe Thales as a political and pragmatic sage, Heraclides turns him into a solitary contemplative. Finally, Heraclides even identified the mythological figure Atlas as a wise astronomer: as he claims, the story

---

[54] See, e.g., Rue 1993; I am much indebted to Long, "Plato's Apologies" (1998), though I do not agree that the digression represents Plato's own view. Note that Plato claims in the *Republic* 600a that Thales is "a *sophos* in practical affairs," adding that "many clever inventions in technical and practical affairs" have been ascribed to him (as well as to the Scythian Anacharsis). Here, as well as at *Protagoras* 343a, Plato reflects the traditional view of Thales as a prototypical sage. It is only in the *Theaetetus* that he reports the story that Thales is a contemplative.

[55] As Blondell (2002, 298–302) rightly argues. According to Blondell, the differences between Socrates and the contemplative philosopher he describes here reveal that Plato "implicitly acknowledg[es] the inadequacy of the ideal in question as a model for actual human life." As she claims, the idealized philosopher in the *Theaetetus* offers a paradigm which is "inaccessible to embodied human beings in any literal sense, but still valuable as a source of inspiration . . ." (p. 292).

[56] Burkert 1960, Nightingale 1995, ch. 1 and *passim*.   [57] Diogenes Laertius (hereafter DL) 1.25–6.

that Atlas carried the world on his shoulders reveals – when interpreted allegorically – that he practiced philosophical speculation.[58] Here, *theoria* is even injected into the mythic realm.

Let me emphasize that the philosophers of the fourth century generally portrayed the early thinkers as engaging in a primitive form of *theoria*: the contemplation of the stars. This kind of *theoria* is astronomical rather than metaphysical, and is therefore identified as a mere precursor of the theoretical contemplation of immaterial "realities." These early thinkers, then, engaged in a form of *theoria* that anticipated – but still fell short of – "true" *theoria*, which is essentially metaphysical. Strictly speaking, they are proto-theorists, since they focused on the cosmos rather than on higher realities.

As I have indicated, the fourth-century philosophers offered an anachronistic account of the early Greek thinkers: in fact, these individuals were far from theoretical contemplatives. Consider, for example, Thales of Miletus, who was ranked by posterity as both a Sage (one of the elite Seven) and a Philosopher. The fifth-century historian Herodotus offers several short accounts of him in the *Histories*. In book I, he tells us that Thales predicted an eclipse and that he engineered the diversion of the river Halys for the benefit of Croesus and his army (when they attempted to invade Persia). Herodotus also reports that, when the Ionians in Asia Minor were being subdued by the Persians, Thales fought to create a confederation of Ionian city-states with a supreme deliberative council in the city of Teos.[59] Diogenes Laertius (third century CE) relates another story about Thales' "cunning intelligence": in order to demonstrate how easy it was to get rich, Thales, foreseeing that it would be a good season for olives, rented all the oil-presses and obtained a monopoly on the proceeds.[60] These stories about Thales portray a man of many skills. Alongside his astronomical expertise and cosmological thinking, he demonstrates a good deal of practical wisdom: engineering the diversion of a river, serving as a leader in

[58] Note that Dicaearchus, in arguing for a pragmatist conception of philosophy, also looks to the ancients for support: he exalts the ancient wise men who "did not philosophize in words [but rather] by the practice of noble deeds" above the later philosophers who turned to discourse and disputation (fr. 31 Wehrli).

[59] Herodotus *Histories* 1.74–5, 170. DL 1.25 reports that Thales advised the Milesians to reject the alliance offered to them by Croesus, which ended up saving them when Croesus was at war with Cyrus.

[60] DL 1.26. Cf. Aristotle, who also reports that this story "is told" about Thales (*Politics* 1.4, 1259a). In fact, this story about Thales conflicts with Aristotle's claim in the *NE* (VI.7, 1141b3–8) that Thales was a contemplative. In the *Politics* (1259a), Aristotle reports the story of Thales and the olive-presses as mere hearsay; as he adds, although the creation of a monopoly "was attributed to Thales because of his wisdom," in fact it is a universal principle of business.

political affairs, and exhibiting a keen understanding of agriculture and commerce.[61]

Pythagoras, too, was a fundamentally practical and political sage.[62] This remarkable figure, who almost certainly did not publish any writings, developed a complete and systematic "art of living." Pythagoras instituted a new mode of life by creating a religious society in the city of Croton. The members of this society, which included women as well as men, lived a life of austerity and discipline that featured a vegetarian diet, the practice of self-examination, obedience to precepts known as _akousmata_, and a strict code of silence about Pythagorean doctrine and practice. Pythagoras and his followers, then, adopted an entire way of life; their ideas and doctrines translated directly into daily _praxis_ (for example, their belief in the immortality of the soul and its transmigration into animals led them to abstain from meat). Insofar as Pythagoreanism offered its members hidden knowledge that could not be divulged, it resembled the mystery religions, which promised to benefit initiates by the revelation of secret wisdom. In addition to these private and secret practices, however, Pythagoras participated fully in political life; in fact, he and his followers are said to have taken over the government of Croton.

It comes as a great surprise, then, when fourth-century philosophers represent thinkers such as Thales, Pythagoras, and Anaxagoras as theoretical philosophers who lived a private life devoted exclusively to contemplation. What is at stake – intellectually and culturally – in the shift from the conception of the wise man as practical, political, and polymathic to that of the contemplative philosopher engaged in metaphysical _theoria_? How did the "theoretical" philosophers of the fourth century conceptualize and legitimize this new form of wisdom?

ARISTOTLE'S "HISTORY" OF PHILOSOPHY

In analyzing this "historicizing" project, we must remember that the history of philosophy, as a genre, did not emerge until the later part of the fourth century BCE (following, as one would expect, the creation of philosophy as a specialized discipline in the first half of the century). Aristotle offers the earliest systematic attempt to organize and analyze the doctrines of his predecessors, and is thus identified as the first historian of

---

[61] See also Aristophanes _Clouds_ 180, and _Birds_ 1009, which identify Thales as a practical/political sage (a view echoed by Plato in _Protagoras_ 343a, and _Republic_ 600a).

[62] On Pythagoras and the early Pythagoreans, see Burkert 1972, Kahn 2001, chs. 1–3.

philosophy.[63] Although Aristotle offers precious evidence of the ideas of the early thinkers, scholars have long recognized that his historical accounts in the *Metaphysics* I (and *Physics*) are highly tendentious. For Aristotle constructs his "history" as a discussion of the evolution of the ideas that he himself sets forth, for the first time, in a full way (especially the doctrine of the four causes). The only early thinkers who qualify as "philosophers" are those who apprehended at least one of Aristotle's four causes and who articulated this in language that was "clear."[64] Aristotle thus separates the early philosophers from nonphilosophical poets and writers by recourse to the clarity of their exposition.[65]

Having thus separated the philosophers from other early authors, Aristotle proceeds to use the same criterion – that of clarity – to distinguish earlier, "immature" philosophy from his own philosophic work. For example, he dismisses Xenophanes and Melissus on the grounds that they are "crude" (ἀγροικότεροι, 986b25–7) and claims that the thinkers up through Empedocles set forth their ideas in a fashion that was "vague and unclear" (ἀμυδρῶς μέντοι καὶ οὐθὲν σαφῶς, 985a13). He then compares these early thinkers to untrained men in battle who "rush around and often strike fine blows but act without understanding"; they "do not appear to understand the things that they say, since they rarely if ever apply them" (985a14–18). Finally, after surveying all his predecessors up through Plato, Aristotle claims that these thinkers were "groping, albeit vaguely" (ἀμυδρῶς) for the ideas that he himself has articulated (988a20–3).

But the early thinkers were not just vague and unclear: as philosophers, they were immature and even infantile. Thus, according to Aristotle, "Empedocles speaks in baby talk" (ψελλίζεται), and therefore one must read him "with a view to his underlying ideas" in order to ascertain the philosophical doctrines hidden in the verse (985a4–6).[66] At the end of the

---

[63] Hippias, in his "Anthology of Related Sayings," and Plato (especially in the late dialogues) both attempt to organize the ideas of their predecessors; so far as we can tell, Hippias' account was very general and sketchy, and Plato discusses the early Greek thinkers only when they are relevant to a given argument in a dialogue. On the pre-Aristotelian discussions of the early thinkers, see Mansfeld 1990, chs. 1 and 2.

[64] For a discussion of Aristotle's use of the notion of "clarity" in his efforts to demarcate poetry and philosophy (and, in turn, immature and mature philosophy), see Mansfeld 1990, 22–83 and cf. 126–46.

[65] As Aristotle says in the *Poetics*, Homer is a poet and Empedocles a philosopher, even though they both write in verse (1447b17–20).

[66] Plato (*Gorgias* 485b) and Aristotle (*Historia Animalium* 536b8 and *Problems* 902b22) use the words ψελλίζεται and the adjectival ψελλός to refer to the speech of babies and small children. *Problems* 902b22 defines "baby talk" as the "inability to join one syllable to another sufficiently quickly" (which is the result of the fact that young children do not yet have control over their tongues – a point which Aristotle reiterates in *HA* 536b8; see also *PA* 660a26).

historical excursus in *Metaphysics* I, Aristotle makes this same claim of all the early philosophers:

> That all seem to have been searching for the causes described in the *Physics*, and that we cannot speak of any cause outside of these [four], is clear even from the things said by earlier thinkers. But they spoke of these things vaguely (ἀμυδρῶς), and although in one sense these ideas have all been stated before, in another they have never been articulated at all. For early philosophy talked, so to speak, in baby-talk (ψελλιζομένη), since it was young and in its infancy (ἅτε νέα τε καὶ κατ' ἀρχὰς οὖσα). (993a11–16)

The "history of philosophy" in *Metaphysics* I, then, offers a biological account in which philosophy started as a babbling infant and then slowly grew into the mature doctrines of Aristotle.[67] For, in Aristotle's view, his predecessors were "groping" to understand the doctrines of causality that he himself has fully articulated. Indeed, according to Cicero, Aristotle explicitly claimed to be bringing philosophy to its perfect *telos*:

> Aristotle, upbraiding the early philosophers for claiming that philosophy had been perfected by their own genius, says that they were either completely foolish or completely conceited, but adds that, as he saw it, philosophy would in a short time be brought to completion (since in a short period of years a great advance had been made). (*Tusculan Disputations* III.28.69)

Although this report may not be fully accurate, it chimes well with Aristotle's evolutionary account of the discipline of philosophy in the *Metaphysics* I.

As a "historian" of early philosophy, then, Aristotle makes a double move: he claims that the ancients attempted to develop and practice theoretical philosophy, but then argues that they could not articulate their theories clearly because philosophy was "in its infancy." The ancients therefore give Aristotle's own theoretical activities a venerable pedigree even as they point up his vast superiority to the entire tradition. Not surprisingly, Aristotle pays no attention to the practical or political activities of the individuals he discusses; rather, he treats them as proto-theorists. To be sure, his "history" of philosophy makes a very important contribution to the history of ideas, but it offers a distorted picture of early Greek wisdom and completely obscures the pragmatic and polymathic nature of the Presocratic thinkers. Ultimately, Aristotle's projection of "theoretical philosophy" onto

---

[67] For example, Aristotle says that Anaxagoras, in claiming that there is *nous* in nature, "was like a sober man in comparison with his predecessors, who spoke incoherently." (984b15–18). But this sign of "progress" does not mean that philosophy had escaped from the "unclarity" of its beginnings: even Plato, Aristotle claims, "uses empty phrases (*kenologein*) and poetic metaphors" when he says that the Forms are patterns (991a20–2).

the ancients has the effect of concealing important differences between the early Greek thinkers and the philosophers of the fourth century.

SOPHIA IN THE SIXTH AND FIFTH CENTURIES BCE

In order to locate the development of philosophic *theoria* in its intellectual and cultural context, I want to discuss, in very general terms, the conception and practice of wisdom in sixth- and fifth-century Greece. A brief look at this period will provide the historical backdrop for the radical turn taken by the fourth-century theoretical philosophers. First of all, the preplatonic thinkers did not conceptualize or formulate a "spectator theory of knowledge," nor did they privilege disinterested contemplation over practical or political activities. In fact, they did not even call themselves philosophers. They did of course engage in some forms of philosophical speculation, but this intellectual activity was not distinguished or detached from other forms of wisdom. Indeed, the preplatonic thinkers did not treat theoretical, practical, and productive wisdom as separate or distinct categories. It is difficult for us to think this distinction away and to imagine a culture that had a completely different sense of the nature and operation of wisdom. But we must remember that the sixth- and fifth-century thinkers did not acknowledge or use Aristotelian categorizations; they had a more fluid and inclusive conception of "higher" wisdom than the philosophers of the fourth century.

In the sixth and fifth centuries BCE, the term *sophoi* had a wide range of application (including poets, prophets, doctors, statesmen, astronomers, scientists, historians, inventors, and various kinds of artisans); it did not pick out a specific kind of wisdom or expertise. Although, in this period, different kinds of wise men were seen to be practicing distinct activities, there was nonetheless a generalized competition among the different groups for the title of "wise man." It was not until the late fifth century that intellectuals began to construct boundaries between disciplines such as philosophy, history, medicine, rhetoric, and various other *technai*, and even then they did not distinguish between theoretical, technical, and pragmatic modes of wisdom.[68] Throughout the fifth century, philosophers, historians, sophists, and physicians worked within a single, quite broad intellectual

---

[68] As Thomas (2000, 31) claims, "there were few demarcations between the various groups who may be categorized by modern scholars as Presocratics, natural philosophers, sophists, and doctors – even if you accept, for instance, the distinction that sophists share their wisdom for money, the interests and methods of prominent individual sophists, as conventionally labelled (e.g. Protagoras, Prodicus) are by no means entirely distinct from some of the *physiologoi* or natural philosophers or from certain writers in the Hippocratic Corpus." See also Nehamas 1990, Vegetti 1999.

matrix: these individuals competed with one another (and, at times, with poets, prophets, and politicians) for prestige and authority.[69] As Rosalind Thomas suggests, there was "no neat and tidy division of specialties, but a community of contemporary interest and debate, theory and counter-theory, in which '*physiologos*,' 'scientist,' 'doctor,' and '*sophistēs*' were not always easy to disentangle."[70]

It was not until the fourth century that thinkers first began to use "sophist" and "philosopher" as technical terms, which they retrojected back onto earlier thinkers and wise men. *Sophistēs*, in fact, was a near synonym of *sophos* until the late fifth century, and did not refer to a particular kind of individual (let alone a "movement").[71] The words *philosophia* and *philosophein*, moreover, were very rarely used until the fourth century and, when they were used, did not pick out a special and distinct group of thinkers. In the fifth century, *philosophia* and its cognates signified "intellectual cultivation" in the broadest sense.[72] In short, none of the wise men in the sixth and fifth centuries called themselves "sophists" or "philosophers" (in the technical sense), nor did others refer to them in this way. If we avoid these anachronistic categorizations, we get a rather different picture of the early Greek thinkers.

We find excellent evidence of the absence of disciplinary distinctions in the work of Heraclitus: in exalting his own brand of wisdom, he debunks not only that of Homer, Hesiod, and Archilochus, but also Hecataeus (a proto-historian), Xenophanes, and Pythagoras (DK B40, B42, B57). Clearly, Heraclitus conceived of himself as rivalling disparate wise men rather than a specialized group of intellectuals (those later identified as philosophers); indeed, he explicitly claims that his rivals have *polumathiē* – wide, non-specialized, learning – but lack true understanding. The fact that Heraclitus' opponents include poets and prose writers as well as a religious/political guru such as Pythagoras gives us a good idea of the milieu in which he was working. He and other early thinkers did seek to distinguish themselves from other "wise men." But these attacks were *ad hominem*, and should not be mistaken for the explicit and systematic differentiation of one genre or discipline from others. Although we see in the early thinkers the

---

[69] Lloyd 1987, ch. 2 and *passim*. In a recent book (2000) on Herodotus, Thomas offers fresh evidence for this position. We should not interpret Herodotus simply within the field of historiography, she claims, since his work responds directly to that of poets, historians, natural philosophers, sophists, and medical writers; rather, we should treat all of these *sophoi* as participating in a broad-ranging, non-specialized analysis of the physical and human world.

[70] Thomas 2000, 160; see also Jouanna [1992]/1999, 366–403, Wallace 1998.

[71] Lloyd (1987, 93n. 153) offers a good discussion of the uses of the word *sophistēs* in classical Greece.

[72] For a list of the few occurrences of the word φιλοσοφεῖν and its cognates in Greek texts before the fourth century, see Nightingale 1995, 14–15 with notes (see also Überweg 1871, 1–4; Havelock 1963, 280–1 with notes, and 1983b, 56–7).

development of the modes and topics of inquiry that we now recognize as "philosophical," these thinkers did not articulate the criteria that distinguished their intellectual endeavors from other disciplines. It is significant, of course, that some opted for prose over verse, and that some repudiated "mythic" modes of wisdom, but this is very far from the explicit definition of a new discipline.[73]

Another early thinker who defies disciplinary categorization is Empedocles, who treated topics ranging from cosmology, anthropology, and religious purification to the transmigration of the soul. This combination of mysticism and rationality has created enormous scholarly problems. Most interpreters have "solved" this problem by separating the disparate fragments of Empedocles into two very different works: *On Nature*, a "naturalist" poem, and *Purifications*, a supernatural story of reincarnation. Recently, however, several scholars have shown that some of the material ascribed to the latter poem belong in the former; as they suggest, the separation of the naturalist from the mythical material is based on the anachronistic assumption that true philosophy has no room for the supernatural.[74] The fact that Empedocles wrote poems (or perhaps a single poem) which included "philosophical" and "nonphilosophical" (i.e. religious) material challenges the standard modern approach to the early thinkers. Among other things, it exposes our tendency to retroject contemporary conceptions of philosophy onto the ancients. If we resist this move, we can see that many of the early thinkers were engaged in complex and broad-ranging projects that do not fall neatly within the boundaries of philosophy as we now conceive it.

Clearly, the fourth-century depictions of earlier thinkers as solitary contemplatives is quite misleading. In particular, they indicate that the wisdom of the early thinkers was confined to intellectual speculation. In fact, there is considerable evidence that most of these men were able performers of practical and political wisdom.[75] For example, Thales played a leading role in Ionian politics, and Anaximander led a colony from Miletus to Apollonia

---

[73] For several recent analyses of the attempts by certain preplatonic writers (including poets and historians) to reject "mythic" modes of thought and/or discourse, see Detienne [1981]/1986, Lloyd 1987, ch. 4 and *passim*, Most 1999. For an excellent study of philosophical conceptions and uses of myth, ranging from the early thinkers to Plato, see K. Morgan 2000.

[74] See Martin and Primavesi 1998, ch. 3.

[75] For the notion of the "performance of wisdom" in Greek culture, see Martin 1993. He uses the word "perform" not in the sense of play-acting or pretending; rather, it signifies the displaying or enacting of wisdom in any public context ("a public enactment, about important matters, in word or gesture . . . [that is] open to scrutiny and criticism," pp. 115–16). Martin focuses on the seven sages, but one could extend the notion of "performing wisdom" to other *sophoi* in the archaic and classical periods. See Lloyd 1987, 89–98, Demont 1993b, and Thomas 2000, ch. 8 on the public "displays" of wisdom by a wide variety of *sophoi* in this period. For Athens as a "performance culture," see Rehm 1992, Goldhill and Osborne 1999. Goldhill (1999a) offers an excellent summary of different conceptions of "performance" in recent scholarship and theory.

on the Pontus (DK12 A3). Pythagoras was part religious guru, part politician, part mathematician. Parmenides is said to have served as a lawmaker in his city (DK28 A1). In Empedocles, we find not only a natural philosopher but a religious thinker, orator, and physician.[76] Anaxagoras enjoyed a close relationship with Pericles; tradition reports that some Athenians considered him so great a threat to the city that they put him on trial for impiety.[77] Zeno of Elea was a fierce advocate of political freedom, taking part in the conspiracy against the tyrant Nearchus;[78] and Melissus served as a general in a sea battle against Pericles in 441/0 (DK 30, A3). Finally, Democritus – now identified almost solely with the theory of atomism – was a political leader who had a coin stamped with his name (indeed this polymathic sage wrote treatises on disparate subjects such as medicine, anthropology, ethics, and politics).[79]

As Paul Cartledge asks, "who are we to say whether Democritus might not himself have seen his 'scientific' work as fundamental but yet subordinated ultimately to an overarching and overriding ethical-political project rather than as an independent end and goal in itself?"[80] We could ask the same question about many other "presocratic" thinkers. Indeed, in the recent *Cambridge Companion to Early Greek Philosophy* (ed. A. A. Long), a number of scholars have argued that these individuals were not only practicing intellectual speculation but were engaged in therapeutic, salvific, theological, and poetic projects akin to those of other nonphilosophical *sophoi* of their day.[81]

As I have suggested, the thinkers of the sixth and fifth centuries did not develop the conception of the spectator theory of knowledge or practice a contemplative mode of life. None claimed that the wise man must detach himself from the world and "gaze upon" truth, or that he should turn his back on practical or political affairs. In fact, in the preplatonic thinkers, there is little if any evidence that knowledge takes the form of "seeing" truth.[82] When the possession or acquisition of knowledge is described by

---

[76] On Empedocles' activities as a physician, see Jouanna [1992]/1999, 262–4. Aristotle claimed in the *Sophist* that Empedocles was the first to invent rhetoric (DL VIII.57).

[77] See Wallace 1994, 136–8 (and notes) for a review of the ancient evidence for this trial. Even if this trial never took place (as he and other scholars believe), the story gives evidence of the widespread belief that Anaxagoras was overly involved in the political affairs of Athens.

[78] Others call the tyrant Diomedon or Demylus. See DK 29, A1, A6, and A7.   [79] Cartledge 1998, 4.

[80] See Cartledge 1998, 8 and *passim*.

[81] Long 1999a. See esp. Long, "The Scope of Early Greek Philosophy" (ch. 1), Broadie, "Rational Theology" (ch. 10), Lesher, "Early Interest in Knowledge" (ch.11), and Most, "The Poetics of Early Greek Philosophy" (ch. 16).

[82] Note that the *mantis* and the *prophetēs* were not represented in Greek texts as "seeing" some invisible spectacle of truth: Teiresias reaches his conclusions when (with the help of his assistant) he attends

preplatonic thinkers (which is quite rare), it generally involves hearing or learning a divine or superhuman *logos*. The emphasis is on discourse and hearing rather than spectating or seeing.[83]

Consider the famous opening of Parmenides' poem, which describes the author's journey towards Truth (DK28 B1). The maiden daughters of the sun escort the poet along the "resounding road of the goddess" to the "etherial gates" at the threshold of "the paths of day and night." A divinity opens the doors. At this point, the reader expects that the poet will now see the truth unveiled. Instead, he encounters a goddess who speaks. There is no description of the appearance of the goddess and, indeed, no visual detail at all. Amazingly (from our post-Platonic vantage point), the poet journeys out of – rather than into – the light: the sun maidens escort the poet into the "House of Night," having ventured from there "into the light" in order to fetch him.[84] What the poet encounters when he crosses the threshold, then, is not a vision but rather the voice of a goddess. "Come now, and I will tell you," she says, "and, when you have heard me (*akousas*), carry my account away" (DK B2). Compare the famous journey in Plato's Analogy of the Cave (*Republic* VII), written over a century later. In Plato, the philosopher moves out of the darkness of the cave and into the light, where he sees with the "eye of his soul" the beings in the metaphysical realm of the Forms. This stands in stark contrast to Parmenides' philosophical revelation, where the truth is revealed in the darkness by a goddess who plays the role of muse. There is no "vision" of truth in this or other philosophical texts of the early period.

to bird-signs and entrails, and Oedipus (after he is blinded) comes to know his own fate by way of a prophetic understanding of a number of different oracles (the physical features of the grove of the Eumenides also provide him with clues). As Fritz Graf has suggested (in a personal conversation), the Greek "seer" does not engage in the act of mental seeing (Cassandra, in the *Agamemnon*, may seem to be the exception, but her vision of what is going on in the palace serves the dramatic spectacle; it does not provide evidence of actual prophetic practice).

[83] Many preplatonic thinkers discussed and speculated about the nature and reliability of physical vision; but they did not articulate a conception of knowledge as "seeing" truth. For discussions of vision and visual artworks in the early thinkers, see Heraclitus DK B101a, Empedocles DK A86, A92, B23, B84, B86, B87, B88, B89; Anaxagoras DK B21a; Leucippus DK A29, 30, 31; Democritus DK A135, B5h, B28a, Gorgias DK B3.86, B4, B5, B26, B28, *Helen* 15–19, Hippias DK A2. Note also that some fragments from the early thinkers make passing references to "seeing" that something is true (e.g. Parmenides DK B4.1, Empedocles DK B129.5, B110.2); but none turns this into an epistemological theory.

[84] As Popper (1992) and Sedley (1999b) have shown. According to Popper, the element of light "intrudes" upon darkness, thus creating the phenomenal world – i.e. light's intrusion creates the dualism that characterizes the cosmos described in the Way of Opinion. As Sedley puts it, "elemental dualism is the physical counterpart of mortals' combination of being with not-being" (1999b, 124). Furley 1989, ch. 3 claims that the poet does journey into the House of Night, but that this is not a place of darkness: rather, it is a region beyond the duality and opposition of light and darkness.

Although our evidence for the preplatonic sages and thinkers is not always adequate, we must nonetheless attempt to locate them in their contemporary intellectual and cultural context. In doing this, we may find it rather difficult to distinguish them from other wise men of the period. First of all, many of these thinkers were famous for their practical and political wisdom. In addition, the ideas and methods they developed were also taken up by other kinds of thinkers and intellectuals (e.g. poets, sophists, doctors, rhetoricians, etc.). On what grounds, then, can we isolate these figures and treat them as philosophers? A. A. Long argues that this group of thinkers was distinctive because they "left an intellectual legacy which could be drawn upon, improved, and criticized"; though they might have initially acted as ambitious individuals staking a claim to *sophia* (rather than as deliberate founders of a new discipline), they nonetheless succeeded in creating an enduring tradition of intellectual thinking. But we must not forget, Long adds, that the sixth- and fifth-century thinkers were engaged in a project that was salvational as well as rational: the cultivation of true *logos*, they claimed, would lead to a happy life.[85] Nehamas captures this well in his conception of the philosophic "art of living" – though in this case we must say *arts* of living, since the early Greek thinkers enacted different modes of life based on different notions of wisdom.[86] These recent studies of the preplatonic thinkers remind us to attend to the pragmatic aspects of early Greek philosophy – to the embodied performance or enactment of wisdom.[87]

Of course the practical, pragmatic conception of wisdom did not disappear when theoretical philosophy was developed. Figures such as Antisthenes, Aristippus, Diogenes, Zeno, Pyrrho, and Epicurus developed and enacted highly practical philosophies. The development of theoretical knowledge did not eclipse practical philosophy, then, but led to new ways of linking theory to practice (which, in turn, led to new attacks on the validity and/or efficacy of theoretical knowledge). In fact, most of the proponents of theoretical wisdom in the Greek and Roman tradition connected it to

---

[85] Long 1999b, 9, 13–14. See also Broadie (1999), who argues that the majority of the early thinkers were engaged in "rational theology."

[86] Nehamas explicates this idea in his superb book, *The Art of Living* (1999a; see also 2000a). He does not discuss the early Greek philosophers in this study, but his conception of the "art of living" would certainly apply to many of these thinkers, since the concept of the specialized, professional "philosopher" did not exist in this period. See also Nehamas (1990) for a discussion of the demarcation of the boundaries between "philosophy" and "sophistry" in the fourth-century BCE.

[87] See also Hadot (1995), who argues that *all* of the ancient philosophers pursued, first and foremost, practical and "spiritual" goals. He claims that ancient philosophy was defined by the cultivation of a distinct "way of life"; it was never simply a cognitive or intellectual activity. This thesis, however, is far too sweeping, for it bunches a multitude of very different thinkers into a single group.

praxis, thus conceiving of the wise man as both a spectator and a performer of wisdom.[88]

****

Why did the thinkers of the fourth century develop a conception of knowledge as "seeing Being"? Why did they consider the practice of traveling abroad and watching the spectacles at religious festivals a compelling paradigm for philosophic activity and apprehension? This book offers an interdisciplinary study of these questions, examining the cultural practice of *theoria* and its appropriation by the fourth-century proponents of theoretical philosophy. Let me emphasize that this is not a study of Platonic and Aristotelian epistemology. This book will approach philosophic *theoria* from a very different angle: it analyzes the mythic, rhetorical, and analytic discussions of philosophic *theoria* in relation to the traditional practice of *theoria*. By examining the link between traditional and philosophic *theoria*, we can locate the creation of theoretical philosophy in its historical context and analyze this discipline as a cultural as well as an intellectual practice.

In chapter one, I offer a detailed examination of the practice of *theoria* in classical Greece. *Theoria* brought foreign Greeks together in shared religious sanctuaries to witness spectacles and participate in rituals. In these religious spaces, the *theoroi* engaged in the act of "sacred spectating," viewing objects and spectacles made sacred by ritual. The *theoroi* attended collective rituals and events designed to knit the participants into a single group. In addition, a panhellenic ideology was explicitly articulated in public discourses. Although a *theoros* never shed his political identity, he participated in an event that celebrated a "Greek" identity over and above that of any individual city-state. The *theoros* was thus encouraged to adopt a broader, more encompassing perspective. The gaze of the *theoros*, then, is characterized by *alterity*: the pilgrim brings his foreign presence to the festival, and he interacts with people from other cities and cultures. He thus returns home with a broader perspective, and brings information and ideas from foreign parts into the city. *Theoria* was at once a religious and a political practice: how did sacralized spectating influence political ideology and praxis? I analyze the interface between religious spectating and political action in the practice of *theoria*.

In chapter two, I discuss Plato's appropriation of the model of traditional *theoria* in his accounts of theoretical philosophy. In particular, I examine his strategic use of the language and structure of *theoria* in the *Phaedo*, *Republic*,

---

[88] For contemporary discussions of the relation of theory to ethical and political practice, see Arendt [1971]/1978, 69–238, Dunne 1993, Bartlett and Collins 1999, Lilla 2001.

and *Phaedrus*. Plato's comparisons of philosophic "spectating" to *theoria* at panhellenic festivals (including the Eleusinian Festival of the Mysteries) have generally been interpreted as ornate metaphors for the mere act of thinking. As a result, scholars have not explored the link between philosophic theorizing and the traditional practice of *theoria* at religious festivals and sanctuaries. This chapter focuses on Plato's deliberate and extensive use of the model of traditional *theoria* in his discussions of philosophy. As I will suggest, this model provided the terminology and narrative structure that Plato used in his foundational accounts of theoretical philosophy. A full understanding of the practice of *theoria* will enable us to examine Plato's conception of philosophy in its social and historical context. In addition, we can investigate the way that Plato attempted to position this philosophic practice in the social and political affairs of the city.

In chapter three, I will analyze Plato's discussion of philosophic *theoria* in the *Republic* v–vii, focusing in particular on the theoric journey depicted in the Analogy of the Cave. Building on the model of traditional *theoria*, Plato constructs a philosophic *theoros* who detaches himself from the social world and "journeys" to see the divine Forms. He is altered and transformed by this contemplative activity, and returns to the city as a stranger to his own kind. This *atopos* individual becomes a sort of agent of alterity, and must confront the problem of bringing alien ideas into the city. As in traditional *theoria* at religious festivals, Platonic *theoria* features a sacralized mode of spectating that differs from mundane modes of viewing. How, then, does Plato conceive of this "theoric" gaze? What does the philosopher see? And what does he fail to see? As I argue, philosophic vision is predicated on periodic bouts of blindness – paradoxically, the philosopher must go blind in order to see. After investigating Plato's accounts of philosophic blindness and insight, I will discuss the theorist's return to the city. How does this estranged individual function in the human and terrestrial world? How do his contemplative activities affect his actions in social and political life?

In constructing the theoretical philosopher, Plato invites his readers to identify with a strange sort of person. In the figure of the philosopher, Plato introduces a new *aristos* – an individual so exalted that he makes all noble, prestigious, and powerful men look common and servile. Using mythic and rhetorical discourse, Plato attempts to make what is familiar strange and what is strange familiar, thus dislodging the reader from his ordinary beliefs. In his efforts to unsettle the reader, Plato uses a very distinctive rhetorical strategy – what I call the "rhetoric of estrangement." For example, in the Analogy of the Cave, Plato portrays our familiar world as a dark and prison-like cavern – a place of exile rather than a true home. Where, we must ask, do we dwell? By estranging the reader from his traditional views and confronting him with the "reality" of the metaphysical region, Plato invites him to look beyond the familiar world and to embrace the alterity of the theoretical perspective.

In the *Republic*, Plato sets forth what is generally considered the standard account of philosophic theorizing: theoretical contemplation is a strictly metaphysical activity in which the mind separates itself from the senses (and, indeed, from the entire physical world) and apprehends the Forms. In the myths in the *Phaedo* and *Phaedrus*, however, Plato suggests that physical vision has a positive role to play in philosophic theorizing. In chapter four, I will examine these mythic accounts of the philosopher's visual apprehension of the physical cosmos and of certain (exceptional) bodies within it. In these texts, Plato identifies certain bodies as perfect (or near-perfect) "images" of the Forms: they are not just shadowy *eidola*, but *agalmata* or "sacred images" of true reality. In viewing these exceptional bodies, the philosophic theorist engages in a form of sacralized spectating right here on earth. The physical sight of these bodies, I argue, makes an important contribution to the philosopher's journey towards the Forms.

Plato takes this idea even further in the *Timaeus*: in this text, the astronomical viewing of the heavens is directly tied to metaphysical contemplation. The cosmos as a whole possesses a perfect body whose motions and revolutions are steered by divine *nous*. When the philosophic theorist looks at the heavens, then, he sees "visible gods." Here, Plato identifies the astronomical contemplation of the heavens as a vital part of philosophic theorizing. In contemplating and imitating the divinities in the macrocosm, the philosopher can bring order and harmony to his individual psyche – he can turn the chaos of his soul into a (micro-) cosmos. The spectacle of the heavens thus translates into virtuous action on earth. Philip of Opus offers a similar account of astronomical *theoria* in the *Epinomis*. But he departs from Plato by dispensing with the theory of Forms and claiming that astronomy is, itself, the highest mode of theoretical wisdom. By theorizing the visible gods in the heavens, Philip claims, the philosopher develops not only wisdom but piety: the philosophic astronomer will thus be the most virtuous individual in practical and political affairs, and the ideal leader of the city.

Aristotle set forth a very different conception of *theoria*. Dispensing with the metaphor of the journey, he focuses almost exclusively on the notion of a sacralized, divine form of viewing. In the act of spectating at religious festivals, Aristotle found the model of a visual activity that is set apart from practical and productive endeavors. Rejecting Plato's claim that contemplation provides the basis for *praxis*, Aristotle argues that *theoria* is a completely disinterested activity that can only be pursued for its own sake. *Theoria* does not lead to action in the practical world; indeed it is defined in opposition to activities that are "useful and necessary." In this chapter, I will examine Aristotle's creation of the distinction between theoretical, practical, and technical forms of reasoning (a distinction that has informed all of Western thinking). I will also discuss his arguments for the superiority of theoretical over practical and productive activities: why (and how) does he privilege "useless" knowledge over that which is useful and beneficial?

In articulating the idea that the highest form of knowledge is neither practical nor productive, Aristotle uses language that has powerful ideological associations. In particular, he claims that *theoria* is not "useful" or "necessary" but rather a completely "free" and "leisured" activity that is an end in itself. In his attempt to demonstrate the superiority of *theoria* over other modes of knowledge, Aristotle makes use of traditional aristocratic rhetoric. According to Greek aristocratic ideology, the truly "free" and "noble" man is self-sufficient rather than subservient; in contrast to "servile" individuals who degrade themselves by working for others (engaging in "productive" labor), the aristocratic gentleman is noble, leisured, and fully free. Aristotle exploits aristocratic discourse to articulate the idea that *theoria* is a completely self-sufficient, independent, and leisured activity. As he claims, *theoria* is never useful or serviceable in the practical world, but is a noble and disinterested activity that is an end in itself.

Unlike Plato, Aristotle almost never uses the "rhetoric of estrangement." Rather, he develops what I call a "rhetoric of disinterest" – a discourse that portrays certain activities as being superior to all endeavors that serve a separate end. By identifying *theoria* as a nonutilitarian ("useless") activity done only "for its own sake," Aristotle sets forth an idea that will have a long history in Western thinking about "pure" intellectual activities and "liberal" education. As I will suggest, he appropriates and transforms traditional aristocratic rhetoric to convey the idea that *theoria* and other "liberal" pursuits are superior precisely because they are "useless" and disinterested. An examination of this rhetoric – which is but one strand in a very complex philosophical project – will help us to locate Aristotle's argument in its cultural context.

Since the fourth-century philosophers used different modes of discourse in articulating their conceptions of *theoria*, I have found it necessary to approach each thinker rather differently. In particular, my examination of Plato and Philip is more literary and less technical than my analysis of Aristotle (though I will analyze Aristotle's rhetoric as well as his arguments).

In spite of their differing methodologies, all of these philosophers were confronted with the same task: the conceptualization and legitimation of a new form of knowledge defined as distant, divine, and "foreign" to the ordinary man. To articulate this outlandish idea, each of these thinkers had to stretch language, creating new vocabularies and discourses. Their intellectual explorations, in short, called for new feats of language. In Thoreau's memorable words:

I fear lest my expression not be *extra-vagant* enough, may not wander far enough beyond the narrow limits of my daily experience so as to be adequate to the truth of which I have been convinced.[89]

The fourth-century philosophers claimed that we must "wander beyond" the familiar limits of experience in order to achieve wisdom. And they themselves wandered outside familiar language to convey this new idea. This book will examine this discursive and philosophical achievement.

---

[89] Thoreau 1983, 372–3.

CHAPTER I

Theoria *as a cultural practice*

Not only does a journey transport us over enormous distances, it also causes us to move a few degrees up or down in the social scale. It displaces us physically and also – for better or for worse – takes us out of our class context, so that the color and flavor of certain places cannot be dissociated from the always unexpected social level on which we find ourselves in experiencing them.

Lévi-Strauss, *Tristes Tropiques*

Thank heaven, here is not all the world.

Henry David Thoreau, *Walden*

The fourth-century philosophers borrow the notion of "contemplating the spectacle of truth" not from the Presocratic tradition but from a specific civic institution – that of *theoria*. In ancient Greece, *theoria* was a venerable cultural practice characterized by a journey abroad for the sake of witnessing an event or spectacle. This chapter will examine the three most prominent forms of *theoria* in the classical period: visits to oracular centers, pilgrimages to religious festivals, and journeys abroad for the sake of learning.[1] In all journeys of *theoria*, the pilgrim or *theoros* traveled away from home to see some sort of spectacle or to learn something about the outside world, thus confronting foreign peoples and places. In classical Greece, the *theoros* could be sent as an official representative of his city, in which case the *theoria* was carried out in a civic and political context. But a *theoros* could also venture forth on his own, enacting a "private" rather than a "civic" *theoria*. In this chapter, I will offer a detailed account of traditional *theoria*, using literary, historical, epigraphic, and anthropological evidence. *Theoria* was one of the most common religious practices in the ancient world, yet it is rarely analyzed in the scholarship on ancient Greek culture.[2]

---

[1] This categorization is quite schematic, and these three forms of *theoria* are not mutually exclusive. For example, one could travel as a *theoros* to a foreign religious festival and also take the opportunity to pursue wisdom in the different places one visited on the journey.

[2] For book-length studies, see Boesch 1908, Rausch 1982. For short discussions, see Bill 1901, Buck 1953, Koller 1957. Recently, Ian Rutherford has been engaged in a thoroughgoing analysis of *theoria* in

This chapter could stand on its own as a contribution to Greek "cultural studies" (and therefore offers a more detailed analysis than the study of philosophic *theoria* perhaps requires). Although much of my data will (perforce) come from Athens, I want to consider the Athenian festivals in the larger context of Greek religious festivals. The big Athenian festivals – the Panathenaia and the City Dionysia – were multi-hellenic religious events that drew *theoroi* from all over the world: they were not exclusively "Athenian" events. By focussing on the foreigners at Athens' festivals, we can look beyond the "democratic gaze" of local Athenian attendants and begin to understand the "theoric gaze" – the gaze of (and at) alterity. In addition, we can explore the ideology and practice of panhellenic events, where individuals from different Greek city-states interacted and negotiated cultural differences. These events featured a specific ideology – the ideology of panhellenism – which was explicitly articulated in public discourses. Although a *theoros* never shed his political and cultural identity, he took part in an event that celebrated a "Greek" identity over and above that of any individual city-state. By participating in collective activities of "ritualized spectating," the *theoros* was encouraged to adopt a broader, more encompassing perspective. After investigating the traditional practice of *theoria* – which is at once social, political, and religious – I will then consider the ways that it informed the fourth-century constructions of philosophic *theoria*.[3] A full understanding of traditional *theoria* will enable us to investigate the philosophic conception of *theoria* from an entirely new angle.

Traditional *theoria* was characterized by a journey "abroad." But what counts as traveling "abroad"? It goes without saying that an individual who travels outside the territory of his own city-state goes abroad (whereas a person who goes to a precinct within his city does not). In cases such as Athens, however, which controlled the entire region of Attica, Athenians often traveled to "extra-urban" sanctuaries or festivals located within the borders of the polis-territory but distant from the city proper.[4] Linguistic evidence indicates that such trips did constitute a *theoria*, presumably

antiquity; his essays (1995, 1998, 2000, 2003) have significantly contributed to my own investigation. For more general discussions of pilgrimage in antiquity, see Coleman and Elsner 1995 and Dillon 1997.

[3] I use the phrase "traditional *theoria*" in contradistinction to "philosophic *theoria*."

[4] As Marinatos (1993, 229–30) suggests, the panhellenic festivals were, for the most part, held in sanctuaries located away from major cities and thus had "an aura of neutrality"; he distinguishes this kind of sanctuary from "urban sanctuaries" located at or near a civic center, which "constitute veritable national monuments representing the power and level of wealth . . . of their respective cities." "Extra-urban" sanctuaries form a third category: located outside of the city proper, often near the borders of the polis-territory, these mark the territorial influence of a given city and operate as regional centers for religious activity.

because they involved a journey of some distance from the city-center.[5] For example, an Athenian who traveled from an urban deme in Athens to participate in the rituals at Eleusis (in Attica, twenty-two kilometers from Athens) or to the sanctuary of Poseidon at Sounion (on the southern tip of Attica) undertook a *theoria*, whereas the Athenian who went to the City Dionysia in Athens did not.[6] In short, theoric spectating could only take place at a distance from the pilgrim's hometown or city: geographical distance was a precondition for the special kind of viewing and apprehension that characterized *theoria*.

When directed towards a religious sanctuary or festival, *theoria* took the form of a pilgrimage in which the *theoros* departed from his city or hometown, journeyed to a religious sanctuary, witnessed spectacles and events, participated in rituals, and returned home to ordinary civic life. How did the separation of the *theoroi* from their native cities affect their social and political identity? To what extent did *theoroi* attending a major oracular center or festival experience a panhellenic, "Greek" identity? How did the journey abroad to a panhellenic (or multi-hellenic) religious event alter the *theoros'* view of the world? Finally, what happened when the *theoros* returned home with a report on foreign affairs and practices – with news from abroad, be it good, bad, or strange? How did his reentry affect civic affairs in his native city?

In their famous study of Christian pilgrimage, Victor and Edith Turner analyze these issues from an anthropological perspective. They break the journey into three phases:

The first phase comprises symbolic behavior signifying the detachment of the individual or group, either from an earlier fixed point in the social structure or from a relatively stable set of cultural conditions; during the intervening liminal phase, the state of the ritual subject (the "passenger" or "liminar") becomes ambiguous – he passes through a realm or dimension that has few or none of the attributes of the past or coming state, he is betwixt and between all familiar lines of classification; in the third phase the passage is consummated, and the subject returns to classified secular or mundane social life.[7]

---

[5] Dillon 1997, xviii; Rutherford 2003. See, e.g., Euripides *Ion* 1074–80 (on the Athenian *theoros* going to the festival at Eleusis), Herodotus VI.87 (on the Athenian *theoria* to the festival of Poseidon at Sounion), Aristophanes' *Peace* 874 (on the Athenian *theoria* to Brauron). In evaluating the linguistic evidence for the practice of *theoria*, one must distinguish the technical terms *theoria* and *theoros* from the non-technical verb *theorein*, which has a very broad semantic range (often signifying simply "to observe" anything in one's visual path) and does not by itself serve as a criterion for identifying an actual *theoria*.

[6] According to C. Morgan (1993, 31–2), the Athenian development of cult sites close to state borders in the sixth and fifth centuries BCE was designed to "consolidate an exceptionally extensive territory"; as she claims, "this sytematic use of cults was largely a matter of defining boundaries and encouraging interaction between the centre and periphery" of the city-state.

[7] Turner and Turner 1978, 2 (see also Turner 1974a and 1974b).

The Turners' discussion places special emphasis on the "liminal" phase, which includes the journey to and the activities at the religious site.[8] During this period, the pilgrim detaches from familiar social structures and enters into foreign and sacred spaces, opening himself to what is new and extramundane. In stark contrast to Durkheim, the Turners argue that pilgrimage brought about the partial (if not complete) abrogation of traditional social structures during the period of the journey: the pilgrims entered a *communitas* that transcended traditional sociopolitical roles and hierarchies.[9] This thesis has of course been extensively analyzed and criticized, but has nonetheless set the terms for a vital debate about the social and ideological aspects of the practice of pilgrimage.

Theoria in the classical period follows the Turners' basic pattern of detachment from the city, the "liminal" phase of the journey itself (culminating in the "witnessing" of events and spectacles in a religious sanctuary), and reentry into the polis. But in the case of "civic" *theoria*, the *theoros* made a journey that was structured by political and religious institutions: his activities abroad were, at least in principle, regulated and monitored. This kind of *theoria*, then, does not completely fit the Turners' model, since some social and political structures remained in place even during the "liminal" phase of the journey. But one should note that the civic *theoros* who journeyed abroad did separate himself, to some extent, from the norms and ideologies of his native city, and he experienced a high degree of freedom during the journey. As C. Morgan observes,

For the individual as citizen of a state, going "beyond the bounds" was a dangerous move, since community boundaries mark the extent of the security and status conferred by group membership. Yet for the individual, it allowed the freedom to act in whatever way he might deem to be in his own interest.[10]

This separation from the city was even more pronounced in the case of "private" *theoria*, since the private *theoros* was in no way answerable to the city and thus enjoyed complete freedom. Whether traveling in a civic or a private capacity, the *theoros* was bound to encounter – and perhaps even embrace – foreign ideas and practices during his journey abroad. There is ample

---

[8] The Turners often use the term "liminoid," since the Christian pilgrimages they study are voluntary rather than "an obligatory social mechanism" (1978, 35).

[9] Cf. Durkheim [1912]/1964. For criticisms of the Turners' thesis, see Morinis 1984, Bowman 1985, Jha 1985 (introduction and essays), Eade and Sallnow 1991 (introduction and essays). Coleman and Elsner (1995, Epilogue) offer a more positive assessment of this thesis, though they too have serious criticisms; among other things, they argue that "*communitas*" is an ideal rather than an actual feature of pilgrimages, which are far more diverse than the Turners acknowledge. See also Elsner's discussion of the "contestation" of meanings and ideologies at pilgrimage centers (1998 and forthcoming).

[10] C. Morgan 1993, 31. As she goes on to explain, the sanctuaries and institutionalized cults within them served (to some extent) to "limit the actions of individuals to those acceptable to the city . . ."

evidence that the Greeks understood that the theoric journey detached the pilgrim from his own community; indeed, this was perceived as potentially threatening to the city, for there was always the possibility that the *theoros* would be "corrupted" by foreign practices and bring harmful ideas into the city. The "liminal" phase of journey, then, presents the *theoros* with foreign perspectives and practices and challenges his original world-view.

In the Greek practice of *theoria*, the pilgrim brings his foreign presence – his otherness – to the festival, and he engages in rituals and activities with other foreigners that offer him an alternative perspective. He enters what James Clifford calls "the contact zones," where different cultures negotiate and interact.[11] By participating in a panhellenic event, he is confronted with difference and alterity and is himself altered by this experience (at least to some extent). He thus returns home with a broader world-view and brings this alterity into the city.

THEORIA AT RELIGIOUS SANCTUARIES

Let us look, first, at the *theoria* sent by a city to consult an oracle. Here, the *theoros* served as an official envoy whose role was to journey to the oracular center, perform specific sacrifices and rites, carry out the consultation, and serve as a first-person witness to the events or activities that transpired there. He then returned to his native city and gave an official account of what he had seen and heard. At this point, the *theoros* communicates to the city what the god has unveiled to him. The task, then, is religious as well as civic, and must be carried out by a good and reliable individual. As the archaic poet Theognis remarks:

A man who is a *theoros* must be more straight . . . than a carpenter's pin and rule and square – a man to whom the priestess of the god at Delphi makes a response, as she indicates the sacred pronouncement from the rich shrine. For you would not find any remedy if you add anything [to the pronouncement], nor would you escape from wrongdoing in the eyes of the gods if you take anything away.[12]

The *theoros*, then, interacts with divine as well as with human beings: since this mission involves a god or gods, he must perform it with religious correctness.

---

[11] Clifford 1997.
[12] Theognis 805–10. Nagy (1990, 164) has suggested that "the word *theoros* means literally 'he who sees a vision'. . . . Thus the god Apollo of the Oracle at Delphi, when he *semainei*, 'indicates', is conferring an inner vision upon the *theoros*, the one who consults him." But the oracular response was transmitted to the *theoros* through the medium of language; the Pythia and her associates communicated the god's response to the *theoros* verbally. I will discuss the visual aspects of *theoria* at oracular centers below.

In the second kind of civic *theoria*, the city sent *theoroi* as official ambassadors to attend and witness a religious festival. The panhellenic festivals – the Olympian, Pythian, Nemean, and Isthmian – included a variety of religious rituals as well as competitions in athletic and artistic events. And the big Athenian festivals – the City Dionysia and the Panathenaia – featured these same kinds of spectacles (with the addition of dramatic contests at the Dionysia). These festivals drew *theoroi* from all over Greece and provided occasions for different cities to interact with one another. A Greek city sending a *theoria* to the major festivals chose its most illustrious men (generally aristocrats) to represent it in the international arena. The members of this embassy, like those visiting an oracular shrine, returned home with an official account of the *theoria*.[13] This kind of *theoria* was both a religious and a political practice, since the polis appointed *theoroi* to represent the city at festivals dedicated to the gods.

Both of these kinds of *theoria* involve journeying to a sacred precinct and witnessing the events that take place there. Ever since antiquity, people have debated whether the word "*theoria*" derives from *theos* (god) or *thea* ("sight," "spectacle").[14] Some modern scholars have been tempted to choose one or the other as the proper and original sense of the term.[15] I follow those scholars who identify *theoria* as both a spectacular and a sacred event – "sacred spectating" captures this dual signification.[16] Kavoulaki reveals the basic connection between seeing and the sacred: *theoria*, she says, "implies and incorporates all possible vantage points: viewing the worshippers from the point of view of the divinity, viewing the divinity among the worshippers, viewing the worshipping community as divine or 'other' and recognizing the power of the divine."[17] She rightly suggests that festival performances and ritual activities are "an invitation for the attention of the superhuman."[18] Thus, at religious festivals and oracular centers, the *theoroi* viewed the rituals, spectacles, and sacred images even as their own religious activities were "viewed" by the presiding god or goddess.

Although the spectacles featured at oracular centers and religious festivals addressed the ear as well as the eye, Greek sources foreground the visual

---

[13] Rutherford (forthcoming) discusses Greek inscriptions that deal with the official reports that the civic *theoroi* delivered upon returning to the city, and the events and/or rituals that took place when they returned.

[14] Rausch (1982, 15–18) reviews the ancient discussions of the etymology of this term. Rutherford (2000, 133–8) offers a good discussion of the word *theoria* and its cognates.

[15] Bill (1901, 198) and Boesch (1908, 4–7) argue that *thea* is the original sense of the word, while Buck (1953, 444) and Koller (1957, 276–9) give primacy to *theos* and *theia*.

[16] Rutherford (1995 and 1998) uses the term "sacred tourism." See also Coleman and Elsner 1995, ch. 1, and Ker 2000, 309.

[17] Kavoulaki 1999, 312.   [18] Kavoulaki 1999, 302.

aspect of *theoria*. Indeed, the *theoros* journeyed to a sanctuary for the purpose of seeing something for himself rather than hearing it reported by others: the "autopsy" or "eye-witnessing" of the spectacles at festivals was a defining aspect of *theoria*. Plato reveals the primacy of vision in his treatment of the practice of *theoria* in the *Laws*, where he discusses the strangers who come to the city of Magnesia for the purpose of attending their religious festivals. The foreign individual who attends such a festival, he claims, is a "*theoros*, in the literal sense, with his eyes, and also with his ears, [attending] all the spectacles of the Muses" (ὄμμασιν ὄντως θεωρὸς ὅσα τε μουσῶν ὡσὶν ἔχεται θεωρήματα, xii.953a). Here, Plato indicates that, in the strict sense, a *theoros* "sees" the sacred spectacles, but that taking in these spectacles "with the ears" still counts as *theoria* (by a sort of metaphorical extension). Plato makes a similar move in the *Republic* v, where he defines the philosophic contemplative by an analogue with the *theoroi* at religious festivals. For he first calls the *theoroi* "lovers of sights" (φιλοθεάμονες, 475d2) but then adds that those people who rush to all the Dionysian festivals are also "lovers of sounds" (φιλήκοοι, 475d3, see also 476b4). Although his own philosophic *theoros* sees rather than hears, Plato acknowledges that the traditional *theoros* uses both his eyes and his ears.[19]

Of course the *theoros* did not go to religious sanctuaries simply to gawk and gaze. As Elsner has suggested, *theoria* at religious sanctuaries was characterized by a specific mode of spectating – what he calls "ritual-centered visuality." The *theoros* witnessed objects and events that were sacralized by way of ritual structures and ceremonies, and was thus invited to engage in a distinct kind of seeing. First of all, the *theoros* enters a sacred space – a "liminal site in which the viewer enters the god's world and likewise the deity intrudes directly into the viewer's world in a highly ritualized context."[20] In this space, the *theoroi* participate in rituals and activities that bring about a certain mode of seeing. This "ritualized" visual mode "denies the appropriateness . . . of interpreting images through the rules and desires of everyday life. It constructs a ritual barrier to the identifications and objectifications of the screen of [social] discourse and posits a sacred possibility for vision . . ."[21] The viewing at oracles and festivals, then, was a religious activity in itself.[22]

Greek religious sanctuaries – with their peculiar blend of icons, statues, showy dedications, treasuries, and temples – offered a wide array of visual

---

[19] I will discuss this passage in detail in chapter 2.   [20] Elsner 2000, 61.   [21] Elsner 2000, 62.
[22] Rutherford 1998, 135. See also Jameson (1999) for an excellent discussion of the spectacular aspect of communal sacrifices (as he rightly observes, certain rituals – or portions of rituals – were "obscure," at times intentionally so).

options to the visitor. As Elsner claims, although "ritual-centered visuality" remained the defining feature of theoric spectating at religious sanctuaries, the *theoros* could opt for different "regimes of spectatorship" during his sojourn – regimes ranging from the aesthetic to the religious. In Euripides' *Andromache*, for example, the *theoros* Neoptolemus spends three whole days enjoying the aesthetic beauty of the sights in Delphi before he turns to his official theoric task: "giving over three bright cycles of the sun to seeing the sights, we feasted our eyes" (τρεῖς μὲν φαεννὰς ἡλίου διεξόδους | θέα διδόντες ὄμματ' ἐξεπίμπλαμεν, 1086–7). In the *Ion*, the members of the chorus in their visit to Delphi describe the spectacle of the sculptures on the temple in vivid detail, gasping with delight at each new scene (184–218).[23] They repeatedly compare these sculptures, and their mythic scenes, with the ones they have back home, thus engaging in a sort of cultural comparison. Their mode of viewing in this scene, then, is aesthetic rather than sacralized.[24]

In journeying to the major festivals and oracular centers, the *theoros* departed from the social and ideological "space" of his city and entered a panhellenic "space" in which Greeks were encouraged to rise above their differences and join together as people sharing a common language, religion, and culture. In this unique "space," the *theoroi* participated in a religious event that transcended – and, to some extent, challenged – the social, political, and ideological structures of any individual city. This is not to say that panhellenic gatherings transcended politics: the panhellenic space was (relatively) neutral, but the people certainly were not. As I will suggest, one cannot understand the practice of *theoria* without attending to its peculiar blend of religion and politics.

CIVIC AND PRIVATE *THEORIA*

All forms of *theoria* could be conducted privately, as well as in the civic context outlined above. The Greeks themselves differentiated these two modes of conducting a theoric journey. Thus Herodotus (to cite but one example) explicitly identifies the *theoria* of Hippocrates to Olympia as private rather

---

[23] They come as the attendants of Creusa and Xuthus, who have journeyed as *theoroi* to consult the oracle.

[24] Interestingly, when they then ask Ion whether they may enter the inner precinct, he tells them to "gaze upon all things with your eyes that are not forbidden" (πάντα θεάσθ', ὅ τι καὶ θέμις, ὄμμασι, 233). The latter sights, we may infer, are completely sacred, and therefore are not subject to ordinary touristic viewing. Note also the scene in Aeschylus' satyr-play the *Theoroi* (or *Isthmiastai*) where the satyrs view the temple and admire the images of the satyrs on the pediments (*TrGF* fr. 78a). And, in the *Thearoi* of Epicharmus, *theoroi* at Delphi gaze at the votive offerings (*CGF* fr. 79).

than civic (ἐόντι ἰδιώτῃ καὶ Ͽεωρέοντι τὰ Ὀλύμπια, 1.59.1).[25] In the case of "private" *theoria*, the individual *theoros* was not appointed or funded by the state, nor did he offer an official account of the *theoria* on his return home. In principle, he was not accountable to the city for what he saw or learned abroad – his activities as a *theoros* were entirely his own affair.

The civic *theoros*, by contrast, provided a direct link between the theoric event and his own city and its affairs. Whether he journeyed to an oracular center or a religious festival, the civic *theoros* was appointed by the city and his trip was payed for by public funds. The civic *theoros*, then, functioned as an ambassador who served as a representative of his city. When he returned, he delivered an official report of the events that took place abroad. Plato discusses this latter aspect of civic *theoria* in the *Laws* (950d–952c). In his legislation for the city of Magnesia, Plato positively forbids private *theoria* to the citizens, and sets forth many strictures for the practice of civic *theoria*, focusing in particular on the rules for the "return" of the *theoros* to the city. As soon as the Magnesian *theoros* gets home, Plato says, he must report "immediately" to the council that supervises the laws and report anything he has learned on his journey concerning legislation, education, or culture. If the council determines that he has brought back valuable information, he may convey this to the people; if not, he will be forbidden to associate with anyone in the city and compelled to live as a private person. If a *theoros* does not comply, they will try him in the courts and, if he is convicted, execute him as a traitor to the city (952c).[26]

Here, the reentry of the *theoros* is treated as a momentous and potentially dangerous political event: the importation of foreign ideas and practices can bring benefits to the city, but it can also bring corruption instead. Plato's attempt to control the reentry of the *theoros* is a reminder that, in civic *theoria*, the ambassador's return home is no less important than the journey abroad:

... in the case of a *theoros* bringing an oracle, the return poses a special crisis because it also represents the moment when a piece of information of immense danger and importance is injected into the community. The danger that a corrupt *theoros* will attempt to exploit the situation is ever present (cf. Theognis, 806). And a *theoros* bringing bad news, like a messenger, stands a good chance of being blamed (like Creon in the *Oedipus Tyrannus*).[27]

---

[25] Goldhill (1999a) and Ker (2000) aim to politicize private *theoria*. I agree that "the *theoros* . . . is always in some sense the city's representative" (Ker 2000, 310), but we must keep in mind the important differences between civic and private *theoria*.

[26] Plato's suggestion that the city should control the content of the theoric reports departs (to some extent) from traditional practice.

[27] Rutherford 1995, 282.

Because the civic *theoros* is a public ambassador and messenger, his *theoria* affects the entire city. Though the civic *theoros* and the private *theoros* have much in common, they nonetheless occupy distinct categories. The civic *theoros*, as a public ambassador, performs specific religious and political duties; this is very different from the private pilgrim or spectator. As we will see, the different practices of *theoria* – civic and private – offered very different models for philosophic *theoria*.

THEOROS VS. THEATĒS

The fourth-century philosophers took as their primary model the *theoria* at religious festivals, and we must therefore investigate this kind of spectating in greater detail. Since most of our evidence about ancient festivals centers on Athens, I will begin first with this material. What constitutes a *theoria* to an Athenian festival? As we have seen, in the texts from the classical period the word "*theoros*" refers to an individual making a journey abroad to a sanctuary or festival.[28] Thus the Athenian spectator at the Dionysia or any other local festival is never called a "*theoros*": he is a "*theatēs*." Thucydides offers a useful clarification of this point: when a city observes religious rites and practices at home, it enacts a *thusia*, not a *theoria* (v.50.25).

Goldhill and other scholars have recently argued just the opposite: that we should categorize the Athenians in attendance at Athens' festivals as *theoroi*.[29] Goldhill bases his argument on the claim that the citizens in classical Athens received handouts from the Theoric Fund at the time of the Dionysian festival. The Athenian citizens, he suggests, were paid by the city to attend the Dionysia in the same way that the civic *theoroi* were funded to undertake a *theoria* abroad; the Athenian spectators thus functioned as local *theoroi*:

---

[28] See, e.g., Koller 1957, 279, Rutherford 1995, 276; 1998, 132, and Ker 2000, 308. Excluding Plato and other fourth-century thinkers dealing with philosophic *theoria* (who expanded the sense of the term), there are very few deviations from the technical sense of the words θεωρία and θεωρός in the classical period. In fact, these all occur in fourth-century texts (Plato's appropriation of the word *theoria* in his middle-period dialogues no doubt influenced other intellectuals and writers in the middle and late fourth century). E.g., Isocrates claims in the *Areopagiticus* 53 (*circa* late 350s) that the early Athenians did not celebrate *ta peri tas theorias* – a periphrasis for "festivals" – in an ostentatious way; here, Isocrates refers to Athens' management of her own festivals or "theoric events"; Demosthenes (*Contra Macarta* 18.4) uses θεωρία to refer to the sight of a diagram drawn on a pinax; similarly, Pseudo-Demosthenes (*Eroticus* 16) identifies the viewing of a work of art as a Θεωρία.

[29] Goldhill 1999a; Monoson 2000, 206–26.

In a sense, every citizen performed the role [of a *theoros*]: the theoric fund (*to theorikon*) was established to enable every citizen to attend the theatre . . . To be a *theoros* is a right and duty of the Athenian citizen, performed in the institutions of the state and institutionally supported by financial and legal means.[30]

Paid by the state to view the religious and political spectacles of their own city, Goldhill claims, the Athenian citizens act as *theoroi* at their own festivals.[31]

We must note, however, that the Theoric Fund did not yet exist in the fifth century: this fund was almost certainly instituted in the mid-fourth century, probably in the 350s.[32] So far from being a venerable demo-cratic institution, the fund was created by certain politicians (most notably Eubulos) in order to gain the support of the *demos* by instituting hand-outs to the citizens. Indeed, as Demosthenes' repeated denunciations of Eubulos and the theoric fund reveal, even when the fund was instituted in the closing decades of the classical period, it was highly contested and hardly a special marker of democratic identity.[33] In addition, the citizens who received handouts from the fund were under no obligation to attend the festival: many of the poorer citizens opted to pocket the money rather than pay the high price of admission for the theatrical events.[34]

The most important piece of linguistic evidence from classical sources for identifying Athenian *theatai* at their own civic festivals as *theoroi* is the very name of the "Theoric Fund" (the *theorikon*).[35] But this term is not found in any text before the middle of the fourth century.[36] Thus, a single term used in the closing decades of the classical period provides the primary linguistic evidence for the identification of the *theatēs* as a *theoros*.[37]

---

[30] Goldhill 1999a, 6–7.   [31] Goldhill 1999a, 7; see also 1994, 352 and 1996, 19.

[32] Van Ooteghem (1932) argues that the fund was created by Eubulos *circa* 360; Buchanan (1962, 28–74) claims that it was originally instituted by Agyrrhios in the 390s (though the sole evidence for this claim is Harpocration in the second century CE) and later expanded by Eubulos; Rhodes (1972, 105–6) suggests that it was created or reorganized after the Social War. See also Pickard-Cambridge 1968, 265–8, Ruschenbusch 1979, Sommerstein 1997, Wilson 1997.

[33] Buchanan 1962, 48–74.

[34] Sommerstein (1997) and Wilson (1997) discuss the role of the theoric fund in relation to the admission fee at the Greater Dionysia (more on this below).

[35] The adjective *theorikos* is seldom used in classical texts. Euripides' *Supplices* 97 refers to the "theoric robes" that foreign *theoroi* would wear, and Heniochus frag. 5 (*PCG*) refers to a "theoric stage" at the Olympian games. In both cases, the adjective simply means "of or pertaining to a festival." This would suggest that the Athenian "theoric fund" was generally "concerned with festivals" (i.e. that the funds were not simply used as handouts to Athenian spectators at the Dionysia but also were spent on the spectacles and events at other festivals).

[36] Rhodes (1972, 105 6) claims that Eubulos (who founded or, possibly, reorganized the Theoric Fund in the 350s) was responsible for the name "*theorikon*."

[37] I do not deny that there is some connection between the activities of the Athenian *theatēs* and those of a *theoros*, but the differences between the *theatēs* and the *theoros* are far greater than the similarities.

In evaluating this evidence, we must keep in mind that the verb *theorein* has a much broader scope than the nouns *theoros* and *theoria*, since it can be used in the general sense of "seeing" or "observing" an object or event in any context.[38] Because of its broad semantic range, the verb *theorein* does not, by itself, identify a viewer as a *theoros* (in the technical sense picked out by the nouns *theoros* and *theoria*).

Goldhill stretches the traditional practice of *theoria* to include all cases in which Athenian citizens gathered for collective viewing. As he claims, *theoria* was a sociopolitical activity performed by citizens not only in the theater but also in the Assembly and lawcourts. He argues for this by identifying the role played by the citizens voting in the Assembly and courts with that of the citizens attending the theater.[39] In all these cases, he claims, the Athenian citizens are *"theatai tōn logōn"* or "spectators of speeches" (as Cleon puts it in Thucydides III.38.4–7).[40] In his view, the *theatai* at the Assembly, the lawcourts, and the theater should be identified as *theoroi*. All are engaging in *theoria*, which is here reconceived as the spectating and judging enacted by democratic citizens at civic and political venues: "*theoria* emphasizes the role of the evaluating, judging spectator as a key factor in the

---

[38] For passages where the verb Θεωρεῖν is used in the non-technical sense of "observing" or "seeing" something, see, e.g., Hdt. III.32, IV.76; Thuc. IV.93.1. For uses of the verb in the technical sense of traveling as a Θεωρός to a sanctuary or festival in a foreign city, see, e.g., Hdt. I.59, VIII.26, Aristoph. *Wasps* 1187–8, 1382, Thuc. III.104, V.50, VIII.10, Xen. *Hiero* I.12, Isoc. *Panegyricus* 44–5. Note that the verb is never used of a person attending a festival in his own city in fifth-century texts (though we do find a few such uses in the mid to late fourth century).

[39] Many scholars have discussed the significant parallels between the citizen "audiences" at political and theatrical gatherings in Athens. They point out that the Pnyx and the theater were similar in spatial organization; that the theater was sometimes used for public meetings in the fourth century; and that the citizen-audiences in both venues offered a collective judgment on discourses that concerned contemporary social and political issues (see, e.g., Ober 1989, 152–5, Ober and Strauss 1990, Winkler 1990, Zeitlin 1990a and 1990b, Euben 1990, Goldhill 1990, 1994, and 1997, Sommerstein et al. 1993, Foley 1993, Rehm 1992 and 2002, Saïd 1998). While these parallels are instructive, we should also attend to the differences between an exclusive audience of male citizens at the Assembly (about 6,000 in number) and a mixed audience of roughly 17,000 people at the theater, which included adult citizens, boys, foreigners, metics, at least some slaves, and possibly also women. For a discussion of the makeup of the audience at the City Dionysia, see Pickard-Cambridge 1968, ch. 6, Goldhill 1997; on the question whether women attended the theater, see, e.g., Podlecki 1990, Henderson 1991, Goldhill 1994.

[40] Note that, in this speech, Cleon draws a sharp *distinction* between the activity of participating in the Assembly and that of "spectating" for entertainment: the Athenians wrongly pursue the "pleasures of the ear" in the Assembly, behaving "more like men who sit as spectators watching sophists than men deliberating about the affairs of the city" (σοφιστῶν Θεαταῖς ἐοικότες καθημένοις μᾶλλον ἢ περὶ πόλεως βουλευομένοις, III.38.7). Cleon does not say that the Athenians are acting in the Assembly like *theatai* at the theater: rather, they are acting like people watching *sophists*, i.e. foreign men who performed not in the theater but rather in the agora, the gymnasia, and in private homes. Cleon does not, then, juxtapose participation at the Assembly with attendance at the Athenian theater (cf. Goldhill 1994, 352–7).

construction of democratic culture."⁴¹ While the analysis of the Athenian spectator in the context of the discourses and practices of the democracy is tremendously valuable, it does not tell us much about the institution of *theoria*. Indeed, this exclusive focus on the Athenian citizen viewing and judging his own polis obscures what is distinctive about *theoria*, namely, that this cultural practice was international and cross-cultural. The study of the political aspects of *theoria* cannot focus exclusively on Athens (or any single city) and its particular political practices.

ELITES AS CIVIC REPRESENTATIVES

Theoria brought different Greek cities and cultures into contact with one another in shared sanctuaries, and featured rituals and events that transcended any single ideological perspective. This does not mean, however, that the *theoroi* shed their political identities in the act of communal celebration. On the contrary, the Greeks who assembled and interacted at the major oracular centers and festivals were members of a panhellenic group by virtue of being members of individual Greek city-states. As Sourvinou-Inwood suggests, in ancient Greece "the *polis* anchored, legitimated, and mediated all religious activity," even in the panhellenic sanctuaries:

> The *theoroi* of each *polis* conducted ritual acts in the Panhellenic sanctuaries in the name of that *polis* . . . The treasuries erected by individual *poleis* in the great Panhellenic sanctuaries are the physical expression of this mediation [of the *polis*], the symbolic representation of the *polis* systems in those sanctuaries.⁴²

At the panhellenic sanctuaries and large religious festivals, one city played host to the *theoroi* from other cities: for example, the Delphians regulated every aspect of the Delphic Oracle, including the admission and exclusion of all visiting *theoroi*, who were "treated on the model of *xenoi* [foreign guests] worshiping at the sanctuary of another *polis*."⁴³ Likewise, the citizens of Elis presided over the Olympian festival, the Delphians over the Pythian festival, the Athenians over the City Dionysia, and so on. Correlatively, the *theoroi* – or "foreign guests" – were received (and perceived) as members of their individual cities.

Theoria not only brought different Greek cities into contact with one another but also the elite members of these cities. For the civic *theoroi* were selected from the highest ranks of society, and were generally wealthy

⁴¹ Goldhill 1999a, 8.   ⁴² Sourvinou-Inwood 1990, 297–8.   ⁴³ Sourvinou-Inwood 1990, 297.

aristocrats.[44] The civic *theoros* did of course represent his city in the panhellenic gathering; but he also pursued private distinction in the world of Greek elites. As Herman observes, the Greek world "was interlaced with a network of *xenia* alliances binding the elites of different communities together"; these kinds of friendships operated outside of – and, at times, in opposition to – the ideology and government of the person's city.[45] The practice of *theoria* enabled elites to form personal friendships and associations with powerful men from foreign (and, sometimes, hostile) cities. The panhellenic festivals, then, effectively created gatherings of Greek elites.

These panhellenic gatherings offered individuals an excellent opportunity to pursue personal status and influence. Consider, for example, Alicibiades' *theoria* to the Olympian games. When serving as an official Athenian *theoros* at Olympia, Alcibiades entered seven chariots in the chariot-race, winning three prizes. In spite of Alcibiades' claim that this brought great luster to the city of Athens, other Athenians believed that he gained power and prestige at the city's expense.[46] Andocides claims that Alcibiades actually upstaged the Athenians on this *theoria* in the opulence of his accommodations, thanks to lavish gifts supplied by non-Athenian communities: the Ephesians erected for him a Persian tent twice the size of the one used by the city; the Chians gave him animals for sacrifices and food for his horses; and the people of Lesbos provided wine and other supplies.[47] Although Andocides no doubt distorted some of the facts, his suggestion that Alcibiades received (and flaunted) costly gifts from non-Athenians shows how elite display could work against the good of the city. The private pursuits of the elite *theoros* did not necessarily serve his city's interests.

The international context of theoric events invited individuals to engage in lavish forms of self-display. The leader of a *theoria* – the *architheoros* – enjoyed an especially visible position. He paid dearly for this position,

---

[44] See, e.g., Plato *Laws* 950e.
[45] Herman 1987, 138 and *passim* (cf. L. Mitchell 1997). See also Kurke (1991, 1993), who discusses the difficult reentry of the victorious athlete at the panhellenic games into his own civic community, which brought about a clash between aristocratic and non-aristocratic members of the city; Ober 1989 (and see also 1998) offers an excellent analysis of the conflict (and the negotiations) between mass and elite in democratic Athens.
[46] Thuc. VI.16; Isoc. XVI.32.
[47] Andocides IV. 29–31. He also claims that Alcibiades borrowed sacred golden vessels from the leader of the Athenian embassy, and then used them in public before the Athenians did, thus creating the impression that the Athenians had borrowed the vessels from him. See also Thucydides VI.15.2, where Nicias argues that Alcibiades indulged in a "private display" during this *theoria*, which was damaging to the public interest.

since it was his duty to arrange and fund the conveyance of the offerings sent to a sanctuary by the city.[48] In Athens, the *architheoros* performed this task as a liturgy, i.e. as a private expenditure on behalf of the city. This office enhanced his reputation among the Athenians, but it also gave him the chance to gain personal authority and fame abroad. According to Aristotle, the *architheoria* was a liturgy that tended to be exceptionally costly (*NE* 1122a25); this would suggest that the *architheoros* went to great expense to make himself conspicuous on the international stage. Nicias, for example, funded a spectacular *theoria* to Delos in which he led an Athenian chorus into the festival over a bridge decorated with gold, fine fabrics, tapestries, and garlands, which he had erected especially for this event. He also bought land in Delos, the revenues from which provided the Delians with sacrificial feasts "at which they asked the gods to bring many blessings to Nicias."[49] Once again, we find a wealthy individual pursuing private as well as civic interests during a journey of *theoria*.

The practice of *theoria*, then, was intensely political, and featured an ongoing negotiation of power and influence both at the level of the city and of the individual. The civic *theoros* serves, first and foremost, as a representative of his city; but he also pursues private distinction in the world of Greek elites.

ATHENIAN FESTIVALS AND THE THEORIC GAZE

The panhellenic festivals (i.e. the Olympian, Pythian, Nemean and Isthmian) attracted Greeks from all over the Mediterranean. As C. Morgan observes, "most pan-Hellenic sanctuaries occupied remote or marginal locations, beyond the borders of the majority of participant states, and usually under the political control of a weak, or subservient, state or institution, and they therefore offered neutral locations for states to meet and compete."[50] Large numbers of *theoroi* also attended the major Athenian festivals – the Panathenaia and the City Dionysia – though these were not panhellenic in the strict sense and did not provide a neutral location for Greek gatherings. But there were many similarities between the Athenian and the panhellenic festivals. A brief examination of Athenian festivals – which are by far the best documented – will offer a more detailed picture of the

---

[48] For references to the *architheoria*, see Andocides 1.132 (on the *architheoros* for the *theoria* to the Isthmian and Olympian festivals, perhaps in 400 BCE); Lysias XXI.5; Demosthenes XXI.115 (on the *architheoros* for the *theoria* to the Nemean festival); *Hesperia* 37 no. 51.26–7 (on the *architheoros* to the Pythian festival, in 331/0). Wilson (2000, 44–6) offers a useful discussion of the *architheoria*, focusing in particular on theoric events involving choruses.

[49] Plutarch, *Nicias* III.4–6.   [50] C. Morgan 1993, 31.

operations of a "theoric event." And it will also show how the presence of foreign *theoroi* – and the alterity of the "theoric gaze" – affected the discourse and practice of the Athenian religious festival.[51]

The Great Panathenaia, held every four years, is generally taken to be Athens' attempt to rival panhellenic festivals such as the Olympic games.[52] In this festival, the procession included not only male Athenian citizens, but also Athenian maidens and priestesses, metics (male and female), freed slaves and non-Greeks living in Attica.[53] The festival also featured athletic and musical contests, open to both Athenians and foreigners. The Panathenaia, with its lavish array of prizes, attracted contestants and spectators from all over Greece. In fact, during the period of the empire, Athens made it compulsory for all the Athenian colonies to participate in the festival by bringing a cow and a suit of armor as offerings to the goddess. In addition, beginning in at least the 450s, Athens laid down a law that imposed this same regulation on the allied cities, thus compelling these foreign peoples to send a *theoria* with offerings to the festival. The seriousness of this law is revealed by a decree dating to the 440s that makes the failure of the allied cities to bring offerings to the festival an offense tantamount to the failure to pay the annual tribute.[54] Since, at the height of her empire, Athens received tribute from roughly 400 communities, the number of *theoroi* from the allied cities alone would have been quite large. Indeed, because of this (enforced) participation of the allied cities, some scholars have described the Great Panathenaia in this period as an "Empire festival."[55]

The City Dionysia, held every year in Athens, took a different form. Though it also began with a huge procession, the competitions at this festival were exclusively artistic (dithyrambic choruses and dramatic productions).[56] The events at this festival featured an interesting and, in certain

---

[51] For an excellent discussion of *theoriai* sent by Athens to other territories, see Rutherford 2003.

[52] For discussions of the Panathenaia, see Parke 1977, 33–50, Neils 1992, Goldhill 1994, Wohl 1996, Maurizio 1998. Neils (1992, 13–27) suggests that the Panathenaia reflected and reinforced the political and social structures of classical Athens. Cf. Wohl (1996, 27), who argues that "reading the Panathenaia as a univocal celebration of Athenian democratic ideology reduces and reifies both the ritual and the ideology until they are both themselves as static as a frieze"; rather, the festival "is multivalent and dynamic, a site of contestation and ideological tension . . ." Following de Polignac's claim that "religious citizenship" represented an axis for defining community that was not coextensive with political citizenship (1995, 78 and *passim*), Maurizio argues persuasively that the Panathenaic procession "presented two visions of Athens simultaneously: in one, Athens was an inclusive community of religious identity; in the other, Athens appeared as an exclusive community of political identity" (1998, 376).

[53] Parke 1977, 38–44.

[54] The penalties being the same in both cases (see Garland 1992, 106–7 for a discussion of these decrees).

[55] Meiggs and Lewis 1969, 91, Garland 1992, 106–7.

[56] For discussions of the City Dionysia, see Parke 1977, 124–36, Pickard-Cambridge 1968, ch. 2 and *passim*, Connor 1989, Winkler 1990, Goldhill 1990, 1994, Sourvinou-Inwood 1994.

ways, surprising mix of Athenian citizens and noncitizens (even though the festival was primarily focused on Athens). First, the procession was made up of Athenian male citizens, young women, metics (and possibly their wives[57]), and *theoroi* from the colonies. In the artistic contests, moreover, the dithyrambic competition was open to foreign poets, though only Athenians could be *choregoi* and members of the choruses.[58] In the dramatic competitions, by contrast, the actors and especially the fluteplayers were very often foreigners, while the *choregoi* and the chorus-members had to be Athenian citizens.[59] Note also that the authors of these "musical" productions did not have to be from Athens: the composers of dithyrambs were often non-Athenians;[60] and even the dramatic playwrights could be foreigners, in spite of the fact that this genre is seen as quintessentially Athenian.[61]

In these musical and dramatic competitions, the Athenians did not simply compete against one another (as in contests between the demes), nor did they simply compete against foreigners (as in the athletic contests at the Panathenaia). Rather, since the participants in musical productions generally included some foreigners, the Athenians often competed with – rather than against – non-Athenians. To be sure, most of the members of dithyrambic and dramatic productions were Athenians, but the fact that the groups included, and were open to, foreigners is a reminder of the inclusive nature of this festival. In addition, other events at the City Dionysia also featured noncitizens and foreigners: the displaying on-stage of the annual tribute, which the allies were required to bring to Athens at this time; the crowning of both citizens and noncitizens for benefactions to Athens; the announcement of the manumission of slaves; and the public enactment of inter-city rituals, such as the enunciation of the oath of alliance between Athens and Sparta, which they agreed to renew annually at the Dionysia and the Hyacinthia (the Spartan festival of Apollo at Amyclae).[62]

---

[57] Sourvinou-Inwood 1994, 271; cf. Goldhill 1994, 362.
[58] The choruses were made up of groups from each of the ten Athenian tribes and thus had a tribal articulation that reflected the Cleisthenic division of the citizenry into demes.
[59] Rehm 2002, ch. 1; on fluteplaying in Athens, see Wilson 1999.
[60] For example, Hypodicus of Chalcis won the first prize at the City Dionysia in 509/8; in the early fifth century, Simonides, Pindar, and Bacchylides entered pieces in this competition; in the mid/late-fifth century, Ion of Chios, Melanippides of Melos, Timotheus of Miletus, and Philoxenus of Cythera participated in the competitions.
[61] E.g. Pratinas of Phlius won in the tragic competition against Aeschylus and Choerilus (in the 490s), and his son, Aristeas, won several prizes; Aristarchus of Tegea wrote seventy tragedies, winning two victories; Ion of Chios, who wrote ten tetralogies, won a first and third prize and celebrated a double victory in tragedy and the dithyramb at the City Dionysia; and Archaeus of Eretria won a victory in the tragic competition. See *TrGF* I (which lists ten non-Athenian tragic playwrights), Pickard-Cambridge 1962 and 1968, 74–9, 79–82, Ostwald 1992, 323–8, and Rehm 2002, ch. 1.
[62] Thucydides v.23.4.

As for the spectators, scholars have generally assumed that Athenian citizens made up the majority of the people at the City Dionysia. But, as Sommerstein has recently argued, the expensive admission fee would have prohibited most working-class citizens from attending the plays, at least before the theoric fund was instituted in the fourth century (and even then the poorer citizens might have preferred to simply pocket the money). According to Sommerstein, noncitizens might well have constituted half of the entire audience at the theater (including foreigners, metics, children, and possibly women).[63] Even if this goes too far, there is no doubt that large numbers of *theoroi* from all over the Greek world regularly attended the festival.[64] The events and spectacles at the City Dionysia were therefore the object of various "theoric gazes" and not just the "democratic gaze" of the Athenian citizen. The distinction between these two is nicely articulated in Aristophanes' *Acharnians*, where Dikaiopolis says to the audience:

Do not begrudge me, spectators (ἄνδρες οἱ θεώμενοι), if I, a beggar, dare to speak before the Athenians about the city in a comic play . . . I shall utter things that are terrible but true. And Cleon cannot slander me now, saying that I criticize the city when foreigners are present (ξένων παρόντων). For this is the Lenaian Festival, and we are all alone. No foreigners are here, for the tributes and allies from the cities have not yet arrived. (498–506)

Here, Aristophanes indicates that the Lenaian festival was attended by Athenians, whereas the City Dionysia drew an international audience. As this passage suggests, Cleon had attacked Aristophanes for criticizing Athens at a City Dionysia, when "foreigners were present." Isocrates makes a similar point when he says that comic poets at the City Dionysia "broadcast the failings of Athens to the rest of the Hellenes" (εἰς τοὺς ἄλλους Ἕλληνας).[65]

---

[63] Sommerstein 1997, 64–8. As he points out, two obols – the admission fee per person per day – was a third of the daily pay of an oarsman or a construction worker, and two thirds of a juror's. Cf. Wilson (1997, 100), who also argues that the admission fee was designed to deter certain people from attending the theater; but, as he claims, because the theoric fund offset this fee for all the citizens, the fee must have been designed to prevent metics, foreigners, and possibly slaves and women from attending. However, as Sommerstein rightly observes (1997, 66n. 19), the fact that the theoric fund was not instituted until the mid-fourth century tells against Wilson's claim; for most of the classical period, the fee functioned to exclude poor and working-class people across the board rather than the foreigners and metics (and, perhaps, women from wealthy families) who could afford these prices.

[64] As for seating in the theater, some seats were reserved for the Athenian Council of 500 (the *bouleutikon*) and their attendant slaves, and the front stalls (*prohedriai*) for dignitaries of state and foreign ambassadors. Winkler (1990) argued that each *kerkis* of the theater was reserved for a particular Athenian tribe (with at least one other *kerkis* for foreigners and/or metics); as Rehm (1992) and Goldhill (1994, 364–5) rightly observe, the evidence for this is poor.

[65] *On the Peace* 14 (I assume that Isocrates refers here to the comic poets, whom he mentions in the previous sentence as indulging in "freedom of speech").

The presence of foreigners, then, made the City Dionysia a very different kind of event from the Lenaia: for, at the Dionysia, the foreign or "theoric" spectators were looking at the Athenians (and each other) from the outside. The spectacles at this festival, then, did not just "represent the city to the city":[66] they also opened Athens to the gaze of foreigners. This is nicely captured by a story reported by Athenaeus: as he claims, the Athenians who received the news of the Sicilian defeat while attending the theater at the Dionysia refused to leave their seats "so that they would not show the spectators from other cities how badly they were taking the disaster" (IX.407a–b).[67] The Athenians at the Dionysia, in short, were confronted with the alterity of the theoric gaze: the participants at the festivals confronted multiple perspectives that challenged their own individual points of view.

Evidence of Athenian awareness of foreign, "theoric" gazes appears in many classical texts.[68] In Aristophanes' *Peace*, for example, the servant feeding the giant dungbeetle wonders what the audience must think of this creature, and speculates that

there is some brilliant young intellectual in the audience asking "what is the substance of this? towards what end does this beetle exist?" And then some Ionian sitting near him will say to him, "Now I've nae doubt but this is aimed at Cleon, it eats the muck sae unco shamelessly." (43–8)[69]

In this scene, Aristophanes conjures up a conversation between two Greeks sitting next to each other at the City Dionysia who speak in different dialects: the first speaker uses Attic Greek (using discourse that is markedly philosophic), and the second an Ionian dialect. Here, we are reminded that the audience at the Dionysia contained diverse gazes and elicited diverse responses. Consider also the parabasis in the *Acharnians*, where the chorus claims that Aristophanes is bringing great benefit to the Athenians by criticizing them and "by showing the people *in the allied cities*

---

[66] Goldhill 1991, 185; Goldhill discusses the presence of the foreigners at the festival in 1990, 239, noting that the "intersections and disjunctions" between the citizens and non-citizens "are largely unexplored."

[67] This story may not be historically accurate but nonetheless paints a plausible picture. Note also the passage in Plato's *Laws* where Megillus offers a glimpse of the Athenian festival from the Spartan point of view: he condemns the riotous and foolish behavior of drunken people whom he saw at the Dionysia in Athens and commends the abstention from drinking practiced in his own home city (637a–b).

[68] Taplin (1993, 3–6) offers a useful discussion of the presence of foreign visitors at the Athenian festivals as well as the importation of dramatic productions and festivals by non-Athenian states in the fifth to the third centuries BCE.

[69] I cite from Rogers' translation (in the Loeb) of lines 48–9; unlike many translators, he makes it clear that the second speaker is using the Ionian dialect.

how they are democratically governed" (καὶ τοὺς δήμους ἐν ταῖς πόλεσιν δείξας ὡς δημοκρατοῦνται, 641–2).[70] In the contest between Aeschylus and Euripides in the *Frogs*, moreover, the latter says that the tragic poets "make people *in the cities* (ἐν ταῖς πόλεσιν) better men" (1009–10). As Taplin observes, "one of the few things that the two great dead poets in the *Frogs* can agree on is that poetry, and in particular tragedy, has . . . a pan-Hellenic value."[71] The presence of foreigners at the Dionysia, then, had an enormous impact on the festival. Indeed this is the major factor in the battle between Aeschines and Demosthenes over the question whether the latter should receive a crown in the theater at the Dionysia or in the Athenian Assembly: while disagreeing on every other count, they both understand that a crowning at the Dionysian festival would take place "in the eyes of all the Hellenes" (ἐναντίον ἁπάντων τῶν Ἑλλήνων) and thus would reach a different, and far wider, audience than it would in the Athenian Assembly.[72]

Even though the Athenian *theatai* at their own festivals are not *theoroi*, then, the festival itself is a "theoric event," i.e. a religious spectacle attended by significant numbers of foreign *theoroi*. The Athenians were clearly quite alert to this fact. For example, Alcibiades claims in Thucydides (vi.16) that he impressed the foreign *theoroi* at the festivals in Athens by funding splendid dramatic choruses that performed at the City Dionysia. In displaying his wealth and generosity at home (as the *choregos* who paid for these choruses), he may have created envy "among the townspeople" (τοῖς μὲν ἀστοῖς) but he presented an image of strength and power "in the eyes of foreigners" (πρὸς δὲ τοὺς ξένους).[73] In this passage, Alcibiades treats the City Dionysia in Athens as a theoric event on a par with the Olympian festival, and even suggests that his funding of choruses in Athens – which was a "liturgy" or benefaction given to the city by its richest members – actually had an important impact on the foreign members of the audience. To be sure, the liturgy was primarily conceived as a "gift" to the Athenian city and its people, and it played a significant role in the internal politics of democratic Athens. Alcibiades does not deny that he performed his liturgies to benefit the people of Athens, but suggests that these benefactions also influenced the non-Athenian members of the audience. As this passage

---

[70] See also Aristophanes' *Clouds*, where the chorus brings greetings from the moon "to the Athenians and the allies" (607–9).
[71] Taplin 1993, 5–6.   [72] The quote is from Aeschines, *Against Ctesiphon* 43 (cf. 49).
[73] See Wilson (1997) for an excellent discussion of the symbolic capital accrued by the aristocratic Athenian *choregos*. As he rightly argues, the *choregos* was a highly visible member of a tragic competition, engaging in "a paradramatic performance" that enhanced his own prestige and power (85–6).

reveals, the Athenians fully acknowledged the international presence in the audiences at their big festivals: the spectacles were presented to Athenians and to foreigners, and evoked different responses from different groups (hence Alcibiades' claim that his expenditure on the choruses affected the locals and the foreigners quite differently).

Isocrates offers an interesting analysis of the international presence at the Dionysia in *On the Peace*, where he castigates the Athenians for offending the foreign members of the audience. As he claims, the Athenians behaved with incredible arrogance during the empire when they divided the money that the allies paid in tribute into talents and brought it onto the stage at the Dionysian festival "when the theater was full." This display of Athenian power at a religious festival was insulting and hubristic, since it was designed to "display *to the allies*" (ἐπιδεικνύοντες τοῖς μὲν συμμάχοις) their dishonorable and subservient position. In addition, he adds, the Athenians "led the sons of the citizens who had died in battle into the theater . . . displaying *to the rest of the Hellenes* (τοῖς δ' ἄλλοις Ἕλλησι) the great number of their own orphans and the misfortunes they had suffered in war" (82–3). Here, Isocrates refers to several of the non-theatrical spectacles at the City Dionysia – the displaying of the tribute brought to Athens by the allies, and the parade in the *orchestra*, in full military regalia, of the Athenian boys whose fathers had died in the war.[74] In this passage, Isocrates conceives of the audience as falling into three groups – the Athenians, the allies, and the "rest of the Hellenes" (including *theoroi* from neutral or hostile nations). Each group, he indicates, had a very different response to these spectacles. This vitriolic passage may not offer an accurate interpretation of the precise reactions provoked by these displays at the Dionysia. Nonetheless, it offers a useful reminder of the mixed nature of the audience at the festival and the different perspectives represented by the members of this audience.

THE POLITICS OF PANHELLENISM

In investigating the political valence of the gatherings at theoric events, one must look beyond the local politics of an individual city such as Athens. Since the major shrines, festivals, and oracular centers attracted people from all over Greece, they brought disparate (and sometimes hostile) peoples into contact. As Rutherford claims,

... an underlying reason for going to a panhellenic sanctuary was to assert the voice of one's own polis in the panhellenic community, and hence to gain recognition

[74] For an excellent discussion of the spectacles and events at the City Dionysia, see Goldhill 1990.

and prestige throughout the Greek world. The panhellenic significance of the great sanctuaries is so central that we should think of the underlying structure of much Greek pilgrimage as a symbolic movement not so much from "secular space" to "sacred space" and back again, but rather between "local space" and "panhellenic space."[75]

Rutherford rightly emphasizes "panhellenic space" as a defining feature of the theoric event. But it is of course Greek religion and its "spaces" that provide the institutional and ideological grounding for panhellenic gatherings.[76]

The very existence of panhellenic festivals testifies to the fact that the Greeks perceived themselves as members of a single religious group. As Sourvinou-Inwood observes, the Greek identity "was cultically expressed in, and reinforced through, ritual activities in which the participating group was 'all the Greeks' and from which foreigners [i.e. non-Greeks] were excluded."[77] This vision of Greek unity and kinship – which formed the very core of the politics of panhellenism – was in fact regularly promoted by the rhetorical speeches composed for these festivals (for example Gorgias' *Olympicus* and *Pythicus* and Lysias' *Olympicus*; Isocrates' *Panegyricus* also belongs to this genre, though the author did not deliver it himself).[78] As Isocrates says in the *Panegyricus*:

Those who founded the great festivals are rightly praised for handing down a custom whereby, proclaiming a truce and resolving our existing quarrels, we come together in one place; then, as we perform our prayers and sacrifices in common, we recall the kinship that exists between us and are made to feel more friendly towards each other in the future. (43)

According to this account, the panhellenic religious festivals – in which all the participants joined in rituals, sacrifices, and prayers – aimed to promote Greek commonality and concord. This encouraged the Greeks to rise above their political and ideological differences and to meet on a higher plane.

To be sure, Isocrates articulates an idealizing portrait of panhellenism. To what extent did the Greeks experience a sense of unity at these religious events? Unfortunately, we do not have enough evidence from the classical

---

[75] Rutherford 1995, 276. See Connor (1988), who offers a persuasive challenge to the idea (articulated by Durkheim) that the "sacred" and "secular" are mutually exclusive in spatial and institutional contexts. As Connor shows, "in classical Athenian culture the sacred was seen as parallel to and co-ordinate with the other [i.e. 'secular'] realm" (p. 164).

[76] It is precisely the confluence of religion and politics that made *theoria* a unique cultural practice, investing it with such great authority and legitimacy.

[77] Sourvinou-Inwood 1990, 300.

[78] For a discussion of this genre (and of Isocrates' place within it), see Nightingale 1995, 96–8.

period to answer this question definitively. Certainly the very existence of common sanctuaries and panhellenic religious events fostered some sense of a shared "Greek" identity. Indeed these sanctuaries offered a panhellenic "space" that transcended civic ideologies and generated a commonality based on a shared religion and culture.

But, as we have seen, Greek religious practices never completely transcended politics. In fact, individuals from different cities often competed at these festivals in contests that pitted one city against another. As Cartledge suggests, "[athletic] competition at Olympia was a paramilitary exercise" where the competitors "channelled their competitive aggression into action that only just stayed this side of outright martial violence."[79] Not surprisingly, political tensions ran high at panhellenic gatherings, especially when individuals at these festivals came from cities that were at war with each other.[80] An example of political hostility at an Olympian festival (occurring in the early fourth century BCE) is recounted by Dionysius of Halicarnassus:

In his Panegyric, the orator [Lysias] summoned the Greeks to expel Dionysius of Syracuse from power and free Sicily, and to start the hostilities at once by plundering the ruler's tent with its adornments of gold, purple finery, and many other riches . . . For the tyrant of Syracuse had sent *theoroi* to attend the festival and offer sacrifice to the god. Their arrival in the sanctuary had been staged on an impressive and lavish scale to enhance the dynast's prestige among the Greeks.[81]

Consider also a fragment of Heniochus (a comic poet of the fourth century BCE), which offers a fascinating picture of the politically charged atmosphere at the panhellenic festival, and the pressures this exerted on the individual *theoroi*. Heniochus creates a scene in which two cities, here personified as individuals, come to an Olympian festival as *theoroi*. First, the cities begin to disintegrate after a long stay in Olympia because of a "lack of counsel" (ἀβουλία); then two prostitutes named "Demokratia" and "Aristokratia" get them drunk and "throw them into confusion" (ταράττετον), presumably vying for their favor.[82] Here, the panhellenic festival provides a context in which the advocates of different forms of government can seduce and

---

[79] Cartledge 1985, 112.

[80] For example, Thucydides reports that at the Olympian festival in 420 BCE, when the Spartans were excluded on the grounds that they had violated the sacred truce, a Spartan man was flogged by the umpires when he entered a team in the chariot-race under a false identity; after that, the people at the festival worried that the Spartans would march on them in arms (v.50).

[81] Dionysius of Halicarnassus, *Lysias* 29. Diodorus Siculus (14, 109) offers a similar account of this *theoria* which Dionysius sent to Olympia, claiming that the crowd mocked and jeered at the poems performed by his Sicilian entourage.

[82] Heniochus frag. 5 *PCG*.

overwhelm the ambassadors of a city who are cut off from home (and its "counsel") during the period of the *theoria*.

In principle then, the panhellenic festivals could include and contain *theoroi* coming from warring cities. Indeed, for the Olympic festival, the Greeks observed a "sacred truce" (*ekecheiria*), which suspended hostilities and guaranteed safe passage to the festival and a peaceful gathering.[83] In particularly bad periods of war, however, the hostility among the Greeks actually obstructed theoric journeys and restricted the practice of *theoria*. This is vividly depicted in Aristophanes' *Peace*, which forges a direct link between the practice of *theoria* and panhellenic peace. The play dramatizes the rescue of the Goddess Peace – whom War has imprisoned in a cave – and her attendant "Theoria," here personified as a character in the drama: when Peace is released from the cave and restored to Greece, Theoria is recovered as well.[84]

Given the peculiar blend of civic rivalry and religious commonality that characterized the big Greek festivals, we may conclude that these events generated a wide variety of religious and political experiences. There was no single or unified theoric gaze, but rather a multiplicity of different points of view. The panhellenic viewpoint existed as an ideal, but was never fully achieved in reality.

THEORIA IN SEARCH OF WISDOM

A third kind of *theoria* takes the form of journey to foreign lands in order to see the world. Here, the *theoros* travels abroad in pursuit of knowledge.[85] In contrast to the first two kinds of *theoria*, this journey is not directed to sacred precincts or gatherings, and is primarily secular in orientation. An example of this kind of *theoros* is Solon, who went abroad for ten years partly in order to avoid repealing his laws but also "for the sake of *theoria*" (καὶ

---

[83] As Cartledge observes (1985, 112), the sacred truce was "a supremely realistic measure aimed at protecting pilgrims and participants in the festival from hostile military activity by states through whose territory they might have to pass or in which the Games were held. The truce never stopped wars between Greek states; it merely prevented wars from stopping the Games."

[84] This fanciful tale has some basis in historical fact, as is evidenced by the peace-treaty between the Athenians and Spartans in 421 BCE. As Thucydides reports (v.18.2), this treaty guaranteed free and safe passage, by land and by sea, for Greeks who wished to visit "the common sanctuaries" for the purpose of "performing sacrifices and *theoria*." Rutherford (1998, 141–5) offers a useful discussion of *theoria* in the *Peace*.

[85] For a general discussion of the "wanderings" of sages and philosophers in archaic and classical Greece, see Montiglio 2000 and Hartog 2001. Helms (1988, 68–9 and *passim*) discusses travel to foreign states for the purpose of acquiring knowledge in premodern societies. E. Cohen (1992) discusses the relation of pilgrimage to tourism.

τῆς θεωρίης . . . εἵνεκεν).[86] According to Herodotus, when Solon visited Croesus in Sardis, the king greeted him as follows: "My Athenian guest, word has come to us of your wisdom and your wandering (πλάνης), how you have traveled much of the earth philosophizing and pursuing *theoria*" (ὡς φιλοσοφέων γῆν πολλὴν θεωρίης εἵνεκεν ἐπελήλυθας, 1.30). Here, Solon's *theoria* – his "wandering" – is linked to the activity of "philosophizing." In interpreting this claim, we need to remember that, in the fifth century BCE, the word *philosophein* did not refer to a specialized discipline but rather to "intellectual cultivation" in the broadest sense.[87] Thus this passage indicates that Solon was cultivating himself as a sage or wise man rather than practicing "philosophy" in our sense of the word. In fact, Herodotus would probably have placed himself in this same tradition, as a *theoros* wandering the world in search of knowledge.

Unfortunately, Herodotus provides very few details about Solon's search for wisdom during the period of his *theoria*. In the scene with Croesus, Solon does not appear to learn anything at all; on the contrary, he attempts to teach the king a lesson. He does of course inspect the wealth and kingdom of Croesus, and thus learns some crucial information about this region. But, for the most part, he performs rather than acquires wisdom. Later, Herodotus tells us that when Solon visited Egypt, he discovered a law made by the ruler Amasis that he decided to implement at home (II.177). This offers one example of the kind of wisdom that Solon pursued. It also gives evidence that this third kind of *theoria* could serve the city as well as the individual. As a political leader, Solon sought more than private edification on his journey of *theoria*; among other things, he set out to discover new ideas that he could bring back to his own city.

Herodotus mentions one other instance of this kind of *theoria*, that of the Scythian sage Anacharsis.[88] Anacharsis journeyed abroad from Scythia to Greece and made an extensive study of the Greeks and their various customs. Herodotus tells two stories about the sage's travels. In one, he says that Anacharsis "was sent to Greece by the king [of Scythia] and became a student of Greek ways" (IV.77). "When he returned," Herodotus continues, "Anacharsis reported to the king who sent him" about the wisdom of

---

[86] Herodotus 1.30.

[87] For a complete list of the occurrences of the word φιλοσοφεῖν and its cognates through the end of the fifth century, see Nightingale 1995, 14–17 with notes (see also Überweg 1871, 1–4, Havelock 1963, 280–1 and 1983b, 56–7). I discuss the creation of the specialized discipline of "philosophy" in the fourth century BCE in Nightingale 1995, 13–21 and *passim*.

[88] IV.76–7. For an excellent discussion of Anacharsis, looking in particular at his relation to Cynicism, see Martin 1996. On the travels of Anacharsis, see Hartog 2001, 108–16.

different Greek peoples (IV.77).[89] Here, the sage was sent on an official "theoric" mission by the king and later returned home with a full report. This is a case of civic rather than private *theoria*, since Anacharsis does not simply journey in search of personal edification.

Herodotus relates another, rather different, story of Anacharsis, which offers us further insight into the practice of *theoria*:

When Anarcharsis had traveled as a *theoros* through much of the world (γῆν πολλὴν 9εωρήσας) and exhibited a great deal of wisdom there, as he was returning to the country of the Scythians he put in at Cyzicus on his way through the Hellespont. He found the people there celebrating a festival for the Mother of the Gods in a very lavish fashion, and he vowed to this goddess that, if he came back to his homeland safe and sound, he would sacrifice to her in the same way in which he saw (ὥρα) the Cyzicenes do this and would institute a nightly rite of worship. (IV.76)

Here, Anacharsis' *theoria* lands him in Cyzicus, where he attends a foreign festival as a *theoros*. In addition to "witnessing" this festival, he vows to bring these foreign rites back home. Upon his return, however, his attempt to import alien religious rituals leads to disastrous consequences: the Scythian king discovers Anacharsis performing the rituals for the foreign goddess, and he kills him with an arrow. According to Herodotus, the Scythians disclaimed all knowledge of Anacharsis after his death "on account of the fact that he went abroad to Greece and adopted foreign customs" (ξεινικοῖσι ἔθεσι, IV.76). This story illustrates the danger of *theoria*, especially when the *theoros* returns with ideas and customs that are alien and unwelcome to the people back home.

Plato offers a detailed account of this third kind of *theoria* in the *Laws*.[90] In book XII, he sets forth laws for the regulation of travel in the city of Magnesia. After outlining the rules for sending *theoroi* to religious festivals

---

[89] Herodotus says that he himself does not believe that Anacharsis' report to the Scythian king is true, since it betrays a clear bias. For my purposes, what matters is the suggestion that the king sent Anacharsis on an official *theoria*. Monoson (2000, 230) wrongly suggests that Plato creates "a new class of official ambassadors" when he describes the *theoroi* who go in search of wisdom as traveling *in a civic capacity* (in the *Laws* XII); for Herodotus clearly identifies Anacharsis as undertaking just such an official *theoria* (Plato does, however, innovate by allowing women as well as men to be *theoroi*; *Laws* 953d9).

[90] Note that the three interlocutors in the *Laws* – a Spartan, a Cretan, and an Athenian – are, themselves, undertaking a *theoria* from Cnossus to the shrine of Zeus on Mt. Ida during the course of the dialogue. According to legend, King Minos went to this shrine to obtain oracles for creating a lawcode (624b); his journey thus provides a model for that of the three men who join together (in a show of panhellenic unity) to construct a lawcode for the city of Magnesia. As Morrow (1960a, 24–8) observes, "the Idaean Cave was a center of worship and a place of pilgrimage throughout the classical periods and on into Hellenistic times" (27–8).

(i.e. the second kind of *theoria*), Plato discusses the regulations for dispatching men on official journeys for the purpose of learning and seeing the world (i.e. the third kind of *theoria*). As he claims, no government can maintain and improve itself without sending *theoroi* to foreign cities – provided that "they perform the *theoria* correctly" (951a–c). Plato indicates that this *theoria* takes as its focus "the affairs of foreign men" (τὰ τῶν ἄλλων ἀνθρώπων πράγματα θεωρῆσαι) rather than sacred festivals and shrines (951a). First, he says, the *theoroi* from Magnesia must go in search of "divine men" (ἄνθρωποι . . . θεῖοι) who are able "to declare some oracle (τινα φήμην) regarding legislation or education" (951b, 952b).[91] But they will also go "to see (ἰδεῖν) some beautiful and noble object which surpasses those in other cities in its beauty (ἐν καλλοναῖς) or else to display something of this kind to another city" (953c–d). This kind of *theoria*, then, is multifaceted, blending elements that are secular (investigating human affairs) and sacred (finding a "divine" speaker of oracles), aural (conversing with wise men) and visual (gazing on beautiful objects).

Plato also discusses the return of this *theoros* to the city. When the Magnesian *theoros* gets home, Plato says, he must report to the council of elders who supervise the laws (952b). If he has discovered men who have uttered "oracles" concerning legislation or education, or if he has any knowledge of his own, the *theoros* shall disclose this to the council (952b). If the council determines that he has brought back valuable ideas, they will allow him convey these to the city (952a); but if they find that he has been "corrupted" by his journey, they will forbid him to associate with anyone in the city (952c). Clearly, the reentry of the *theoros* is treated as a momentous and potentially dangerous political event: the importation of foreign ideas and practices can bring benefits to the city, but it can also lead to corruption. Plato offers detailed legal measures for the practice of *theoria* precisely in order to avert this danger.

Since this kind of *theoria* takes the form of a journey in search of knowledge, we can place at least some of the travels of the early Greek thinkers under this heading. In the classical period, many intellectuals journeyed abroad in pursuit of wisdom. Some of them went as *theoroi* to religious festivals, using this opportunity to interact with the wise men they found there. In the drama of Plato's *Parmenides*, for example, Parmenides and Zeno of Elea have come to Athens for the Great Panathenaia (127a–c). Other thinkers traveled as ambassadors for their cities, using this occasion

---

[91] In using the word "oracle" in this passage, Plato injects a sacralizing element into this kind of *theoria*, thus emphasizing its potential affinities to journeys of *theoria* to oracular centers and religious festivals.

to seek out foreign men of learning. In some cases (one thinks especially of the sophists), they did not journey to discover wisdom so much as to display their own expertise, and thus were not *theoroi* in the strict sense.[92] But many thinkers did travel in search of wisdom (while also sharing their own as well).[93] The proto-historian Hecataeus claimed to be "a man of much wandering" (*anēr poluplanēs*), and numerous historians wrote on topics that must have involved some traveling.[94] Among these wandering thinkers, I find especially interesting the claim of Democritus: "I covered more of the earth as a wanderer (ἐπεπλανησάμην) than any of the men of my time, making the most extensive investigations (ἱστορέων τὰ μήκιστα), and I saw more regions and lands and listened to more men of learning."[95] Guthrie, in fact, compares Democritus to Herodotus as an intellectual wandering the world in search of knowledge.[96] This reminds us that intellectual *theoroi* came in many forms in this period and were not limited to sages. Like Herodotus, Democritus both "saw" and "heard" things on his travels. It is the activity of traveling abroad to "see" and learn about the world, of course, that makes these intellectuals *theoroi*.

Of course the practice of *historiē per se* does not make a thinker a *theoros*. In fact, as Thomas shows, *historiē* was defined by the inquiry into nature based on methods "ranging from highly theoretical speculation to the use of visual evidence, experience, empirical evidence, or logical proof; *historiē* is clearly not confined to the process of using personal experience or visible

---

[92] The Socratic dialogues portray many sophists visiting Athens, including Protagoras, Prodicus (*Protagoras*), Gorgias (*Gorgias*), Thrasymachus (*Republic*), and Hippias (*Protagoras, Hippias Major*, and *Hippias Minor*, cf. Xenophon's *Mem.* IV.4.5–25), Euthydemus and Dionysodorus of Chios (*Euthydemus*), Cephalus of Clazomenae and some fellow "philosophers" (*Parmenides*), Evenus of Paros (Plato, *Apology* 20b–c), and Stesimbrotus of Thasos (Xenophon, *Symposium* III.6). The sophists, of course, traveled to many other Greek cities: for example, Gorgias gave exhibitions at Olympia, Delphi, Thessaly, Boeotia, and Argos; Hippias performed at Olympia and traveled extensively in Greece, and Prodicus and Protagoras are said to have visited many Greek cities (Plato, *Apology*, 19e–20a, *Meno* 70b, *Gorg.* 449b–c, Aristotle, *Rhetoric* 1414b31–3, Philostratus 1.9.4; see Kerferd 1981, 42–9 and Thomas 2000, 10–11).

[93] For example, in the fifth century, Parmenides, Zeno, Anaxagoras, and the mathematicians and astronomers Oenopides of Chios, Hippocrates of Chios, and Theodorus of Cyrene all journeyed to Athens (see Ostwald 1992, 349–50).

[94] *FGrHist* 1 T 12a. Dionysius of Halicarnassus (*Thuc.* V.1) identifies a number of the predecessors and contemporaries of Thucydides. For a useful discussion of these early "historians," see Fowler 1996.

[95] DK 68 B299, listed among the "Unechte Fragmente," though Guthrie takes it more seriously (1965, 387 and n.1); see also DK A1, 9, 12, 13, 16, B116, B246.

[96] Guthrie 1965, 386–7. As Kirk, Raven, and Schofield observe (1983, 403), five treatises concerned with foreign travels are not included by Thrasyllus in his collection and arrangement of the writings of Democritus (they think that these treatises were "probably not genuine," which does not of course mean that Democritus did not travel widely). As Thomas rightly argues (2000), Herodotus needs to be placed in the broad context of intellectual activity in fifth-century Greece: his work interacts with that of sophists, natural "philosophers," and especially medical scientists and writers.

evidence, for it can equally involve theoretical argument . . ."⁹⁷ To be sure, Herodotus explicitly calls attention to the things that he "saw" as an eyewitness; he even distinguishes between what he saw with his own eyes (ὄψις) and what he "heard" from others (κατὰ τὰ ἤκουον, 11.99). Herodotus and other ancient historians did take visual evidence seriously. But this does not mean that *historiē* was defined by the use of visual, eyewitness evidence; in fact, historical inquiries dealt as much with the invisible as they did with the visible.⁹⁸ A *histōr*, then, was not necessarily a *theoros*. In many cases he simply had no access to foreign regions and had to rely on hearsay and conjecture (often based on analogy, polarity, or some sort of natural or historical "laws"). Only when the historian personally journeyed to a city or region – when, in short, he traveled as a *theoros* – could he offer an eyewitness account of the things he had seen and learned.⁹⁹

FROM TRADITIONAL TO PHILOSOPHIC *THEORIA*

In sum, the defining feature of *theoria* in its traditional forms is a journey to a region outside the boundaries of one's own city for the purpose of witnessing some sort of spectacle or learning about the world. *Theoria* involves "autopsy" or seeing something for oneself: the *theoros* is an eyewitness whose experience differs radically from those who stay home and receive a mere report of the news. On the journey as well as at its destination, the *theoros* encounters something foreign and different. This encounter with the unfamiliar invites the traveler to look at his own city with different eyes. As Coleman and Elsner observe,

Pilgrimage . . . not only involves movement through space but also an active process of response as the pilgrim encounters both the journey and the goal. It is the experience of travel and the constant possibility of encountering the new which makes pilgrimage distinct from other forms of ritual.¹⁰⁰

---

⁹⁷ Thomas 2000, 166–7. Cf. von Fritz (1936, 255), who claims that *historiē* designated "knowledge of all sorts which was not based on speculation, demonstration, intuition, practice or the like but on personal experience. It meant all that a man could tell, because he had been a *histōr*, a personal witness." Lateiner (1986) argues that *historiē* is based on empirical research that favors visual evidence (but note that he modifies these claims in 1989, 84, 255). Cf. Connor's discussion of *historiē* in reference to the archaic *histōr*, who serves as a mediator and arbitrator (1993).

⁹⁸ On Herodotus' discussions and treatment of the "invisible," see Thomas 2000, 200–12; as she points out, Herodotus' approach has much in common with the early medical practitioners and "scientists."

⁹⁹ Redfield (1985) discusses Herodotus' travels as a form of scientific *theoria*. Many scholars have doubted Herodotus' claims to have visited all the places he claims to have gone (see, e.g., Fehling 1989).

¹⁰⁰ Coleman and Elsner 1995, 206.

The journey abroad may end up confirming the theorist in his original perspectives and prejudices, but it may also function to unsettle him and even to transform his basic world-view. *Theoria*, in short, brings an individual into contact with what is foreign and different: it is an encounter with otherness. In the case of the first two kinds of *theoria* – i.e. journeys to a religious festival or oracular center – the *theoros* not only encounters foreign peoples and places but also interacts with the god who presides over a given festival or shrine (by participating in the sacrifices, prayers, and rituals). Here, the *theoros* approaches the ultimate and most distant "other," a divine being.[101]

The three kinds of *theoria* that I have discussed above could overlap in various ways – they were not necessarily mutually exclusive. But the *theoria* to see and learn about the world differed from other theoric journeys in that it was not directed towards a sacred shrine or festival, and was primarily secular in its orientation. Given that this kind of *theoria* was generally enacted by sages and thinkers, it provided an obvious model for the fourth-century thinkers who developed the concept of philosophic *theoria*. But these philosophers made surprisingly little use of this model. Indeed, in their appropriation and transformation of traditional *theoria*, they placed the greatest emphasis on theorizing at religious festivals and their sacred precincts (both in its civic and its private forms).

The fourth-century philosophers favored this paradigm for several reasons. First, they sought to conceptualize a mode of apprehension that took the form of "seeing" divine essences or truths. *Theoria* at religious festivals – in which the pilgrim viewed icons, sacred images, and spectacles – offered a good model for this conception of philosophical "vision." As we have seen, *theoria* at religious sanctuaries and festivals was characterized by a sacralized, "ritualized" visuality. The fourth-century philosophers conceptualized a mode of "seeing" that resembled ritualized vision in some key ways. First of all, philosophic *theoria* "views" and apprehends objects that are identified as sacred and divine. In this activity, the "spectating" operates outside of traditional social and ideological spheres. Like the *theoros* at religious festivals, the philosophic theorist detaches himself from ordinary social and political affairs during the period of *theoria*. But this theorist goes well beyond the traditional *theoros*: he completely detaches himself from his city – and, indeed, from the entire human world – and engages in activity that is impersonal, disinterested, and objective. Indeed, he practices

---

[101] Though the *theoros* does not literally "see" this being, he does look at sacred images and symbols and, by way of ritual, enters into a relationship with a god.

an entirely new form of spectating that the philosophers attributed to the gods themselves. Whereas the spectatorial activities of the traditional *theoros* were not neutral, objective, or independent of the views of others (he was, after all, one of a multitude of *theoroi*), the philosopher theorizes alone or with a few like-minded associates, seeking to perfect his understanding by turning his back on traditional views.[102] It is only when he ceases from contemplation that the philosopher experiences an individual or political identity.

Theoria at religious festivals also offered the philosophers the model of a panhellenic "space" which (at least in principle) transcended political differences and encouraged a sense of identity that was much broader and more universal than that defined by the individual polis. At panhellenic festivals and gatherings, people from different cities could affirm a single Greek identity based on a shared religion, language, and culture. While the traditional *theoros* at a panhellenic festival did not abandon his political identity, he participated in a religious gathering which operated above and beyond any single political ideology. The fourth-century philosophers took this model to its extreme: philosophic *theoria* operates in a sphere that completely transcends social and political life. In the activity of contemplation, the theorist rises above all earthly affairs – including his own individual human identity – in order to "see" eternal and divine beings. Building on the practice of traditional *theoria*, the philosophers developed the notion of the transcendental, impersonal, and impartial "space" of theoretical activity. This radical separation between theoretical and social/political "space," of course, inevitably raised the question whether the wisdom acquired in metaphysical contemplation could (or should) play a role in civic affairs. The philosophers thus had to address the question of the theorist's "return" to the city with a new and foreign kind of wisdom. This presented a problem similar to that of the return of the traditional *theoros* to his native city: what sort of "report" does he bring back to the city, and how will this be received by the people back home?

****

The fourth-century philosophers appropriated and transformed the model of traditional *theoria*. Each put the basic model to different uses, emphasizing different aspects of this practice as it suited his own purposes. For example, in the *Republic* Plato makes full use of the entire journey of *theoria* (including the departure, the activity of spectating, and the return home),

102 Arendt [1971]/1978, 94.

whereas in the *Timaeus* he emphasizes the visual aspects of *theoria* and downplays the metaphor of the journey. In some texts, Plato takes private *theoria* as his model, and in others he uses civic *theoria*. Philip of Opus and Aristotle, moreover, completely abandon the notion of the journey, focusing exclusively on the spectatorial activity of contemplation. These philosophers did not make a single or schematic use of their model but rather shaped and transformed it to illustrate different aspects and/or conceptions of *theoria*.

CHAPTER 2

Inventing philosophic theoria

What distinguishes the higher human beings from the lower is that the former see and hear immeasurably more, and see and hear thoughtfully . . . The higher human being always becomes at the same time happier and unhappier. But he can never shake off a *delusion*: he fancies that he is a *spectator* and *listener* who has been placed before the great visual and acoustic spectacle that is life; he calls his own nature *contemplative* and overlooks that he himself is really the poet who keeps creating this life.

Nietzsche, *The Gay Science*

The most sublime speculation of the contemplative philosopher can scarce compensate the neglect of the smallest active duty.

Adam Smith, *Theory of Moral Sentiments*

In the fourth century BCE, Greek thinkers first articulated the idea that supreme wisdom takes the form of *theoria*. These philosophers defined their new conception of knowledge in different ways, using different modes of discourse. In addition to offering philosophic analyses and discussions of *theoria*, the fourth-century philosophers employed powerful rhetoric in the attempt to define this new intellectual practice. None offered a completely neutral or analytic account of theoretical activity; all developed what G. E. R. Lloyd calls "a discourse, or one might say a rhetoric, of legitimation."[1] In this chapter, I will examine one of the central strategies deployed in the attempt to conceptualize and legitimize philosophic *theoria*, namely, the frequent use of the discourse and structures of traditional *theoria*. The fourth-century philosophers took over the cultural practice of *theoria* and transformed it for their own purposes. In the venerable and authoritative institution of *theoria*, they found a model that helped them define and defend the new discipline of "theoretical" philosophy.[2]

[1] G. E. R. Lloyd 1990, 43.
[2] This does not mean, of course, that the cultural practice of *theoria* determined or explained fourth-century epistemological theories.

Scholars have generally treated Plato's comparisons of philosophic "spectating" to "*theoria*" at panhellenic festivals (including the Eleusinian Festival of the Mysteries) as superficial metaphors. For this reason, they have not examined the vital link between philosophic theorizing and the traditional practice of *theoria*. In this chapter, I will analyze Plato's deliberate and quite extensive use of traditional *theoria* in his accounts of theoretical philosophy in the *Republic*, *Symposium*, and *Phaedrus*. As I shall argue, the model of *theoria* at religious festivals offered Plato a way to structure and describe the new discipline of theoretical philosophy. I am not suggesting that the cultural practice of *theoria* was causally related to the development of philosophical contemplation. Nor do I claim that an analysis of traditional *theoria* will address technical questions of Platonic epistemology. Rather, by investigating the links between traditional and philosophical *theoria*, we can examine Plato's foundational account of theoretical philosophy in its cultural context. In addition, we can analyze the relation of Plato's theoretical philosopher to the polis.

Plato's appropriation and transformation of traditional *theoria* is found in the dialogues that expound the theory of Forms and related metaphysical subjects (traditionally identified as "middle dialogues").[3] In the ethical, aporetic texts (the "early dialogues"), Socrates neither discusses nor enacts the activity of *theoria*: rather, he claims that he does not possess knowledge and makes no mention of the Forms. In these dialogues, Socrates uses an interrogatory, nondogmatic style and focuses almost exclusively on ethical and political questions. In addition, he is firmly embedded in his native city of Athens, claiming in the *Apology* that he is god's gift to the city and refusing the penalty of exile even when the alternative is execution.[4] In the dialogues dealing with the theory of Forms, Plato introduces a new kind of philosopher, a sage who journeys away from the world in pursuit of a vision of metaphysical "reality."[5] We see hints of this change in the behavior

---

[3] In light of several recent and quite powerful attacks on the distinction between the early, middle, and late dialogues (favored by interpreters for decades), I have chosen to avoid this terminology to the extent possible (or, alternatively, to put it in quotation marks). See especially Annas 2002 and Griswold 2002.

[4] See Goldhill and von Reden 1999, who claim that Socrates was a "performer in exile," since he did not display his wisdom at the Assembly or other political gatherings. To be sure, Socrates played by his own rules, rejecting traditional social, political, and economic exchanges; but his *ad hominem* interrogations of his fellow Athenians kept him intimately tied to the city. On Socrates' bodily performance of wisdom (including that of his death), see Loraux 1989. Nehamas (1999a, chs. 1–2) analyses the Socrates of the early dialogues as a unique practitioner of a distinct "art of living."

[5] I do not discuss the *Theaetetus* in this study of *theoria*, since it is an aporetic dialogue that does not deal with the theory of Forms or with metaphysical "vision." As I suggested in the Introduction, the brief "digression" (173c–177c) in this text depicts a radically contemplative philosopher. But, although this passage begins with Thales' observation of the stars, it does not develop the notion of the rational "vision" of the Forms (and does not even press the metaphor of "seeing").

of the character of Socrates, such as when he wanders off to a stranger's porch to enjoy a period of silent contemplation on his way to the party in the *Symposium*, and when he stands up all night long "inspecting" a philosophical problem during a military expedition.[6] Here, Socrates seems to be engaging in the novel activity of theoretical contemplation, withdrawing from the world as he journeys in thought.[7]

Contemplation, however, is only one stage in the activity of philosophic *theoria*. Even though the theoretical philosopher departs from the world to "see Being" in the metaphysical realm, Plato has certainly not given up on politics or *praxis* (his two most monumental works, after all, are the *Republic* and *Laws*). In fact, as Plato claims, the philosopher who has journeyed to contemplate the Forms must "return" to a life of virtuous action in the practical sphere (and, in ideal circumstances, to rule the city).

CIVIC *THEORIA* IN THE *REPUBLIC*

The *Republic* exhibits especially clearly Plato's use of the model of festival *theoria* in his conceptualization of theoretical philosophy. Indeed the traditional practice of *theoria* features quite prominently in this text.[8] At the very opening of the dialogue, Socrates describes his trip to Peiraeus to "theorize" the festival sacred to the goddess Bendis (327a–b). As he says in the opening lines:

I went down yesterday with Glaucon the son of Ariston to the Peiraeus in order to offer my prayers to the goddess [Bendis] and also because I wanted to see (θεάσθαι) how they would conduct the festival, since this was the first time they celebrated it. I thought that the procession of the citizens was quite fine, but the procession sent by the Thracians was no less fine. After we had offered our prayers and theorized the spectacle (θεωρήσαντες), we began to head back to the city. (327a)

---

[6] *Symposium* 174d–175a, 220c–d. This does not mean, of course, that we should identify Socrates with the perfected theoretical philosophers described in the *Republic* (note that Socrates repeatedly says in the middle dialogues that he does not possess knowledge).

[7] It may seem that Aristophanes' *Clouds* portrays Socrates as a contemplative, for he first appears suspended in a basket and says: "I walk on air and give thought to (περιφρονῶ) the sun." He explains that he raises himself up in order to "mingle" his thoughts with the air (225–30). While this may seem to identify Socrates as a detached thinker speculating about the heavens, the text depicts him first and foremost as a teacher of rhetoric and shady business dealings. As many scholars have observed, Socrates in this play is a polymathic sophist rather than a philosophic contemplative.

[8] Interestingly, two of Plato's metaphysical dialogues open with a scene involving civic *theoria*. At the beginning of the *Phaedo*, we are told that, when Socrates was in prison, the Athenians sent a *theoria* to the oracular center on the island of Delos (58a–c). And the *Republic* opens with Socrates' description of his visit to the festival of the goddess Bendis (327a–b).

Here, Socrates describes his (private) *theoria* at the festival of Bendis, a Thracian goddess whose worship had just been instituted in Attica.[9] Although we do not know the precise date of this inaugural festival, evidence from inscriptions indicates that it was sometime before 429 BCE.[10] The bustling port of Peiraeus no doubt attracted *theoroi* from many different places; Socrates explicitly mentions a procession "sent" by the Thracians (no doubt because Bendis was a Thracian goddess), thus reminding us that the festival had international spectators and participants. The fact that this was the first celebration in Athens of a Thracian festival gives it a peculiar status as both Athenian and foreign: while Athens officially instituted and sponsored the festival, the Thracians played a key role in "introducing" it and participating in its rituals. The festival, then, is not simply a local Athenian gathering but a true "theoric event."[11] Note that Socrates calls into question the Athenocentric point of view when he claims that the Thracian procession was as fine as the Athenian: here, he deliberately adopts a panhellenic viewpoint.

This instance of *theoria* at the very opening of the *Republic* is carefully woven into the text, and it proleptically anticipates the discussion of metaphysical *theoria* set forth in books v–vii.[12] In the scene at the beginning of book i, some friends who have come as *theoroi* to the festival apprehend Socrates as he is heading back to Athens, informing him with great excitement that there will be a torchlit relay-race on horseback in honor of Bendis that evening, as well as an all-night celebration "well worth seeing" (ἄξιον θεάσασθαι, 328a). These friends compel Socrates to stay in the Peiraeus so they can see the spectacles together later that night (328a). They then take him to the festival dinner at Cephalus' house, where Socrates begins the long discussion that occupies the rest of the dialogue. Interestingly, the group never returns to the festival, opting instead to engage in a philosophic search for the nature of justice. This philosophic journey towards Justice, then, interrupts and supplants the *theoria* at the festival.[13] This move from traditional to philosophic *theoria* is clearly emphasized later in the book, when their conversation is said to be the "feast" at the festival of Bendis

---

[9] The Athenian polis had the power to include and exclude forms of worship in this region, and people who wished to introduce new cults or festivals had to seek official sanction (Burkert 1985, 176–9, Garland 1992, 14, 19, 137 and *passim*).

[10] Garland (1992, 111–14) suggests that the foundation of the festival was directly connected with interstate politics, since the Athenians were keen to form an alliance with the Thracian potentate Sitalces at the outbreak of the Peloponnesian War (see also Ostwald 1992, 313 and von Reden 1995).

[11] Thucydides ii.29. See Garland 1992, 112 and Ostwald 1992, 313.

[12] See Clay 1992b, 128–9 for a discussion of the ways that the opening scene anticipates the account of the philosopher in book v.

[13] I am indebted to Charles Griswold for this idea.

(354a–b): here, the actual festival feast is recast as a "feast" of words. In the opening scene of the *Republic*, then, Plato introduces several key ideas that will reemerge later in the dialogue: the activity of spectating at a religious festival; the theme of light and darkness; and the notion of spectacles "worth seeing."

The *Republic* also closes with an account of *theoria*: the Myth of Er features a traditional *theoria* enacted in an untraditional place. This myth depicts souls making a journey to a religious festival located in the afterlife. In this eschatological drama, a man named Er plays the role of an official *theoros*. According to the story, Er was slain in battle and taken for dead, but when he was brought home and placed on the funeral pyre he woke up and related to his own people the spectacle that he had seen on his visit to the land of judgment. Socrates places great emphasis on Er's journey and its destination: "Er said that when his soul departed (ἐκβῆναι) he journeyed (πορεύεσθαι) with a great many people, and they came to some sort of divine region" (ἀφικνεῖσθαι σφᾶς εἰς τόπον τινὰ δαιμόνιον, 614b–c). Er, then, has made a pilgrimage with other souls to a foreign and divine place – the region where the souls are judged after death. In this precinct, he sees the souls coming down from heaven and those coming up from hell who "appeared to have made a long journey" (ἐκ πολλῆς πορείας). As Er relates, the souls camp here in the meadow "as at a festival" (ἐν πανηγύρει). And, as at a festival, the souls who know each other embrace, and "those coming from beneath the earth asked the others about the conditions up above, and those coming from heaven asked how it fared with them" (614d–e). The gathering that Er witnesses, then, is described as a religious festival (a *panegyris* is the standard term for a panhellenic festival). The souls at the gathering meet both friends and strangers and, like people on a traditional *theoria*, they give and receive information. The "space" in which they meet is located outside of ordinary social and political affairs, and transcends the ideology of any given city. The festival is thus a panhellenic or, perhaps better, "pan-human" event. At the same time, the souls in attendance maintain the identity of their former life: civic and personal affairs are not completely left behind.

The judges explain to Er that "he must be the messenger to mankind to tell them of the things here," and they bid him "to hear and to see everything in this region" (ἀκούειν τε καὶ θεᾶσθαι πάντα τὰ ἐν τῷ τόπῳ, 614a). Er, then, takes on the official task of witnessing the "sights and sounds" in this place (the phrase recalls the "lovers of sights and sounds" in book v who, as we will see, are *theoroi* at Dionysian festivals). And he must also bring this information back to the human world, thus performing the duties of the civic *theoros*: as Socrates reports, when Er was "brought home" (κομισθεὶς δ' οἴκαδε) and restored to life, "he related the things that he saw there" (ἔλεγεν ἃ ἐκεῖ ἴδοι).

Plato thus portrays Er as a *theoros* at a religious festival who interacts with divine and human beings and brings back a report from this distant and sacred place. In his visit to this "festival," Er bears witness to competitive and theatrical "spectacles" (*theamata*, 615d). He watches the newly dead souls being judged for their performance on earth and then rewarded and punished – he sees, in short, the winners and losers in the game of life. He also watches the souls who have returned from heaven and hell choose their next life. This spectacle takes the form of a sort of drama, complete with famous characters like Ajax and Agamemnon and Odysseus, which Er calls a "pitiful . . . and ridiculous sight to see" (619e–620a) – pity, of course, conjures up the genre of tragedy, while the ridiculous invokes comedy.[14]

Finally, Er says that this spectacle "was a sight worth seeing" (ταύτην . . . τὴν θέαν ἀξίαν εἶναι ἰδεῖν), which recalls the scene at the opening of the dialogue where the visitors to the festival of Bendis tell Socrates that the torch-race and nightly events will be "worth seeing" (328a). This verbal echo reminds us that *theoria* is featured at the very beginning and the very end of the dialogue. Plato's deliberate placement of theoric events at the opening and close of the dialogue serves to highlight its central books. As we will see, traditional *theoria* plays a prominent role in the very middle of the *Republic*, offering a direct model for the philosopher's journey to the metaphysical realm of the Forms and his return "home" with a report from this region.

In books v–vii of the *Republic*, Socrates sets forth for the first time in Plato's corpus a detailed account of a new practice that he calls "philosophy."[15] In fact, when Socrates brings up the topic of "philosophy" in book v, his interlocutors do not understand what he means by this term. It is worth repeating that, before the fourth century BCE, the word *philosophein* (and its cognates) meant "intellectual cultivation" in the broad sense; it did not refer to a specialized discipline or mode of wisdom. It was in fact Plato who first appropriated this term for one particular intellectual discipline. He therefore had to define and describe the "philosopher" with great care and specificity.[16] Part and parcel of this construction of the specialized discipline

---

[14] In one passage, Plato also depicts Er as a *theoros* sent to an oracular center (thus mingling together two different kinds of civic *theoria*): "And then the messenger from that region [i.e. Er] announced that the prophet (προφήτην) spoke in this way: 'even for him who comes forward last, if he chooses intelligently and lives earnestly, there remains a satisfying life'" (619b).

[15] I discuss Plato's construction of the specialized discipline of philosophy in Nightingale 1995.

[16] See Nightingale 1995, ch. 1 and *passim*.

of philosophy was the identification of "*theoria*" as the quintessential activity of the true philosopher.

From the very beginning of his definition of the philosopher in the *Republic* v, Socrates describes him as a new kind of *theoros*. At the opening of this discussion, in fact, Socrates explicitly gestures towards the traditional practice of *theoria*. Here, beginning with the "love" portion of the "love of wisdom," Socrates invites his interlocutors to consider individuals who are "lovers of sights" (φιλοθεάμονες) and "lovers of sounds" (φιλήκοοι, 475d). Out of all the varieties of "lover," these will provide the model for the lover of wisdom. Who and what are the "lovers of sights and sounds"? Socrates describes them as people who "run around to all the Dionysian festivals, never leaving a single one out, either in the towns or in the cities" (475d). The lovers of sights and sounds, then, are clearly identified as *theoroi* who journey abroad to religious festivals to witness the events there.[17] These *theoroi*, in fact, call to mind the men who encounter Socrates at the festival of Bendis at the opening of the dialogue: as we have seen, these men were enthusiastic viewers of the spectacles at that festival. Socrates' friends, then, are living examples of "lovers of sights and sounds." In short, all of these *theoroi* – both the friends in book I and the (nameless) "lovers of sights and sounds" in book v – provide an analogue for this new man called the "philosopher." Like the "lovers of sights," the philosopher loves seeing. But the philosophers love one single kind of spectacle – they are "lovers of the sight of truth" (τῆς ἀληθείας . . . φιλοθεάμονας).

Plato uses the "lover of sights" rather than the "lovers of sounds" as the most direct analogue for the philosopher: having acknowledged that the *theoroi* at religious festivals use both their eyes and their ears, he focuses exclusively on visual spectating when he makes the move from the traditional to the philosophic *theoros*. Whereas the "lovers of sights and sounds" delight in the multiplicity of beautiful spectacles performed at Dionysian festivals, the philosopher "journeys to and looks upon (ἰέναι τε καὶ ὁρᾶν) Beauty itself" (476b–c). The philosopher, then, is a new kind of *theoros*: a man who travels to the metaphysical realm to see the sacred sights in that region.

Plato depicts the journey of the philosophic *theoros* in the Analogy of the Cave (*Republic* VII). Since I will discuss the Analogy in detail in the next chapter, I will confine myself to some introductory remarks here. The story

---

[17] The fact that Socrates mentions that these individuals journey to "towns and cities," never missing any of the Dionysian festivals (which were held in Greek cities all over the Mediterranean), indicates that the "lovers of sights and sounds" are men who journey abroad as *theoroi* and do not simply attend local festivals.

begins in a dark cavern, which houses all human beings in the terrestrial realm; living in chains, these souls are condemned to watch shadowy images of earthly things flickering on the back wall of the cave – a shadow-play that they mistake for substantial reality. Released from bondage, the philosophic soul slowly makes his way up to the mouth of the cave: he makes a sort of journey abroad, experiencing real terror as he leaves the familiar region of the cave and turns towards the light. Eventually, the soul comes to the mouth of the cave and enters the metaphysical "realm" of the Forms, a realm full of light. As he gazes upon true reality and goodness, the philosopher now recognizes that the shadow-figures in the cave were all copies of the beings in this realm, and that this region is the locus of "true being."

After gazing upon the Forms and thus achieving knowledge, the philosopher returns home, journeying with reluctance back into the cave. Temporarily blinded by the darkness in that realm, his eyes must slowly adjust, at which point he can see in that realm better than the prisoners within it (*Rep.* 520c). If the philosopher returns to a bad city and communicates his visions to the people there, Socrates says, they will mock and revile him and perhaps even put him to death: the return and reentry of the philosophic *theoros* from the foreign realm of the Forms is a potentially dangerous operation. But if the philosopher lives in a good city, his theoretical discoveries are (as it were) good news, and they provide the basis for government and politics.

Plato knows that this is a novel and somewhat paradoxical idea, and he takes pains to explicate this new kind of "seeing." First of all, he claims, the objects of true knowledge are metaphysical entities called *eidē*, a term which is generally translated as "Forms." More literally, the word *eidos* means the "aspect" or "shape" or "look" of something: Plato conceptualizes the Forms, then, as visual objects. Plato regularly identifies the Forms as true "being" or "the really real"; they are not concepts or ideas but rather beings that enjoy the fullest kind of existence. According to Havelock, "[t]he trouble with the word 'Form' is precisely that as it seeks to objectify and separate knowledge from opinion it also tends to make knowledge visual again."[18] It is unfortunate, he adds, that Plato did "not always succeed in shielding himself rigorously against this visual contamination."[19] But so far from "shielding himself" from the "contamination" of visual imagery, Plato positively revels in it. To be sure, Plato distinguishes the "eye of the soul" from the physical eyes, and tends to denigrate sensory perception. In addition, the method used to search for the highest form of

[18] Havelock 1963, 268.   [19] Havelock 1963, 268.

knowledge – dialectic – is of course based on verbal analysis and discussion. But by using the phenomenon of vision as an analogue for the apprehension of the Forms, Plato clearly conceptualizes the attainment of knowledge as a "seeing" of Being.

How, then, does the philosopher achieve this vision of truth? As Socrates suggests in *Republic* v, the philosophers must receive a special education designed to lead them to the "*theoria* of all time and of all being" (θεωρία παντὸς μὲν χρόνου, πάσης δὲ οὐσίας, 486d). Traditional modes of teaching, Socrates observes, claim to "put knowledge into a soul that does not yet possess it, as if they were implanting sight in blind eyes" (518b–c); here, he refers to an education that is exclusively aural – the teacher sets forth a *logos* (in poetry or prose) which the student is expected to learn and memorize. True education, by contrast, aims to "turn" the soul in the direction of reality: "it is not the art of implanting vision in the soul but rather, assuming that it already possesses vision but is not turned in the right direction or looking where it should, an art that brings this [turning] about."[20] In describing the activity contemplation, Plato uses the metaphor of the soul's capacity for "vision" or "sight" again and again. Indeed, his philosophic educational system aims, first and foremost, to develop and train the "eye of the soul" (τῆς ψυχῆς ὄψιν, 519b). According to Socrates, most humans direct their gaze "downwards" towards feasting and other physical pleasures, but we can also direct our gaze "upwards" towards truth and reality (519b). Only an extensive education in philosophy can "draw the soul away from the world of becoming and towards true being" (521d).

This higher education (which begins when the students are twenty) focuses exclusively on disciplines that train the soul in the activity of contemplation or "seeing reality." The first area of study is that of number and calculation which, according to Socrates, serves to draw the mind towards "being" (οὐσία, 523a). For when the soul receives confusing messages from the senses – when, for example, the same thing appears to be both great and small – the art of "number and calculation" enables the mind to "view" (ἰδεῖν) the great and the small in themselves, abstracted from their concrete manifestations (524c). Ultimately, the students must "come to the vision (θέαν) of the nature of number by pure thought" (525c). The second area of study is plane geometry, which "enables one to see (κατιδεῖν) goodness . . . since it compels the soul to be turned towards that region in which the most blessed part of reality lies." In this region, the soul "gazes

---

[20] τέχνη ἂν εἴη τῆς περιαγωγῆς, τίνα τρόπον ὡς ῥᾷστά τε καὶ ἀνυσιμώτατα μεταστραφήσεται, οὐ τοῦ ἐμποιῆσαι αὐτῷ τὸ ὁρᾶν, ἀλλ' ὡς ἔχοντι μὲν αὐτό, οὐκ ὀρθῶς δὲ τετραμμένῳ οὐδὲ βλέποντι οἷ ἔδει, τοῦτο διαμηχανήσασθαι (518d).

upon the spectacle of being" (οὐσίαν . . . θεάσασθαι, 526e). Geometry, in short, will make us "direct upwards the [faculties] which we now direct downwards" (527b).

Astronomy serves the same function, at least when it is studied in the proper fashion. We may imagine, as Glaucon does, that looking at the stars will necessarily lead the soul to "look upwards" (εἰς τὸ ἄνω ὁρᾶν, 529a). But Socrates insists that the man who "gazes up" at the stars does not in fact study the higher realities; rather, when gazing at the physical heavens, "the soul does not look upwards but downwards" (529a–b). True astronomy, by contrast, studies the mathematical principles that govern the motions of the heavenly bodies: it involves "gazing with the mind and not the eyes" (νοήσει ἀλλ' οὐκ ὄμμασι θεωρεῖν, 529b). Here, Plato reminds the reader to interpret the numerous descriptions of the philosopher "looking upwards" metaphorically rather than literally. According to this conception of *theoria*, the philosopher sees truth by transcending the bodily realm altogether.[21]

At the age of thirty, the students who have successfully mastered these disciplines come to the pinnacle of their education. For the next five years, they study "dialectic." In book VII, Socrates describes dialectic as the "journey" of the mind to the Forms in a passage that directly recalls the Analogy of the Cave:

There is first the release from bonds, and the turning away from the shadows to the images and to the light of the fire; then, there is the ascent out of the cave into the sunlight and the inability to look at the plants and animals and the light of the sun . . . All this labor in the disciplines we have mentioned has the power to lead the best part of the soul up to the vision (θέαν) of the best among realities. (532b–c)

Socrates claims that dialectic is the only discipline that enables the philosopher to give "an account of the essence of each thing" (534b). Unfortunately, Plato does not offer a technical definition of dialectic.[22] But he clearly links the "journey of dialectic" (διαλεκτικὴν ταύτην τὴν πορείαν, 532b) to the soul's journey out of the cave towards the contemplation of "true being." Of course dialectic involves speaking, whereas contemplation involves seeing. As this passage indicates, the practice of dialectic leads to the "visual"

---

[21] Note that Plato indicates in other dialogues (especially the *Phaedrus* and *Timaeus*) that the physical sense of sight plays a positive role in the practice of *theoria*. I will analyze this alternative account of theorizing in chapter 4.

[22] There are numerous discussions of the precise nature of "dialectic" and of Plato's puzzling suggestion in *Republic* 533b–c that it "does away with the hypotheses" and thus leads to knowledge of "first principles." See, e.g., Robinson 1941, chs. 6, 7, and 10, Crombie 1963, 548–62, White 1976, 95–104, Annas 1981, 277–93, Reeve 1988, 71–9 and *passim*, Mueller 1992, and Kahn 1996, ch. 10.

contemplation of the Forms. In addition, the philosopher engages in dialectic after he has achieved a vision of the Forms, at which point (like a good
theoros) he returns and "gives an account" (διδόναι τὸν λόγον) of the
things he has seen.[23]

In the *Republic*, in sum, Plato identifies the philosopher as a new kind of
theoros, an intellectual ambassador who makes a journey to a divine realm to
see the spectacle of truth and then brings a report of his findings back home.
Note that, in this and other dialogues, Plato often identifies the Forms as
"blessed" and "divine" essences, even though they are not living beings.
The philosopher who gazes upon the Forms contemplates divinity, an act
replete with wonder and reverence. In the *Republic*, in fact, Plato calls the
philosopher's vision of the Forms a "divine *theoria*" (θείων . . . θεωριῶν,
517d), and he identifies the movement of the philosopher from the cave to
the Forms as a journey "from Hades to the gods" (521c). Like traditional
theoria at religious sanctuaries and festivals, philosophic *theoria* has a religious orientation. Indeed, this is one of the main reasons why Plato takes
as his primary model the *theoria* to religious festivals rather than the *theoria*
in search of wisdom.[24] Although the latter is associated with the travels of
sages and intellectuals, it is a secular form of *theoria* that focuses on the
human and terrestrial world. Since Plato's sage journeys to see "the most
blessed of beings" (τὸ εὐδαιμονέστατον τοῦ ὄντος, 526e), the model of
the religious festival is far more apt. The "sacralized visuality" that characterized the viewing at religious festivals and sanctuaries offered a direct
model for the "divine" contemplation of the theoretical philosopher.

Like civic *theoria*, philosophic *theoria* also has a practical and political
dimension. For just as the civic *theoros* must return home to relate the news
to his fellow citizens, the philosophic *theoros* depicted in the *Republic* returns
to the city to impart and implement the truths that he has "witnessed." As
Plato asserts in book VII, the good city will train its philosophers to ascend
to the contemplation of reality but will also require that they spend part
of their lives in political pursuits (519c–520e, 540a). Although they have
no desire for political power, the philosophers will nonetheless agree to
spend fixed periods of time governing and serving the city.[25] The official
requirement that the philosophic *theoros* must return to the city to utilize
and disseminate his wisdom clearly gestures towards the practice of civic
theoria.

---

[23] I will discuss dialectic and contemplation in more detail in chapter 3.
[24] Cf. Goldhill 1999a, 6, who places Platonic *theoria* under the heading of (secular) private travel in
search of wisdom.
[25] I will discuss this point in chapter 3.

The *Republic* has a political orientation that gives the text a specific bias. We must remember, however, that even in the *Republic*, Plato's philosophic theorist does not journey to the Forms simply to apprehend truths that will best serve the city. The activity of philosophic *theoria* serves, first and foremost, to transform the individual soul, conferring upon it a state of wisdom, happiness, and blessedness.[26] Contemplation is a blessed activity in itself, and it also provides the grounding for virtuous action in the practical world.

In the *Republic*, Plato constructs an ideal city that trains the philosopher to journey to the Forms but also requires him to "return" afterwards and play a role in the government of the city. The model of "civic" *theoria* works well for this philosophic theorist, since his *theoria* is prepared for and carried out in a political context. But what about philosophers living in non-ideal cities? These individuals, Plato states, will stay out of politics altogether (496a–c). The philosopher who lives in a bad city will still make the journey of philosophic *theoria*, but he will do this in a private rather than civic capacity.

PRIVATE *THEORIA* IN THE *SYMPOSIUM* AND *PHAEDRUS*

In developing the notion of "private" philosophic *theoria*, Plato takes as his model the *theoria* at the festival of the Greater Mysteries at Eleusis.[27] Consider, for example, the "Diotima" speech in the *Symposium*, where Socrates explicitly compares the philosopher's vision of the Forms to the mystic revelation at Eleusis.[28] Though brief, the passage nonetheless offers a vivid description of the philosopher's theoric journey away from the physical realm and towards the mystic revelation of Beauty.[29] After going through each step of the journey (ἰών, 210e; ἰέναι, 211c; ἐπανιέναι, 211c), the philosopher reaches his final destination:

[26] For example, Socrates says that the philosopher who engages in *theoria* will, when contemplating, think that he has arrived at the Islands of the Blessed (518b, 519c; cf. 540b). He also argues that the philosopher who practices dialectic and contemplates the Forms experiences supreme pleasure (book IX).

[27] On the Eleusinian Mysteries, see Mylonas 1961, Parke 1977, ch. 3, Burkert 1987, Clinton 1993. Riedweg (1987) offers a useful discussion of Plato's use of the terminology of the Mysteries; see also M. Morgan 1990, ch. 4 and *passim*.

[28] See also *Phaedo* 69c–d and 81a, where Socrates compares philosophers to those who have been "purified" and "initiated." As Rowe rightly suggests (1993, 151), Socrates refers in the *Phaedo* to "initiatory rites in general" (rather than to the Eleusinian Mysteries in particular).

[29] In the *Symposium*, the soul is not divided into "parts." But Plato does mention that the soul sees the Form of Beauty "with that by which it is necessary to see [it]" (212a) and "with that to which it is visible" (212a). It is clear that he means that the soul possesses a faculty or (in the non-technical sense) a part which is rational; it is with this faculty that it "sees" the Forms.

When he views beautiful things, one after another in the correct way, he will suddenly see, at the end, a wondrous (θαυμαστόν) vision, beautiful in nature, which is the final object of all his previous toils. (210e)

The philosopher who beholds the Form achieves the vision of "divine Beauty" (τὸ θεῖον καλόν), which makes him "beloved of god and – to the extent possible for any man – immortal" (211e–212a).[30] By contemplating the Forms, the philosopher becomes both wise and happy. And this activity also enables him to "give birth to virtue." The vision of Beauty thus renders the philosopher virtuous as well as wise: theoretical contemplation leads to the production and enactment of virtue in the practical sphere.[31]

In describing the philosopher's *theoria*, Diotima compares the contemplation of the Forms to the *epoptika* or the moment of revelation at the Eleusinian Mysteries (210a). For example, just before she describes the ascent, she says to Socrates that while he might be initiated (μυηθείης) into the matters discussed thus far, he cannot yet advance to the next stage to see the "final rites and revelations" (τὰ δὲ τέλεα καὶ ἐποπτικά, 209e–210a). Here, Diotima uses the technical language of the Eleusinian Mysteries, explicitly referring to *theoria* at this famous festival. There were two classes of initiates who came as *theoroi* to this festival: the μύστης ("initiate"), who took part in the festival and mystery rites for the first time, and the ἐπόπτης ("watcher"), who came to the festival for (at least) a second time to see the ἐποπτικά or "highest mysteries."[32] Diotima identifies Socrates as a *mustēs* – an initiate who has come to the festival for the first time. He is not, she claims, an *epoptēs* and thus cannot be granted the vision of the highest mysteries. When Diotima goes on to describe these "*epoptika*" in the passage that follows, she is clearly referring to the contemplation of the Forms. As she explains, the philosopher who ascends correctly moves from the "sight" of the beautiful body of a boy to the beauty of all bodies and, from there, to the beauty of the soul; he will then "behold" the beauty of laws and institutions and, finally, "theorize" (θεωρῶν) the Form of the Beautiful (210a–d). In this passage, then, Diotima clearly identifies philosophic *theoria* with the revelation of the highest mysteries at the initiation ceremony at Eleusis.

---

[30] Plato repeatedly uses the language of vision to describe the philosopher's encounter with the Form of Beauty (θεωρῶν, κατίδῃ, 210d; θεώμενος, κατόψεται, 210e; καθορᾶν, 211b; θεωμένῳ, ἴδῃς, 211d; κατιδεῖν, 211e; βλέποντος, θεωμένου, ὁρῶντι ᾧ ὁρατὸν τὸ καλόν, 212a).

[31] Of course the *Symposium* offers a far simpler account of theorizing than the *Republic*, which sets forth a theory of the soul and an extensive discussion of ontology and epistemology.

[32] Burkert 1985, 287.

Although the festival of the Greater Mysteries at Eleusis was sponsored by Athens, it was attended by *theoroi* from all over Greece. While this festival featured rituals and spectacles similar to those at other religious festivals, it culminated in the unique ritual of initiation (sometimes called the *teletē*). The festival was a public and international event lasting many days, but the initiation ceremony focused on the private individual, offering him or her salvation in the afterlife.[33] After journeying as a *theoros* to the festival of the Mysteries, the person seeking initiation underwent rites of purification and participated in various rituals. Eventually, this individual obtained a view of the *hiera* or sacred objects, which the hierophant revealed at the climax of the ritual. Interestingly, the mystic ceremony featured the movement from darkness to light. At the beginning of the ritual, the initiates stood in darkness in a building called the *Telesterion*; when the hierophant opened the door of the *Anaktoron* – a stone chamber at the center of the *Telesterion* – a stream of light blazed forth from the interior. To receive the revelation, the *mustai* enter the *Anaktoron*, where the *epoptai* are gathered with thousands of torches.[34] The precise difference between the experience of the *mustēs* and the *epoptēs* is not quite clear: both "saw" the sacred objects, though the *mustēs* might have been veiled during part of the revelation; alternatively, the *epoptēs* might have seen additional sights or perhaps had a closer look at the sacred objects.[35]

The Greeks believed that initiation into the Mysteries guaranteed a good fate in the afterlife: "blessed among mortals on earth is he who has seen (ὄπωπεν); but the uninitiated never has the same lot once dead in the dreary darkness" (*Homeric Hymn to Demeter* 480–2). We find a similar claim in Sophocles: "thrice blessed are those mortals who have seen these rites and thus enter Hades: for them alone there is life, but for the others all is misery" (fr. 837 Pearson–Radt).[36] Interestingly, some Greeks thought that the mystic revelation had an epistemic as well as a salvific aspect; as Pindar says in an important fragment, "blessed is he who, seeing these things (ἰδὼν κεῖνα), goes beneath the earth; he knows (οἶδε) the end of life, and he knows (οἶδεν) the god-given beginning" (fr. 121 Bowra).[37] By all accounts,

---

[33] Initiation into the Mysteries was open to all Greek speakers, including women and slaves. On the festival and rituals of the Eleusinian Mysteries, see Parke 1977, 55–72, Burkert 1985, 285–90, Dillon 1997, 60–70.

[34] Burkert 1985, 287, Clinton 1993, 118–19, Dillon 1997, 67. Sources from late antiquity provide evidence for certain details of the ceremony.

[35] Parke 1977, 71, Burkert 1985, 287.

[36] As Isocrates puts it, the *mustai* "have better hopes for the end of life and for all eternity" (IV.28).

[37] Cf. Aristotle, who claims that "it is not necessary for those being initiated to learn something but to experience and be put into a certain state" (fr. 15 Ross=15 Rose 3rd ed.).

initiation into the Mysteries focused on the afterlife rather than earthly life. The rite of initiation served the individual rather than the community or civic body: it offered personal salvation and blessedness. Note also that the initiate took an oath to keep the central revelation a secret. The *theoros* who gets initiated does not, then, return home with a report of the vision (though he may have brought news of the other events at the festival). The initiation at Eleusis thus offered the model of an exceptionally private form of *theoria*.

It is easy to see why Plato was attracted to this religious festival, since it featured a vision that transformed the initiate and granted him or her salvation in the afterlife. The personal nature of the initiation ceremony offers a model of private *theoria* that has salvific as well as epistemic associations. Just as initiation at Eleusis transformed the individual so that he would achieve salvation in the afterworld, the "initiation" of the philosophic *theoros*, Plato claims, purifies and transforms the soul and guarantees it a blessed destiny. To be sure, Plato believed that philosophic *theoria* makes the soul wise and happy in this life as well as the next – indeed the philosopher practices *theoria*, first and foremost, to live well in the present. But in other respects the philosopher has much in common with the initiate at the Mysteries: in both cases, the *theoros* "sees" a divine revelation that transforms his soul.

Let us turn, now, to the *Phaedrus*, which makes an even more prominent use of the model of mystic initiation. In Socrates' second speech, he describes the experiences of the human soul before incarnation on earth. In this period, he says, souls traveled around the cosmos seeking "initiation" into wisdom. The human souls follow in the train of the gods, who periodically ascend to the very edge of the universe to contemplate the Forms:

Those that are immortal, when they get to the top, pass outside it and take their stand on the outer surface of the heaven; the revolution of the cosmos carries them around as they stand there and they theorize (θεωροῦσι) the things outside the heaven. (247b–c)

Even the gods, as it seems, make a journey of *theoria* to the Forms (247e): traveling to the most distant part of the universe, they "see the spectacles and have a feast" (as though at a festival) and, after contemplating, return "back home" (*oikade*).[38] During this *theoria*, the gods gaze upon "really real Being" (οὐσία ὄντως οὖσα – a term that Plato often uses for the Forms). As Socrates explains, along with the gods, preincarnate human

---

[38] On this startling image, see Griswold 2003.

souls also attempted to make this upward journey, hoping to gain a vision of reality. Some of these souls failed to reach the edge of heaven and "went away uninitiated in the vision of reality" (ἀτελεῖς τῆς τοῦ ὄντος θέας ἀπέρχονται); others were more successful, though they achieved at best an unstable and partial view of the Forms (247a–b).[39] Socrates describes the "initiation" into the knowledge of the Forms as follows:

The soul . . . rejoices in seeing being (ἰδοῦσα . . . τὸ ὄν) for a time and, by theorizing (θεωροῦσα) the truth, it is nourished and made happy until the revolution brings it again to the same place. In the revolution it beholds (καθορᾷ) justice itself, and temperance, and knowledge . . . and beholding the other true beings in the same way and feeding on them, it sinks back down within the heaven and goes home. (247d–e)

Here, Socrates identifies the "realities" that the souls behold as the Forms of Justice, Temperance, etc. But he also calls them "blessed" and "holy sights" (μακάριαι θέαι, 247a; ὧν τότε εἶδον ἱερῶν, 250a), thus emphasizing the divinity of the Forms. The soul that views these beings, he suggests, experiences a sort of religious revelation.

This primordial initiation, Socrates claims, can be reenacted in one's earthly life. For the "initiated" soul, when incarnate on earth, can "recollect" the Forms and contemplate them through the practice of philosophy. In particular, the sight of bodily beauty can trigger the recollection of the Form of Beauty (though recollection leads to true knowledge only after long philosophic labor):

When the recent initiate (ἀρτιτελής), who beheld many of those realities there, sees [on earth] a godlike face or the form of a body that offers a good imitation of the Beautiful, he shudders at first and some of the former awe takes hold of him; then, as he looks at it, he reveres (σέβεται) it like a god . . . [As he looks upon the beautiful boy,] his memory is borne back to the true nature of Beauty, and he sees it standing together with modesty upon a holy pedestal, and when he sees this he is afraid and falls backward in reverence (ἰδοῦσα δὲ ἔδεισέ τε καὶ σεφθεῖσα ἀνέπεσεν ὑπτία). (251a, 254b)

In this passage, Socrates describes the process of the recollection of the Form of Beauty. The beautiful body on earth, shining with the radiance of true Beauty, is an "*agalma*" (251a, 252d) – a sacred statue or object that embodies and represents the divine (a point to which I will return in chapter 4). This

---

[39] Cf. 249b, which asserts that the soul who has never seen the truth cannot pass into a human form, and 249e–250a, which says that all souls who become human on earth must have "beheld the realities." Socrates' suggestion in 247a–b that some souls did not see the Forms before birth is presumably meant as one chapter in a long psychic history.

body – a sort of sacred image on earth – "reminds" the soul of its earlier vision of divine Beauty.[40]

Although the primordial initiation offered the soul a vision of all the Forms, the sight of the Form of Beauty had a particular force. For, unlike the other Forms, Beauty possesses its own special brilliance:

> Beauty shone with light at that time when our souls, with a blessed company, saw the blessed sight and vision (μακαρίαν ὄψιν τε καὶ θέαν) . . . and were initiated into that which is rightly called the most blessed of mysteries (εἶδόν τε καὶ ἐτελοῦντο τῶν τελετῶν ἦν θέμις λέγειν μακαριωτάτην), which we celebrated in a state of perfection, when we were without experience of the evils in the later time to come, being initiated and seeing the mysteries in the clear light (μυούμενοί τε καὶ ἐποπτεύοντες ἐν αὐγῇ καθαρᾷ) – sights that were perfect and simple and calm and blessed . . . (250b–c)

The radiant light of the Form of Beauty is brilliantly instantiated in earthly beauties, whereas the earthly copies of other Forms such as Justice and Temperance "contain no light" (250b). This is because Beauty "shone with light" (ἔλαμπεν) when mortal souls viewed it before birth, "and now that we have come here we grasp it shining most clearly through the clearest of our senses" (250d).[41] In recollecting the Form, then, the soul experiences its previous, preincarnate "initiation." But the person who practices philosophy also undergoes an abiding and continuous initiation in the present: for if he "employs such recollections rightly," the philosopher "is always being initiated into perfect mysteries, and he alone becomes truly perfect" (τέλεους ἀεὶ τελετὰς τελούμενος, τέλεος ὄντως μόνος γίγνεται, 249c).

Throughout this speech, Plato compares the philosophic recollection and contemplation of the Forms with the mystic revelation at the Eleusinian festival (especially the vision of the "sacred objects" in the initiation ceremony). Both the initiate at the Mysteries and the philosopher theorizing the Forms see a vision that transforms them and brings joy and a blessed destiny. Unlike the ordinary initiate, however, the philosopher looks directly at "divine" beings (and not just at sacred objects and symbols) and his experience of *theoria* brings him wisdom as well as blessedness. For this vision fulfills the soul's innate desire for truth: "when it sees Being, the soul attains the knowledge that it longs for, and it encounters true reality" (248b). In this text, Plato uses the discourse of myth and Analogy and does not offer a technical account of his epistemology. But by comparing philosophic *theoria* to the initiation into the Mysteries, Plato offers a vivid picture of the salvific and epistemic aspects of the practice of theoretical philosophy.

---

[40] Griswold [1986]/1996, 111–21 and *passim*.   [41] I will discuss this passage in detail in chapter 4.

As I have suggested, the model of the *theoria* at the Mysteries also conjures up secrecy and exclusion: the initiate is forbidden to talk about the mystic revelation to noninitiates (though he may discuss the other parts of the *theoria* at Eleusis). As Jameson observes,

[At the Eleusinian festival of the Mysteries,] certain sights seen and actions performed distinguished the admitted and the excluded. Here performance was prominent, sometimes spectacular, such as the procession of initiates from Athens to Eleusis, but the central elements were hidden and the very fact of their obscurity defined the participants. This is an example of what has been called "advertised secrecy."[42]

The person initiated at the festival, then, experiences a sort of *theoria* within a *theoria*: the pilgrimage and public activities at the sanctuary take the form of traditional *theoria*, but the initiation ceremony offers a vision of a secret and exclusive spectacle. This ritual separates the initiated from the uninitiated.

To a Greek audience, Plato's description of philosophic *theoria* as a sort of mystic initiation may have conveyed the idea that his philosophic "initiation" involved secrecy and exclusivity. Clearly, Plato does represent the philosophers as forming an exclusive and specially favored group: indeed, he deploys a great deal of rhetoric in distinguishing the true philosopher from imposters and nonphilosophers.[43] In addition, he frequently suggests that the philosopher cannot communicate the truth to the masses (even if he wanted to) because they do not have the capacity to understand it. This kind of rhetoric, then, serves to "advertise secrecy," since it represents philosophic truth as available to only a tiny group of elites.

While Plato's depiction of philosophers as an elite group of initiates no doubt appealed to aristocrats and educated intellectuals, ordinary people might have held it in suspicion. In the *Clouds*, for example, Aristophanes criticizes Socrates for offering esoteric ideas to students as though they were mystic initiates:

STUDENT (OF SOCRATES): It is not permitted for me to tell these things to anyone except students.
STREPSIADES: Then you may go ahead and tell me; for I have come to be a student at this think tank.
STUDENT: I will speak. But you must remember that these are high mysteries (*mustēria*)

(140–3)

---

[42] Jameson 1999, 334.   [43] As I argue in Nightingale 1995, ch. 1 and *passim*.

Later in the play, when he begins to teach Strepsiades, Socrates makes him put on a chaplet for the initiation ceremony, telling him that "we do all this to those who are being initiated" (*teloumenous*, 258). The *Clouds*, of course, portrays Socrates as training students to engage in unjust activities that will bring harm to the city and its people. The suggestion that Socrates' teaching offers an "initiation" into a secret society makes him look suspicious: Socrates' secrecy indicates that he has something to hide. Given that Aristophanes, a writer whose discourse appealed to the broader public, pours scorn upon the private "initiations" offered by sophistic educators (here represented by Socrates), we may wonder how the ordinary Athenian would have reacted to Plato's use of the model of initiation in the Mysteries.

This raises an important question: does Plato's philosophic initiate hide something from the masses? As I have argued elsewhere, the Greek *sophos* possesses intellectual "property" that can be owned and disowned in the same way as material wealth.[44] He can offer it up for public scrutiny or hide it away so as to benefit only himself and his associates. If he hides this property, he may appear to behave like the evasive Athenian taxpayer, who makes his wealth "invisible" so as to avoid spending it on liturgies for the city.[45] As Polanyi has suggested, in pre-market economies, economic relations are "embedded" in the social system, whereas in the market economy, they are "disembedded" from the social structure and operate in an independent sphere not subject to social control.[46] The Greek man who hides

---

[44] Nightingale 1995, ch. 1; see also Gernet ([1968]/1981, ch. 16), who discusses the philosophic distinction between the "visible" and the "invisible" in relation to the distinction between visible and invisible property in the economic sphere.

[45] Finley 1952, 53–6, Kurke 1991, 227 and *passim*. E. Cohen (1992, 190–206 and *passim*) builds a powerful case for an extensive "invisible economy" in fourth-century Athens. Consider, for example, the *antidosis* trial, which arose when an Athenian assigned to perform a compulsory public service or "liturgy" sought exemption on the grounds that another individual was wealthier than him and should shoulder the financial burden in his stead (see, e.g., MacDowell 1978, 162–4, Gabrielsen 1987, Christ 1990). The person assigned the liturgy challenged this wealthy individual either to pay for the liturgy or to accept an exchange of property. In the trial, the defendant was required by law "to make visible" (ἀποφαίνειν) his wealth in a right and just manner (Demosthenes 42.11 and 18); he would also have to convince the jury that he was not "hiding" any wealth. As Gabrielsen (1986, 104) suggests, "*acknowledgement of ownership* (formally an ὁμολογία or δήλωσις) is the fundamental and necessary step for converting property into visible [wealth]; failure to do so allows the property to remain in the area of the invisible and marks the act of concealment (ἀπόκρυψις οὐσίας)." The material possessions that a person claims as his own, then, are "visible property" and those which he disclaims (or refuses to claim) are "invisible property."

[46] Polanyi 1957, 68 and *passim*; for an analysis of Polanyi's thesis and its impact upon the modern debates about the ancient Greek economy, see Humphreys 1978, ch. 2. Many scholars claim that it is in fourth-century Athens that a disembedded economy begins to emerge (Humphreys 1978, chs. 6 and 7, Thompson 1982, Osborne 1991, Burke 1992, E. Cohen 1992, 4–5 and *passim*; but

his wealth effectively disembeds himself from the social economy of the city. By concealing his property and opting out of traditional civic systems of exchange, he becomes a sort of outsider in his own city.

Does Plato's philosopher engage in activities that are disembedded from the sociopolitical structure? I believe that he does, though this is not because he actively hides his intellectual property. Rather, the philosopher is disembedded because he rejects traditional social and political systems of exchange. This is true even of the philosopher in the ideal city in the *Republic* (whose *theoria* is civic rather than private): although he serves as a ruler, he maintains the status of a disinterested "outsider." This philosopher engages in an activity radically opposed to traditional forms of social exchange: he will never exchange his wisdom for material, symbolic, or political capital.[47] Indeed the philosophic rulers in the ideal city in the *Republic* will not touch gold and silver or own any private property, thereby avoiding all material transactions. Interestingly, Adeimantus compares these rulers to "hired mercenaries" who work for a foreign city (ἐπίκουροι μισθωτοί, 419a). Socrates is quick to agree with Adeimantus, saying that the philosophers *are* like foreign mercenaries except that they "serve for food and receive no wage in addition, as other mercenaries do" (420a). The philosophic rulers are, in crucial ways, foreigners in their own city.

Paradoxically, then, Plato's philosopher is a mercenary who receives no wage. The philosophic ruler is, as it seems, a non-mercenary mercenary: *an outsider who serves the city free of charge*. According to Plato, this extreme foreign and "outside" position ensures that the ruler will act in a disinterested and impartial fashion in political life. The philosopher, then, offers the city a new kind of liturgy: he performs a civic benefaction, but does not ask for *charis* in return. Indeed, Plato's philosopher – as an outsider serving for no wage – stands in stark contrast to the liturgist in Athens, who offers his wealth to the community in the expectation of some sort of return recompense.[48] Whereas the Athenian liturgist participates in a social system in which he can "buy" *charis*, the philosopher engages in virtuous action for its own sake, categorically refusing any sort of economic or political payback. Plato positions the philosophers outside the traditional

---

cf. Rostovtzeff 1941, 100–1, Polanyi 1957, Finley 1970, Austin and Vidal-Naquet 1977, 147–52). Of course the development of a disembedded economy need not destroy or replace the previously existing embedded economy; as Millet observes (1990, 1991), gift-exchange and market exchange (together with the ideologies that attend them) can coexist in a single city-state, and did so in fourth-century Athens (1990, 171).

47 I will discuss this point in detail in chapter 3.

48 For discussions of the liturgy system in Athens and the liturgists' bids for *charis*, see Davies 1981, 88–105, Ober 1989, 226–36.

systems of exchange (economic, social, and political), thus guaranteeing their freedom and impartiality.[49]

Plato's philosopher, then, is in some sense disembedded from the social and economic fabric of his city. In addition, his wisdom is inaccessible to the common man and is, to that extent, "invisible." But the philosopher does not endeavor to hide and hoard his wisdom, nor does he use it to enrich or advance himself privately.[50] The philosophic *theoros* in the *Republic*, in fact, uses his private (intellectual) wealth for public purposes. Of course, the philosopher can only practice this "civic" *theoria* in the truly good city. In an ordinary city, the philosopher will stay out of politics and lead a private life. Nonetheless, Plato makes it quite clear that the private (nonpolitical) theorist will translate his contemplative wisdom into the practical sphere: metaphysical contemplation provides the ground for virtuous action, which the philosopher performs when he "returns" (again and again) from contemplative activity. In fact, this practical instantiation of theoretical contemplation is a crucial part of the theoric journey taken as a whole. To the extent that the philosopher embodies his wisdom and exhibits his virtue in the practical realm, he makes it visible and efficacious. In addition, the philosopher will "give an account" of his wisdom to his friends and associates, thus opening it up to scrutiny. He does not, then, hide his wisdom from view – on the contrary, he attempts to communicate it by way of rational argumentation that is open to inspection.[51]

Plato's account of the theoretical philosopher, then, manifests an interesting tension. On the one hand, the philosopher's activities in the practical sphere are disembedded from traditional social, economic, and political systems of exchange. But, at the same time, he benefits his society by instantiating his contemplative wisdom in both his words and his deeds. While his contemplative activities pull him away (for a time) from human affairs, Plato's philosopher acts virtuously when he engages in social and practical activities. This is, no doubt, one of the reasons why Plato preferred oral or "living" discourse to the disembodied voice of the written text: for Plato, philosophic wisdom must be enacted by a living soul in a human body.

In this chapter, I have examined Plato's appropriation of the discourse and structure of traditional *theoria* in his explication of philosophic theoria. Plato turned to traditional *theoria* as a cultural practice that had authority and currency in Greek society in this period. By associating his own

---

[49] Note that Plato himself, in creating the theoretical philosopher, makes a bid for symbolic capital: he wants his philosophers to be recognized as supremely wise and virtuous.

[50] As the Athenian tax-evader does, who hides his property and makes it "invisible."

[51] Cf. Szlezák 1999, who argues for the esotericist position.

philosophic practice with that of *theoria*, Plato claimed legitimacy for theoretical philosophy and found a way to structure philosophic practice and make it more intelligible to the layperson. Plato's foundational conception of "theoretical" philosophy raises important questions about the relation of philosophic *theoria* to politics and *praxis*. What is the place of contemplation in the social and political lives of human beings? What is the precise relation between contemplation and action? To what extent should the contemplative and other-worldly activity of *theoria* be privileged over practical and political "performances" in the human world? How could an activity that transcended human affairs recommend itself as the highest form of wisdom? These issues and questions will be central to all of the fourth-century discussions of *theoria*.

CHAPTER 3

The fable of philosophy in Plato's Republic

When you consider the radiance, that it does not withhold/ itself but pours its abundance without selection into every/ nook and cranny not overhung or hidden . . .

A. R. Ammons, "The City Limits"

When one spends too much time travelling, one becomes at last a stranger at home.

Descartes, Discourse on Method

Not till we are completely lost, in other words, not till we have lost the world, do we begin to find ourselves, and realize where we are and the infinite extent of our relations.

Thoreau, Walden

Plato offers a detailed discussion of philosophic *theoria* in the *Republic* books V–VII. He locates this discussion in the context of a conversation between quite specific characters, one of whom has dedicated his life to the search for wisdom. As in all his dialogues, Plato places the specificity of the characters in a dialogical relation to the general and abstract ideas under discussion. The drama of the dialogue, in short, corroborates but also complicates the issues set forth in the arguments and myths.[1] This drama features characters in a particular historical context engaging in philosophical discussions on various topics. In the dialogue as a whole, the characters' lives and personalities enrich and illuminate the intellectual arguments. In the *Republic* and other dialogues dealing with *theoria*, Socrates' highly idiosyncratic persona affects our interpretation of the text and its account of theorizing. Socrates' personal search for wisdom and self-knowledge is

---

[1] On Plato's use of the dialogue form, see Griswold [1986]/1996, chs. 1 and 6, 1988, Frede 1992, Nightingale 1995, Clay 2000, 79–176, K. Morgan 2000, chs. 6–8, Blondell 2002. On Socratic and/or Platonic irony, see Friedländer 1958, ch. 7, Rowe 1987, Vlastos 1991, ch. 1, Nightingale 1995, ch. 3, Nehamas 1999a, chs. 1–3, Griswold 2000.

placed in a fruitful interaction with his accounts of the impersonal, transcendental activity of theoretical contemplation.

By composing philosophic dramas, Plato created a sort of dialogue between the concrete and the abstract, the particular person and the metaphysical pilgrim. On the one hand, he reminds us, the activity of theorizing takes place in the context of a personal life that is historically specific. But, at the same time, the particular person is an immortal soul whose life on earth is but one chapter in its lengthy history.[2] The philosophic theorist, then, acts at the interface between time and eternity, the personal and the transcendental. The dialogues dealing with *theoria* offer a literary and philosophical exploration of this dynamic tension.[3]

In addition to his philosophic discussions of the theory of Forms, Plato depicts the discipline of *theoria* in numerous myths and rhetorical passages. Indeed the most famous account of theoretical philosophy is found in the Analogy of the Cave. In this philosophic fable, Plato portrays the rational part of the soul as a living, changing person making an arduous pilgrimage. Here, Plato personifies this part of the soul, representing it as a whole person possessing intellectual, erotic, and affective faculties. This personification represents the rational part of the soul as a sort of "homunculus" – a full person rather than a single part of the soul. Interpreted in analytic terms, the personification of the rational part of the soul conflicts with Plato's philosophic analysis of the tripartite soul (in *Republic* IV). But the very effort to translate mythic into analytic discourse is, I believe, methodologically unsound.[4] For the myths are not doing the same work as the arguments (or vice versa): these different modes of discourse present different kinds of ideas and address different sorts of questions. As McCabe has argued, Platonic myth is a discourse that contains a "surplus of meaning": the literary language of myth presents the reader with multiple interpretive

---

[2] Blondell (2002) offers an eloquent discussion of this issue.

[3] According to Plato, the Forms are eternal and changeless, whereas the soul is everlasting but exists in time (it is subject to motion and change). Plato does not offer a technical analysis of the soul's interaction with Beings that exist outside of time. Rather, he uses the narrative mode, which depicts the soul's theoretical journey as taking place within time. The philosopher's journey unfolds step by step; even when gazing on the Forms, the philosopher does not escape from time. Thus, in the soul's encounter with the Forms, a being that exists and evolves within time confronts and attempts to comprehend a timeless, changeless Being.

[4] In my view, the polysemic discourse of metaphor and myth cannot be fully translated into analytic argument; for, in this kind of translation, some aspect of the myth is inevitably distorted, devalued, or ignored. For some recent investigations of Plato's myths and strategies for interpreting them, see Brisson 1982, Griswold [1986]/1996, ch. 4; Detienne [1981]/1986, Rowe 1991, 1999, McCabe 1992, Gill 1993, Nightingale 1995, chs. 2 and 4, Laird 1999, ch. 2; K. Morgan 2000, chs. 6–8, Blondell 2002, ch. 1 and *passim*, Lear forthcoming. Lloyd (1987, ch. 4) discusses the language of metaphor in ancient Greek scientific and philosophical texts.

Detienne, The Creation of Mythology

options, and cannot be neatly translated into analytic arguments.[5] This does not mean that the myths are unphilosophical; rather, they approach (certain) philosophical questions in a different key.

In representing the activity of *theoria*, Plato uses a very distinctive rhetorical strategy. In particular, he develops a rhetoric designed to spirit the reader to new and unknown regions. In the Analogy of the Cave, for example, Plato creates a sort of topography of the physical and metaphysical regions, which border one another at the mouth of the cave. He uses highly visual, physical language in his description of these regions, offering the reader a vivid spectacle of the realms of being and becoming.[6] By portraying the people in our world as deluded cave-dwellers, and by depicting a radiant metaphysical region located (so to speak) above and outside our own, Plato attempts to unsettle his readers from all that is familiar. He develops a rhetoric that says to the reader: you know not where you are. I call this the "rhetoric of estrangement," since it aims to uproot and displace us, portraying the familiar world as strange and the strange reality of the Forms as kindred to the human soul. By using this kind of rhetoric, Plato invites the reader to enter into the perspective of the philosophic *theoros* – to adopt the alterity of the theoric gaze.

Of course the reader who witnesses Plato's metaphysical "spectacle" is not in fact "seeing" truth: reading this mythic discourse is no substitute for discovering or contemplating the Forms. The Analogy of the Cave is a protreptic discourse that urges the reader to embrace the life of philosophic *theoria*. Distancing us from our traditional world-view, it encourages us to accompany the mythic philosopher on his journey to the Forms. If the reader accepts this rhetorical invitation, he will depart from his present point of view (and, in some sense, from the familiar world in which he lives) and enter into the *aporia* and *atopia* that characterize the activity of philosophic theorizing. The reader's response is affective as well as cognitive: the rhetoric of darkness and light, imprisonment and freedom, exile and return plays on the emotional and erotic parts of his/her psyche. In addition, the myth depicts distant and strange beings as the objects of the deepest human longing – beings which the philosophic soul discovers by practicing dialectic. Of course this is representation, not reality. In the Analogy, the

---

[5] McCabe 1992.

[6] In the analogies of the Sun and the Cave, Plato uses visual language even as he tells the reader that physical vision has no access to truth. This move – together with Socrates' disclaimers of knowledge and his pointed reminders that he is (uncharacteristically) using *eikones* – is unsettling, and raises difficult questions about the philosophical status of literary (non-analytic) discourse (see note 5 above).

reader observes a drama in which the philosophic soul exits from the cave and "sees" the Forms: the reader sees the theorist see.

In this chapter, I want to focus on one particular part of the *Republic*, namely, the discussion of philosophic *theoria* set forth in books v–vii. I will not offer an interpretation of the dialogue as a whole, or attempt to examine Plato's epistemology in analytic terms. Rather, I will look at Plato's foundational account of philosophic *theoria*, focusing in particular on the Analogy of the Cave. In this philosophic fable, the *theoros* journeys "abroad" to see the sacred spectacle of the Forms. This experience alters and transforms the philosopher: by engaging in contemplation, he achieves wisdom and a radical form of freedom which affect his actions in the practical realm. As in traditional *theoria* at religious festivals, Platonic *theoria* features a sacralized mode of spectating that differs from mundane modes of viewing. What is the nature of this new kind of "theoric" gaze? What does the philosopher see? And what does he fail to see? What sort of freedom does the philosopher achieve? Finally, how do his contemplative activities affect his actions in the social and political world?

In the *Republic*, Plato divides the "journey" of *theoria* into the three phases found in traditional *theoria*. In the first, the philosopher departs from the human and terrestrial world and goes in search of the Forms; having detached himself from society, he enters into a state of *aporia* and *atopia*. In the second, the philosopher reaches the metaphysical "region" of reality and engages in the contemplation of the Forms. Paradoxically, the precondition for this metaphysical "vision" is blindness to the human and terrestrial world. Theoretical contemplation, I argue, is not panoptic. Nor is it neutral or dispassionate: the philosophic gaze is erotic as well as intellectual. Finally, in the third phase, the philosophic *theoros* "returns" to the city and uses his contemplative knowledge as a basis for action. But he returns home as a different man, and has a new orientation to his fellow humans and to the city as a whole. For the detachment from the world and the contemplation of the Forms radically transforms the philosopher, both ethically and epistemically. When he returns to the human realm, he sees (and is seen) very differently: the philosophic *theoros* will henceforth dwell in a world where he is never fully at home. The philosopher has become a sort of stranger (*atopos*) in his own land. Yet it is precisely this "outside" status that enables him to achieve the radical freedom necessary for impartial and virtuous action.

The very notion of a philosophic "journey" to "see" the truth is of course a metaphor, and is thus articulated in literary, rather than analytic discourse. Read as a philosophical myth, the Analogy of the Cave offers a vivid account of the life and activities of the theoretical philosopher. This myth does not, by itself, provide definitive evidence for Plato's metaphysical theories, but it does offer an account of philosophy which scholars who wish to analyze Plato's epistemogy, ontology, and psychology cannot ignore. In this chapter, I will interpret the Analogy of the Cave as a philosophic fable – a myth that defines and defends *theoria* as a new intellectual practice that has a specific place in the social and political realm.

THE IDEAL VS. THE HUMAN PHILOSOPHER

In books v–vii of the *Republic*, Plato introduces a new kind of sage – a philosophic *theoros* who "loves the spectacle of truth." The discussion in these books focuses on the activity of turning the "eye of the soul" upwards towards reality rather than downwards towards earthly affairs. Plato illustrates this in the Analogy of the Cave, where the philosopher looks away from the terrestrial world, and directs his "eyes" to the region of true reality. For a time, he is blinded by the light of the sun that shines there. But his eyes slowly adjust, and eventually he is able to gaze upon the beings in this metaphysical realm, including the Being that illuminates this region, the sun-like Form of the Good. He now sees that the shadow-figures in the cave were (at best) copies of the true beings in this realm, and that this region is the locus of the "really real." With reluctance, he goes back into the cave and is initially blinded by the darkness in that realm. When he returns, the people who dwell there say that his eyes have been ruined by his journey; they mock him and say that he has lost his mind (517a).

The philosopher depicted in the Analogy of the Cave is an idealized figure who makes a journey that no human being could ever accomplish.[7] For, in this myth, the philosopher makes his way towards the direct contemplation of the Form of the Good – a vision that renders him a perfected soul akin to the gods. The very idea of a person looking directly at the sun suggests that the tale is an *adunaton*: no ordinary human could do this without being permanently blinded. As Socrates himself indicates, the perfected philosophers in the ideal city should be treated as "divinities" or, at least, as "blessed and divine men" (540b–c); they are, in some sense, superhuman. In addition, Socrates also suggests that the philosophers who have journeyed to the Forms could – if they chose – stay in this region and never return

---

[7] See Blondell 2002, 225–6 on this "impersonal ideal of philosophic perfection."

(517c–d, 519d).[8] But surely a human soul cannot, during incarnate life, make a permanent escape from the physical and social world – only a divine soul would have this option.

Let us grant that this is a highly idealized narrative. The Analogy of the Cave (and the portrait of the perfected philosophers educated in the ideal city) does not offer a literal and realistic account of the philosophic life: it tells the story of a *sophos* rather than a *philosophos*. In fact, the ordinary human philosopher never achieves perfect knowledge, nor could he make a permanent abode in the region of the Forms. Socrates himself more or less admits that his Analogy sets forth an unrealizable ideal. In particular, he says that he "hopes" that his story of the philosophic ascent is true, though this is only how it "seems" to him:

> . . . if you assume that the ascent and the contemplation of the things above is the soul's ascension to the intelligible region, you will not be wrong about what it is that I hope for (ἐλπίδος), since you wish to hear these things. God knows if it is true. But it seems to be the case – it seems to me, at any rate (τὰ δ'οῦν ἐμοὶ φαινόμενα οὕτω φαίνεται) – that the last thing to be seen – and it is hardly seen – is the Form of the Good . . . (517b)

Again, when Glaucon asks him later in book VII about the dialectical journey and its culmination in the vision of the Forms, Socrates asserts that the story should not be taken for literal truth: "whether it really is true or not, this is not worth affirming, but that it looks something like this I do affirm" (533a). The Analogy of the Cave, then, portrays a successful theoretical journey culminating in a full and direct vision of the Forms (including the Form of the Good). This mythic account does offer essential information about philosophic *theoria* – about what sort of activity it is and how it is structured – but we must keep in mind that it offers an idealized portrait which is, in certain ways, at odds with the human experience of philosophic *theoria*.

Where does this leave the ordinary, nonideal philosopher (a particular individual like Socrates)? As a human being, he must journey again and again to the metaphysical region, each time gaining a partial view of the Forms. And he must "return" each time to the terrestrial and human world, since he is an incarnate human being. In short, he must shuttle back and forth between two worlds in an ongoing endeavor to contemplate the Forms

---

[8] Since they would, if left to themselves, choose to remain there, the perfected philosophers in the ideal city must be "compelled" to return so that they can take their place as rulers of the city (more on this below).

and to imitate and instantiate them on earth. The human philosopher can never become the idealized *theoros* depicted in the Analogy; though he can, over a lifetime, make real progress in contemplating the Forms, he will fall short of the complete wisdom and happiness achieved by the perfected philosopher. As I will suggest, the human philosopher dwells in a permanent condition of *aporia* and *atopia*, and never achieves the tranquillity depicted in the myth. The Analogy of the Cave, then, tells the story of a *philosophos* becoming a *sophos*; the human *philosophos*, we may infer, will have a rather different experience of theoretical activity.

DISTANCE AND DETACHMENT

Plato's notion of the philosophic journey to a foreign land – with its condition of radical detachment from the world – is an important part of his appropriation of traditional *theoria*. In traditional *theoria* the traveler detaches himself, for a time, from his own city and journeys to a distant land. As we saw in chapter 1, the traditional *theoros* enters into a "liminal" space when he departs from the city and goes on a pilgrimage: according to Victor Turner, during the period of the journey, pilgrims (even those traveling with people from their own city) enter into a zone where ordinary civic institutions and structures are temporarily suspended. In this "liminal" phase, the *theoros* departs from traditional social and political structures, thus opening himself up to new experiences and perspectives. Plato's philosophic *theoros* also enters a "liminal" space, but he achieves a much more radical kind of detachment than his traditional counterpart. For the philosopher's "journey" not only cuts him off from the city but leads to a metaphysical "region" that transcends social and political life altogether. This detachment, of course, is only temporary: as we have seen, continuous contemplation is not possible for human beings. But, this detachment is, while it lasts, total and complete. As Plato indicates, this detachment is the precondition for philosophical contemplation as well as for virtuous action in the world. The detached activity of contemplation transforms the philosopher, rendering him wise and truly free; this, in turn, enables him to play the role of a virtuous and impartial "outsider" in his own city.[9]

---

[9] I will consider later the precise ways in which the philosopher is "truly free" and how the activity of "seeing" and "spectating" is connected with both detachment and freedom.

The claim that the philosopher must detach from the human and terrestrial world and journey to "see" truth is a commonplace in the dialogues
that deal with *theoria*. In the *Phaedo*, for example, Socrates argues that
philosophy aims at the "separation" of the soul from the "prison" of the
body. This state of detachment can only be fully achieved at death, he
claims, when the philosophic soul "travels" to the divine region of reality
(61d–e, 67b–c, 67e–68a, 69c, 80d, 81a, 114b–c); but the soul can make a
similar "journey" in his present life by practicing philosophy (79c–d). In the
Symposium, too, Socrates emphasizes the philosopher's detachment from
the bodily world: the "ascent" up the "ladder of love," which culminates
in the vision of the "divine" Form of Beauty (211e–212a), is depicted as a
journey out of the corporeal world (210a, 210e, 211b, 211c).

Consider also the central speech in the *Phaedrus*, which contains a vivid
depiction of the soul's contemplation of reality before it is born on earth.
This myth portrays both the divine and the preincarnate human souls as
"traveling" up to the very "edge" of the universe and, after taking a stand
there, looking "outside" it at the region of the Forms (247a–c). In this first,
preincarnate, chapter of the story, the soul is of course fully detached from
the social and the terrestrial world when it "contemplates" the spectacle
of the Forms – indeed, it has not even entered this world at all.[10] As the
story goes, every human soul is later incarnated on earth; but it can regain
its original theoric vision by practicing philosophy and "recollecting those
things which it once saw, when it journeyed with the god, lifting up its
vision to the things which are really real and disregarding (lit. over-looking)
those things which we now say are real" (ἀνάμνησις ἐκείνων, ἃ ποτ᾽ εἶδεν
ἡμῶν ἡ ψυχὴ συμπορευθεῖσα θεῷ καὶ ὑπεριδοῦσα ἃ νῦν εἶναί φαμεν,
καὶ ἀνακύψασα εἰς τὸ ὂν ὄντως, 249c). The philosopher on earth, then,
recollects and reenacts a primordial "journey" that preceded civic life; when
he practices theoretical contemplation after incarnation, he looks "up" at
reality and "disregards" or "overlooks" the human and terrestrial world.
While contemplating the Forms, both before and after incarnation, he
doesn't see the world at all.

The *Republic* discusses the journey and detachment of the philosophic
theoros in elaborate detail. The Analogy of the Cave, as we have seen,
portrays the theoretical philosopher as escaping from a prison-like "home"
(*oikesis*) and traveling to a foreign land; in order to see the Forms, he must

---

[10] Note that the preincarnate soul already possesses nonrational impulses that pull away from the
bidding of reason.

depart from the dark cave where non-philosophers dwell in bondage.[11] At first, he has to be released from his chains by another person, presumably a theoretical philosopher (515c, 532b). But once released, he makes a journey that leads him out of this dark region. This journey, as I have suggested, is conceptually linked to the practice of traditional *theoria*, where the *theoros* travels to a foreign city or country. But, by introducing the notion of escaping from a prison, Plato reconfigures the traditional theoric journey: the philosophic *theoros* departs from a sort of jail, and goes to a metaphysical region where he completely transcends human affairs. He travels to an utterly foreign "place" to engage in a new kind of spectating.

Plato, then, has transformed the traditional journey of *theoria* into a story of bondage and freedom, darkness and light. Socrates even compares the region inside the cave to the land of the dead (516d–e), identifying the soul's journey back into the cave as a "*katabasis*" (516e) – the standard term for a journey to Hades. By depicting the inside of the cave as Hades and the outside as the region of true life and reality, Plato indicates that the philosophic theorist travels to a realm that is maximally distant from and alien to his original abode. In fact, the philosopher who journeys to contemplate the Forms cuts himself off from the social and physical world so fully that he is temporarily blinded to it. While the philosopher engages in contemplation, he has turned away from the darkness of the human and terrestrial world. At times, Plato seems to say that the philosopher *will not* look back at the human world while he is contemplating, since it does not interest him.[12] More often, however, Plato indicates that the philosophic theorist *cannot* do this because he is, at least temporarily, blinded to it.

THE BLINDNESS OF THE PHILOSOPHER

In the Analogy of the Cave, Socrates describes the philosophic theorist as experiencing bouts of near total blindness. Why, we may ask, does a story about "seeing" the truth have so much to say about blindness? In the middle books of the *Republic*, Plato repeatedly indicates that the philosopher's eyes are, while he contemplates the Forms, blind to the human world. The philosopher turns his back on humanity, journeys out of that dark prison,

---

[11] ἐν δεσμοῖς, 514a; τοῦ δεσμοῦ, 514b; τῶν δεσμῶν, 515c. The scholarly literature on the Analogy of the Cave is of course vast, and raises a huge number of questions that are not pertinent to my study. Since my primary focus is the interaction between traditional and Platonic *theoria*, I will confine myself to the scholarship that contributes to this (rather narrow) investigation.

[12] For example, as Socrates asserts early in book VI, "to the person whose mind is occupied with grandeur and the *theoria* of all time and of all reality . . . this human life [does not] seem a thing of great concern" (486a).

and is, during that time, cut off from the world. As Socrates says in book VI:

There is no leisure for the man who directs his mind towards true realities to look downwards (κάτω βλέπειν) on the affairs of humans and, wrangling with them, to be filled with envy and hostility; but, gazing on things that are orderly and unchanging, and seeing that these things neither do wrong nor receive wrong from one another but are all in an orderly state in accordance with reason, he will endeavor to imitate these things and liken himself to them as much as possible. (500b–c)[13]

Here, the philosopher does not scorn or look down from on high on the human world: while gazing upon the Forms, he does not see it at all. Note also that Plato describes the education of the theoretical philosopher as the "turning" of the eye of the soul away from the world of becoming and towards that of being, from darkness to light: this "turning-around" (στρέφειν, 518c; περιαγωγή, 521c) of the soul effectively turns it away from the human world and redirects it to objects in the realm of true being. In the activity of seeking and "seeing" the Forms, the philosophic soul turns its back on "a day that is like night" and looks towards "the true light of day" (521c).

According to Socrates, the theoretical journey leads the philosopher to experience different kinds of blindness. When he first departs from the cave, the philosopher is initially blinded by the dazzling light in the region of the Forms; his eyes are "filled with its radiance," and he cannot see anything at all (515e–516a). Gradually, he grows habituated to this light, and he can eventually see the beings in this region; in the ideal case, he can even gaze upon the source of the light itself (516a–b). After achieving this vision, the theorist returns to the human world and is initially blinded by the darkness inside the cave; although he eventually regains his vision in that dark region, it takes a long time for his eyes to adjust (ὁ χρόνος μὴ πάνυ ὀλίγος εἴη τῆς συνηθείας, 517a).[14] As Socrates observes,

[When the philosopher reenters the cave,] he would have his eyes filled with darkness (σκότους ἂν ἀνάπλεως σχοίη τοὺς ὀφθαλμούς) . . . And if he had to contend with the perpetual prisoners [in the cave] in judging those shadows – he whose vision was dim (ἀμβλυώττει), before his eyes had recovered . . . would he

---

[13] Note that this passage suggests that the philosopher imitates the divine Forms rather than the gods (cf. the *Phaedrus*, *Timaeus*, and the "digression" in the *Theaetetus*, where the soul imitates the gods). On Plato's conception of the "likeness to god," see Annas 1999, ch. 3 and Sedley 1999a. I will discuss this issue in chapter 4.

[14] At 508d, Socrates claims that, when the philosopher views things in the world of becoming, he can only achieve opinions (which are themselves susceptible to change).

not produce mockery? And wouldn't people say that, having made the journey upward, he had come back with his eyes ruined . . . ? And if they were able to lay hands on that man who was trying to release people and lead them upwards, would they not kill him? (516e–517a)

Of course an intelligent person would not unthinkingly mock the blind philosopher; rather, he would realize that "there are two different disturbances of the eyes caused by two different things, depending on whether the eyes have shifted from darkness to light or from light to darkness." And if he should come upon a person who "could not see" (ἀδυνάτουσάν τι καθορᾶν), he would ask himself whether that person "had come from a brighter region and was blinded (ἐσκότωται) by his lack of habituation or whether he had moved from a deeper ignorance into a brighter place and had been blinded when filled with the light in this brighter place" (518a–b).

Plato's theoretical philosopher, in sum, has blind spots: the vision of the theorist is not panoptic, since he sees differently – and different objects – in each realm.[15] When contemplating the Forms, he does not see the world, which now appears dark; and when he pursues practical and political activities back in the cave, he sees the Forms less clearly. Since the eye of the soul "is destroyed and blinded (ἀπολλύμενον καὶ τυφλούμενον) by [nontheoretical] pursuits" (527e), the philosopher will have to keep renewing and increasing his knowledge via philosophical discussion and contemplation. In my view, Plato's extensive discussion of philosophic vision conveys an important point: that the theorist's (temporary) blindness to the world is necessary for metaphysical "seeing." The philosopher must accept the condition of blindness as the precondition for philosophic insight. He goes blind in order that he may see. The activity of metaphysical contemplation does not, then, offer a "gods-eye view," i.e. the simultaneous and panoptic vision of all things, both human and divine.[16] Rather, the philosophic

---

[15] Socrates does claim at 486a that the philosopher seeks "that which is whole and comprises everything, both divine and human" (τοῦ ὅλου καὶ παντὸς ἀεὶ ἐπορέξεσθαι θείου τε καὶ ἀνθρωπίνου). But even if the philosopher could achieve complete knowledge, the activity of contemplation, by itself, is not panoptic, since it focuses only on metaphysical reality. Cf. Nietzsche's attack on the "blind-spot" of philosophers at the opening of *The Genealogy of Morals*; see Nehamas (1985, 107) for an excellent discussion of this issue. Though the Platonic philosophers have a different sort of blind spot, it is significant that their vision is not panoptic.

[16] Note that the god's-eye view differs from "the point of view of the universe," which was first defined by Sidgwick in a utilitarian context, and later seen as originating in Platonic and especially Stoic philosophy (on the Stoics, see Annas 1993, ch. 5, Long 2002, ch. 7.3; on Sidgwick's position and its later variants, see Williams 1995, ch. 13, Griswold 1999a, 3.2, esp. 140–2). Annas (1999, ch. 3) claims that the notion of the "point of view of the universe" first emerges in the middle dialogues of Plato. I believe that Plato first articulated this idea in the eschatological discourse in the *Laws* x; here, Plato

theoros blinds himself to the human realm in order to see a vision that transforms his soul and gives him a radically different perspective on the world when he returns to it.

APORIA AND ATOPIA

If the ideal philosopher in the Analogy suffers blindness in certain phases of the journey, the ordinary human philosopher will no doubt fare even worse. As I have suggested, the human philosopher will spend his entire life shuttling back and forth between the human world and the Forms, and his vision of the Forms will be, at best, only partial. He will not, like the ideal philosopher, make a direct and straightforward journey to enlightenment, but will be compelled to return again and again without achieving perfect knowledge. He may, of course, bring back a partial view of reality after making many journeys, but even then he will have to set out again in search of greater knowledge. The human philosopher, in short, will experience a great deal of *aporia* and achieve a less-than-complete understanding of truth. For the human philosopher, *aporia* is an integral part of the theoretical life: he will do far more wondering and wandering than the ideal theorist in the Analogy.

The idealized *theoros* in the Analogy makes a single and straightforward journey that culminates in a complete vision of truth: unlike the human philosopher, he escapes from *aporia*. Note that the ideal philosopher does experience *aporia* at the beginning of his journey, when he is first released from bondage and "compelled suddenly to stand up and turn his head and to walk and look upwards towards the light" (515c). At this point, the light blinds his eyes and he cannot see clearly in either direction. The philosopher has entered a sort of existential and epistemic no-man's-land, since he can no longer recognize the images at the back of the cave but has not yet journeyed into the light: "and if someone should compel him, by questioning, to say what each of the things at hand really is, don't you think that he would experience *aporia* and believe that the things he saw before were truer than the things that are now being revealed to him?" (515d).[17] His confusion at this point is so great that "if he were compelled to look at the light, he would feel pain in his eyes and, turning around,

encourages the reader to adopt the point of view of the universe (in which he sees himself as part of a perfectly good whole) and to transcend the realm of chance and contingency (Nightingale 1999b).

[17] Plato also discusses philosophic *aporia* in the section in book VI dealing with "provocatives" (524d–525a).

he would flee back (φεύγειν ἀποστρεφόμενον) to those things which he could see" (515d–e).

To become a philosopher – to escape from the bondage of opinion and set out on a quest toward unknown truths – one must be exiled from one's original "home" and experience a profound sense of *aporia* (515e). The fact that the perplexed soul wishes to flee back to its original dwelling is truly poignant: *aporia* is depicted as (among other things) a state of homelessness. The soul has, both cognitively and existentially, left home, and thus suffers deracination and disorientation. Of course the ideal philosopher does not flee back into the cave, but recognizes his ignorance and undertakes a journey that will end in the contemplation of the Forms. But the ordinary human philosopher will never achieve complete knowledge and therefore will always experience *aporia*: though he will discover some truths, there will always be others that he does not know. To be sure, he will not always suffer the radical, confusing state of *aporia* experienced by the person first released from bonds. But, insofar as he knows that there are things that he does not know, he will experience an abiding sense of *aporia*. I take this to be a positive, if not always comfortable, condition (though it perhaps looks negative when compared with a perfected ideal): it is a fertile self-awareness of ignorance that is a fundamental aspect of *theoria*. In the activity of theorizing, *aporia* works together with *eros*, which compels the philosophic soul to seek and find a path towards truth (again and again).

In addition to the experience of *aporia*, the philosopher's departure from home leads to a permanent state of *atopia*. For the person who has detached himself from society and gone on the journey of philosophic *theoria* will never be fully "at home" in the world. *Theoria* uproots the soul, sending it to a metaphysical region where it can never truly dwell and from which it will inevitably have to return. As a *theoros*, the Platonic philosopher must journey to "see" truth (in various degrees of fullness) and bring his vision back to the human world. In the ideal city, of course, the perfected philosophic *theoros* will take up an official position in the civic structure. But he does not gladly accept this burden and, in spite of his position as ruler, he lives as a sort of foreigner in his own city (a point to which I will return). The ordinary human philosopher, by contrast, will return to a non-ideal city, where he may be mocked and abused: his *theoria* and *atopia* put him in a far more precarious position. The philosopher who journeys to the Forms, in sum, becomes a new and different person: the activity of contemplating the Forms transforms him, giving him a new set of capacities, dispositions, and values. The soul that "sees" the Forms (even partially) comes into a specific value system together with the capacity to put it into practice. When he returns to the human world, then, he is *atopos*, not fully at home: having seen truth and divinity, he has become a stranger to his own kind.

PHILOSOPHIC SIGHT-SEEING

Thus far, we have discussed the "journey" of *theoria* that detaches the philosopher from the world. But there are different kinds of journeying and different modes of detachment, and these need not feature (or feature centrally) the activity of spectating. I want to turn now to the notion of "seeing," a defining aspect of traditional *theoria* that plays a key role in Plato's accounts of philosophic *theoria*. To be sure, the journey to "see Being" is a literary analogy, and can be treated as a more or less empty metaphor. One could argue, for example, that Plato simply wants to convey the idea that, when we attain knowledge via dialectic, we directly grasp and understand the truth of a given subject matter. Plato certainly does, at times, describe knowledge as a discursive achievement. Clearly, the Platonic philosopher must practice dialectic in order to attain knowledge and, after achieving knowledge, must "give an account" of the Forms to himself and others. Plato could have left it at that. He could have described and conceptualized the attainment of philosophic knowledge as an entirely discursive activity. But he went further than this – for he conceived of knowledge as involving both "saying" and "seeing." What, I want to ask, does the metaphor of "seeing" capture that is not conveyed by the notion of correct and irrefutable argumentation? What, if anything, does this metaphor add to Plato's conceptualization of philosophic knowledge?

Scholars have debated this issue for centuries. Some interpreters have argued that Plato took seriously the notion of a "vision" of the Forms, and that he identified this as a non-discursive activity which goes above and beyond the practice of dialectic. Cornford, to cite but one famous example, claims:

A defining formula is expressed in words; it can be written in a book and intellectually understood, like the definition of any other idea. By means of it the dialectician can "give an account" of derivative moral truths, and even teach them to men who will never be philosophers. But the intellectual understanding of formulae expressed in words is not the same as the intuitive vision of the reality which the formulae profess to describe.[18]

---

[18] Cornford 1965, 94; see also Festugière 1950, Cherniss 1965 and Bluck, 1965. Cf. Annas (1981, 282–4), who rejects the idea that there are two stages in the philosophic grasp of truth – first, the practice of dialectic and, then, the ineffable "vision" of reality. She argues that rigorous and consistent reasoning must reach a level of "insight that requires a certain kind of vision"; but, in her view, "the verbal and visual descriptions [of knowledge] do not clash" (p. 284).

In recent decades, scholars have become uncomfortable with what they take to be a "mystical" interpretation of Plato – the notion of a nonverbal "vision" of truth smacks of an "unphilosophical" religiosity. According to these interpreters, Plato conceived of the pursuit and attainment of knowledge as a fully discursive enterprise. Thus Kahn, for example, argues:

> It is a mistake to suppose (as some critics have done) that the etymological connections of the terms *idea* and *eidos* with the verb *idein*, "to see," are in any way essential or decisive for Plato's conception of the Forms. The metaphor of vision for intellectual access to the Forms is useful but altogether dispensable. The expressions for "hunting," "grasping," "hitting upon," or simply "thinking" and "recognizing" (*gnōnai*) will do as well. The fundamental conception of the Forms is, from the beginning, linguistic rather than visual in its orientation.[19]

I do not intend to offer a philosophical analysis of Plato's epistemological theories. But I do want to address the question of the significance of Plato's visual metaphors. For, contrary to Kahn and others, I believe that the metaphors which Plato used in his discussions of epistemology are not simply interchangeable. Certainly the visual metaphors are by far the most dominant in Plato's discussions of knowledge. If the metaphor of seeing the Forms is "dispensable," then why would Plato adopt the model of the traditional practice of *theoria* with its emphasis on the act of spectating? Why make so much of the notion of the soul's "vision" of the Forms? This is an indispensable part of Plato's mythic account of *theoria*, and it should not be ignored by scholars attempting to analyze his epistemology (though it cannot be interpreted in strictly analytic terms).

Let us look briefly at Plato's discussion of dialectic in the *Republic*. Note, first of all, that Plato repeatedly identifies dialectic as a "journey" (διαλεκτικὴν . . . τὴν πορείαν, 532b, cf. 532e; πορεύεται, 533c; διαπορεύεται, 534c). In fact, Plato explicitly identifies the journey of dialectic with the itinerary described in the Analogy of the Cave:

> [And dialectic is] the release from bonds, and the turning away from the shadows to the images and to the light of the fire and then the ascent out of the cave into the sunlight and, there, the inability to look at the plants and animals and the light of the sun, though one can see the phantasms of these reflected in water and the

---

[19] Kahn 1996, 354–5. But note that Kahn, throughout his discussion of the theory of Forms (ch. 11), talks about the discovery of the Forms as a "revelation" and claims that "the figure of the philosopher with his gaze fixed upon the Forms" is "the master Analogy of the *Republic*" (p. 361). See also Crombie 1964, 112–13 and Hare 1965, who suggest that Plato failed to observe a contrast between the conception of knowledge "as if it were something analogous to sight" and that of knowledge as propositional. Cross goes so far as to claim that "a Form, so far from being 'a substantial entity', is much more like 'a formula'. It is the logical predicate in a logos, not the logical subject. It is what is said of something, not something about which something else is said" (1965, 27–8).

shadows of real things, not the shadows of images cast by a light which is quite different from the true sun. All this labor in the disciplines we have mentioned [including dialectic] has the power to lead the best part of the soul up to the vision (θέαν) of the best among realities. (532b–c)

Given that dialectic is the process that leads the philosopher to apprehend the Forms and later enables him to "give an account" of them and serve as a teacher to others (532a–b, 534b–c), we may assume that the "journey" of dialectic involves both the movement to the Forms and the return back to the human world. Dialectic is thus closely associated with the journey of *theoria* as a whole. We must remember that *theoria* in the traditional sense encompassed the entire journey from beginning to end: this included traveling abroad, seeing spectacles, and returning home. Can we say, then, that dialectic is coextensive with the journey of the philosophical theorist in its entirety? Does it include all theoretical activity, including that of "seeing" truth?

Unfortunately, Plato offers only a very general discussion of dialectic here and elsewhere, which makes it difficult to answer this question with certainty.[20] In the *Republic*, Plato identifies dialectic as a *technē* and, indeed, a technical method of the highest order. For dialectic enables the philosopher "to define in *logos* the Form of the good, abstracting it from all other things . . . and, as though in battle, going through every kind of test and striving to examine things not in accordance with opinion but in accordance with essential reality – in all these cases making this journey with a *logos* that does not trip or fail" (534b–c). The ability to "give an account" of something is associated with the possession of *technē* from the earliest dialogues of Plato.[21] Indeed, Plato clearly associates dialectic with the technical discipline of mathematics (which, as he says in a number of dialogues, distinguishes the "pure" and "precise" *technai*).[22] To be sure, dialectic

---

[20] Indeed, as Robinson has rightly observed (1941, 74), "[t]he fact is that the word 'dialectic' had a strong tendency in Plato to mean 'the ideal method, *whatever that may be*'. In so far as it was merely an honorific title, Plato applied it at every stage of his life to whatever seemed to him at the moment the most hopeful procedure." See Nehamas (1999b, esp. 113–18), who indicates that dialectic can never be reduced to a formal method, since it cannot be dissociated from the metaphysics of Plato, particularly the theory of Forms (see also Guthrie 1975, 524–5, Kerferd 1981, 65, Griswold 1988). Cf. Irwin (1986, esp. 54), who argues (unpersuasively) that in the *Republic* dialectic is "the familiar Socratic conversation."

[21] See, e.g., *Republic* 531e, 533c, 534b. Roochnik (1996) offers a detailed study of *technē* in preplatonic and (primarily) early Platonic texts. Note that the question whether dialectic is technical is different from the question whether Plato in the early and/or middle dialogues believed that ethical virtue was a *technē* (the scholarly debate on this issue is summarized in Roochnik 1996, 1–10). I will discuss this latter issue in chapter 5.

[22] *Republic* 522c, *Statesman* 258d–260b, *Philebus* 55e–56e; see Roochnik 1996, 36–9, 278–81.

is superior to mathematics and its related disciplines, being the "coping-stone" of all the other philosophical studies (534e), but it is nonetheless a *methodos* (533b, 533c). In short, Plato identifies dialectic as the *technē* which enables the philosopher to journey to the Forms and to give an account of them after periods of contemplation.[23]

In the passage quoted above (532b–c), Plato indicates that dialectic (and the other disciplines studied by the philosophers) "leads" the rational part of the soul to the "vision" of the Forms. Here and elsewhere, he appears to distinguish the "vision" itself from the discursive activity of dialectic.[24] Indeed, Plato repeatedly isolates the act of "seeing" the Forms in his descriptions of the journey of philosophic *theoria* and treats it as a unique kind of activity. Though the notion of "seeing Being" is of course a metaphor (and must be interpreted as such), I believe that the descriptions of the philosophic soul gazing on the Forms capture something essential about the experience and nature of knowledge as Plato conceived it.

First of all – and here I state the obvious – this metaphor emphasizes the nature of the Forms as ontological presences: the Forms are metaphysical beings that are substantial, have independent standing, and possess determinate boundaries which distinguish them from one another. Of course Plato can and does make this point without recourse to visual metaphors, i.e. by identifying the Forms as "beings" or "substances" and defining them as noncorporeal, changeless, everlasting, and separate from particulars. But he opts to emphasize their "visibility" to the mind, partly in order to confer on them a substantiality and presence akin to the "apparent" beings in the physical world. In other words, Plato first borrows the notion of visibility and substantiality from the physical world, and then denies that the things in this lowly realm are fully real. The "visibility" of the Forms to the mind, in short, reveals their substantiality and ontological presence. Metaphors from the concrete, physical world do an excellent job of conveying this ontological point, even though we must always remember to treat these as iconic, abstracting from the world of physical particulars when we attempt to understand the Forms.

But the visual metaphors do much more than this, for they also present us with a particular model of apprehension. In the act of theoretical

---

[23] See *Phaedo* 90b–d, where Socrates discusses arguments conducted with and without "*technē*." Nehamas offers a useful discussion of this passage (and of dialectic in the middle dialogues) in 1999b, 116–17 and *passim*.

[24] These passages do not, by themselves, demonstrate that contemplation of the Forms is a non-discursive mode of thought; this is a mythic "story" rather than an analytic argument. For discussions (and criticisms) of the notion of non-discursive thinking, see A. Lloyd 1969, 1986, Sorabji 1982.

contemplation, the philosopher views a reality or being that he cannot touch, change, or in any way affect. We construct language and arguments; but reality is something that we see. The Forms are ontologically independent of the viewer, and are in no sense created or produced by the human mind. This strikes us, now, as a naïve metaphysical realism that falsely lays claim to objective truth. According to many modern interpreters, Plato ignores the fact that all human apprehension is subjective and perspectival. In addition, as some critics claim, he wrongly believes that the philosopher can apprehend reality from a single, "frontal" perspective, and does not allow for alternative perspectives and interpretations.[25]

Although these criticisms have some force, we must remember that Plato's theoretical philosopher only attains a partial vision of the Forms and therefore does not achieve a perfect "frontal" view. And, since all human souls are imperfect, the contemplation of the Forms will be to some extent distorted by the viewer. Plato fully understands that there are manifold social, psychic, and bodily conditions that distort a person's vision of the Forms. This does not mean, however, that the philosopher constructs or fabricates the Forms, or that the Forms themselves can in any way be altered by human apprehension. In Plato's view, perfectly good and wise souls will see the Forms clearly; if our own view is limited, this is not because of their obscurity but because of the dimness of our vision. As for the criticism that the theoretical journey is entirely private and subjective, we should bear in mind that the philosopher will, both before and after contemplating the Forms, discuss and analyze them with other people (and be engaged in dialectic over the course of a lifetime).

For Plato, the objects of knowledge are entities that must be discovered and contemplated by arduous philosophic effort. But this vision is also, in a sense, granted to us as a gift. As Plato indicates in the Analogy of the Sun, it is the Form of the Good that illuminates all the other Forms and makes them "visible" and knowable.[26] Plato begins this analogy by describing the faculty of vision in the physical world, which is activated by the sun. The sun is a divinity which "dispenses" or bestows light on humans "as from a treasury" (ταμιευομένην, 508b): light is a dispensation or gift given by the sun. The eye, in turn, is said to have been created for humans as a "lavish expenditure" (πολυτελεστάτην) by a divine maker (507c).[27] In

---

[25] For a critique of the notion of the "frontal" view (from a Heideggerian perspective), see Levin 1993a, 202–3 and *passim*.
[26] Indeed the other Forms owe their existence to the Form of the Good.
[27] Miller (1985) offers an interesting discussion of the "generosity" of Goodness.

fact, unlike the other senses, the faculty of vision can only apprehend its objects because of the bestowal and "flowing forth" (ἐπίρρυτον) of light, which "yokes" the subject and object of knowledge together (507e–508a). Indeed, as Socrates says, human *opsis* or vision is by nature "related" to the sun (508a).

Plato now turns from the physical sun to the Form of the Good – that divine hyper-being which illuminates the entire realm of the Forms, "bestowing (παρέχον) truth upon the objects of knowledge and giving (ἀποδιδόν) the power of knowledge to those who know" (508e). As Socrates explains, the Form of the Good "is the cause for all things of all that is right and beautiful, giving birth (τεκοῦσα) to light in the visible realm and to the lord of this light [i.e. the sun], and itself being the lord in the intelligible realm, furnishing from itself (παρασχομένη) truth and intelligence" (517c). The Good bestows the gift of light, both metaphysical and physical. By analogy, the human knower, i.e. the rational part of the soul, is "related to" or fitted for the Forms just as the physical eye is "related to" its objects (508a). Indeed, in this and other dialogues, Plato indicates that the rational part of the human soul is divine in nature and "akin" to the Forms.[28] There are, of course, essential differences between reason and the Forms (unlike the Forms, the rational part of the soul – and, indeed, the soul in its entirety – moves and changes). We must remember that the soul has its own ontology and is encountering, in the Forms, beings that are divine and ontologically different from it. Nevertheless, the rational part of the soul is said to be kindred (συγγενής) to the Forms. Indeed, it is precisely because reason has this kinship with the Forms that it can apprehend and associate with them at all. However, without the illumination of the Form of the Good, this kinship would not result in knowledge. It is the divine gift of light – the metaphysical light of the Good – that confers on the human soul the ability to know and "see" being.

We may object to a philosophical theory based on a "metaphysics of presence" which does not acknowledge human subjectivity (i.e. that the human subject constructs what it perceives, apprehends, or knows). In addition, Plato's divinization of the Forms and his comparison of the activity of contemplation to a religious revelation will strike many modern readers as objectionable. Nonetheless, we must acknowledge that, for Plato, the

---

[28] For some examples of the assertion of the "kinship" of the rational part of the soul to the Forms or the "intelligible" realm, see *Phaedo* 79d, *Republic* 490b, 585c, 611e, *Phaedrus* 246d–e, *Timaeus* 47b–e, 90a, 90c–d, and *Laws* 897c (the word that Plato generally uses to express kinship is *sungenneia* and its cognates, but there are many terms and locutions that articulate this idea).

activity of *theoria* takes as its model a cultural practice that was essentially religious, i.e. *theoria* at religious sanctuaries and festivals. Plato could have focused on the third, more secular, kind of *theoria*, in which the traveler goes abroad to see the world. But, while this kind of *theoria* does inform Plato's account of philosophic theorizing, it is the *theoria* at religious festivals that plays the leading role in his discussions of philosophical contemplation. The "sacralized visuality" that characterized *theoria* at religious sanctuaries offered the most direct model for the philosophic vision of "divine" realities.

HEAT AND LIGHT

Plato's account in the Analogy of the Sun is itself quite "lavish" – too lavish for many interpreters. Glaucon, in fact, exclaims that Socrates' discourse here is "divinely hyperbolic" (509c).[29] And the discourse gets even more lavish when Socrates moves to the Analogy of the Cave. For, while the Analogy of the Sun is iconic and representational, it does not offer an account of philosophic seeing from the point of view of the human theorizer. It is by adding a living, individual person to his account – by entering into the discourse of narrative – that Plato can communicate the experience of theoretical vision from a human and existential point of view. Indeed it is only by entering into the narrative mode and introducing a living protagonist that he could have offered this kind of account. In the Analogy of the Cave, Plato sets forth a narrative in which a human soul journeys to enlightenment – a sort of "story of the soul." This includes an account of the philosopher's existential experience of *theoria* and the transformation that this brings about in the soul. In the language of myth and narrative, Plato was able to convey the soul's experience of the "vision" of reality. This experience, as we will see, is emotional and affective as well as intellectual: *theoria* is not simply a cognitive or epistemic activity but a discipline that involves and affects the philosopher's entire being.

Let us look first at the *pathos* of the philosopher as he pursues and contemplates the Forms. As we have seen, in the Analogy of the Cave, Plato depicts *theoria* as a journey to a distant and completely foreign region. In this "story of the soul," Plato emphasizes the discomfort and difficulty that the philosophic *theoros* experiences on the journey to the Forms: he feels

---

[29] In my view, Plato deliberately chose to use different styles and genres of discourse to convey a metaphysical theory that was too complex to set forth in one discursive mode. See Nightingale (1995) for a discussion of Plato's use of multiple genres of discourse in the dialogues.

pain (ἀλγοῖ) when he first sees the light of the Forms from the depths of the cave (515c); even from this distance, its powerful radiance hurts his eyes (ἀλγεῖν . . . τὰ ὄμματα, 515e). In addition, he finds the rough and steep ascent out of the cave "painful and vexing" (ὀδυνᾶσθαι . . . ἀγανακτεῖν, 515d–e). Indeed, the philosopher experiences profound *aporia* as he makes his way towards the light (515d–e), and an abiding sense of *atopia* when he returns to the world.

We have seen that Plato calls dialectic a "journey" and compares dialectical activity to a "battle" which subjects the philosopher to endless tests, challenging him to confront every argument without slipping or falling in his reasoning (534c). This dialectical "journey," then, is hard and difficult work: it is an effortful, methodical, technical activity. But contemplation is described as a distinct activity which differs from dialectic in fundamental ways. Thus Plato says in book VII that dialectic "leads to a place where, for the person who arrives (ἀφικνομένῳ), there is (as it were) a rest from the road and an end to the journeying" (ὁδοῦ ἀνάπαυλα ἂν εἴη καὶ τέλος τῆς πορείας, 532e).[30] As this metaphor indicates, the philosopher who achieves a vision of the Forms is at rest or repose (ἀνάπαυλα) rather than doing battle: he is gazing upon – rather than battling for – the truth. To be sure, the philosopher will not be able to remain in this state of repose, but he will at least experience a temporary "rest from the road" when he has achieved the vision of some aspect of truth. The activity of seeing Truth, then, differs from that of hunting and pursuing it. To "see" Being involves a state of receptivity on the part of the soul: the soul, in short, is gazing and receiving rather than hunting or grasping.[31] Likewise, though the philosophic *theoros* makes a journey that is painful and toilsome, he experiences intense pleasure and happiness when he contemplates the Forms (and even imagines that he is in the Islands of the Blessed, 519c). Here again, the journey is distinguished from the activity of contemplation. Contemplating the Forms is depicted as an intellectual activity that is not technical or methodical or effortful.

Let me emphasize that theoretical contemplation is not merely intellectual: this activity has important erotic and affective aspects. As Socrates reminds us in book IX, all three parts of the soul have their own desires and pleasures (580d): the rational part has its own *eros* (the desire for truth

---

[30] Although this phrase is put in the mouth of Glaucon, Socrates' response suggests that he considers this a valid metaphor for the activity of philosophic "seeing."

[31] As we have seen, the Form of the Good gives light as a sort of divine gift that makes intellectual vision possible. The soul that pursues the Forms via the *technē* of dialectic will not achieve its goal unless it *receives* the gift of light.

and goodness) as well as its own particular *hedonē*.[32] Thus both *eros* and reason – both heat and light – are at work in the activity of contemplation (as well as in the journey towards it). Plato makes this point quite explicitly in his identification of the philosophers as "lovers of the spectacle of truth" (475e) and "lovers of truth and of being" (τοῦ ὄντος τε καὶ ἀληθείας ἐραστάς, 501d).[33] Philosophers, then, are both lovers and spectators of truth – in these passages, love is directly linked to spectating. How, then, does *eros* function in the activity of contemplation *per se*? What is the relation between *eros* and gazing?[34]

Plato does not give a detailed or technical answer to this question in the *Republic*. But he does claim that the journey of *theoria* is both fueled and sustained by *eros*.[35] Consider the extraordinary passage in *Republic* VI:

> It is the nature of the true lover of learning to battle for being (πρὸς τὸ ὄν . . . ἁμιλ-λᾶσθαι), and not to loiter around the many particulars that are the objects of opinion; he will keep journeying (ἴοι) and will not be blunted or desist from *eros* until he lays hold of the nature of each thing in itself with that part of the soul for which it is fitting to grasp this [i.e. the rational part] . . . and with that part he draws near to and has intercourse with the really real (πλησιάσας καὶ μιγεὶς τῷ ὄντι ὄντως) and, giving birth to intelligence and truth, he achieves knowledge and lives truly and is nourished, and is thereby released from his birthpangs (ὠδῖνος). (490a–b)

In the first part of this passage, the rational part of the soul battles for truth – the verb ἁμιλλᾶσθαι signifies a contest or military struggle – and does not cease from this struggle until it "grasps" the Forms. But, at this point, there is an abrupt change of metaphors. For Socrates now portrays the apprehension of truth as a sexual activity: the soul "draws near to and has intercourse with (makes love to) reality"! Here, the soul plays the role of the receptive, female partner in intercourse – it suffers labor pains and gives birth to intelligence and truth. This image of psychic birthgiving

---

[32] This claim that the rational part of the soul has its own erotic desires creates the "homunculus" problem (as does Plato's tendency to describe the journey of the rational part of the soul as a journey of a whole person). While Plato's description of the rational part of the soul as a sort of person creates problems for his psychology and epistemology, it powerfully conveys the idea that theoretical philosophy is an entire way of life rather than a merely intellectual activity. By personifying the rational part of the soul and placing it in a heroic narrative, Plato creates a compelling and memorable account of the philosophic life.

[33] Note that Plato uses *philia* words interchangably with *eros* words in this passage: φιλοῦντα, 474c; ἐρωτικῷ, 474d; ἐραστοῦ, 474e; ἐρωτικῶν, 475a; φιλοίνους, φιλοτίμους, 475a; φιλοθεάμονες 475d, e). Note also ἐρῶσιν, 485a, c (and cf. 499c).

[34] For an excellent discussion of the erotic gaze in Roman texts (in the early Empire), see Bartch forthcoming.

[35] For an interesting study of this issue, see Rosen 1988, ch. 6.

recalls the *Symposium*, but here the soul seems to have been (somehow) impregnated by the Forms. In this act of sexual union, the Forms play the role of the father, and the soul that of the mother. As the female partner, the soul opens to and receives the Forms and subsequently produces offspring. Thus the journey of *theoria* is portrayed as having three phases: in the first, the soul struggles and strives after the Forms (via dialectic); in the second, it apprehends and receives them; and in the third, it produces offspring in the world as a result of the experience of apprehension.

Plato mixes a number of potent metaphors in this passage, and it would be foolish to press them too hard. How, one may ask, could the apprehension of the Forms be an act both of sexual coupling and of intellectual gazing (which involves at least some distance between subject and object)? One could simply say that Plato uses disparate metaphors to suggest that *theoria* involves both the heat of *eros* and the light of truth. But the metaphors do have some elements in common. For both metaphors portray the apprehension of truth as a receptive activity that brings an end to pain and striving. Of course, in both of these metaphorical scenarios, Plato is describing perfect (and therefore idealized) instances of theoretical contemplation: in each case, the soul goes all the way (so to speak). We must remember that, unlike the perfected wise man, the human philosopher never attains full erotic or intellectual satisfaction, since he only achieves partial truth even after a lifetime of theoretical journeying. This means that he abides in a condition of *eros* even after achieving a view of the Forms. Indeed, even as he contemplates some aspect of reality, the philosopher experiences a taste of things to come, a longing for things not yet seen.

But *eros* is not simply a matter of unfulfilled desire – it is not just a feature of the *journey* towards truth. In my view, the activity of contemplative gazing is itself erotic, for the philosophic soul will look with love at the Forms that he does see, as a lover gazes upon the face of a beloved. For Plato, then, the philosophic gaze is an erotic gaze. The Forms, when they come into view, stoke the heat of *eros* rather than cooling its fires.[36]

In the *Republic* and other texts from the middle period, the "vision" of the Forms transforms the soul both ethically and epistemically. The soul is, in this process, moved, affected, and radically reconfigured. When the theoretical philosopher "returns," then, he will be a different person with a completely new perspective on the world. Although Plato does not spell out the precise ways in which contemplation translates into ethical thought

---

[36] I take it that the *eros* that drives the rational part of the soul does not belong to or derive from the appetitive part (as Nussbaum 1986, ch. 5 suggests; cf. Griswold [1986]/1996).

or action, he makes it clear that the contemplation of the Forms will lead to virtuous *praxis* when the philosopher "returns" to the world. Contemplation and action are thus conceived as two distinct activities (in constant alternation) in the theoretical life: in contemplative activity, the philosopher is completely detached from, and blind to, the world; in practical activity, he acts within the world, using his knowledge of the Forms. Just as the traditional journey of *theoria* includes the departure, the spectating, and the return, philosophic *theoria* comprises both the journey to contemplation and the return to action. It is for this reason that the education of the philosophers in the ideal city aims at both contemplation and virtuous *praxis*: after they spend fifteen years studying arithmetic, geometry, stereometry, astronomy, harmonics, and dialectic, the philosopher-kings are subsequently trained for fifteen years in practical and political activities based on "experience" (*empeiria*, 539d–540a). Practical and experiential wisdom, then, forms a crucial part of the theoretical life taken as a whole.

But how do these two activities relate to one another – how, in short, does theoretical contemplation affect one in the practical realm? As we have seen, the philosopher is initially blinded when he reenters the cave, and it takes a long time for him to get accustomed to the darkness of that region (517a). Why is it that a person who has blinded himself to the human world will understand it better when he returns (at least after he acclimatizes; 520c)? How does the vision of Being help one to understand and respond to the world of becoming? Plato does not offer a systematic or technical response to these questions, though he is emphatic about the link between contemplation and virtuous action.

In order to tease out Plato's position on the relation between contemplation and action, we must piece together images and arguments from different parts of the text. As I have argued, Plato both appropriated and transformed the cultural practice of *theoria* in his effort to define theoretical philosophy. Like the traditional *theoros*, the philosophic theorist must "return" home and share what he has learned. In traditional *theoria*, as we have seen, the *theoros* might well have been changed – and, in the eyes of his fellow citizens, corrupted – by his experience of foreign parts. In philosophic *theoria*, this change is quite extreme: the theoretical philosopher becomes a sort of stranger to his own kind. According to Plato, *theoria* transforms the philosopher in such a way that he becomes wise, virtuous, and fully free. In the case of traditional *theoria*, the *theoros* experienced freedom from ordinary domestic and civic affairs during the period of the journey; but this condition was temporary, and ceased upon his return. The philosophic *theoros*, by contrast, achieves a more radical form of freedom, for the practice of *theoria* makes the philosopher (among other things) free at soul.[37] In addition, he continues to experience this (internal) freedom even after he comes "home" to the practical and political world.

Contemplating truth, then, makes a man free as well as wise: the theoric journey, with its necessary condition of detachment and (temporary) blindness, frees the soul from the influence of social and civic ideology.[38] And the "vision" and love of truth ensures that this freedom will be a permanent psychic condition. As I will suggest, freedom plays a fundamental role in good and virtuous action. But what sort of freedom does the theoretical philosopher achieve and how does this play out in the context of civic and practical affairs? Plato examined the philosopher's freedom from many different angles, using both rhetoric and argument in the explication of this important concept. In examining the freedom of the philosopher in the context of social and political affairs, we must distinguish it from self-control, i.e. the rule of reason over the irrational parts of the soul (which plays a key role in the psychology of the *Republic*).[39] Self-control is a precondition for engaging in philosophical activity, but it differs from the radical freedom and detachment achieved by philosophical *theoria*.

THE RHETORIC OF PHILOSOPHIC "FREEDOM"

I want to look, now, at one of the key strategies that Plato uses to portray the freedom of the philosopher: his use of the rhetoric of *banausia*. As we will see, this kind of rhetoric defines freedom in opposition to servile and productive labor. It was traditionally used by aristocrats to assert their superiority over people who worked for a living, but Plato deploys it for very different purposes. Take, for example, the passage at *Symposium* 203a:

The god does not mix with the human, but it is through this being [i.e. the intermediary called a *daimon*] that all intercourse and conversation takes place between the gods and men, whether they are awake or sleeping. And the person

---

[37] For an excellent discussion of Plato's notion of freedom (and slavery), see Vlastos [1941]/1981.

[38] Note the reference to the creators and purveyors of ideology inside the cave at 514b–515a: "[Picture a scene in which] a low wall has been built, just like those who put on puppet shows have, which is placed in front of the men, above which they put on their shows . . . See also on the other side of this wall men (ἀνθρώπους) carrying all kinds of implements rising above the wall: human images and various animals, crafted in wood and stone and all sorts of materials. Some of the men doing the carrying will be talking, and others will be silent."

[39] Socrates introduces this idea in the discussion of *sophrosunē* in the city and soul in book IV, and uses it to distinguish the philosopher from the tyrant in book IX.

who is wise in this regard is a daemonic man (δαιμόνιος ἀνήρ), but the person who is wise in any other regard, whether in the realm of arts and sciences or manual labor, is a banausic man (βάναυσος).[40]

The dichotomy drawn here between the "daemonic man" (i.e. the philosopher) and the "banausic" individual recurs at *Theaetetus* 176c–d, where Socrates says:

The god is in no way unjust, but is as just as it is possible to be, and there is nothing more similar to god than the man who becomes as just as possible. It is concerning this activity that a man is revealed as truly clever or else worthless and cowardly. For the knowledge of this is wisdom and virtue in the true sense, and the ignorance of it is manifest folly and viciousness. All other things that appear to be cleverness and wisdom – whether their sphere is politics or the other arts – are vulgar or banausic (βάναυσοι).

By interacting with the divine and assimilating himself to god, the philosopher acquires the only kind of wisdom that is not vulgar or "banausic." What Plato suggests in these passages, then, is that *all* nonphilosophic activities are "banausic." In other words, all the varieties of human wisdom and expertise – together with their instantiations in one or another occupation – are now recategorized as either "philosophic" or "banausic." But what precisely does Plato mean by *banausia*?

A brief digression is in order. Here, I will examine the notion of *banausia* in some detail, since all the philosophers that I discuss in this book made use of this rhetoric in their attempts to define and defend *theoria*. As we will see, this discourse played a prominent role in aristocratic self-fashioning in the late fifth and fourth centuries BCE. In using this discourse, the fourth-century philosophers tapped into – and, in some cases, subverted – a rhetoric and an ideology that had a powerful currency in their culture. What is the valence of this rhetoric of *banausia*? Although the word "illiberal" (*aneleutherios*) clearly designated a person as "unfree," the term "banausic" (*banausos*) is harder to comprehend. Yet fourth-century writers regularly link these two words together, and sometimes use them as virtual synonyms. Unfortunately, the word *banausos* is generally rendered as "mechanic" or "base mechanic" by English translators (including Liddell and Scott). But the word "mechanic" (at least in modern parlance) conjures up something quite different from the banausic worker, and actually obscures the true nature of *banausia*.

---

[40] As Dover observes in his commentary on the *Symposium*, "[i]n *Rep.* 495d–e Plato probably (though the interpretation is not certain) extends it [i.e. the word *banausos*] to the arts of the sophist and rhetorician, and that would accord with the sentiment given here to Diotima" (1980, 141).

In the most general terms, *banausoi* is the label for people who earn their living by plying a "craft" that involves the use of the hands. *Banausos*, however, is not merely a descriptive term, since it invariably marks a person as mercantile and servile. Thus Aristotle places the "banausic" arts in the category of "wealthgetting that involves exchange" and identifies them as a form of "labor for hire" (μισθαρνία).[41] In texts from the classical period, the word *banausia* and its cognates is virtually monopolized by Xenophon, Plato, and Aristotle; this language is almost never used in oratory or comedy (whose authors tend to reflect democratic sentiments).[42] As Whitehead has rightly observed, "the 'definition' of a *banausos* . . . can only be articulated by someone *outside banausia* . . ."[43] In short, the label carries with it the perspective and prejudices of the leisured elite.

How, then, and in what contexts is this concept articulated? First of all, aristocratic writers use the term to define a group of people as "by nature" inferior and unfit for participation in politics. Aristotle, for example, says that a city should not award citizenship and political privilege to any person who performs a banausic occupation; and, correlatively, citizens and rulers should not engage in *banausia*:

> In ancient times the banausic class in some cities consisted of slaves or aliens, for which reason the majority of artisans are still [slaves and aliens] today. But the best ordered city will not make the *banausos* a citizen. And if the *banausos* is a citizen, then what we said to be the virtue of a citizen cannot be said to belong to every citizen, nor even be defined as the virtue of a free man, but will only belong to those individuals who are released from occupations which provide the necessities of life. (*Politics* III.5, 1278a6–11)

Aristotle goes on to say that the mere fact that a person learns or uses a craft does not make him banausic; rather, the defining criterion is the goal or end

---

[41] *Politics* I.11, 1258b20–6. I follow the chapter breakdown and numeration in Ross's *OCT* edition of the *Politics*.

[42] Exceptions are: Sophocles, *Ajax* 1121; Herodotus 11.165; and Hippocrates, *De morbo sacro* 18 (Littré) and *De decente habitu* 2, 5 (if indeed this is a fourth-century text). For passages in Xenophon, Plato, and Aristotle dealing with *banausia*, see Xenophon, *Oec.* IV.2–3; VI.5–8; *Symp.* III.4.; *Cyrop.* V.3.47; Plato, *Alc.* 1 131b; *Amat.* 137b; *Symp.* 203a; *Rep.* 522b; 590c; *Tht.* 176c–d; *Laws* 644a; 741e; 743d; *Epin.* 976d; Aristotle, *EE* 1215a; *NE* 1107b; 1122a; 1123a; *MM* 1205a; *Pol.* 1258b; 1260a–b; 1264b; 1277a–b; 1278a; 1289b; 1291a; 1296b; 1317a–b; 1319a; 1321a; 1326a; 1328b–1329a; 1331a; 1337b; 1338b; 1339b; 1340b–1342a; *Rhet.* 1367a.; *Metaph.* 996a; *Oec.* 1343b. Rössler (1981, 203–43) offers a detailed survey of the notion of *banausia* in the fifth and fourth centuries BCE.

[43] Whitehead 1977, 119. See also E. Wood, who suggests that we need to separate the "*disdain*" for dependent labour," which was probably a "universal cultural norm in Athens," from the "outright *contempt* for labour and labourers" exhibited by aristocratic writers such as Xenophon, Plato, and Aristotle (Wood 1989, 139, my italics). On Greek attitudes towards labor and laborers, see Glotz [1926]/1987, 160–7; Vernant [1965]/1983, chs. 10–11; Mossé [1966]/1969, ch. 2; Burford 1972, 25–6, 184–218 and 1993, ch. 5; Rössler 1981; Ste. Croix 1981, 179–204; Wood 1989, 137–45.

that he aims at. As he claims, "it makes a great deal of difference what end one has in view in an activity or course of study; if one does these things for one's own sake or for the sake of one's friends or for the sake of virtue it is not illiberal, but a person who does the same thing for the sake of other people often appears to be acting in a menial and slavish manner."[44] The *banausos*, then, is a servile or wage-earning individual, and thus unsuited for the activity of governing.[45]

Xenophon, too, claims that *banausoi* should not participate in politics, since they lack the leisure required for participating in civic affairs in a responsible and beneficial manner:

Men speak against those arts called "banausic" and rightly look down upon them . . . For these so-called banausic arts offer no leisure (ἀσχολίας) for taking care of one's friends and one's city, so that such people are thought to be bad at dealing with friends and poor defenders of their cities; indeed, in those cities which are reputed warlike, the citizens never engage in banausic occupations. (*Oec.* IV.2–3)

Aristotle agrees with Xenophon that only men of leisure can manage the affairs of the city properly, but he notes that in certain cities – and especially radical democracies such as Athens which pay the poor to participate in government – *banausoi* may well have free time on their hands.[46] According to Aristotle, however, the mere possession of free time does not make *banausoi* "leisured." For banausic activities inevitably make the *mind* of the worker "unleisured and petty" (ἄσχολον γὰρ ποιοῦσι τὴν διάνοιαν καὶ ταπεινήν, *Pol.* VIII.2, 1337b14–15). Thus a *banausos* who possesses free time can never have true leisure, since his banausic occupation destroys his capacity for experiencing leisure.[47] Whether literally or metaphorically, then, the *banausos* is unleisured and therefore unfit for rule.

Clearly, then, *banausia* is a loaded and highly derogatory term. Note in particular Aristotle's claim that many *banausoi* were *nouveaux riches*, i.e. wealthy members of the non-aristocratic class (*Politics* III.5, 1278a21–5).[48] He

---

[44] *Politics* VIII.2, 1337b19–21; cf. VIII.6, 1341b8–15.
[45] *Politics* III.5, 1278a21–2. For detailed analyses of Aristotle's conception of *banausia/banausos* in the *Politics*, see Lévy 1979 and Rössler 1981, 226–31.
[46] See, e.g., *Pol.* VI.4, 1319a26–30: "there is no element of virtue in those occupations which the multitude of *banausoi* and market-people and hired laborers pursue, but the fact that they loiter around the agora and the city means that almost everyone in this class finds it easy to attend the assembly."
[47] For discussions of Aristotle's notion of leisure, see Solmsen 1968b and Demont 1993a.
[48] This claim forms part of the argument that, in an oligarchy, while it is impossible for the *thetes* to be citizens since they are too poor to meet the property qualifications, many of the *banausoi* will make the grade because they are rich (1278a21–5). Note that Aristotle exaggerates the number of wealthy *banausoi*: as Lévy (1979, 39–40) and Ste. Croix (1981, 271) observe, the evidence strongly indicates that the majority of *banausoi* were poor (or at least not rich).

and other aristocrats who inveighed against the *banausoi*, we can infer, were especially concerned to distinguish themselves from the upwardly mobile (rather than the poor): the fact that the *nouveaux riches* could acquire privileges and offices that were originally the prerogative of the aristocracy would suggest that these people in particular needed to be put in their place. A passage in the *Nicomachean Ethics* offers clear evidence of this point. In book IV, Aristotle identifies *banausia* – generally translated as "vulgarity" – as the opposite of *mikroprepeia* or "paltriness." Here, *banausia* is the vicious extreme of the virtuous mean identified as "magnificence" (*megaloprepeia*):

The person who exceeds this mean [of "magnificence"], the *banausos*, exceeds by virtue of spending beyond what is appropriate. In situations calling for small expenditures he spends a great deal and he makes himself conspicuous in a tasteless way, for example by feasting the members of his club in a manner fitting for a wedding or, when financing a comic chorus, by bringing them on in purple garments in its first entrance . . . And he will do all these things not out of goodness or nobility but in order to display his wealth, thinking that he is admired on account of these things, spending a little where he should spend alot and spending alot where he should spend a little. (*NE* IV, 1123a18–27; see also II, 1107b16–20; IV, 1122a28–33)

This passage vividly reveals the aristocratic anxiety about the wealth and power of the successful *banausos*.[49]

In this period, then, we find a rhetoric and ideology which set the "truly free" individual in opposition to men who were free in a merely legal and civic sense. The free or "liberal" man, in short, is leisured, educated, independent, and "truly" fit for rule, whereas the "banausic" or "illiberal" individual is slavish, servile, wage-earning, uneducated, and unfit for rule. As Raaflaub has shown, the rhetoric of "liberal" and "illiberal" activities contributed to a larger ideology constructed by aristocrats hostile to democracy; in the later fifth and fourth centuries, the critics of democracy "began to politicize the notion of *eleutherios* and to develop the concept of the *truly* free citizen in order to bolster their aspirations to exclusive government and power in the polis."[50] I have discussed this ideological and political program because it provides the context for the fourth-century discussions of the "free" activity of *theoria*. This rhetoric of "freedom" and "*banausia*" plays an important role in all the fourth-century discussions of *theoria*. As we will see, the philosophers put this rhetoric to different uses: Plato subverted this kind of discourse by turning it against the aristocrats themselves, whereas

---

49 Von Reden 1995a, 85.   50 Raaflaub 1983, 534.

Philip and Aristotle affirmed aristocratic ideology and used its rhetoric in a more straightforward fashion.[51]

THE PHILOSOPHER VS. THE *BANAUSOS*

The passages we examined from the *Symposium* and *Theaetetus* suggested that *everyone* is "banausic" except the true practitioner of philosophy. These passages, though tantalizing, are quite cursory. The *Republic* fleshes out these claims, especially in the section that describes the theoretical philosopher (books v–vii). In these books, Plato defines the philosopher, in part, by way of opposition: he juxtaposes this new kind of sage to a disparate group of individuals identified as nonphilosophers. In particular, Plato targets intellectuals and sophists who offered serious competition to his own programme – men reputed to be wise and powerful. As we will see, Plato portrays these kinds of men as banausic "laborers for hire" in contrast to the philosophic theorist: the servility of the nonphilosophers stands in diametrical opposition to the freedom of the theoretical philosopher. According to Plato, only the philosopher is truly free. To achieve this kind of freedom, the philosopher must transcend false ideologies as well as the systems of exchange – social, political, and economic – that support and reflect these ideologies. By achieving this radical kind of freedom, the philosopher can act impartially in his practical and political activities in the human realm.

Plato conveys this conception of freedom, in part, by recourse to the rhetoric of *banausia*. Consider, for example, Socrates' description of the false pretenders to philosophy in book vi:

. . . just as men run away from prison to take sanctuary in temples, so these [pretenders] joyously leap from *technai* to philosophy, those that are the most clever in their little crafts. For in comparison with the other arts the prestige of philosophy even in her present state retains a superior dignity; and this is the ambition and the goal of that multitude of pretenders unfit by nature, whose souls are cramped and crushed by their banausic occupations (διὰ τὰς βαναυσίας) just as bodies are deformed by arts and crafts. (495d–e)

Socrates concludes this overheated passage with an *eikōn*, comparing the philosophic pretender to "a small, baldheaded tinsmith who has recently been freed from prison bonds and taken a bath"; this man, having made some money, "puts on a new cloak and, dressed like a bridegroom, comes to

---

[51] Note that Plato uses the rhetoric of *banausia* in the *Laws* (644a; 741e; 743d) in a straightforward fashion which affirms aristocratic ideology. But the *Laws* does not deal with *theoria* or the Forms; indeed, this text espouses views that are more traditional and conservative than those set forth in the middle dialogues.

124   *Spectacles of Truth in Classical Greek Philosophy*

marry the daughter of his master, who is poor and abandoned" (496e–496a). This is powerful rhetoric. In the first part of the passage, the pretender to philosophy is described as a prisoner as well as a banausic craftsman; and, in the second part, he is compared to a slave who has bought his freedom and is pursuing a marriage above his station. Plato could not have gone further in his emphasis on the illiberal nature of the nonphilosophers: they are prisoners and slaves and servile banausic workers.[52]

Let us look more closely at the comparison of nonphilosophers to tin-smiths and other "banausic" craftsmen. Who exactly are these pretenders to wisdom, and why does Plato portray them as *banausoi*? Although Adam rightly rejects the notion that the passage is directed against specific individuals who have turned to philosophy from a craft-profession, he rather hastily concludes that "Plato is describing a familiar phenomenon of his own times, when clever and ambitious young men were in the habit of forsaking their handicrafts and devoting themselves to 'culture'."[53] This literal reading, I believe, ignores the rhetorical nature of the passage. In less than a single Stephanus page (495c–496a), Plato mixes an extraordinary number of potent metaphors: the escaped criminal taking refuge in a temple, the base suitors courting an abandoned maiden, the bald-headed tinsmith freed from slavery who gets dressed up to marry his impoverished master's daughter, and the bastard children that issue from such a marriage. In describing the suitors of philosophy who attempt to escape their banausic professions, moreover, Plato moves into the diminutive mode: they are "little men" (ἀνθρωπίσκοι) practicing some "little art" (τεχνίον; 495d). This passage is a metaphorical depiction of counterfeit wise men: Plato is not describing an actual group of artisans who have overstepped their station but rather a much larger group of individuals who resemble wage-earning craftsmen by virtue of their servile activities.

At the end of this passage, Socrates says that the false consorts of philosophy produce "*sophismata*" rather than true knowledge (496a). This would indicate that Plato is attacking sophists and rhetoricians rather than ordinary artisans. And this fits well with the peculiar argument that precedes the passage about the *banausoi*. This begins at 493a, where Socrates describes the sophists as "teaching nothing other than the opinions of the many – the

---

[52] Note that this passage dealing with the pretenders to philosophy in book v, which compares these men to prisoners in bonds (δεσμῶν, 495e; cf. τῶν εἱργμῶν, 495d), proleptically anticipates the Analogy of the Cave, where all nonphilosophical people are said to be imprisoned in a dark cavern "in bonds" (ἐν δεσμοῖς, 514a; τοῦ δεσμοῦ, 514b; τῶν δεσμῶν 515c). Although the pretenders run away from prison (495d), and thus appear to escape, it is clear that this "escape" is merely illusory.

[53] Adam 1902, 28 (at 495d).

things which they opine in public gatherings." On the basis of this claim, Socrates proceeds to argue that poets and politicians are, in essence, no different from "wage-earning" sophists (μισθαρνούντων, 493a). As Socrates says:

How, then, does the man who considers it wisdom to have learned the passions and pleasures of the variegated multitude when it is assembled – whether in the case of painting or poetry or, for that matter, politics (εἴτε δὴ ἐν πολιτικῇ) – differ from the sophist? For if a person associates with these people, exhibiting either his poetry or some other piece of craftsmanship or else his political service to the city, and granting the multitude mastery over him (κυρίους αὐτοῦ ποιῶν τοὺς πολλούς) beyond what is necessary, the proverbial necessity of Diomedes will make him do the things which these people praise. (493c–d)

The servility of the poets and the politicians assimilates them to the banausic, "wage-earning" sophists. For they offer the products of their wisdom – whether poems or political speeches – in exchange for some kind of recompense. Since they give the people what they want in exchange for power, honor, and money, they are as servile and illiberal as any wage-earner. Like the sophists, they are pretenders to wisdom whose activities are fundamentally banausic.

As we have seen, in classical Greece the aristocratic rhetoric of *banausia* served to mark out manual and productive laborers as servile wage-earners who were not fit to participate in politics. But Plato is not simply parroting aristocratic ideology. On the contrary, he turns the rhetoric of *banausia* against the aristocrats themselves: *all* pursuits and arts are "banausic" and "illiberal" except that of philosophy.[54] Upper-class citizens pursuing honor and political office are no less banausic than the "servile" wage-earners. In the *Republic*, Socrates even suggests that *banausia* is a servile condition of the soul rather than a matter of a person's education or occupation:

Why is it, do you think, that *banausia* and working with one's hands is a matter of reproach? Shall we not say that it is because that part which is by nature the best in a man is weak, with the result that it is unable to rule the beasts within him, but serves them, and can learn nothing but the means of flattering them? (590c)[55]

---

[54] Here, I am dealing with the *rhetoric* of *banausia* rather than with Plato's refusal to allow banausic and other hired laborers any political role in the cities he constructs in the *Republic* and *Laws* (in the *Laws*, in fact, they are also barred from citizenship). While Plato's political constructs are certainly elitist, the rhetoric of *banausia* that he uses to define the theoretical philosopher is directed against the aristocrats who are working inside contemporary political systems. For an interesting analysis of Plato's approach to *banausia* and banausic laborers, see Wood and Wood (1978, 143–64, esp. 158–60); their reading, which places Plato squarely within aristocratic ideology, does not account for his *assimilation* of aristocrats to banausic laborers in his definitions of "philosophy."

[55] As Rössler rightly observes (1981, 217–18), Plato's use of the discourse of *banausia* differs from that of other writers: "So sind die Bezeichnungen βάναυσος oder βαναυσία bei Platon nie-wie

Here, Plato redefines *banausia* as a condition of the soul rather than a class category. For the "servile" or banausic soul is found in both upper and lower class individuals. (Indeed, far from attacking banausic labor *in toto*, Plato offers a quite positive assessment of a number of *technai* in many of his dialogues, including such lowly arts as weaving, carpentry, and metallurgy.[56])

In contrast to the "banausic" poets and politicians, Plato's philosopher avoids traditional social and political modes of exchange. As Socrates says in book VII:

> There is some tiny (πάνσμικρον) group remaining which consists of those who consort with philosophy worthily, whether it be a noble and well-born character constrained by exile who, in the absence of people who would corrupt him, remains true to [philosophy] in accordance with its nature, or when a great soul who is born in a small town disregards and disdains the affairs of the city . . . And the bridle of our companion Theages may provide a restraint. For all the other conditions for falling away from philosophy were at hand in the case of Theages, but his sickly constitution restrained him by keeping him out of politics. (496a–c)

Plato distinguishes the true philosophers precisely by the fact that they do not participate in civic or political affairs – by their refusal to negotiate with the crowd. This does not mean that the philosopher is useless or impractical; Socrates in fact insists that philosophers would be eminently useful if people understood how to put them to use (489b). Rather, the philosopher seeks for truth and wisdom rather than the rewards of the city and its people.

Only the philosopher is truly free, since his discipline is radically opposed to servile and mercantile activities: this individual will never exchange his wisdom for material or symbolic capital. It is for this reason, in fact, that Plato insists that the philosophic rulers in the ideal city in the *Republic* will not touch gold and silver or own any private property, thus avoiding all traditional systems of exchange (economic, social, and political). As we have seen, Socrates compares the rulers to "hired mercenaries," i.e. individuals working for a *foreign* city (419a).[57] But the philosophic mercenaries (paradoxically) receive no wages. The philosophic rulers are, as it seems, foreigners in their own city – outsiders who serve the city free of charge.

noch bei Herodot (2.165) oder später wieder bei Aristoteles-eindeutig auf eine bestimmte soziale Gruppe bezogen . . . Für Platon ist βαναυσία eine Sache der Erziehung, gewissermaßen der negative Gegenpol zu einem pädagogischen Ideal."

[56] For Plato's conflicted views on the subject of craft (*technē*) and craftsmen, see Vidal-Naquet [1981]/1986, ch. 11; Bergren 1992, esp. 262–9. Brumbaugh (1989, ch. 16) describes Plato's extensive knowledge of the crafts and his many positive assessments of craft labor.

[57] ἐπίκουροι μισθωτοί, 419a.

Only by occupying this foreign and "outside" position can the philosopher act virtuously and impartially.

Plato's philosopher achieves a condition of freedom that makes him an impartial "outsider." Only by attaining this freedom can the philosopher rule himself and others in a just fashion. The practice of *theoria*, which detaches the philosopher from the world and even blinds him (for a time) to it, enables him to occupy a unique position when he comes back to the social realm. For the philosophic theorist can judge the affairs of his city as an impartial outsider (from a position of freedom) even as he lives and acts within it. This peculiar brand of freedom is, in Plato's view, a precondition for truly just and virtuous behavior.

In the *Republic*, Plato makes a paradoxical and controversial claim, namely, that turning away from the world of becoming and contemplating an unchanging reality will give us better insight and virtue in the earthly realm. Indeed, Socrates explicitly states that the philosopher who contemplates the Forms will, when he returns, "see" better inside the cave than any of the prisoners dwelling there (520c). In short, blinding oneself to the world is a precondition for seeing the Forms, and contemplating the Forms is a precondition for seeing clearly and acting virtuously in the human realm.

CONTEMPLATION AND ACTION

In a recent essay entitled "What Use Is the Form of the Good?", Annas has suggested that the metaphysical theories adumbrated in the *Republic* are not much use for practical and ethical life. For one thing, she argues, the moral theory in this text is not derived from the metaphysics (nor is it clear how it could be so derived) and does not in fact depend on it. Indeed, the activity of theorizing the Forms runs counter to practical activities, for "reflecting on the theoretical basis of your own virtue turns out to inhibit you from practicing it."[58] I would agree that the philosopher is "inhibited" from action during the period in which he is contemplating the Forms; at this point he is in fact blind to the world. But this does not mean that contemplative activity will inhibit the philosopher from practical action when he "returns." Although the philosopher does not want to lead a political life, he does not shrink from other practical activities and

---

[58] Annas 1999, ch. 5 (the quote is found on p. 105); she makes a similar (if less polemically expressed) argument in 1981, 259–71. Cf. Reeve (1988, 82–4), who argues that "it is a mistake to accuse Plato of giving the philosopher kings the wrong credentials for ruling well," since "dialectic is not simply a faculty of theoretical or propositional knowledge, but a complete psychological power" (see also Cooke 1999, Dorter 2001). For an insightful discussion of Annas' position, see Long 2000.

affairs. Indeed, throughout the *Republic*, Plato suggests that the philosopher embraces virtuous action (to behave in a less than virtuous fashion would in fact harm the philosopher's soul). I also agree that in the *Republic* Plato does not explain how metaphysical contemplation generates a moral theory with a specific content. The practice of *theoria* does, however, produce a moral agent who will be just and impartial in his dealings with the world, using the apprehension of the Forms as a "measure" for all his actions. The activity of contemplation transforms the philosopher epistemically, ethically, and erotically – he "returns" from his theoretical journey a changed man.

As Plato suggests, theoretical contemplation leads to a sort of "conversion" of the soul. The philosopher who sees the Forms comes to view the world in a radically different way:

When he recalls (ἀναμιμνησκόμενον) his first habitation and the "wisdom" there and the fellow-inmates that he formerly (τότε) lived with, wouldn't he consider himself happy in his transformation (τῆς μεταβολῆς), and pity those others? (516c)

Here, the philosopher remembers his "former" life in the cave and rejoices in the change that he has undergone (a sort of reverse recollection). He now rejects the moral and ideological systems of his city, since he has discovered a different locus of value; true goodness exists above and beyond civic life.[59] But what use do these other-worldly "goods" have in the distant world of human pursuits?

The question of the usefulness of *theoria* was raised and debated throughout the fourth century BCE. In the *Republic*, we find plentiful evidence of this contentious debate. Indeed, Socrates explicitly addresses the charge that philosophers are "useless" (ἄχρηστοι).[60] He responds as follows:

Say [to the man who calls the philosopher useless]: "you are right in claiming that the best men among the philosophers are useless (ἄχρηστοι) to the multitude." But bid him to blame this uselessness (ἀχρηστίας) on the men who do not know how to put them to use rather than on the philosophers themselves. (489b)

According to Socrates, the theoretical philosopher is eminently "useful" in the practical and political sphere; indeed "it is by reference [to the good] that just things and other such things become useful and beneficial (χρήσιμα

---

59 "And if there were honors and praises which they bestowed on one another in his former life, and prizes for the man who identified most swiftly the things that were passing in front of him and who most of all remembered what generally came before, after, and at the same time as these things, and who was most proficient at divining what was to come – do you think that the philosopher would be desirous of these things and would emulate those who were honored among those people and who held positions of power . . . ?" (516c–d).

60 See, e.g., 487d–e, 488d, 489b, 490d, 499b.

καὶ ὠφέλιμα, 505a; see also 505e, 518e–519a, 531d, etc.). In short, one cannot perform useful actions without some apprehension of true goodness. To be sure, the human philosopher will not achieve a complete vision of goodness, but he can make progress in contemplation by practicing philosophy over the period of a lifetime, and this intellectual progress will be matched by a progress in virtue in the practical sphere. Plato states quite emphatically, then, that the contemplation of the Forms is "useful" in the world of politics and *praxis*.

How does the philosopher translate his contemplation into action? Plato does not offer a philosophic analysis of this activity, but he repeatedly emphasizes the link between theoretical contemplation and virtuous action in books v–vii. And he also addresses this issue in a more implicit and indirect fashion, especially in his discussions of the philosophic and non-philosophic life. At the most general level, theoretical contemplation trans-forms the human soul, making it increasingly wise and good: by associating with beings that are "divine and orderly," the philosopher becomes divine and orderly himself (500c–d).[61] The apprehension of the Forms also pro-vides the soul with a sort of model or paradigm for virtuous *praxis*; as Socrates puts it, "lifting up the vision of their souls [the philosophers] will look at that which sheds light on all things and, having gazed upon the good itself, they will use it as a pattern for setting in order (*kosmein*) the city, the citizens, and themselves . . ." (540a–b). Only by contemplating the Forms can one discover a "measure" (*metron*) according to which one can live a virtuous life (504c).

Plato tends to use metaphors from the crafts to convey the movement from theoretical contemplation to virtuous action.[62] This raises the ques-tion whether this move involves the technical or methodical application of abstract rules to the shifting and chancy world of phenomena.[63] Does Plato offer a technicist account of moral action in the *Republic*? One should note

---

[61] Annas (1999, ch. 3) offers a rich examination of Plato's different conceptions of the philosopher's "assimilation to God." As she argues, the *Phaedo* and *Theaetetus* manifest an "unworldly strand" in Plato's thinking on this topic – "the idea that virtue is not a matter of coping with the good and evil that we find in our lives, but rather a matter of fleeing from the whole thing, escaping to a realm that is not human at all" (65). In the *Republic*, she claims, "although the strongest possible contrast is drawn between worldly and God-given rewards, virtuous assimilation to God is not said to be a flight from the human world" (62). Cf. Annas 1981, ch. 10 for a discussion of the larger question of the relation of *theoria* to *praxis*.

[62] Dorter 2001, 337 argues that *technē* "creates the bridge between the intelligible and practical realms that enables us not only to move from the practical realm to the contemplative realm but also to function subsequently within the practical realm without abandoning the intelligible one."

[63] For discussions of "technicism" in the Western tradition (beginning with Plato) and modern criti-cisms of this approach to ethics and politics, see Dunne 1993, and Volpi 1999.

that most of the references to *technai* are artistic rather than mathematical or methodical: the philosopher "imitates" the Forms in the medium of actions (and words) rather than applying a system of rules or a technical method. For example, the philosophers are compared to artists who "mould and sculpt both themselves and the city" – they are "painters (*zographoi*) who use a divine paradigm" (500c–e). Like artists imitating a model, the philosophers "will frequently look in each direction – at that which is by nature just, beautiful, temperate, and the like, and then, in turn, at that which they are producing in mankind . . ." (501a–c).[64] This process is quite different from a technical application of rules or formulae to action.

When the philosopher engages in *praxis*, he looks back and forth from this world to that of the Forms: "like painters, looking away towards the truth (εἰς τὸ ἀληθέστατον ἀποβλέποντες) and, always referring back to this and gazing at it with as much exactitude as possible (ἀκριβέστατα)," the philosopher will "establish in this world too the laws of the beautiful and the just and the good" (484c–d). As this passage suggests, the philosopher can envision the Forms which he has already contemplated even when he is engaging in practical activities. Once the philosopher attains some knowledge of truth, he has access to it when he returns to the cave. As Socrates claims, the philosopher who has returned from contemplation will "know what each of the images (τὰ εἴδωλα) [in the cave] is and of what it is a semblance on account of having seen true beauty and justice and goodness" (520c). The philosopher who has contemplated reality will understand the nature of Form and particular and the ontological relation of the one to the other: he knows that the entities in the cave are in fact *eidola* and also understands what they are "images" of.

This leads to a surprising conclusion: that the philosopher's vision and understanding are broader when he dwells in the world than when he engages in theoretical contemplation (at which point he sees only the Forms). Although the human world and its affairs are no doubt dark and distracting, it is in this realm that the philosopher attends to both "worlds"

---

[64] Detienne and Vernant (1991, 315) claim that Plato condemned all knowledge and skills based on stochastic intelligence, and believed that only that which is measurable can belong to exact science and the domain of truth: "Although Plato makes an exception for the art of building (because of measurement), he is uncompromising in his condemnation of medicine, the arts of the *strategos* and the shipwright, not to mention rhetoric and the tricks of the sophists. *Sophia* becomes contemplative and ceases to refer to the art of skillful craftsmen." In my view, contemplation is very closely tied to verbal and practical *technai* – Plato has not abandoned *metis*, but attempts to tether it to the knowledge of the Forms.

as he strives to live and act according to truth. Of course he can do this only after he has contemplated the Forms and then returned (and readjusted) to the phenomenal realm: at that point, he can rely on what he has already seen and understood about reality as he makes his way in the world of becoming.

As I have suggested, the activity of theoretical contemplation – during which time the philosopher is blind to the world – is a prerequisite for virtuous behavior in the human world. The detachment involved in the journey of *theoria*, which leads to the vision of true goodness, engenders in the philosopher a new perspective and a radical freedom. In Plato's view, only a person who has achieved the wisdom and radical detachment of the theoretical philosopher can be truly free and therefore act in an impartial fashion in the human world.[65] While the detachment and blindness of theoretical contemplation are temporary (since they are confined to periods of contemplation), the freedom that this produces is permanent – it is an abiding quality of the soul transformed by the vision of the Forms. Paradoxically, it is only by journeying away from the world that one can live freely and virtuously within it.

RETURN AND REENTRY

The Analogy of the Cave offers an especially vivid depiction of the philosopher's "return" to the world. According to Socrates, when the philosophic *theoros* reenters the social and political realm after a period of contemplation, he runs the risk of mockery and even violence at the hands of his fellow citizens (517a). If he returns to a bad city, he will be scorned and maligned, and his fellow citizens will see him as foolish and possibly even dangerous. In the ideal city, however, he has been trained and sent on an official mission by the polis: his "return" is enacted in the context of the political life of the city. In the case of traditional *theoria*, as we have seen, the reentry of the *theoros* is a crucial part of the journey as a whole. This marks a critical moment for the city, since the *theoros* may have been transformed (or "corrupted") by his travels and thus bring alien ideas into the polis. Plato's account of philosophic *theoria* clearly recognizes that the return of the *theoros* poses problems both for him and for his fellow citizens.

---

[65] See Griswold (1999a, 129–46 and *passim*) for a discussion of "the impartial spectator" and its relation to the "love of virtue" (though this argument is developed in the context of Enlightenment thinking, especially that of Adam Smith, its juxtaposition with Plato's notions of impartiality and the love of the good is instructive).

The traditional civic *theoros*, of course, is a man of power and influence: sent by the city as its representative, he returns in this same capacity. In the *Republic*, Plato's philosophic *theoros* also undertakes his journey in a civic context. But Plato transforms the traditional model in important ways. In particular, he claims that the philosopher has no desire to return to the city to participate in political affairs. The person who has received a philosophic education and achieved theoretical contemplation is loathe to enter the world of politics and must in fact be compelled to do so:

> It is the task of the founders to compel the best natures to come into the learning which we have said is best – to see the good and to make that ascent (ἀναβῆναι ἐκείνην τὴν ἀνάβασιν). And, when they have ascended and gained a sufficient view, they must not be allowed to do what is permitted at present (ὃ νῦν ἐπιτρέπεται) . . . namely, to remain there and to refuse to go down (καταβαίνειν) among those prisoners and to have a share in their labors and honors (μετέχειν τῶν παρ' ἐκείνοις πόνων τε καὶ τιμῶν). (519c–d)

What are we to make of this claim? Is Plato saying that the philosophers do not want to return from the realm of the Forms at any time, whether it be to rule or just to engage in ordinary life? Or is he saying that they do not want to rule the city and to lead a political life? The text, in fact, is ambiguous. It may seem that the philosophers who have made the *anabasis* out of the cave and achieved the vision of truth will not want to make the *katabasis* at all.[66] Certainly the rhetoric that Plato uses in the Analogy of the Cave indicates that the cave is a dark prison from which any intelligent person would want to escape.

The passage quoted above, however, is more focused and specific than the Analogy as a whole. In particular, Socrates claims that the philosophers do not want to go back "down" because they will be required "to have a share in the labors and offfices" of the people in the cave: this indicates that the philosophers do not wish to serve as political leaders in the city rather than that they eschew virtuous action in the private sphere. Socrates' claim that philosophers are "permitted at present" to abide in philosophical activity is also significant. Clearly, he does not mean that "present" philosophers in the non-ideal world have found a permanent dwelling in the region of the Forms (thus making a complete escape from human life). Rather, Socrates describes the "present" practice of allowing men to avoid

---

[66] As Annas argues (1999, 62–3, n. 29), "the philosophers will not want to 'return to the Cave' from their own point of view; but the insight into virtue which they get from studying and assimilating themselves to the order and structure of the intelligible world makes it clear that they are not to escape the task of concerning themselves with others." It is unclear, however, that the philosopher can be said to have his "own point of view" during the time that he is contemplating.

all forms of political engagement and to lead a private life devoted to philosophical activities (which includes a wide range of practical activities). The
philosopher rejects politics and the political life, and in this sense "remains"
in the realm of truth and virtue.

Plato does not, then, oppose the *contemplative* to the *practical* life; rather,
he differentiates between the *philosophical* and the *political* life even as he
tries to bring them together in a utopian context. The opposition between
these two kinds of life is, of course, a topos found in other Platonic texts.
In the *Gorgias*, for example, Socrates represents and defends the life of the
philosopher, while Callicles champions the political life. Callicles claims
that "philosophy is a fine thing if someone engages in it in moderation in
his youth; but if he spends time at it (ἐνδιατρίψῃ) longer than is right, it is
destructive"; it is good, he adds, to study philosophy when one is young, but
a man who continues this pursuit in his adulthood is foolish and unmanly.[67]
When Callicles attacks individuals who "spend time" in philosophy, he
clearly refers to an entire mode of life (rather than to a single contemplative
activity). In the *Republic*, too, Plato draws a stark contrast between the
philosophic and the political life. As Socrates claims in book vi, the group
of true philosophers consists of individuals who have avoided political life
(496a–c). Philosophy, as it seems, is not compatible with politics. But, after
constructing this opposition between the philosopher and the politician,
Plato claims in book vii that the two lives must be brought together in the
context of the ideal city.

In the *Republic*, then, Plato does not attempt to define or defend the
notion of a *contemplative life*. Rather, he focuses on the *philosophic life* –
a life that combines contemplation and action. Contemplation is not the
only activity in the philosophic life, since the philosopher is a human being
who cannot live the disembodied life of the gods. Human beings dwell,
for the most part, in the practical and social realm; even the activity of
theoretical contemplation must be arranged for by practical reasoning and
supported by virtues such as courage, temperance, and justice. Dialectical
discussion – a central feature of philosophy – involves other people and has
a necessary social and interpersonal dimension: in this activity, practical
virtue operates in conjunction with theoretical activity. Likewise, when the
philosopher turns from contemplation to practical or political activities, he
will use his theoretical wisdom as a basis for action in the social and civic
realm. It is not the case, then, that *theoria* "inhibits" the philosopher from
acting virtuously. Insofar as he is human, the philosopher will desire and

[67] *Gorgias* 484c–485b; see also *Republic* 487c–d, 497e–498a.

embrace practical virtue and understand that virtuous activity is a necessary part of the philosophical life as a whole. For Plato, theoretical philosophy is an art of living, not just of thinking.

In the *Republic*, then, a tension arises not because the philosophers must engage in different *activities* – contemplative and practical – within a single, philosophical life, but rather because they are asked to engage in two different *lives* which, by definition, are opposed. The city requires the philosophers to do something that, by definition, they do not want to do: to take up the task of ruling. Plato's theoretical philosopher willingly engages in virtuous action, but does not want to lead a political life. While Plato clearly believes that philosophy is antithetical to political life in ordinary, nonideal cities, he attempts to bring these lives together in the context of the ideal city. *If* there is an ideal city – and it is by no means clear that Plato believed in its possibility – then it can and must be ruled by philosophers.[68] In this case alone, the philosopher must live a double life (as it were): he will practice philosophy and serve as a ruler. To qualify for this position, an individual must possess theoretical wisdom and practical virtue; in addition, he or she must not want to rule or lead a political life (347c–d, 521a–b, 540b). A person who does want to rule is, by definition, not a true philosopher and is thus disqualified from ruling. The philosopher in the ideal city, however, will agree to rule, in spite of his disinclination to do so. Since he is a "just" person responding to a "just command," the philosopher is "willing" to return and rule the city (520d–e).

Plato's suggestion that the theorizing philosopher does not want to return to rule the city has left some scholars puzzled and disturbed. According to Irwin and Annas, Plato's glorification of contemplative activity and denigration of the politics in books v–vii is an unfortunate aberration from the task of the *Republic*, which is to define justice and demonstrate why the just life (which includes practical and political activities) is the happiest and best for human beings.[69] Irwin argues that Plato "mistakenly suggests that the philosopher will want to stay contemplating the Forms and

---

[68] In book IX (592a–b), Socrates reiterates his earlier claim that the philosopher will refuse to participate in politics in an ordinary city, though he will do so in the ideal city (592a). When Glaucon responds by saying that this latter city "resides in words, but does not exist anywhere on earth," Socrates replies: "but perhaps there is a paradigm laid up in heaven for the man who wishes to behold it and, by beholding it, to found a city in himself." Here, Socrates raises the question whether the ideal city can ever come into being (see also 473a; but cf. 456c, 499c–d). Burnyeat (1999) argues that the ideal city can be realized on earth; cf. Clay 1988, Annas 1999, ch. 4.

[69] For recent arguments against Irwin and Annas' view, see Reeve 1988, 201–3 and *passim*, Kraut 1991, and Gill 1996, 303 and *passim*.

will not voluntarily *undertake public service.*" What Plato must really have meant, according to Irwin, is that dialectic will produce in the philosopher a conception of himself as a rational agent who "has reason to *include just action in his life.*"[70] But one can "include just action in one's life" without "undertaking public service" as a *politikos*: philosophic *praxis* need not be political. As I have suggested, the life of the theoretical philosopher combines virtuous action and contemplation – it is *political life*, rather than practical virtue, that conflicts with *theoria*.

Annas claims that Plato refused to face the fact that practical and contemplative wisdom "ever could conflict." As she argues, Plato never acknowledges the fact that "the philosophers may suffer real loss, because their own prospects of happiness are sacrificed" – that, in short, "justice is not in their interests."[71] But the fact that the philosopher does not want to rule or live a political life does not mean that he is loathe to act at all. It is the life of politics, rather than virtuous activities *in toto* that goes against the philosopher's interests. In fact, Plato is not even consistent on this last point. On the one hand, Socrates seems to agree with Glaucon's claim that forcing the philosophers to rule in the ideal city will mean that they live less good and happy lives than they would if they did not have to rule (519d–e). But Socrates says in book VI that the philosopher in an ordinary city who looks after his own soul and stays out of politics ("standing apart, behind a wall") will not have accomplished anything very great: "only in a city that is fitting for him will he attain his full stature and preserve the commonwealth as well as his private interests" (ἐν γὰρ προσηκούσῃ αὐτός τε μᾶλλον αὐξήσεται καὶ μετὰ τῶν ἰδίων τὰ κοινὰ σώσει, 496d–497a). This indicates that the philosopher is happier in a city where he both theorizes and rules than in one where he engages in *theoria* as a private person.

Gill offers a more persuasive interpretation of the philosopher's "return" to the city. He focuses on Socrates' claim that the philosophers in the ideal city will agree to rule because, being "just men obeying just commands," they are eager to pay back their city for the education and rearing that has been granted them (520b–e). As Gill argues, it is an "ethics of reciprocity" – which forms the basis of the entire Greek ethical and political tradition – that drives the philosophers to return to the city and become rulers. According to Gill,

---

[70] Irwin 1977, 237–45 (my italics).
[71] Annas 1981, 267–9. Annas adds that if the philosophers "view their own happiness as rationally and impersonally as they do everybody else's, then justice seems to demand an ideal, impersonal viewpoint which it is not in the interests of any actual people to adopt" (p. 269).

. . . the philosopher-rulers' acceptance of the "just demand" made of them is presented as an act of reciprocal exchange. Unlike philosophers in other communities, the philosopher-rulers in the ideal state should "be keen to pay back the cost of their upbringing" [520b4–c1], which has made them uniquely capable of looking after themselves and the city by developing the dual capacities for dialectic and government. This response seems better explained as an attitude associated with a polis-centred version of the (mutually benefiting) relationship of generalized reciprocity than as an attitude which expresses the desire to benefit others for its own sake.[72]

In the *Republic* vi–vii, the philosopher's activity is indeed "polis-centered" and based on reciprocity.[73] As I would urge, this is because the philosopher in the ideal city serves as a civic *theoros*. He is trained and sent on an official mission to "see" divine reality, and is also required, on legal and moral grounds, to return to the city to impart and implement the things he has learned. His return is "polis-centered" precisely because his philosophical *theoria* takes place in a civic and political context. As a civic *theoros*, he has a political and a religious obligation to bring his vision back to the city.

To be sure, it is only in the ideal city that the theoretical philosopher lives a political life and serves as a civic *theoros*. The philosopher who lives in a nonideal city will not serve in a civic capacity but will play the role of a private *theoros*.[74] This does not mean, however, that the theoretical philosopher will never have to return from contemplation and engage in action in the practical sphere; as I have suggested, insofar as he is a human being the philosopher will make many "journeys" to the Forms (never gaining a full or perfect view), and will come back just as many times. Even as a private man, the philosopher will wish to share the vision he has achieved with his associates, and to give a dialectical account of his findings. In this case, he still brings back what he has learned, but does this in a private rather than a civic context.

---

[72] Gill 1996, 303. See also Ober (1998, 241–2), who suggests that this passage in the *Republic* comes close to a "contractual" agreement; Ober compares this to the passage in the *Crito* where the (personified) Laws argue that Socrates is obliged to stay in Athens and follow its laws because he was reared by the city and never made any attempt to express his opposition by leaving.

[73] Gill's claim here is part of a much larger argument against theories that ascribe to Plato's philosophers either a Kantian (or neo-Kantian) sense of "duty" or an ethic of altruism. He argues that the "ethic of reciprocity" (seen in this passage) is at the core of Plato's entire moral theory. But this passage does not offer decisive evidence for Plato's moral positions or theories in the *Republic* as a whole, since it is articulated in a very specific context and cannot be generalized into a "moral theory."

[74] I refer here to Plato's view of the philosopher in the *Republic* and "middle dialogues." Plato set forth a very different political philosophy in the late dialogues (such as the *Statesman* and *Laws*).

The *Republic*, of course, has a political orientation that gives the text a specific bias: it therefore emphasizes civic rather than private *theoria*. But, as I have suggested, Plato's philosophic *theoros* will "return" to the human and civic realm regardless of whether he theorizes in a private or a political capacity. In fact, even in the ideal city, the philosopher does not seek truth simply in order to serve the city. The soul aims, first and foremost, at wisdom, virtue, and *eudaimonia*. According to Plato, *theoria* will render the philosopher happy whether or not he dwells in an ideal city. In addition to being good in itself, moreover, contemplation provides the basis for all virtuous action on earth. Whether the philosopher practices *theoria* in a civic or a private context, he can and will translate his contemplative wisdom into virtuous deeds: the philosophic spectator, who has gazed upon reality, will later "perform" his wisdom (in word and in deed) in the practical realm. Platonic *theoria* encompasses both contemplative and practical activities and should not be identified as a merely intellectual activity.[75]

We need not worry, then, that the philosophic rulers in the ideal city have sacrificed their full opportunity for happiness. But we should perhaps worry about their subjects: for the nonphilosophers in the ideal city have no power and they dwell in a "closed" society with a rigid class system. Many thinkers have attacked Plato's political theory on the grounds that it is a blatant power grab posing as a disinterested and noble enterprise: even as Plato claims that his philosophers are unwilling to rule, he writes a text that installs them as rulers. This leaves him open to the charge of bad faith. One could argue, of course, that Plato created a fictional utopia rather than a blueprint for governing society, and that he explicitly recommended that philosophers stay out of politics in ordinary cities. But even if his ideal philosophers renounce wealth and political power, it is clear that Plato himself was pursuing cultural capital in the world of Greek elites. As I have suggested, in his foundational construction of theoretical philosophy, Plato presided over the inauguration of a new and prestigious elite – that of the cultured, educated philosopher who is above political affairs even though he possesses the wisdom most necessary to the city.

In the *Republic* and other middle dialogues, Plato cleaves quite closely to the metaphors and structures offered by the model of traditional *theoria*, especially those of journeying, spectating, and returning home to bear

---

[75] As Kraut (1991, 58–9) suggests, "if there is a single goal towards which [the philosopher] should be striving, then it is the *imitation* of the Forms, not, more narrowly, their contemplation." I agree that the "imitation" of the Forms "is diverse and does not consist solely in one kind of activity."

witness. In his later work (especially the *Timaeus*), Plato offers a different account of *theoria*, which dispenses with the metaphor of the journey and focuses on the activity of "sacred spectating" and the virtuous action that this produces. As we will see, Philip of Opus and Aristotle also focus on the activity of spectating, though each of these philosophers offers a radically different conception of theoretical philosophy.

CHAPTER 4

Theorizing the beautiful body: from Plato to Philip of Opus

Beauty is momentary in the mind –
The fitful tracing of a portal;
But in the flesh it is immortal.

Wallace Stevens

It's not my fault that we are made so, half from disinterested contem-plation, half from appetite./ If I should accede one day to Heaven, it must be there as it is here, except that I will be rid of my dull senses and my heavy bones./ Changed into pure seeing, I will absorb, as before, the proportions of human bodies, the color of irises, a Paris street in June at dawn,/ all of it incomprehensible, incomprehensible the multitude of visible things.

Czeslaw Milosz, trans. Robert Hass

Plato is famous for his denigration of the physical world. In the myths in the *Phaedo* and *Phaedrus*, however, and in the "likely account" in the *Timaeus*, Plato offers a very positive account of the physical cosmos as a whole and of certain (exceptional) bodies within it. In particular, he identifies certain bodies as perfect (or near-perfect) "images" of the Forms: they are not just shadowy *eidola*, but *agalmata* or "sacred images" of true reality. These bodies are either exceptionally beautiful bodies in the terrestrial realm or the heavenly bodies in the celestial sphere. Although Plato generally has a very negative view of the sensible world, he makes an exception in the case of physical beauty: beautiful bodies have a sort of sacred status which generates, for the philosopher, the kind of sacralized visualization that *theoroi* experience at religious festivals and sanctuaries. In fact, one of the most common objects of the theoric gaze in these sanctuaries were *agalmata* (images of the gods) and other sacred spectacles. In the myths in the *Phaedo* and *Phaedrus*, Plato indicates, the philosopher who looks at a beautiful body sees a "sacred image" (*agalma*) of the Forms. And in the *Timaeus*, the philosopher who gazes on the heavens sees, in the cosmos as a whole, an *agalma* of the intelligible realm, as well as the "visible star-gods" within the cosmos. These sacred sights lead the philosopher both to revere and to emulate the divine. The physical vision of these bodies does not mire the soul in the corporeal "mud" but makes a positive contribution to the philosopher's journey towards the Forms.

In the myths in the *Phaedo* and the *Phaedrus*, Plato goes even further than the *Republic* in his efforts to visualize and spatialize the regions of being and becoming. In the *Phaedo*, I will suggest, Plato uses the discourse of geography to portray the "true earth" and its relation to metaphysical realities: rather than using the fictional image of a cave, he opts for the more "natural" discourse of geography, i.e. of earth and its atmosphere. Adopting this genre of discourse, Plato reconceives the earth (as it was traditionally conceived) and links it to an immaterial "reality": in this narrative, the earth and its many physical particulars are conceived as participating in – and, indeed, "caused" by – the Forms. This myth, in fact, focuses almost exclusively on the concrete, physical region on the surface of the earth – a region that Socrates calls "a spectacle for blessed spectators to see" (111b). The eschatology in the *Phaedo*, then, speculates on a journey to the surface of the "true earth," where the *theoros* can behold radiant and "perfect" bodily beings; indeed, it draws a sort of map connecting the various regions of earth, the heavens, and the metaphysical regions "above."

In the myth in the *Phaedrus*, Plato moves from earth to the cosmos as a whole, depicting the "space" of the heavens and the metaphysical realm "outside" the physical universe. Here, Plato begins to set forth the basic elements of his cosmology, in which soul (as "self-moving motion") initiates the motions of all bodily beings in the universe, with divine souls regulating the cosmos as a whole. This myth sketches out a sort of topography of the heavens, taking the reader up to the very "edge" of the physical universe (traced by the fixed stars). In Plato's elaborate narrative, the soul journeys through the heavens to the very edge of the physical universe, where it contemplates the "region beyond the heavens" – the *hyperouranios topos* (i.e. that of the Forms). In both the *Phaedo* and the *Phaedrus* myths, I will argue, the physical vision of (certain) bodily beings plays an important role in the activity of *theoria*.

The *Timaeus* takes this in a new direction. This text sets forth a full-blown cosmology, portraying the universe as a god made up of a divine World-soul and a "perfect" World-body. In addition to the World-Body (of the cosmos), the individual heavenly bodies are "visible gods" which are moved in their rotations by divine *nous*. In looking at the heavens, then, the human being sees the motion of divinity – motions which he can imitate, making of himself a (micro)cosmos. This cosmological theory – with its claim that the physical universe is good and divine – encourages the human theorist to take a closer look at the corporeal realm. Here, Plato suggests that the practice of astronomy plays a key role in the theoretical investigation of truth and reality: astronomical *theoria* works in conjunction with metaphysical *theoria*. In his explication of astronomical *theoria*, Plato focuses exclusively on the visual aspect of traditional *theoria* – placing special weight on the viewing of *agalmata* at sacred precincts – and makes no use of the metaphor of the journey. As we will see, Philip of Opus takes this a step further, claiming in the *Epinomis* that astronomy is the *sole* activity of *theoria*, completely abandoning the *theoria* of the Forms.

As in the *Republic*, Plato uses the "rhetoric of estrangement" in the *Phaedo, Phaedrus*, and *Timaeus*. This rhetoric aims to loosen the reader's ties to the human world and to reveal his essential kinship with the divine. To cite one of the most memorable examples:

> God has given to each of us that kind of soul which dwells in the top of our body [the head] and which raises us up from earth towards our kindred in heaven (τὴν ἐν οὐρανῷ ξυγγένειαν) – since we are not an earthly but a heavenly plant (φυτὸν οὐκ ἔγγειον ἀλλὰ οὐράνιον), if we are to speak truly. For it is by suspending our head and our root (ῥίζαν) from that region whence the substance of our soul first came that the divinity keeps our whole body upright. (90a–b)

Here, Timaeus compares humans to upside-down plants with roots located in the heavens. This rhetorical strategy offers the readers a radically new perspective on the world, inviting us to attend to a strange and wondrous spectacle. In using this kind of discourse, Plato both dislocates and relocates the human being in the cosmos, thus preparing us to theorize the heavenly bodies and to pattern our "kindred" souls on their orderly and divine motions.

PHAEDO: *THEORIA* AT THE ENDS OF THE EARTH

Towards the end of the *Phaedo*, just before he drinks the hemlock, Socrates narrates an elaborate eschatology.[1] In this myth, he offers a lengthy description of an "other world" which is located on the borders of "this world" when it is viewed from a larger perspective. Like all eschatological narratives, this discourse not only conjures up regions and beings that are ontologically different from one another, but it also forges a vital link between these regions. Eschatology is defined by a *logos* about the *eschata*, i.e. about things

[1] For discussions of the myth in the *Phaedo*, see Annas 1982a, esp. 126–9; Burger 1984, 194–7, Sedley 1989, Rowe 1993 ad loc., K. Morgan 2000, 192–201.

that are distant or at the edges of space or time ("outermost," "utmost," "farthest," "remotest"), or that serve as an end or limit to human life as we know it.[2] Socrates' eschatology in the *Phaedo* offers a detailed account of our world and the one at its distant edge, and explores the juxtaposition and the interaction between them.

In this text, Plato conceives the "other" world in physical and geographical terms: located on the surface of the earth in the "aether," it occupies a region directly above (and adjacent to) our world, which is located in the hollows of the earth (109b–e).[3] According to the myth, in this region wise and pure souls behold corporeal bodies that are "perfect" and radiantly beautiful.[4] As I will argue, by portraying a purified form of physical vision in the upper regions of the material cosmos, Plato introduces (albeit tentatively) the notion of "theorizing" perfect or heavenly bodies. This kind of *theoria* differs from traditional metaphysical *theoria* and thus deserves a separate treatment. Though metaphysical *theoria* remains the highest goal of the philosopher, this theorizing of "perfect" bodies plays an important role in philosophical activity. Although the *Phaedo* explores this idea in mythic and rather fanciful terms, this text anticipates later dialogues in which Plato offers a full-blown cosmology that links the cosmos to the Forms (and, correlatively, connects the vision of the heavens with the "vision" of the Forms).

The eschatology in the *Phaedo* portrays a higher world that is not metaphysical: in this myth, Socrates describes the uppermost part of the physical universe (rather than the region of the Forms). He does gesture at one point to the realm of the Forms (114b–c), in whose pure reality all physical particulars "participate" to a greater or lesser degree. But the myth makes no attempt to depict or discuss that realm; it deals exclusively with that part of the cosmos which houses "aetherial" bodies – the best and most beautiful entities in the physical universe, located in the aether. This otherworldly myth differs from the Analogy of the Cave, which focuses on the world of the Forms rather than that of the cosmos or heavens: though it describes the region outside the cave in physicalist terms, the Analogy represents a metaphysical "region" outside of space and time. Like the *Republic*, the *Phaedo* uses highly metaphorical discourse. But, in this case, Plato uses these

---

[2] I have offered a detailed discussion of the genre of eschatology in Nightingale 2001. As Bakhtin says of this genre, "in essence these [eschatological] forms strive to make actual that which is presumed obligatory and true, to infuse it with being, to join it to time, to counterpose it – as something that actually exists and is at the same time true – to the available reality . . ." (1981, 149).

[3] For a discussion of the "aether" in the (preplatonic) literary and philosophical tradition, see Rowe 1993, 273. As he rightly suggests, in Plato's myth aether is "treated as a stuff as well as a location."

[4] For a critique of Plato's orientation towards "perfection," see Griswold 2003.

metaphors to describe a higher region of the physical world. As Socrates says, it is difficult to journey to the edge – the *eschaton* (ἐπ' ἔσχατον) – of the earth, where air gives way to aether. But if someone should reach the upper limit of the air and "lift his head above it,"

He would see [the upper region] (κατιδεῖν ἂν ἀνακύψαντα); just as, in our region, fish lift their heads above the water and see the things here, this person would see the things there (τὰ ἐκεῖ κατιδεῖν). And if his nature were strong enough to endure the *theoria* of that region (εἰ ἡ φύσις ἱκανὴ εἴη ἀνέχεσθαι θεωροῦσα), he would recognize that it is the true heaven and the true light and the true earth. (109e–110a)

Here, Socrates depicts a (hypothetical) philosopher making a journey to the upper *eschaton* of our region – where air gives way to aether – and "theorizing" the true earth and the true heaven. What, we must ask, is the nature and the object of this *theoria*?

Socrates claims that he will describe the "earth" as it really is. Indeed, he devotes much of the myth in the *Phaedo* to a detailed discussion of the "earth" and its "many wonderful places" (πολλοὶ καὶ θαυμαστοὶ τῆς γῆς τόποι, 108c). The region where we dwell, he claims, is located beneath the surface of the earth, in hollow crevices sunk into the ground:

The earth is very large, and those of us located between the river Phasis and the pillars of Heracles dwell in a small portion of it, living by the sea like ants or frogs around a pond, and many other people live in many other such regions. For everywhere around the earth there are many hollows of every shape and size . . . Moreover, it has escaped our notice that we dwell in the hollows of the earth, but we think that we live up above, on the surface of the earth . . . (109a–c)

In this lower region, nothing is "perfect" or "pure," since everything is corroded with brine and mud (110a). Due to the impurity of the locale, the human dwellers have dim and distorted vision, and thus have a quite limited view of the physical world.

In contrast to the subterranean regions, the region on the surface of the earth – located in the aether – is a "blessed" place that contains physical bodies and entities that are perfect and pure and radiantly beautiful. As Socrates asserts, "the earth itself is pure and is situated in the pure heaven (τὴν γῆν καθαρὰν ἐν καθαρῷ . . . τῷ οὐρανῷ), where the stars dwell." This realm is, quite literally, aetherial. And it is a wonder to behold:

The earth when seen from above looks like those balls made up of twelve pieces of leather, variegated and divided into patches of color, of which the colors we see here are (as it were) samples, such as painters use. But there the earth has colors that are much brighter and purer (λαμπροτέρων καὶ καθαρωτέρων) than those here. For one part is purple, wondrous in its beauty (θαυμαστὴν τὸ κάλλος), and another is golden, and yet another is white – whiter than chalk or snow. And the earth is made up of other colors of a similar kind, which are more numerous and more beautiful than those we see here. (110b–c)

Socrates offers an elaborate description of this region, with its beautiful plants, trees, flowers, and fruits, its mountains with their lovely colors, its stones made up of jewels, and its landscape adorned with gold and silver – all of which things are "in plain sight" (110d–111a). Plato could not have gone further in emphasizing the physicality of the region. To be sure, the things in that region are, like all physical entities, phenomena – they are part of the world of becoming rather than being. But they occupy a higher level of the universe and thus have a special status as objects of vision.

Given the metaphorical cast of the discourse, it may seem at first glance that Plato is depicting the metaphysical realm of the Forms in overly phys-icalist terms.[5] But this interpretation does not stand up to scrutiny. For the myth indicates that the people dwelling on the surface of the earth are embodied, mortal beings rather than disincarnate souls: though they live exceedingly long lives, they eventually grow old and die (111b).[6] Even more importantly, Socrates asserts at the end of the eschatology that there are regions superior even to this one. For, as he claims, while people who have led exceptionally good lives in the subterranean world will migrate to the surface of the earth after they die, those who have lived as theoretical philosophers will depart entirely from the bodily realm and will inhabit "abodes even more beautiful than these, which are not easy to describe" (114b–c). The surface of the earth, then, is not the highest or best realm, since it is still a place of embodiment. Certainly we should not identify it with the region of the Forms (such as the realm outside the cave in the *Republic* or the *hyperouranios topos* in the *Phaedrus*).

Although the discourse in the *Phaedo* is fanciful in many ways, we should take seriously its depiction of the aetherial region as part of the physical cosmos. Blessed, radiant, and beautiful, this region is also material and incarnate. In spite of the *Phaedo*'s denunciations of the physical realm in the arguments that precede the eschatology – this is arguably the most body-hating of all the dialogues – its myth asserts the existence of heavenly

---

[5] See, e.g., Hackforth ([1955]/1972, 174–5), who says that the myth has a "metaphysical symbolism": "the 'true earth' is another version of the world outside the cave." But he adds that Plato offers a confused picture, since he later indicates that the realm of the Forms is in a region higher and "more beautiful" than that on earth and in the aether (114c). Gallop ([1975]/1988, 222) makes a similar move, claiming that Plato's account of the earth "symbolizes the distinction between the sensible world and the world of Forms." Cf. Rowe 1993, 275–6.

[6] As Rowe (1993, 277) suggests, the "men" in the aether are "presumably, combinations of soul and something which is at least comparable to our bodies." Cf. Burger 1984, 194–6.

bodies that are splendid to behold. To be sure, Plato repeatedly reminds us that this is just a story. In the opening section, for example, Socrates begins with the cagey assertion: "it is said that after death . . ."[7] And, in the long passage on the "earth," Socrates claims that he has been "persuaded [of the tale] by someone" (108c) – a "someone" who is never identified and who can hardly serve as an authority.[8] Indeed, Socrates repeatedly says that he has been "persuaded" of the things which he relates (108c8, e1; 108e4, 109a7) and suggests at the end that no one can "assert with confidence that such things are exactly as [he has] described them" (114d). Nonetheless, he adds, it is best for a person to "run the risk" or "take the chance" that something "like" what he has narrated is true, and to "repeat these things to himself like magic charms."[9] Clearly, Plato did not set out to compose a detailed scientific discourse on the cosmos: this is not a true cosmology.[10] But the eschatology in the *Phaedo* does put forth some ideas that are central to the cosmologies in the *Timaeus*, *Laws* x, and *Epinomis*. For – albeit in mythic and highly provisional terms – it posits the existence of perfect and pure bodies and indicates that a philosophical soul can "theorize" these aetherial beings.

In order to substantiate these claims, we must look more closely at Socrates' discourse on the "earth." In discussions of the sources of this tale, scholars have generally focused on two genres of discourse: Orphic and Pythagorean depictions of the judgment of souls in the afterlife, and philosophic texts on the earth and cosmos.[11] But Socrates' discussion of the judgment of souls is a small piece of a much larger story, and the discourse as a whole contains only a few clear allusions to Presocratic philosophy.[12]

---

[7] λέγεται, 107d5; cf. λέγεται, 107d4, φαίνεταί μοι, 108a2.

[8] As Burnet (1911, 127) observes, there is no (known) philosopher or scientist from this period who can be identified as the "someone" whom Socrates mentions here.

[9] χρὴ τὰ τοιαῦτα ὥσπερ ἐπᾴδειν ἑαυτῷ, 114d.

[10] Sedley (1989) rightly argues that the myth in the *Phaedo* offers "an introduction to teleological cosmology" (p. 360).

[11] Hackforth ([1955]/1972, 172–5) offers a useful summary of the scholarship on these issues; see also Friedländer 1958, 261–85, Annas 1982a, Sedley 1989. Kingsley (1995, chs. 7–10) offers a detailed discussion of the Pythagorean and Orphic elements in the *Phaedo*.

[12] The passages dealing with the judgment and peregrination of souls after death are 107d–108c, 113a, 113d–114c. The one dealing with philosophic speculations about the earth/cosmos is at 108e–109a (on the shape of the earth and the cause of its stability, which was a question raised by the Presocratics). The references to *aithēr* at 109b and 111b may allude to Anaxagoras and/or Empedocles, who use the word to refer to cosmic fire; but, as Rowe points out (1993, 273), the term is also used by poets (especially Homer) to designate the sky or heavens. Finally, the physical model of the earth depicted in this myth may be intended as a response to the physicalist philosophers whom Socrates criticized earlier in the dialogue (108e–109a, 110e). See Sedley (1989) for a detailed discussion of Plato's allusions to materialist explanations of the earth and cosmos; he argues that Plato countered these by offering a teleological account (see also Rowe 1993, 280–2).

In fact, the myth breaks into two unequal parts, the second being (roughly) twice as long as the first. In the first part, Socrates discusses the judgment of souls after death (107d–108c); in the second, he offers a lengthy account of the "true nature of the earth." To some extent, the second part of Socrates' tale serves to locate the after-life narrative sketched out in the first: Plato's "earth" will turn out to contain the places where souls are punished and rewarded after death. But the second part contains a huge amount of material that does not serve this purpose, and thus needs to be considered as a separate discourse with its own form and logic. This latter discourse commences at 108c, where Socrates says rather abruptly: "there are many marvellous regions of the earth, and the earth itself is not of the nature or size that it is thought to be *by those who customarily speak about the earth*" (ὑπὸ τῶν περὶ γῆς εἰωθότων λέγειν, 108c7). Simmias responds that he himself "has heard many things about the earth," but would gladly learn what Socrates thinks on the subject (108d). Here, Plato deliberately locates the narrative in the context of a specific genre: that of geography or the account of the "earth" (*gē*) and its inhabitants.[13]

Ancient geography was an enterprise that engaged both poets and prose writers, and often contained a blend of fact and fiction.[14] The technical term for a geographic discourse or text was a "*periodos gēs*": a "circuit" or "mapping" of the earth. This term generally designated prose writings, but was also used of poetic descriptions of the earth and its *topoi*.[15] Some geographers attempted to draw a pictorial map of the earth, but many preferred to set forth a descriptive cartography. Geographic texts in the archaic and classical periods shared the following prominent features. First of all, these texts set out to identify what the early poets called the *peirata gaiēs* – the "boundaries" or "edges" of the earth. Within these boundaries lay the realm of the "known world" – which Herodotus and other

---

[13] Although scholars have analyzed the myth in the *Phaedo* as a "geography," they tend to approach this solely in the context of philosophical speculation about the earth and cosmos – i.e. as "geophysics" or "geography as a science" (see, e.g., Friedländer 1958, 261–85; cf. Clay 1985, 233n. 7, and Clay and Purvis 1999). I propose to locate the myth in a much broader generic context which includes non-philosophical discourses – in poetry and in prose – on the subject of geography.

[14] Nicolet 1991, 58–66; Romm 1992, 27. On the genre of geography in the ancient Greek and Roman worlds, see Nicolet 1991, Romm 1992, and Clarke 1999. Hartog (2001) discusses travel in the ancient world and the representation of "barbarians" in Greek and Roman texts. Clarke (1999, ch. 1) offers an excellent discussion of (post)modern theoretical approaches to geography and their application to ancient texts and ideas. Note also that, insofar as they deal with the inhabitants of the different regions of "earth," ancient geographies can also be categorized as ethnography.

[15] As Romm (1992, 27) shows, this notion goes all the way back to Homer and Hesiod. For a fascinating analysis of Hesiod's "world," which investigates his somewhat paradoxical portrayal of the earth as both bounded by Ocean and (from the human perspective) unlimited and unbounded, see Clay 1992a.

fifth-century writers called the *oikoumenē*. As a rule, ancient geographic texts subscribed to the notion that the outer limits of the earth were surrounded by "Ocean," which was conceived as a river encircling the lands of Europe, Africa, and Asia (a depiction of which is found on the first Greek maps of the world).[16] Although one could, theoretically, reach the river Ocean by journeying in any direction, in early Greek thought the gateway to Ocean was located at the "Pillars of Heracles" (which refer to the rocks standing at each side of the Straits of Gibralter). The Pillars of Heracles thus functioned as a symbol of the far edges of the earth – of those distant places where the earth comes to an end and gives way to Ocean.[17]

Ancient Greek geographic texts, then, dealt with both the "known world" and with the regions at the edges or borders of this world. The latter, of course, were distant and mysterious, but contained vital information about the structure and nature of the world and its inhabitants (both human and non-human). Interestingly, these distant lands were denoted by the term *"eschatiai"* or *"eschata"* starting at least as early as Herodotus. As Romm observes, the word *"eschatiai"*

> becomes the standard geographic usage from this time forward . . . Herodotus [III.106, III.116] uses the feminine form of the adjective *eschatios*, "distant" or "uttermost," so as to agree with an implied noun *gê*, "land"; later authors generally prefer a substantival neuter form, *ta eschata*, sometimes qualified by *tês gês*, "of the earth." In either case the word is declined in the plural yet functions as a collective noun, essentially singular in meaning. Thus . . . the furthest reaches of the earth, in all directions, form a continuous belt of lands, closely joined by common characteristics just as they are set apart from the rest of the world.[18]

Insofar as it focuses on "distant" regions and beings – offering a *logos* about the *eschata* – geography in this period intersects with the genre of eschatology. Given that even an empirically oriented geographer like Herodotus dealt with semi-mythical regions at the distant edges of the earth, the interaction between the genres of geography and eschatology should come as no surprise.

---

[16] Herodotus is a rare exception, since he rejects the traditional conception of Ocean as a river encircling the earth: not only is there no evidence for this supposition, he suggests (II.23, IV.8), but the fact that land extends beyond the Caspian Sea (which he claims is landlocked) indicates that Europe may not be bounded by Ocean in the north and the east (IV.45). Herodotus, then, reconceives the "edges of the earth," indicating that he can only vouch for the world which is inhabited or known by human exploration. On early cartographic maps of the earth (which are briefly described in Herodotus IV.36), see Nicolet 1991, 71–2, Romm 1992, 14, Clay and Purvis 1999; for a more broad-ranging history of cartography, see Harley and Woodward 1987.

[17] See, e.g., Pindar *Ol.* 3.43–5, *Isthm.* 4.11–13, *Nem.* 3.20–3.   [18] Romm 1992, 39.

A few examples from Herodotus will illustrate this point:

The most *distant* places of the inhabited world (αἱ δ'ἐσχατιαί κως τῆς οἰκεομένης) have been allotted the finest things . . . As I said earlier, India is located at the most distant region in the east; and in this land the animals, both four-footed and winged, are much bigger than those in other lands, except for the horses . . . and the gold there is abundant . . . And the trees in the wild produce wool which is finer and more excellent than that which comes from sheep. (III.106)

It is clear that in the north of Europe there is much more gold than elsewhere. How it comes into being, I cannot say with certainty, but it is reported that the one-eyed Arimaspian men steal it from the griffins. I do not believe that there are men with only one eye, having a nature similar in every other way to humans. But I do believe that the most *distant* places of the world (αἱ δὲ ὦν ἐσχατιαί οἴκασι), since they shut in and bound all other lands, possess those things that we consider the finest and most rare. (III.116)[19]

By definition, the most "distant" places differ from the interior: the people are exotic, the flora, fauna, and weather are (in one way or another) extreme, and the lands are replete with gold and other precious goods. This logic, together with the fact that eyewitness reports from these regions are rare, leads Herodotus to offer speculative accounts of distant peoples and places. His accounts of the *eschata*, moreover, deal either explicitly or implicitly with the boundary between humans and nonhumans, between men and animals and/or gods. This geographic "eschatology," then, both explores and negotiates the boundaries of the human. Finally, it enables its author to view "normal" people such as the Greeks from a distant and alien vantage point: the Greek world is defined (either positively or negatively) in opposition to regions at the *eschata*. In Herodotus, for example, the Ethiopians are reported to be the tallest and fairest of men (III.20), to have a 120-year life-span (III.23), and to feast from a "Table of the Sun" whose viands are spontaneously provided by the earth itself (III.18). Herodotus portrays these extraordinary and exotic Ethiopians as mocking the opulent gifts sent them by the Persians, thus representing these distant people as critics of the men

---

[19] Consider also the *Arimaspeia*, a poem by Aristeas of Proconnesus (*circa* sixth century BCE). According to Herodotus (IV.13), Aristeas says that he learned about the Arimaspians (one-eyed men of the far north) from the Issedones, who lived directly south of the Arimaspians. This poem idealized the Arimaspians (frr. 4, 5) and criticized the "pitiful" seafaring men of the interior (fr. 7). By locating himself at the edge of the known world – in the land of the Issedones – Aristeas claimed to have access to the regions of the *eschata*. Herodotus IV.27 attributes this account of the Arimaspians to the Scythians, who (he claims) have heard about these men from the Issedones (who live to the north of the Scythians). Note that Aristeas' poetic account anticipates later geographical texts that are more empirical in orientation. The gap between Aristeas' mythic account and those of the later geographers should be seen as a difference in degree rather than in kind, since the genre in the classical period was never exclusively empirical.

from the interior (III.20–4). This scene is a sort of "ethnologic satire," representing "the master races of the world humbled in the eyes of indifferent aliens."[20]

Consider, finally, the fourth-century historian Theopompus, who tells of people who live *beyond* the Ocean.[21] In brief, Theopompus describes a continent beyond the circle of Ocean where there are "many great cities, and where laws have been instituted which are the opposite of those laid down by us." He goes on to discuss, in some detail, the magnitude of this land, the great size of its animals, and its extraordinary human inhabitants (who are twice the size of those here and who live twice as long).[22] Theopompus thus sets forth a speculative and mythic geography that bears a direct resemblance to Herodotus' discourses on the "*eschatiai*." Theopompus portrays the cultures at the *eschata* as superior to those of ordinary humans, thus providing an external standard against which to measure the ordinary human world. In a similar fashion, his contemporary Ephorus, in a geographic text entitled *Europe*, praised the distant Scythians at the expense of the Greeks.[23]

To the extent that they deal with the *eschata*, geographic writers in the classical period speculate on earthly regions which are unseen and not fully known. They depict these unseen regions as both similar to and different from our own world. As we have seen, Herodotus and other geographic writers describe the places at the "edges" of the known world as alien and exotic, and even posit different temporalities for these distant lands (e.g. longer or reversed life spans, perfect weather, semi-divine inhabitants, etc.). They also suggest that the *eschata* provide a different scale of measure than the ones used in "this world." In many cases, the distant regions provide a

---

[20] Romm 1992, 59. Romm offers a detailed discussion of this and other examples of "ethnologic satire" on pp. 45–9, 67, and 71–4.

[21] Theopompus' story (which appears to derive from the discussion of marvels in book VIII of his *Philippica*) is described in detail by Aelian in the *Varia Historia* (III.18). See Flowers 1994, Appendix I and Clay and Purvis 1999 for useful analyses of the relation of Theopompus' tale to utopian discourses.

[22] Theopompus describes three cultures living in this distant land: the *Eusebeis*, the *Machimoi*, and the *Meropes*: the *Eusebeis* are free of disease, have an abundance of food that is obtained without toil, and are so just that the gods visit them in person; the *Machimoi* cannot be wounded by iron and possess piles of gold and silver; and the *Meropes*, when they eat from the tree of pleasure, grow younger and younger until they disappear. Theopompus has his *Machimoi* travel across the Ocean and come to the land of the Hyperboreans, who dwell in the far north: "but when they learned that these men were considered the very happiest in our world, they disdained to advance further, since they scorned the base and humble lives of the Hyperboreans." Here, the most blessed people dwelling in our world are judged and found wanting by the exotic men from beyond the Ocean. By conjuring cities even more distant than the Hyperboreans, Theopompus invites his readers to view all the peoples and places in the "known" world from the outside.

[23] Ephorus' idealizing account of the Scythians is described by Strabo (VII.3.9).

vantage point from which traditional ethical and cultural norms are assessed *ab extra*. Finally, geographic discussions of the *eschata* explore the nature and boundaries of the human – its relation to and difference from superhuman or subhuman beings.

Of course geographic treatises in this period were by no means confined to fanciful speculations on unseen worlds: what was seen and known was at least as important as what was unknown. By the fifth century, geographers were making a serious attempt to understand the scope and nature of the physical world, and to analyze the operations of material and bodily phenomena. Herodotus, for example, enters into a detailed investigation of the topography of the earth and the functioning of various natural phenomena (though he does not of course abandon mythic thinking). As Thomas has shown, Herodotus was directly influenced by the natural philosophers, medical writers, and other scientifically oriented thinkers of the sixth and fifth centuries.[24] Herodotus clearly attempted to develop a more empirical and methodological approach to geography (though the *History* as a whole is encyclopaedic, containing a broad spectrum of material ranging from empirical investigation to speculative inference to fanciful discussions of wonders and marvels).[25] On the one hand, Herodotus emphasizes the importance of *opsis*, criticizing other geographers for making dogmatic claims not based on visual evidence; indeed he makes a point of telling us when he has seen something for himself.[26] But he also draws inferences based on analogy, theorizing about what is unseen on the basis of what has been seen – or, to put it in his words, "gaining evidence for what is unknown from things that are clearly visible" (II.33).[27] For example, Herodotus speculates on the unseen source of the Nile based on an analogy with the source of the river Ister (II.33).

This use of analogical argument, as Thomas shows, is also prominent in medical and philosophical texts of the classical period, and is an important feature in the early development of empirical fields of study. Numerous classical thinkers investigating the body and/or the physical world – even those with a strong empirical bias – were seriously engaged in speculation

---

[24] Thomas 2000.

[25] Though, as Thomas observes (2000, ch. 5), Herodotus (like the *physiologoi*) often uses wonders as clues to the investigation of nature rather than as merely entrancing tales.

[26] See., e.g., II.99; cf. II.23. Many scholars have doubted the veracity of Herodotus' claims to have seen the things that he says that he saw. Even if Herodotus is not being completely honest, these claims make an important methodological point about the difference between evidence based on sight, hearsay, and speculation.

[27] Jouanna [1992]/1999, ch. 12, Thomas 2000, 200–12. For a discussion of the use of analogy in Greek thinkers and scientists, see Lloyd 1966 and 1987, 179–89.

about things that were unseen or invisible to the naked eye.[28] For these thinkers, the "invisible" was part of the physical world – it was a category for earthly phenomena that humans had not yet seen or were not in a good position to see. In his geographic discourses, Herodotus deals with things he has seen as well as with unseen or inaccessible physical phenomena. He carefully marks the boundaries between the seen and the unseen even as he extends his inquiry, by way of analogy and conjecture, into the unknown parts or features of the earth.

As I have suggested, when Plato sets forth an account of the *gē* that differs from those offered by "the men who customarily speak about the earth," he deliberately invokes the genre of geography. Although Socrates has already described the judgment and reincarnation of souls in the opening section of the story (107c–108c), he proceeds to situate this drama in the present world by describing the "true" nature of the earth and its many inhabitants. Socrates' account, of course, will contest earlier geographies: as he claims, the land between the pillars of Heracles and the river Phasis (in Colchis) – the "edges" of the earth in traditional geographies – is only one of many earthly regions (109a–b). In addition, Socrates locates this "known world" *beneath* the surface of the earth, making it part of an elaborate subterranean system. Interestingly, he keeps the river Ocean, which encircles his new and expanded earth (112e).[29] In this scheme, the *eschata* are located on the surface of the earth, where everything is superior to the things in our subterranean region (110a–b). On the earth's surface, the flora and the fauna are exceedingly beautiful and various, and the terrain is made of jewels and precious metals (110d–111a). The people there are free of disease and live much longer than those here; and they are also superior to us in sight, hearing, and wisdom (111b). Finally, these people can communicate directly with the gods, who actually dwell in the temples there (111b).[30] As in earlier geographies, the peoples and regions of the *eschata* provide

---

[28] Thomas 2000, 200–12; see also Lateiner 1986.

[29] Clearly, Plato departs from the *details* of his generic models in locating "our" region beneath the earth and in reconceiving the regions above us; but in representing the "distant" regions as heterochronic and heterotopic, Plato adheres to the central *principles* of ancient geographic thinking.

[30] Although the stories of the Golden Age and/or the Islands of the Blessed may seem to provide the primary models for Plato's "geography," one should note that many features that are central to both of these stories are conspicuously absent from Socrates' tale: an easy life without toil, the land's spontaneous and unstinting production of food, and the continuous merrymaking and feasting of the inhabitants (see, e.g., Hesiod *Works and Days* 109–19, 170–3; Pindar *Ol.* 2.61–7). I believe that the Greek geographic writings offer a more direct model for most of the key elements in Socrates' tale: the references to Earth, Ocean, and the Pillars of Heracles; to the region at the edges or distant parts of the earth; to the weather in these regions, their flora and fauna, and their abundance of gold and other precious goods; and, finally, to the life-span of its inhabitants and their physical and moral superiority to the people in "our world."

a different standard for measuring and judging ordinary human life. But Plato's account of the "earth" is more overtly prescriptive, since it urges us to leave our dark and muddy region and journey up to higher realms.

Geography, as we have seen, was a mode of discourse that posed specific questions and used particular modes of logic and analysis. Why, we must ask, did Plato incorporate this genre of discourse into his eschatology in the *Phaedo*? Certainly he did not do this in any of his other eschatologies. Clearly, Plato turned to this genre for specific reasons. First, Plato wanted to offer his own account of the "edges" of the earth. And, second, because geography was a field of inquiry that focused on the physical world – the world of bodies and material phenomena that were, at least in principle, accessible to the senses (especially that of vision).[31] In ancient geographies, as we have seen, an investigation of the "known world" (the *oikoumenē*) led to an inquiry into its "edges" (*peirata*) and the distant regions situated at these edges. This, in turn, confronted thinkers with the boundaries of the known and the question of how to extend their understanding into regions that were unseen and unknown. Plato uses the discourse of geography in the *Phaedo* because he is dealing with both known and unknown physical regions and exploring the connections between them. In fact, he even employs the method of analogical argument found in empirically oriented thinkers such as Herodotus, using the known and visible world as the basis for speculation on the invisible regions of the *eschata*: "what water and the sea are in our lives, air is in the lives of the aether-dwellers, and what the air is to us, aether is to them" (111a–b). Indeed Socrates twice uses the phrase *ana logon* to indicate that the life forms on the surface of the earth are "analogous" to ours, but more beautiful and perfect and pure (110d, 110d).

To be sure, Plato uses the genre of geography for his own purposes. But he preserves the basic discursive and conceptual features of this genre, which give him a way of articulating alternative modes of life. By entering into the discourse of geography, Plato draws a new map of the earth and invites us to reimagine our own place in the cosmos. It goes without saying that the myth in the *Phaedo* has an ethical orientation; but, unlike Plato's other eschatologies, it does not simply depict a mythic place of judgment and the fate of the souls after death. For it also speculates on the higher regions of the physical cosmos, which house the best bodily entities and beings. I have called these "aetherial" bodies, since they are located in the aether and are the most perfect of physical beings. These bodies are the objects of a form of philosophic *theoria* quite different from that discussed in the

---

[31] This raises the question of the relation of the myth to Socrates' repudiation of natural science earlier in the text. In my view, Plato offers in the myth a corrective to the solely materialistic approach by linking the physical to the metaphysical world.

last chapter – a *theoria* that does not focus exclusively on the Forms. The myth not only describes and discusses "aetherial" bodies, but identifies the contemplation of them as a form of *theoria*. This idea, which is set forth in rather sketchy terms in the *Phaedo*, will find its full explication in the cosmologies of the *Timaeus* and *Epinomis*.

I have already quoted the passage where Socrates says that when a human soul raises himself up to the aetherial region, he will "theorize" the "true heaven and the true light and the true earth" (109e–110a). Socrates also claims, quite strikingly, that "the earth is a spectacle for blessed spectators to see" (αὐτὴν ἰδεῖν εἶναι θέαμα εὐδαιμόνων θεατῶν, 111a). Socrates describes this "spectacle" in the most loving detail, viewing it both from the ground and from above. On the ground – that is, if one stands on the surface of the earth – the "blessed spectator" can see a full spectrum of bodily beings, animate and inanimate, all of which are wondrously pure and beautiful: the aetherial region as a whole is a "pure abode" (114c). This spectator sees "beautiful" things on earth (110c1–3; c6, d6–7, e2), and also looks up at the "true heaven" in the upper regions of the aether, where he sees the sun, moon, and stars "as they really are" (111c). This vision of the heavens is clearly marked as a serious philosophical activity. As Sedley suggests, "this [passage] is readily understood as symbolizing the contribution of astronomy to man's goal of narrowing the gap between himself and God."[32]

While the beings and entities on the upper earth are "aetherial" bodies, the stars are heavenly as well as aetherial. Indeed the myth clearly indicates that there is a difference between higher and lower bodies in the aetherial realm. The bodies of the souls dwelling on the surface of the earth are mortal, whereas there is no death in the heavens. Even in the aetherial realm, then, some bodies are more perfect than others. The very fact that the heavenly bodies inhabit a higher region of the aetherial realm indicates that they are superior to the aetherial bodies on earth, presumably because they are more perfect instantiations of the Forms.[33] Nonetheless, in spite of this differentiation in the aetherial realm, all of the bodies in this region

---

[32] Sedley 1989, 379.
[33] On the ontological status of the stars and heavenly bodies in the cosmos, see Hackforth [1955]/1972, 180 and Sedley 1989, 378–9. As Rowe (1993, 275–6) indicates, the hierarchical ordering of the bodily realm – with stars at the highest level, then the entities on the earth (in the realm of aether), in the hollows (in the realm of air), and in the sea (in the realm of water) – suggests that each level of the physical cosmos participates in the Forms in a different degree (he rightly adds that the myth does not provide "any further useful information about the form-particular hypothesis"). Cf. Nehamas (1999b, ch. 7), who argues that particulars are not "imperfect" approximations of Forms, claiming that there is no evidence that "particulars participate in the Form . . . in different degrees" (p. 145). I discuss this debate further in note 37 below.

are exceptionally pure and beautiful, and they are "theorized" by good and wise souls.

How, we may wonder, can a dialogue that repeatedly condemns sense perception and the bodily world assert, even in mythic terms, that "the earth is a spectacle for blessed spectators to see" (111a)? In the arguments that precede the myth, Socrates explicitly claims that sight and the other senses are not "accurate" (*akribeis*) or "clear" (*sapheis*, 65b) and that bodily entities – things that are "visible" and perceived by the senses – are always changing (78e–79d). Thus when the soul "makes use of the body for inquiry, either by seeing or hearing or any other of the senses . . . it is dragged by the body to things that never stay the same and it wanders and is confused and dizzy, like a drunken man" (79c). As Socrates asserts, the soul can only attain truth by inquiring "itself by itself" and "withdrawing from the senses, except insofar as their use is necessary, collecting and concentrating itself into itself" (79d, 83a). The man who is truly a philosopher

approaches each thing, as much as he can, with thought alone, not introducing sight into his reasoning or dragging in any of the other senses as an accompaniment to reason. Making use of pure thought, itself by itself, he endeavors to track down each constituent of reality, itself by itself, in complete purity, and he removes himself, as much as is possible, from the eyes and the ears and in general from the whole body; for he knows that, when the body is the soul's partner, it overwhelms the soul and does not allow it to attain truth and wisdom. (65e–66a)

This insistence on the need for the soul to "withdraw" and "separate itself" from the body, and to make use of reason alone, "itself by itself," seems to leave no role for vision or the senses to play in philosophic activity.

We find an important qualification of this extreme position, however, in the arguments for recollection (72e–77a). Socrates says there that it is the sensory perception of things in this world which leads us to remember the Forms; as he indicates, "we acquired [knowledge] before we were born and lost it at birth, but afterwards by the use of our senses (ταῖς αἰσθήσεσι χρώμενοι) regained the knowledge which we once possessed" (75e). When a person experiences sensory perceptions that trigger recollection, he will come to understand that all of the phenomena in the physical realm "strive" after one or another of the Forms even as they fall short of these absolute essences (75b). The properties of a physical object, then, remind the perceiver of a given Form by virtue of being like it at least in some small degree; at the same time, the soul becomes aware that this object is unlike the Form since it "falls short" of its true being.[34] The properties of things in

---

[34] To be sure, Socrates says that both "like and unlike things" can instigate recollection (74a), but it is clear that a physical object must have at least a minimal likeness to a Form in order to trigger recollection.

the physical world are impure and unstable and distant from reality – they are, after all, phenomena – but they do "participate" in the Forms. Indeed the Forms actually "cause" physical beings to have the qualities that they do by virtue of their "presence" (*parousia*) and "association" (*koinonia*) with them (100c–d).[35] As these passages indicate, sensory perception plays at least a small role in the activity of recollection. To be sure, the philosopher will use the senses only as a starting point for recollection. But Socrates' suggestion that we "make use of the senses" (75e) in the process of recollecting the Forms offers an important qualification of his vitriolic attacks on sensory perception elsewhere in the text.

According to Plato's metaphysical doctrines, the properties of bodily entities in this world both "participate in" and "fall short of" the Forms. It was open to Plato, then, to emphasize either the similarity or the dissimilarity between the physical properties and the Forms. In the dialectical arguments in the *Phaedo*, he focuses almost exclusively on dissimilarity – on the ontological deficiency of physical phenomena and the false picture that they present to the senses.[36] Indeed, even in the passages that offer a more positive view of the senses, Plato continues to emphasize the vast ontological gap between Forms and particulars, Being and becoming. The overall picture is one of radical unlikeness.

In the mythic account of the pure bodies dwelling in the aether, by contrast, Plato chooses to emphasize the similarity or *likeness* of certain particulars to the Forms. To be sure, he does not mention the Forms explicitly in the myth. But, if the properties of all bodies participate in and instantiate the Forms in different degrees, then the impure bodies in the hollows of the earth differ from the ones in the "pure abode" of the aether. According to this view, the properties of the bodies in the aether are better and purer instantiations of the Forms – and thus more "like" them – while those beneath the earth are poorer instantiations.[37] In fact, Plato not only draws a distinction between the bodies in the aether and those in the air (i.e. in our region), but he also differentiates between the ones in the air and those

---

[35] On Forms as "causes" in the *Phaedo*, see Vlastos 1971a; cf. Mueller (1998), who offers a persuasive argument that the Forms have causal efficacy.

[36] This is also true of the *Republic* (see, e.g., 476c).

[37] This is a matter of considerable controversy. For arguments in favor of a theory that particulars "approximate" the Forms in different degrees, see, e.g., Burnet 1911, n. ad 74a9 [1924]/1979, n. ad 6e4; Taylor 1929a, 187, Ross 1951, 23–5 and *passim*; Allen 1971 and Nehamas 1999b, ch. 7 reject this view. Vlastos (1981c) offers a useful discussion of the conception of "degrees of reality." My own position is similar to Crombie's (1963, 284–311; see also Patterson 1986, esp. 92–5). Crombie attacks the doctrine of "imperfect embodiment" but concedes that "this does not mean that Plato thought that there were all around us innumerable perfect instances of the intelligible natures." Rather, "the arguments which Plato uses do not commit him to the doctrine that it is in principle impossible that a physical object should ever perfectly embody a form" (p. 310).

in the sea: "in the sea things are corrupted by the brine, since nothing of any account grows there, and in general there is nothing that is perfect, but caves and sand and endless muck and mud . . . and there is nothing at all that is worthy to be compared to the beautiful things in our [aerial] world (πρὸς τὰ παρ᾽ ἡμῖν κάλλη)" (110a). Here, Plato affirms the presence of beautiful beings in our world and says that they are superior to the things in the sea. As this passage indicates, the properties of the bodies in our region are purer than those in the sea (though they fall short of those in the aetherial region). Even the beautiful bodies in our world, in short, bear some likeness to the Form of Beauty.

Here and elsewhere in the myth, Plato bears witness to the beauty in this world as well as the one above. He makes no mention of the powerful presence of beauty in the physical world in the rest of the dialogue (though he does identify a Form of Beauty that is the "cause" of beautiful particulars). But in the myth, he repeatedly remarks upon the beauty in our world, using it as the primary comparandum for the "more beautiful" bodies in the aether (110c, 110d, 110e). After the denunciations of the physical world in the earlier parts of the dialogue, one is amazed to find Plato exclaiming over the beauty of colors and jewels and gold and silver in our own world, not to mention his celebration of the "wondrous beauty" of the bodies and entities in the aether (110c).

In the aetherial realm, on the surface of the earth, people have the priv- ilege of viewing these wonderful spectacles all the time. These individuals have exceptional "sight and hearing and wisdom," and are even able to see the gods in their temples directly, by means of the senses (*aistheseis*, 111b). In this region, the senses are closely connected with wisdom.[38] The myth as a whole, then, celebrates the visual contemplation of perfect bod- ily instantiations of the Forms – this activity has a positive role to play in the philosophic life. Plato does not say precisely how the contemplation of these bodies affects the philosophic soul (ethically or epistemically), but he does suggest that this is a form of *theoria*, and thus opens the door to the notion of "theorizing" (exceptional) bodies. Although he does not offer a philosophical analysis of ontology or cosmology in this myth, he does put forth an idea that will be fully explicated in other dialogues – namely, that

---

[38] As Rowe (1993, 278) observes, if the aether dwellers' senses "are superior to ours, because of the greater purity of the medium . . . then the point Socrates made in his defence about the obstruction caused by the senses to the acquisition of φρόνησις (65a9–b6) will be less applicable; indeed now . . . the senses will even be an aid to its acquisition, since things are seen as they really are." Cf. Burger (1982, 196–7), who argues that the aether dwellers lack "noetic vision," since their cognition has been reduced to bodily sensation.

there are "perfect" bodies in the aether and the heavens which are "a sight for blessed spectators to behold."

In the *Phaedo*, Plato offers only a brief glimpse of the *theoria* of aetherial and heavenly bodies. This is not, of course, an alternative to metaphysical *theoria*; rather, this visual activity can accompany and reinforce the theoretical contemplation of the Forms. Since the aether dwellers are at a more advanced stage of virtue and wisdom than we are, their physical vision does not obstruct philosophic contemplation. On the contrary, they can see the physical world clearly, as it really is, presumably because they have a better understanding of the true nature of Forms and particulars. These souls are not perfect, but they dwell in a pure region of the cosmos where sensible and intellectual apprehension are mutually reinforcing. Their *theoria* of the beautiful and pure bodies in the aether goes hand in hand with their metaphysical theorizing of the Forms.

PHAEDRUS: THEORIZING THE *AGALMATA* OF BEAUTY

"Whither and whence?" asks Socrates at the opening of the *Phaedrus*, thus thematizing the journey in the very first line. Phaedrus answers that he is "going for a walk outside the city wall"; he induces Socrates to follow him by promising to share a brilliant speech of Lysias on love (227a–c). When Socrates agrees to follow him into unknown parts, Phaedrus exclaims:

> You, my divine friend, are the most outlandish man (ἀτοπώτατος). Indeed you seem exactly like a stranger being guided around (ξεναγουμένῳ) rather than a native to the region (ἐπιχωρίῳ). For you do not journey abroad – leaving the city and crossing the border – nor do you even go outside the city walls. (230c–d)

Socrates, as it seems, is not only *atopos* but a *xenos* in his own region. While Phaedrus attributes Socrates' unfamiliarity with the locale to the fact that he never leaves the city, it soon becomes clear that his *atopia* is due to his exploration of higher regions. As scholars have observed, the physical journey enacted by Phaedrus and Socrates proleptically anticipates the journey of the souls articulated in Socrates' second speech.[39] In that speech, Plato will replay the themes of journeying and seeing in a metaphysical key.

In the dramatic action of the dialogue, Plato emphasizes another theme that is prominent in Socrates' second speech – that of blindness and vision. Note, in particular, that Socrates covers his head (and thus blinds himself) while giving his first speech (237a), and then uncovers his head for the

---

[39] See, e.g., Griswold [1986]/*1996*, 33–4, Ferrari 1987, 21–5; K. Morgan 2000, 228–9.

second, palinodic speech. In the latter passage, he explicitly gestures towards Stesichorus, who was blinded for composing an impious poem, but regained his sight by writing a "palinode" retracting his original discourse (243a–b). Like Stesichorus, Socrates delivers a second speech that "takes back" the claims of the first; although Socrates is not of course blinded as a punishment for the first speech, he effectively blinds himself by covering his head. The act of uncovering his head for the second speech clearly signals that his vision has been restored.

Socrates' second speech in the *Phaedrus* contains Plato's most elaborate "story of the soul," beginning with its early, pre-incarnate history and moving to its sojourn on earth. In this speech, Socrates claims that all human souls beheld the Forms before incarnation, though some got a better look than others. At that time, souls were winged and could fly up to the edge of the cosmos; some could even "journey outside" the universe (ἔξω πορευθεῖσαι) and station themselves (ἔστησαν) on its outer surface (247b–c). The revolution of the cosmos then carried them around, and they beheld the Forms from this position. Here, the souls "journey" as *theoroi* to the edge of heaven and take their seats (as it were) on its outer edge, like spectators. At this point, the souls enjoy the contemplation of the Forms:

The mind . . . of every soul which is destined to receive (δέξασθαι) that which befits it rejoices in seeing Being (ἰδοῦσα . . . τὸ ὄν) for a time and, by theorizing (θεωροῦσα) the truth, it is nourished and made happy until the revolution brings it again to the same place. (247d–e)

The superior human souls, then, "receive" what is fitting, namely the vision and knowledge of the Forms.[40] After incarnation, though the souls have lost their wings and forgotten their vision of truth, the philosophic soul can develop the capacity to "recollect" the Forms and to theorize them again while dwelling on earth. Indeed, even a proto-philosopher can experience a fleeting recollection of the Form of Beauty when beholding exceptional beauty in the physical world.[41]

Socrates proceeds to describe the philosophic person encountering a beautiful boy on earth. As he gazes with love on the boy, he is "driven out of his mind" (ἐκπλήττονται, 250a), and perhaps the best word for

---

[40] Socrates goes on to identify these "realities" as the Forms of Justice, Temperance, etc.; he also says that these are "blessed" and "holy sights" (μακάριαι θέαι, 247a; ὧν τότε εἶδον ἱερῶν, 250a), thus emphasizing that the Forms are divine and that the viewing of these beings is a kind of religious revelation. This is in keeping with the many comparisons in this speech of the activity of philosophic theorizing to the revelation at the Eleusinian Mysteries (see chapter 2).

[41] For an excellent discussion of Plato's theory of recollection (and of the various scholarly interpretations of this theory), see Scott 1995, chs. 1–2.

his condition thereafter is *permeable*. For when the philosophic lover sees the boy, he is the recipient of a variety of influxes: "nourishment" from the Forms "flows in upon" him (ἐπιρρυείσης δὲ τῆς τροφῆς, 251b5); he "receives the stream of beauty in through the eyes" (δεξάμενος γὰρ τοῦ κάλλους τὴν ἀπορροὴν διὰ τῶν ὀμμάτων, 251b1–2); and, as he gazes upon the beauty of the beloved, his soul "receives particles from there that come at him in a stream" (ἐκεῖθεν μέρη ἐπιόντα καὶ ῥέοντ'. . . δεχομένη, 251c). In these passages, Plato portrays the soul as the receptacle of various streams that "flow into it" and "fill" it.[42] As Nussbaum observes, the lover "receives a mysterious substance that begins by being light, but transforms itself into fluid." Indeed, as she claims, the rational part of the soul is here portrayed as "sexual" in the sense that it is "open and receptive."[43] One could argue that, when it beholds beauty, the soul plays a role analogous to that of the female partner or passive male partner in sexual intercourse (a point made explicit in the *Republic*).[44]

The philosophic lover sees the beauty of the beloved, and he is instantly transported back to the realm of the Forms. The effect is, quite literally, staggering. When he recollects the Form of Beauty, "his memory is carried back to the true nature of Beauty," and he immediately feels a powerful sense of awe and reverence (254b).[45] Thus begins the transformation or the μεταβολή (251a) that the soul undergoes as a result of the experience of recollection. As the philosopher stands again in the presence of Being, he begins to regrow his wings, and the very boundaries of his psyche are radically altered and transformed. It is this transformation that enables him to love his beautiful boyfriend and yet behave with restraint and self-control. The recollection of the vision of the Forms transforms the lover

---

[42] See also 251e, where the lover is "irrigated by the streams of desire" (ἐποχετευσαμένη ἵμερον). At 255c, the beloved receives the "overflow" of the effluences that strike the lover (ἡ μὲν εἰς αὐτὸν ἔδυ, ἡ δ' ἀπομεστουμένου ἔξω ἀπορρεῖ); and at 253a, the philosophic lovers are said to "draw the liquid of inspiration from Zeus like the bacchantes" and to "pour this out over the soul of the beloved" (κἂν ἐκ Διὸς ἀρύτωσιν ὥσπερ αἱ βάκχαι, ἐπὶ τὴν τοῦ ἐρωμένου ψυχὴν ἐπαντλοῦντες). This last passage cited is difficult to construe; Hackforth (1952, 100n. 2) seems right in suggesting that "[t]he point is that in both sorts of divine madness [i.e. that of the bacchant and that of the lover] the immediate subject of possession 'infects' another or others"; see also Carson 1986, 157. On Plato's representation of love and the body, see Foley 1998, 44–51.

[43] Nussbaum 1986, 216–17. Nussbaum is wrong to claim here that the intellect is, in the *Republic*, "purely active" and not "sexual" or "open and receptive" (as it is, she claims, in the *Phaedrus*). As I argued in ch. 3, the rational part of the soul in the *Republic* is explicitly described as sexually receptive.

[44] See Nightingale 1995, 160.

[45] The most common words for "reverence" in this passage are *sebesthai* and *aideisthai* (250e, 251a, 252a, 254e), but Plato also uses *deima* (251a) and its cognate *deidō* (254c, 254e) and *thambos* (254c). As Prier shows (1989, 87–91, 107), *thambos* and *sebas* are closely related to *thauma*.

from a predatory, lustful man to a person who sees divine Beauty in physical particulars: his actions are governed not only by truth but also by feelings of awe and reverence for its sacred presence. Instead of lurching forward in an aggressive and rapacious fashion, the philosopher stands in awe before the Form of the Beautiful.

As in the *Republic*, Plato describes theoretical activity as a journey to "see" the Forms which radically transforms the philosopher and governs his behavior on earth. But the *Phaedrus* differs from the *Republic* in important ways. As I will argue, the depiction of the activity of *theoria* in the *Phaedrus* contains a number of elements that align it with the *Timaeus*, *Laws* x, and *Epinomis*.[46] In the *Phaedrus*, Socrates articulates some basic principles of cosmology that will be given a full treatment in these latter texts. This account gives a new and very prominent role to the gods, who not only inhabit and order the universe but also serve as moral exemplars for humans. In addition, the *Phaedrus* gives the beautiful physical body an almost divine status, thus bringing it closer to the Form of Beauty. Visual perception, at least when it beholds beauty, now plays a very constructive role in the philosophic life. For, when the philosopher sees the beautiful body of his beloved, he sees a near-divine *"agalma."* He theorizes a body of near-heavenly beauty right here on earth. Finally, this text highlights the philosopher's experience of reverence and awe as he beholds the "divine" Forms. As we will see, this feeling of reverence has a direct impact on the philosopher's actions in the human world. The *Phaedrus*, then, offers an account of the link between contemplation and action very different from that of the *Republic*.

In the *Phaedrus*, Socrates articulates a number of ideas that are not found in the *Symposium*, *Phaedo*, or *Republic*. First, he defines the soul as "self-moving motion": in contrast to physical entities, which cannot move themselves but must be moved by forces external to them, the soul is a being that moves itself (245c–e). Soul, in fact, not only moves itself but also serves as the "first principle of motion" in the physical cosmos. For it is the *"archē"* or source of the motions of bodily entities in the universe.[47] As Socrates explains, "all soul has the care of all that which is soulless, and it

---

[46] I do not discuss *Laws* x in this book, since it makes no explicit reference to *theoria*. It offers arguments for the existence and goodness of the gods, but does not deal with epistemology (except in the brief passage in book xii dealing with the Nocturnal Council, which is highly general and makes no mention of *theoria*). For a discussion of the intended audience of the *Laws*, see Nightingale 1993 and 1999b.

[47] On Plato's definition of the soul as the "self-moving motion" which is the *archē kineseōs* in the cosmos, see Demos 1968. Demos offers a useful discussion of the different "proofs" of the latter claim offered in the *Phaedrus* and the *Laws*.

pervades all of heaven, sometimes in one form and sometimes in another" (246b). When a soul is divine, it "pervades the highest regions and orders the whole cosmos" (πάντα τὸν κόσμον διοικεῖ, 246c). Divine souls regulate the physical universe, and thus play a key role in both the cosmology and the psychology of the *Phaedrus*. The divine soul is "beautiful, wise, and good" (246e) – it is an epistemically and ethically perfect being. Importantly, the gods derive their divinity from the perfect apprehension of the Forms, and thus the human soul who cultivates this apprehension can itself become godlike. As Socrates puts it, the philosopher gets "as close as possible, via recollection, to those things by being close to which the gods are divine" (249c). As in the *Symposium*, *Phaedo*, and *Republic*, the Forms are "divine."[48] But the *Phaedrus* brings another class of divine beings into the discussion of *theoria*, namely, the perfected souls of the gods.[49] It locates these souls within the universe and gives them the role of "ordering" the physical cosmos. We can infer that those parts of the physical universe which the gods control and order are good (as good as it is possible for a material entity to be). Socrates says that the upper regions of the cosmos are the dwelling-place of the gods (246d) and contain "many blessed sights and pathways" (247a). This part of the universe is superior to the earthly region where humans dwell, and is "closer" to the "*hyperouranios*" region of the Forms (ontologically speaking, since the Forms are outside of space and time).

Here we have the beginnings of a true cosmology, though Plato does not develop these claims in any detail. He clearly indicates that the gods are immanent in the physical cosmos, but does not discuss the nature or the status of the celestial regions that they inhabit. The fact that the gods, when they engage in the *theoria* of the Forms, stand on the outer edge of the heaven and are carried around by its "revolution" (247c) would suggest that their contemplative activity is connected with the circular motion of the fixed stars. But Plato stops short of drawing a direct link between the circular motion of the stars and the activity of divine *nous* (as he will do in the *Timaeus* and *Laws* x). Nor does he suggest that the practice of

---

[48] In the latter part of the *Phaedrus*, Plato sets forth a different conception of dialectic than that found in the *Republic* – the method of "Collection and Division" (also featured in the *Sophist* and *Statesman*). Some scholars claim that this change provides evidence for Plato's departure from the theory of Forms as it is set forth in the "middle" dialogues. The alleged changes in Plato's doctrines are not pertinent to my argument. Likewise, the fact that the *Republic* and *Phaedrus* offer rather different accounts of the psyche is not relevant here, since I am only concerned with the rational part of the soul and its contemplation of metaphysical reality.

[49] Obviously, gods are mentioned in the other dialogues, but they do not play a central role in those texts (which is accounted for, at least in part, by the fact that those texts do not contain cosmologies).

philosophy includes the contemplation of the heavenly bodies of the stars (though we are told that there are "blessed sights" – μακάριαι θέαι – in the heavens, 247a). Thus Plato does not draw any explicit connection between metaphysical *theoria* and the *theoria* of heavenly motion in the cosmos. But he does lay the groundwork for this connection. And he makes a significant move in this direction in his discussion of the philosophic lover's vision of the beautiful, near-divine body of his beloved.

In the *Phaedrus* myth, Plato discusses the visual perception of beauty in some detail. In particular, he links this bodily perception directly to the soul's "vision" of the Form in its preincarnate state: "beauty was radiant to see (ἦν ἰδεῖν λαμπρόν) at that time when the souls, with a blessed company, saw the blessed sight and vision" (μακαρίαν ὄψιν τε καὶ θέαν) (250b). As Socrates goes on to explain, since the Form of Beauty "shone with light (ἔλαμπεν) among those visions, when we came to" earth we found it shining most clearly through the clearest of our senses" (αὐτὸ διὰ τῆς ἐναργεστάτης αἰσθήσεως τῶν ἡμετέρων στίλβον ἐναργέστατα) (250c–d). Socrates makes a very striking claim here: that we can "clearly" see the Form of Beauty "shining" when we look at beautiful bodies in the physical world. This comes as a surprise, given Plato's repeated assertion in other dialogues that the senses are deceptive and unclear. In this text, we find an exception to this negative view of the senses. For, although no "clear image" (ἐναργὲς εἴδωλον) of the other Forms "comes through our sight" (εἰς ὄψιν ἰόν), "beauty alone has this privilege" since it is "the most clearly visible" (ἐκφανέστατον) of the Forms (250d–e). This is because "there is no light in the earthly copies" (ἐν τοῖς τῇδε ὁμοιώσασιν) of the other Forms (250b), whereas the Form of Beauty radiates its own light. Beautiful bodies on earth, then, offer a "clear image" of the Form of Beauty, which is apprehended by the sense of sight. As these passages indicate, the visual apprehension of the beautiful body offers – at least to a philosophic soul – a simultaneous "vision" of the Form.

What, then, is the ontological status of the beautiful body? Plato does not offer a straightforward answer to this question in the *Phaedrus*. But he does address it indirectly, in his description of the relationship between the philosophic lover and his beloved. The faculty of vision plays a leading role in this drama, since it is the sight of the beautiful boy which first attracts the lover and which leads to his recollection of the Form of Beauty. Plato's drama takes us inside the human soul, where we view the pathology of a philosophic love affair from within. Socrates has already described the inner structure of the human soul, comparing the rational part to a charioteer and the irrational parts to a white horse and a dark horse. He now relates what happens when the philosophically inclined lover comes into contact with the boy he loves. "When the charioteer sees the beloved face of the boy (ἰδὼν τὸ ἐρωτικὸν ὄμμα), his whole soul is warmed by the sight" (αἰσθήσει, 253e). The vision of the beautiful boy gets the whole soul involved, generating disparate desires within it. These lead to a conflict between the charioteer and the dark horse, which are pulled in two directions by this apprehension of bodily beauty. When the lustful horse drags the lover up to the beloved, aiming for sexual contact, the charioteer sees the face of the boy, "which is flashing like lightning" (τὴν ὄψιν τὴν τῶν παιδικῶν ἀστράπτουσαν, 254b). The beauty of the boy flashes with light because of the special radiance of the Form of Beauty. Thus the physical sight of the boy's beauty offers to the mind an immediate glimpse of the Form: "when the charioteer looks upon [the boy], his memory is carried back to the true nature of beauty, and he sees it again standing together with Temperance upon a holy pedestal" (254b).

This close connection between bodily beauty and the Form of Beauty confers a special status on the beautiful body. The body which possesses this beauty is identified as an *agalma* (251a, 252d–e). An *agalma* is no ordinary image but a "sacred image" of a god. In the classical period, the word *agalma* referred exclusively to the statues and images of gods.[50] As sacred images, *agalmata* were featured in every religious festival and were regularly housed in temples and sacred precincts. They were one of the most important "spectacles" seen by the traditional *theoros*. In fact, the *agalmata* of the gods played a key role in the "ritualized visualization" that characterized theoric viewing at religious sanctuaries. It is significant, then, that Plato compares the beautiful body not just to an *eikōn* or "image" but to an *agalma* or "sacred image."

Socrates offers a vivid description of the lover's apprehension of the *agalma* of Beauty:

When the lover sees a godlike face or the form of a body that is a good imitation (εὖ μεμιμημένον) of the beautiful, at first he shudders and some of the former awe takes hold of him; then, as he looks at it he reveres him like a god (ὡς θεὸν σέβεται) and, if he didn't fear that he would be thought completely mad, he would sacrifice to the boy as though to an *agalma* and a god (ὡς ἀγάλματι καὶ θεῷ). (251a)

---

[50] As Lewis and Stroud (1979, 193) point out, in the archaic period the term *agalma* referred to a broader range of statues and images, whereas in the classical period it designated only sacred images. On *agalmata* and sacred images, see Vernant 1991, ch. 8; Gernet [1968]/1981, 73–111. For a discussion of *agalmata* or statues of victors in the games in the archaic period (which possessed a talismanic quality akin to the images of gods), see Kurke 1993. Osborne (1994b) analyzes the "*agalmata*" of *korai* (and their viewing audiences) in the archaic period; Steiner (2001) offers a wide-ranging discussion of statues in the archaic and classical periods.

The beautiful body of the boy, then, is an image or "imitation" of the Form of Beauty; since the Form is divine, its image is sacred and closely linked with divinity. It is for this reason that the lover is inclined to offer sacrifice to the boy as though to "an *agalma* and a god."[51]

As Vernant observes in his discussion of *agalmata* and divine images, the purpose of such an image "is to establish real contact with the world beyond, to actualize it, to make it present, and thereby to participate intimately in the divine; yet by the same move, it must also emphasize what is inaccessible and mysterious in divinity, its alien quality, its otherness." In other words, the sacred image functions "to inscribe absence in presence, to insert the other, the elsewhere, into our familiar universe . . . revealing the elsewhere in what is given to view." But, as Vernant adds,

> In its attempt to construct a bridge, as it were, that will reach towards the divine, the idol must also at the same time mark its distance from that domain . . . It has to stress the incommensurability between the sacred power and everything that reveals it to the eyes of mortals.[52]

The *agalma*, in short, both is and is not divine – unlike an ordinary image, it is sacred and in some sense replete with divinity, yet it is not itself a god. We see this playing out in Plato's drama, which treats the body of the boy as a near-divine being that demands reverence and religious respect. As Socrates says again later in the passage, the lover "adorns [the boy] like an *agalma*, as though he were a god" (252d–e).

As I have suggested, the *Phaedrus* gives a positive role to the sense of sight, at least when used by the philosophic soul. In this dialogue, the visual perception of beauty triggers the immediate recollection of the Form. Interestingly, the soul does not experience uncertainty or confusion when it has a visual perception of the beautiful body of the beloved. The lover is quite certain that the boy is beautiful, and is clearly struck by the likeness of this bodily beauty to the Form of Beauty. Since the beautiful body is a "clear image" and, indeed, an *agalma* of the Form, it does not lead the soul into confusion. On the contrary, it is precisely because this beauty is such an

---

[51] Though this phrase seems to conflate the god and his sacred image, the two are of course not identical. Note that statues are thematized earlier in the dialogue, where Phaedrus claims that if Socrates delivers a better and completely different speech than Lysias, he will set up a statue of Socrates and himself in Delphi ("like the nine archons" 235d); if he delivers a better and more copious speech, Phaedrus says, he will erect a statue of Socrates at Olympia next to those dedicated (in the Temple of Hera) by the Cypselids (236a–b). Since these are statues of human beings, they are not (in this period) *agalmata* (cf. *Symposium* 216e–217a, where Alcibiades claims that Socrates has "*agalmata*" inside him that are wondrous and divine"). For an excellent discussion of statues in the *Phaedrus*, see K. Morgan 1994.

[52] Vernant 1991, 153.

extraordinary instantiation of the Form that it leads the viewer to experience recollection. There is no suggestion that the lover experiences confusion or aporia when he beholds the boy.[53] He does, to be sure, experience a kind of madness – the *mania* of a soul being transformed by *eros* and truth. But he is in no way uncertain about the beauty of the boy: his vision is clear and accurate. Of course he will have to conduct a lengthy philosophical investigation to discover the ontological difference between bodily beauty and the Form; he is, after all, only beginning a life of philosophy and must engage in serious intellectual labor if he is to achieve knowledge and truth. As he advances in philosophy, the lover will confront epistemic *aporia* and deal with the disparity between the one and the many, the Form and the particulars. But it is the clear image of Beauty in the physical world which turns this lover into a philosopher.[54]

This differs from Plato's account in other dialogues, where he claims that the senses cannot offer anything clear or certain. As we have seen, the arguments in the *Phaedo* set forth a quite negative account of sensory perception. At best, the senses serve as an aid to recollection insofar as they present the soul with something that announces itself as ontologically deficient; indeed the confusion and unclarity of sense data are what drive the philosopher to search for the reality behind the appearances. The instability and unreliability of sense perception lead him into uncertainty; and the discomfort of uncertainty pushes him to seek clarity and truth in the intelligible realm. We find a similar position in the *Republic*, where Socrates says that "some of our sensory experiences do not provoke the mind toward inquiry, since they are adequately judged by the senses, whereas others always invite the mind to inquire insofar as the sensory perception produces nothing that can be trusted" (523a–b). For example, when the senses report to the soul that something is both hard and soft, "the soul experiences *aporia*" since it cannot understand how the same thing can be both hard and soft (524a). This also occurs in the perception of number, for the same thing can appear to be both one and many. "But if something opposite to it is always seen at the same time, so that it no more appears to be one than the opposite of one, there would then be need of something to judge the matter, and the soul would be compelled to experience aporia and to inquire, and to arouse the thought within it, and to ask what the one is in itself . . ." (524e–525a). The soul, then, enters into a state of uncertainty and *aporia*, which leads it towards the study of metaphysical entities and ends in the

---

[53] Though he does feel *aporia* in the face of the fluctuations of pleasure and pain caused by the sprouting of the wings of his soul (251d–e).
[54] Griswold [1986]/1996, 121–33.

"vision of being" (ἐπὶ τὴν τοῦ ὄντος θέαν, 525a). In short, it is the sensory perceptions which generate conflicting interpretations that incite the soul to the practice of philosophy. As in the *Phaedo*, the soul cannot settle this matter except by turning away from the confusion of the senses.

In the *Phaedrus*, Plato sets forth a quite different idea – an idea which was adumbrated but not developed in the *Phaedo* myth: that seeing a beautiful body plays a vital role in the activity of philosophic *theoria*.[55] In beholding the beautiful *agalma*, the lover contemplates a body that is near-divine in its beauty. We are one step away from the notion of "theorizing" a heavenly body. To be sure, Plato is using mythic discourse in the *Phaedrus* (as Socrates himself points out at the end of his speech, 257a). But this myth offers a detailed account of the soul and a serious introduction to cosmology. It thus anticipates the cosmological discussions in other Platonic dialogues.

Before turning to those texts, I want to look at the way that this kind of *theoria* affects *praxis*. As we have seen, when the charioteer beholds the beautiful body of the boy, he is immediately led to recollect the Form of Beauty, which he sees "standing together with Temperance upon a holy pedestal" (254b). He reacts to this vision as though he has come face to face with a divine being: "when he sees this he is stricken with awe and falls backwards in reverence (ἰδοῦσα δὲ ἔδεισέ τε καὶ σεφθεῖσα ἀνέπεσεν ὑπτία), and he is thus compelled (ἠναγκάσθη) to pull the reins back so violently that both horses are brought down to their haunches" (254b–c). Here, the *theoria* of the Form of Beauty produces both a reaction and, in turn, an action. The lover reacts with a powerful sense of reverence and awe, and these feelings play a significant role in governing his behavior: they "compel" him to stop in his tracks and jerk back the reins. In recollecting and "theorizing" the Form, the lover apprehends the nature of Beauty. But the activity of *theoria* includes not only rational understanding but also a direct sense of the divinity of the Form. When it "sees" the Form, the soul of the lover confronts a divine reality that elicits feelings of religious awe and reverence.[56]

The experience of reverence directly affects the lover's actions. In particular, this response to the Form translates into a reverential attitude towards the beloved: when the lover recollects the Form, "some of that former awe takes hold of him (τι τῶν τότε ὑπῆλθεν αὐτὸν δειμάτων), and then, as he looks at [the boy], he reveres him like a god" (ὡς θεὸν σέβεται, 251a).

---

[55] See, e.g., Nussbaum 1986, ch. 7, Griswold [1986]/1996, ch. 3.
[56] Note that the forward motion of eros is checked by the arresting experience of *sebas* (which does not mean that eros disappears; quite the contrary).

This encounter with the divine Form has a powerful impact on the lover, leading him to restrain himself and approach the boy in a completely different way from the lustful lover – in a reverential fashion, as if the boy were sacred. Plato returns, again and again, to the reverence that the lover experiences as he theorizes the Form through the body of the boy (250e, 251a, 252a, 254c, 254e, 251a, 254c, 254e). This feeling or *pathos* accompanies the rational apprehension of the Form, and it plays a major role in the redirection or turning of the philosopher away from bodily desires and towards reality. Awe and reverence do important work in the ethical sphere, since they directly influence the philosopher's values and actions. Of course Plato offers here only a partial account of philosophic *praxis*, since the *Phaedrus* focuses on the transformation of the soul of the budding philosopher rather than on the more advanced stages of philosophy. But we should take seriously its suggestion that the lover experiences a profound sense of awe when encountering the Forms – an awe that he also feels towards the boy who is the *agalma* of Beauty. As in other dialogues, the philosophic soul will "imitate" or liken himself to the divine (see, e.g., 252c–d). But, in the *Phaedrus*, this activity produces a soul that does not turn away from the physical world in its entirety but rather finds something sacred in it. Thus, after repeatedly recollecting the Form of Beauty while gazing on the boy, "the soul of the lover follows the beloved in reverence and awe" (αἰδουμένην τε καὶ δεδιυῖαν, 254e).

The *Phaedrus* contains a vivid picture of the metaphysical *theoria* of the Forms, and in this regard resembles other middle dialogues dealing with theoretical contemplation. But it differs from these texts in some key ways. For, in addition to discussing the basic relationship of the soul and the Forms, it locates the soul within the physical cosmos – a cosmos that is divinely ordered. As the self-moving motion that initiates the motion of bodily entities, the soul is the primary causal power in the physical universe. Correlatively, the cosmos and its bodies – both in the heavens and on earth – are the site and the sign of psychic virtue and vice. Bodies that exhibit orderly motion point to the presence of divine guidance, whereas those that produce disorder are associated with the souls of humans and animals. The gods, then, play a key role in this cosmological myth. These perfect souls engage in both contemplative and practical activities: they gaze on the Forms "outside" the revolution of the heavens, but they also control the motion of the cosmos and the bodies within it, making them move in circular and orderly revolutions. These divine souls serve as a model for humans to follow. Rather than "imitating" the Forms, as the philosopher did in the *Republic*, the philosophic soul in the *Phaedrus* imitates the gods (252c–d): he develops his capacity to contemplate the Forms and also learns how to control his bodily impulses and engage in virtuous action.

The fact that the physical universe is governed by divine and rational beings gives it a more positive status, in spite of its ontological distance from the Forms. In addition to identifying the heavenly bodies as divine and "blessed sights" (247a), Plato recognizes the presence of bodies of near-heavenly beauty right here on earth. Of course he still subscribes to the doctrine that physical particulars fall short of the Forms in which they participate. But, in this text, Plato chooses to emphasize the likeness of certain particulars to at least one of the Forms, namely, the Form of Beauty. It is for this reason that he focuses on the beautiful body that contains a "clear image" of the Form. The physical world, then, is not just a region of uncertainty and unlikeness (to borrow Augustine's term); and, correlatively, the senses are not necessarily misleading and deceptive. As we have seen, vision has a positive role to play in the philosophic activity of *theoria*. In stark contrast to the other middle dialogues (with the possible exception of the myth in the *Phaedo*), the philosophic lover in the *Phaedrus* theorizes the beautiful body and the Form of Beauty at the same time. The beauty of the body is not located at the lowest rung of a tall ladder, soon to be transcended in the pursuit of the vision of the Forms. Rather, the lover in the *Phaedrus* sees the Form's radiance in the *agalma* of the beloved. It is as though the person still living in the cave were able to recollect the Form of Beauty while looking at an exceptionally beautiful image projected on its wall – as though the shadowy image could (somehow) shine.

TIMAEUS: VISIBLE GODS

The *Timaeus* offers a "likely account" of the cosmos and the human place within it (which is first called a *muthos* and later a *logos*).[57] At the opening of this discourse, Timaeus describes the creation of the universe. In the beginning was the gaze:

When an artificer (*demiourgos*) keeps his gaze permanently fixed (βλέπων ἀεί) on that which is uniform [i.e. the Forms], using a model (*paradeigma*) of this kind, and in this way creates his work in shape and in quality, the object will necessarily

---

57 *Timaeus* 29d, 48d. For a discussion of Plato's (less than consistent) use of the distinction between *muthos* and *logos*, see Brisson 1982, Lloyd 1987, 181–3, and K. Morgan 2000, 156–84 and *passim*. On the genre and/or "likely" discourse of the *Timaeus*, see Hadot 1983, Brague 1985, Ashbaugh 1988, K. Morgan 2000, 271–81.

be beautiful; but when he gazes at the world of becoming, and uses a model in this realm, the object will not be beautiful . . . Which of these models did the Creator use in constructing the universe? . . . If this cosmos is beautiful and its artificer (demiurge) is good, his gaze was fixed on that which is eternal (πρὸς τὸ ἀΐδιον ἔβλεπεν). (28a–29a)

The Demiurge, then, gazes at the Forms and creates the world. From this primal act of *theoria* comes the cosmos (with its body and soul) and, later, divine and human beings (each with its respective body and soul). All of these souls – the World-Soul and the individual souls of the gods and humans – have the capacity to theorize the cosmos itself and the intelligible world on which it is patterned.

To understand Plato's account of *theoria* in the *Timaeus*, we must first consider the basic cosmological principles in this text.[58] First of all, like the *Phaedrus* and *Laws* x, the *Timaeus* asserts that soul is self-moving motion, and that it is the "primary" causal principle in the created universe.[59] The entities in the physical world, by contrast, are secondary causes, since they lack reason and can only generate motion by being moved by others (46de).[60] The primary causes, in short, are those that "together with *nous*, are artificers (*demiourgoi*) of things that are beautiful and good" whereas the secondary causes are "devoid of intelligence" and always produce "accidental and disorderly effects" (46e). Soul, then, is not just a self-moving metaphysical being but a demiourgic power in the physical cosmos. But

---

[58] The question of the appropriate hermeneutic strategy to adopt for the *Timaeus* (literal vs. allegorical), which leads to the question of the relation between the *Phaedrus*, *Timaeus*, and the *Laws* x, has generated a debate that goes back to antiquity. Mohr (1985, 116–18) summarizes three basic approaches to this problem. One attempts to reconcile the three dialogues by rejecting a literal reading of the precosmic period depicted in the *Timaeus* and denying the existence of motions independent of psychic causes described in that text (see, e.g. Cornford [1937]/1952, Skemp 1942, and Cherniss 1944 and [1954]/1977). A second and third group read the *Timaeus* literally, but the former aims to unify the dialogues by suggesting that soul is the cause of all motion in the created universe ([early] Vlastos [1939]/1965, Hackforth 1936, Easterling 1967, and Robinson 1970), whereas the latter – which I endorse – argues that Plato was simply not consistent in his views on physical causation and the soul's role therein ([later] Vlastos 1965, Herter 1957, Mohr 1985). Cf. Taylor (1928), who argues that the *Timaeus* is an amalgam of "Pythagorean religion and mathematics with Empedoclean biology" which is not "distinctively Platonic" (p. 11). Gadamer 1980 and Ashbaugh 1988 probe more deeply into the hermeneutic problems posed by this dialogue.

[59] 37b5, 46d–e, 77e5–c3, 77c4–5, 89a1–3, 46d–e. The *Phaedrus* and *Laws* x, however, assert that soul is the primary source of all bodily motion in the universe, whereas the *Timaeus* indicates that there was motion in the pre-cosmic chaos which preceded the formation of the world. Whether or not it is the source of *all* motion, soul is clearly the primary causal principle in the created universe.

[60] "They are thought by most men not to be the auxiliary causes (συναίτια), but the actual causes (αἴτια) of all things, because they freeze and heat, and contract and dilate, and the like. But they are not so, for they are incapable of reason or intellect; and the only being which can properly have *nous* is the invisible soul, whereas fire and water, earth and air are all visible bodies" (46d).

souls come in different varieties: only the divine souls have perfected noetic capacities and are therefore able to create beauty, order, and goodness in the material universe.

Thus far, the account of the cosmos resembles that of the *Phaedrus*. But the *Timaeus* goes much further. Let us consider, first, the role of *nous* in the universe. According to Timaeus, *nous* is "present in" the cosmos by virtue of being "present in" soul, for "*nous* cannot be present in anything which is devoid of soul" (30b). Timaeus also draws an explicit link between *nous* and circular motion (34a, cf. 89a).[61] The absence of intelligence, moreover, is assimilated to disorderly movement: "motion which is never uniform or regular, never in the same compass, around the same center, in the same direction or in a single place – motion which has no order, plan, or formula – is akin to unreason of every kind."[62]

Since soul is the primary causal power in the physical cosmos, divine souls create the orderly motions in the physical cosmos, and lesser souls the disorderly motions. *Nous*, then, is not just "like" the circular motion of the heavenly bodies but is in fact its cause: the *nous* of the World-Soul causes the entire World-Body to revolve in a circle, carrying the fixed stars in its outermost orbit; and the *nous* of the divine souls who inhabit the stars makes each of the individual star-bodies rotate around its own center (34a–37a).[63] In addition, Plato claims that the World-Soul is constructed out of two circular "bands" of soul-stuff – the Circle of the Same and the Circle of the Different – which rotate at different angles (36b–c). Here, Plato speaks metaphorically, since the soul is an invisible being that lacks a physical shape and structure. But his imagistic account clearly portrays the motion of both the World-Soul and the World-Body as circular.[64] Note that the human soul, too, has an immortal part (*nous*) which is made of the same materials as the World-Soul: human *nous* has the same structure, motions, and activities as divine *nous*, even though it does not operate

---

[61] As Plato explains in the *Laws* x, the motion of *nous* is a "revolution" which actually resembles circular motion, since both "move regularly, uniformly, within the same compass, around the same center and in the same direction, according to one formula and one ordering plan" (ἕνα λόγον καὶ τάξιν μίαν, 897e–898b).

[62] *Laws* 897e–898b. For an investigation into the *nous*–circular motion analogy, see Lee 1976. Note also Aristotle's attack on this analogy in the *De Anima* 1.3.407a2–b11.

[63] That the World-Soul is autokinetic is made clear at 89a, where Timaeus says that "of all motions that is the best which is produced in a thing by itself (ἡ ἐν ἑαυτῷ ὑφ' αὑτοῦ ἀρίστη κίνησις, a1–2), for it is most akin to the motion of thought and of the universe." Cornford ([1937]/1952, 95 n. 2), citing the reference at 37b5 to "the thing that is self-moved", says that "the self-moved thing is the Heaven as a whole, which, as a living creature, is self-moved by its own self-moving soul" (see also Taylor 1928, 148, 178; cf. Mohr 1985, 174).

[64] Cf. Sedley (1999a), who argues that Plato intends this literally rather than metaphorically.

perfectly. The rational part of the human soul, then, is akin to the divine World-Soul.[65]

I want to look, now, at Plato's account of the World-Body, which houses the best and most perfect psyche, the World-Soul.[66] As Brague rightly observes, the interpreter of the *Timaeus* must grasp "the structure of the world as an animal," i.e. as a combination of a body and a soul.[67] According to Timaeus, the Demiurge took over the physical realm, which was in a state of chaos and disorderly motion, and "brought order out of disorder." He designed a cosmos that was "exceedingly good and most beautiful," modeling his creation on the "intelligible" cosmos (30b–d). In fashioning the World-Body, the Demiurge used the four elements – earth, fire, air, and water – which are made up of "corpuscles" shaped and bounded by triangles of different sizes and configurations. The World-Body, then, is composed of the same constituents that make up all bodies, but is shaped and constructed so as to be, "so far as possible, whole and perfect (τέλεον), with perfect parts" (32c–d). The Demiurge created the World-Body to be "perfect and ageless and free of disease," giving it a spherical shape, which is "the most perfect and the most self-similar of all shapes" (33a–b). Unlike mortal bodies, the World-Body does not need eyes, ears, hands, feet, or a digestive system: it is "self-sufficient" (αὔταρκες) and free of all needs (33d). The World-Body, moreoever, has a single motion – it revolves in a circle – and can never engage in any other kind of motion (34a; cf. 43b). For this reason, the Demiurge made the World-Body "smooth and even and equal on all sides from the center, a whole and perfect body" (ὅλον καὶ τέλεον . . . σῶμα, 34b).[68]

This body is perfect in itself, i.e as a living body: it is made of corporeal entities yet lacks all the vagaries and deficiencies of mortal bodies. But it is also perfect as an image of its intelligible model – it is a perfect instantiation of the Forms on which it is modeled. It is therefore called "an *agalma*

---

[65] Human *nous*, however, is less "pure" than that of the World-Soul (41d–e).

[66] Assuming that the Demiurge is not a soul. As Mohr (1985, 178) observes, ever since Cherniss' (1944) *Aristotle's Criticism of Plato and the Academy* vol. I, "there has been nearly universal agreement among critics that Plato's God or divine Demiurge is a soul." Mohr gives a cogent argument against this view: the Demiurge is transcendent rather than immanent in the universe (pp. 178–83).

[67] Brague 1985, 56. Brague offers an excellent discussion of the "body" of the world in the *Timaeus*.

[68] Compare Vernant's description of the notion of a "divine" body in the poets and philosophers of the archaic and early classical period (1989, 21): these authors "do not oppose the corporeal to the noncorporeal, a pure spirit. Rather, [they] contrast the constant and the changing, the immutable and mutable, that which is eternally accomplished and in plenitude with that which is incomplete and imperfect, divided, dispersed, transitory." The mortal body, in short, "does not possess, completely and definitively, that set of powers, qualities and active virtues which bring to an individual being's existence a constant, radiant, enduring life" (p. 25).

of the eternal divinities" (37c). This "perfect" cosmos is rightly called an "*agalma*," since it is the sacred image of its divine intelligible model.[69] Timaeus makes it clear that the intelligible model is "the most beautiful and the most perfect in all ways" (30d). The cosmos and its heavenly bodies fall short of the perfection of the Forms, but are nonetheless a perfect "image" of wholeness, sphericity, beauty, order, and harmony. The star-bodies of the lesser gods, too, are "perfect" images of the Forms: made of fire, and spherical in form, these divine bodies are "as radiant as possible to look upon and exceedingly beautiful" (40a).

The World-Body, together with the heavenly bodies within it, bears a resemblance to the "aetherial" bodies of the *Phaedo* and the *agalmata* of Beauty in the *Phaedrus*. In each of these texts, we find bodies that are supremely radiant and beautiful. But the *Timaeus* introduces a new idea: namely, that part of the beauty and perfection of the heavenly bodies is located in their orderly, circular *motions*. These motions are caused by divine *nous*, which makes the heavenly bodies move in beautiful, orderly revolutions.[70] Whereas the shape, constitution, and appearance of the cosmos and heavenly bodies are simple material qualities, their motion is directed by divine souls.

According to Timaeus, the created universe could not be "eternal" (αἰώνιος), like its intelligible model (37d, 38b–c). Thus the Demiurge, in imitation of the eternal Forms, made the cosmos to be "a moving image of eternity" (εἰκὼ ... κινητόν τινα αἰῶνος, 37d).[71] The World-Body and the heavenly bodies of the stars trace this "moving image." Though the cosmic image – unlike the model – must move, its motions and revolutions are organized according to mathematical principles: the cosmos "moves according to number, which phenomenon we call time" (37d).[72] It is not just the physical properties of the cosmos and the stars, then, which "imitate" the essences in intelligible model; their motions form another

---

[69] As Taylor (1928, 184) observes, the suggestion that the cosmos is an *agalma* of "the eternal gods" is troubling, since it seems to indicate that it is an image of gods, i.e. divine souls, rather than the intelligible Forms. But since, in Plato's metaphysics, the Forms are divine, it is not difficult to see the reference to the "eternal gods" as a reference to the Forms.

[70] The fixed stars, carried by the Circle of the Same, move in perfectly circular revolutions (40a–b), whereas the sun, moon, and planets, whose motions are affected by both the Circle of the Same and the Circle of the Different, move in spirals, which is still a form of circular movement (38c–39b).

[71] Note Socrates' claim at 19b–c that he would like to see the city whose structure and constitution he has described be set in motion, just as one might want to see a "beautiful creature," whether a real one or an artistic rendering, moving and engaged in activity. This emphasis on motion is not found in earlier dialogues. Broadie (2001) offers an excellent interpretation of this passage (and of the relation of politics to cosmology in general); see also K. Morgan 1998.

[72] On Greek conceptions of time, see Ricoeur 1984 vol. 1, ch. 1 and G. Lloyd 1993, ch. 1.

kind of image – an image of the eternity of the model. These motions, as I have suggested, are governed by the self-moving World-Soul. The motion of the heavenly bodies, then, is a visible manifestation of divine *nous*. In thus connecting divine intelligence with the bodily motion of the stars, Plato can claim that the heavenly bodies are "visible gods" (θεῶν ὁρατῶν, 40d). The universe, then, is "a visible living creature . . . and a perceptible god" (θεὸς αἰσθητός); it is, as Timaeus says in the last line, "a visible image of intelligible being – a single and unique cosmos, being the greatest and the best and the most beautiful and perfect" (92c).

When philosophers gaze up into the heavens, then, they are looking at "visible gods." They are seeing the *agalma* or divine image of the intelligible world. The visual contemplation of the heavens thus plays a positive role in the philosophic life. In fact, Plato claims that philosophy has its origin in the vision of the heavenly bodies:[73]

Vision (*opsis*) is the cause of the greatest benefit to us, since no account of the universe would have ever been given if men had not seen (*idontōn*) the stars or sun or heaven. The vision of day and night and the months and the revolutions of the years has created the art of number, and it has given us the notion of time as well as the ability to investigate the nature of the universe. From these things we have procured philosophy – and there is no greater good which the gods have given us than this. This, I claim, is the greatest benefit of eyesight. (47a–b)

The practice of astronomy, then, plays an essential role in philosophy, since it enables us to investigate and understand "the nature of the universe."[74] According to Timaeus, "without recourse to [the physical world], we humans cannot discern by ourselves alone the divine objects for which we strive, or apprehend them or in any way partake of them" (69a). This text, then, issues a strong endorsement of visual perception, at least when it is directed towards the "visible gods." As Sedley suggests, in the *Timaeus* "astronomy becomes *par excellence* the discipline which can bridge the gulf between the sensible and intelligible worlds."[75] To be sure, one can practice astronomy incorrectly: one must not study the heavens in the belief that "the most sure proofs about these matters come through sight" (91e). True philosophers will engage in the visual contemplation of the heavens, but they will seek "proofs" about the motions of the universe via mathematics.[76]

---

[73] Cf. *Theaetetus* 155d, which claims that philosophy began in wonder.

[74] For some useful analyses of Greek astronomy, see Heath [1913]/1981, Dicks 1970, Lloyd 1979, 169–225, 1987, 235–41, 304–19. See Ostwald 1992, 349ff. for a discussion of the activities of astronomers in Athens in the fifth century BCE. Blumenberg (1987, esp. chs. 1–3) analyzes the conception of man as "*contemplator caeli*" in the ancient, mediaeval, renaissance and modern periods.

[75] Sedley 1989, 377 (see also Sedley 1999a).

[76] On Plato and Greek mathematics, see Cherniss 1951, Burnyeat 1987, and Mueller 1992.

Let us compare this to the discussion of astronomy in the *Republic*.[77] In his brief account of astronomical study in book VII, Socrates says that the only discipline which turns the soul's gaze upwards is that which deals with "being and the invisible"; anyone who tries to learn the truth by investigating the physical world – even if he is looking up at the stars – is turning his intellectual gaze downwards (529b–c). Socrates grants that the heavenly bodies are "the most beautiful and most exact" of physical things, but says that they "fall far short of true realities" (529c–d). One cannot, by studying the heavens, apprehend real speed and slowness or true number and its ratios; nor can one understand the proportional measurement of day to month and month to year, since the heavenly bodies do not move "always in the same way, without deviation" (529d–530b).[78] Socrates does claim that the creator of the universe made it "as beautiful as possible" and that we can "use the embroidery in the heavens as a pattern to aid in the study of reality" (529d–530a). But the philosopher must practice astronomy "by means of problems, just as in the study of geometry." If we practice astronomy in a philosophic fashion, we must "leave the things in the heaven alone" (τὰ δ' ἐν τῷ οὐρανῷ ἐάσομεν, 53a–b).

The *Timaeus* shares a number of these same views: the created cosmos is only an "image" and, as physical and phenomenal, it falls short of intelligible reality; studying the heavens can be an aid to philosophy but will not, by itself, lead to the apprehension of its intelligible model. But the *Timaeus* goes beyond these claims in identifying the heavenly bodies and their motions as the visible manifestation of divine *nous*. In this text, the person who contemplates the heavens sees "visible gods," whereas in the *Republic* he sees only "diagrams" (529d–e). The *Republic* does indicate that the cosmos is organized by reason (530a), and we may infer that it operates according to mathematical principles. But this text makes no mention of the presence of divine souls in the heavens, and does not conceive of the soul as "self-moving motion."[79] The *Timaeus*, by contrast, explicates these

---

[77] For analyses of Plato's astronomical theories in the *Timaeus*, see Heath [1913]/1981, ch. 15, Cherniss 1944, Appendix VIII, Dicks 1970, 92–150, Vlastos 1975, 31–65, and Brisson and Meyerstein 1995, part 1. Scholars have debated whether Plato claims in the *Republic* that the practice of astronomy should be pursued as a pure science, with minimal recourse to empiricism (see esp. the essays in Anton 1980). Mourelatos (1981) claims that Plato's "astronomy" centers on kinematics rather than the study of celestial motion; cf. Vlastos 1980, Sedley 1989, esp. 377, and Mueller 1992, 192–4. In my view, the *Timaeus* gives more positive weight to the visual contemplation of the heavens than the *Republic* does.

[78] As Patterson (1985, 93) rightly observes, "it should not be inferred from this that, were the paths of stars forever regular (as in the cosmology of the *Timaeus*), their visible characteristics would be proper study for geometry or astronomy. On the contrary, they would still be only visible models of invisible, intelligible realities."

[79] At *Republic* 508a–c, Socrates refers to the sun as one of the "gods in heaven," but this is in keeping with popular religious ideas and has little cosmological import.

ideas in great detail, placing special emphasis on the orderly motions of the heavenly bodies and their correlation with *nous*. As we will see, the contemplation of these motions not only aids in the study of cosmology and metaphysics but plays a crucial role in the ethical development of the human soul.

Scholars generally agree that Plato's cosmological texts reflect his awareness of Eudoxus' mathematical model of the heavens, particularly his claim that the motions of heavenly bodies (including that of the planets) is circular.[80] In the *Laws* VII, the Athenian asserts that "not long ago," he learned that "the belief that the sun, moon, and other heavenly bodies wander is incorrect – on the contrary, each of these bodies moves in a circle on one and the same path . . ." (821e–822a).[81] This "recent" discovery, he says, changed the look of the heavens, which can now be seen to exhibit orderly motion. It was because Plato associated order and harmony with rationality that he ascribed the circular motions of the heavens to divine *nous*. And, once he forged this link between divinity and the movements of the stars, he could argue that astronomy – if practiced correctly – generates both knowledge and piety. As Plato says in the *Laws*, even in the olden days the men who seriously studied the heavens

were not, as people commonly believed, impious or godless – quite the contrary, they were affected (ἔπαθεν) in the exact opposite way . . . For even then a sense of wonder (θαύματα) at the heavens entered into them, and they began to suspect what is now known, at least those who studied them with accuracy – namely, that [the stars] would never have been able to move according to such wonderful (θαυμαστοῖς) calculations with so much accuracy if they were soulless and lacking in *nous*. (966e–967b)

The contemplation of the heavens, in short, leads not to atheism but to a heightened sense of piety. Indeed the man who studies these in a serious way will experience wonder and reverence, since he is beholding the motions of divinity.[82]

---

[80] Simplicius reports that Plato set a problem for astronomers to account for the complex phenomena of the "wandering" planets in terms of a definite number of uniform and orderly motions (*in De Caelo* II, 12, 219a23). Eudoxus' system of concentric circles offers one "solution" to this problem. See Heath [1913]/1981, ch. 16 and Dicks 1970, ch. 6 for discussions of Eudoxus' theory.

[81] If this passage is saying that the planets move in perfect circles, it would contradict the *Timaeus*, which claims that the planets move in spirals. But it is likely that the *Laws* is claiming that each planet has a fixed and orderly (spiral) path, from which it does not deviate (see, e.g., Cornford [1937]/1952, 90, Dicks 1970, 138–9, Tarán 1975, 102–3). In both texts, then, the motions of the heavenly bodies are circular in the sense that both the revolutions of the fixed stars and the spiral motions of the sun, moon, and planets are steered by *nous* and are completely devoid of rectilinear motion.

[82] Note that in the *Laws* the ordinary citizens are required to learn astronomy (817e–818a); according to the Athenian, it is a mark of piety, rather than impiety, to study the stars (821a–822c).

How, then, does the contemplation of the heavenly bodies generate a virtuous character? According to Timaeus,

God devised and bestowed upon us vision (ὄψιν) in order that we might behold (κατίδοντες) the revolutions of *nous* in the heavens and use them for the revolving of the reasoning that is within us, since our [noetic revolutions] are akin (ξυγγενεῖς) to those, the peturbable to the impeturbable; and in order that, by learning and sharing in calculations that are correct by nature, and imitating (μιμούμενοι) the unwandering revolutions of the god, we might set in order those that are wandering in us.[83] (47b–c)

As this passage suggests, the philosopher must gaze at the visible gods in the heavens in order to theorize the motion of *nous* and, having apprehended this, must attempt to imitate its orderly motion by the activity of his own mind.[84] As Timaeus suggests, the motion of our human reason is "akin" to that of the cosmos, though our thoughts are perturbed and need to be set in order. Indeed, as he says later in the text, a human being must "nourish" each part of his soul – both the mortal part and the "divine" noetic part – "with its proper motions":

For the divine part [of the human soul], the kindred (ξυγγενεῖς) motions are the thoughts and revolutions of the universe. Each of us, then, must follow together with these celestial motions (ταύταις . . . ξυνεπόμενον), rectifying the revolutions within his head (ἡμῶν περιόδους ἐξορθοῦντα), which were corrupted at birth, by learning the harmonies and revolutions of the universe, and thus assimilating his thinking part to the object of his thought, in accordance with its original nature (κατὰ τὴν ἀρχαίαν φύσιν). (90c–d)

As we have seen, the divine part of the human soul is akin to cosmic *nous* – it is made of the same material and has the same structure and motion. It can therefore "follow together with" the motion of the heavens and "rectify" its own vagaries (which are deviations from its natural motion). By theorizing the heavens, then, the human being can recover his "original nature."

What does Plato mean when he says that we should "assimilate" our minds to divine *nous*? Clearly, he is advocating the practice of "becoming like god" but, as Annas suggests, this can mean different things depending on one's conception of god:

---

[83] It might seem that this passage is trying to make a distinction between *nous* and *dianoia*, since we are said to "behold the revolutions of *nous* (τὰς . . . τοῦ νοῦ . . . περιόδους) in the heavens and use them for the revolving of the *dianoesis* (τὰς περιφορὰς τὰς τῆς παρ' ἡμῖν διανοήσεως) that is within us." But Plato later uses the word *dianoesis* for the revolutions of divine intelligence (90c–d), which indicates that he does not make a firm distinction between them. See also *Laws* 898e, where Plato conflates *nous* with *dianoesis*.

[84] See Sedley 1999a for a fine discussion of this conception of "likeness to God" (though his interpretation is more literal than mine).

If becoming like God is living according to your reason, then it need imply no more than a very ordinary, indeed traditional, practice of virtue, understood as a rational activity. God here is just reason . . . [i.e.] something which can guide practice as well as theory. But if becoming like God is actually a flight from the mix of good and evil in our world, then God is . . . something perfectly good outside human experience and not to be characterized in human terms.[85]

In the *Timaeus*, humans souls must imitate a divine reason that is both contemplative and practical. On the one hand, divine reason contemplates the Forms, but the gods are makers and doers as well as theorizers. The Demiurge both "gazes on" (28a, 29a) the intelligible world and also creates the cosmos; and the lesser gods act in the same fashion.

As I indicated above, souls "together with *nous*," are the "*demiourgoi* of things that are beautiful and good" (46e). *Nous*, then, is not just a contemplative faculty but a demiourgic power in the physical cosmos. In fact, when the divine souls create mortal beings, they proceed by "imitating" (41c, 44d, 69c) the Demiurge's creative act. Plato places great emphasis on the productive, artistic nature of this activity: the gods mix and sift and knead and weld the elements.[86] The creative activities of the divine souls, then, are directly connected with that of the Demiurge.[87] Divine *nous* is, among other things, a productive power – that which makes order out of chaos. As Timaeus famously puts it, *nous* "persuaded" necessity to form a cosmos (48a).[88]

In "becoming like god," then, the human soul must engage in contemplative, ethical, and productive activities. Indeed our task as human souls is to make of ourselves a cosmos:

---

[85] Annas 1999, 64.

[86] At 73b8, for example, a god is said to take the atomic triangles that were straight and smooth and create bone marrow by separating off the most perfect triangles and mingling them in the proper proportion. Again, at 73d–e, he makes bone by sifting pure and smooth earth, kneading and wetting it with marrow, and dipping it in fire and water; and at 77a the gods "mingle" the elements to create trees and plants. Brisson (1974, 27–106) discusses the *demiourgos* in early antiquity, and offers a detailed analysis of Plato's Demiurge as a craftsman. Brumbaugh (1989, ch. 16) offers a useful analysis of Plato's attitudes to the "arts and crafts."

[87] The similarity between the Demiurge's act of creation and that of the gods is further underlined by the fact that, in the discussion of the creation of the human body (at 69c, where the Demiurge is said to hand over the creation of mortal creatures to the gods), Timaeus refers to these creators now in the plural and now in the singular: μηχανώμενοι (70c4), θεός (71a7), οἱ συστήσαντες ἡμᾶς (71d5–6), θεός (71e2), οἱ συντιθέντες (72e4–5), ὁ θεός (73b8), τοῖς δημιουργοῖς (75b7–8), ὁ θεός (75d1), οἱ διακοσμοῦντες (75d7), ὁ ποιῶν (76c6), οἱ συνιστάντες (76e1), θεοί (77a3), οἱ κρείττους (77c6), ὁ θεός (78b2), θεός (80e1).

[88] In the *Timaeus*, ἀνάγκη is defined as a secondary and "wandering cause" (48a) that comprises all the causal powers operative in the physical world which, "being destitute of reason, produce on each occasion that which is chancy (i.e. random: τὸ τυχόν) and disordered" (46e5–6). For an account of "necessity" and "chance" in the *Timaeus*, see Morrow [1950]/1965, 432–5, and Brisson 1974, 469–78.

He who has seriously pursued learning and true thoughts, and has developed these qualities above all others, will necessarily think thoughts that are immortal and divine, if he lays hold of the truth . . . and inasmuch as he is always tending his divine part and keeping the daemon that dwells within him as well ordered as a cosmos (κεκοσμημένον), he will be supremely blessed. (90b–c)

This task is at once intellectual and ethical: to imitate the orderly motion of the heavens is to become orderly and virtuous oneself.[89] Note that the *Timaeus* does not suggest that the soul can ever escape or "flee" the physical universe, even after death. In fact, the soul has its native home in the stars:

[The Demiurge] divided souls equal in number to the stars, and he assigned each soul to a star; placing them as though in a chariot, he showed (ἔδειξε) them the nature of the universe (τὴν τοῦ παντὸς φύσιν) and declared the laws of destiny . . . [And he stated that] the person who lives virtuously for his appointed time will return again to his home (οἴκησιν) in his native star, and will have a happy and congenial life. (41d–e, 42b)

This scene resembles the passage in the *Phaedrus* where the preincarnate souls ascend with the gods to the edge of the universe and theorize the Forms. But in the *Timaeus* each soul views "the nature of the universe" or (more literally) "the all," which includes the physical as well as the metaphysical realm. The soul, then, gazes upon the order and harmony of both the Forms and the cosmos. When incarnated on earth, the philosophic soul must study the noetic motions of the physical cosmos in order to apprehend the intelligible realm.

But how does this lead the person to become virtuous in the practical sphere? We may wonder why it is that the person who "draws himself along with (ξυνεπισπώμενος) the revolution of the Same that is within him" and "conquers by his reason the irrational and tumultuous mass [of his body]" (42c–d) necessarily becomes a good man. To be sure, he will be self-controlled and temperate. He will imitate all that is orderly, patterning his own actions on the perfect motions of divine *nous*. As we have seen, Plato claims that we must make of ourselves a cosmos, which is a beautiful and good and orderly being – an image, in turn, of the intelligible realm.[90] Note that we "imitate" the intelligible model by patterning

---

[89] Brague 1999, 44–7; cf. Sedley (1999a), who argues that the human soul "becomes like god" by emulating the contemplative (but not the ethical or productive) activities of the divine World-Soul. Annas (1999, 59–71) shows how various Middle Platonists interpreted Plato's notion of "becoming like god" in different ways – some claiming that this involved a combination of theoretical and practical activities and others that it was exclusively contemplative.

[90] See Broadie 2001, 26 and *passim* on the need for human souls to "craft" themselves and the city as a cosmos.

ourselves on a mediating model: we assimilate ourselves to the Forms by imitating the divine souls in the heavens. This imitative act centers on motion and action: we must make our own motions orderly and attempt to trace in the microcosm of our own souls a "moving image of eternity." Finally, when we view the "visible gods" in the heavens, we are moved both by our "kinship" to these divinities as well as by a profound reverence for beings greater than ourselves. In fact, the demiurge created humans to be "the most god-worshiping" (θεοσεβέστατον) of creatures (42a1). And he gave them sight in order that they might behold the gods whom they revere and emulate.

The *Timaeus*, then, subscribes to the theory of Forms with its dualistic ontology, but it also allows for the presence of "heavenly bodies" whose contemplation contributes to good and wise behavior.[91] This does not mean that these bodies have some special ontological status, i.e. that they differ in some essential way from other bodies. They are phenomena that possess their properties as form-copies entering the receptacle.[92] They may be better instantiations of the Forms than other corporeal entities, but they are nonethelesss a part of the realm of becoming and, like all particulars, are subject to change and dissolution. Plato, however, hedges on this last point. For he claims that the cosmos is indissoluble except by the agency of its own creator, and that the Demiurge will never dissolve it because this would be an evil deed (41a–b; cf. 32c, 38c–d). It will therefore have an "unceasing life" (37c) and be an "everlasting image" of its intelligible model (αἰώνιον εἰκόνα, 37d; cf. 38b–c). Given that it is everlasting and retains its fundamental structure and order throughout all of time, the World-Body differs from mortal bodies. But this is accomplished through the "will" of the Demiurge rather than because of any corporeal factor (41a–b). The World-Body and the heavenly bodies, then, are phenomenal particulars, but are also the vehicles of the divine motion of *nous*. They thus have the ambiguous status of *agalmata* – on the one hand, they are sacred and divine, and on the other, a mere image of the true divinity of the Forms.

In the *Timaeus*, I have suggested, we find some additions to the basic two-world theory advanced in texts like the *Republic*. We still have the ontological distinction between "being and becoming," i.e. the Forms and the sensible particulars (27e–28a). Timaeus makes it clear that the Forms

---

[91] For references to the Forms, see 51c, 51e–52a (and see also 29b, 48e–49a, 50c–d).

[92] Scholars differ over the status of phenomenal particulars in the *Timaeus*. For the argument that the phenomenal particulars are not objects, and thus should be identified by way of their properties, see Cherniss [1954]/1977, [1957]/1965, Lee 1966, Mohr 1980, Silverman 1992; cf. M. Gill 1971 and Zeyl 1975.

in no sense "enter into" any other thing, be it the receptacle or the corporeal particulars (51e–52a, 52c). The Forms are not incarnate in bodies;
rather, bodily phenomena are images or "imitations" (*mimemata*) of the
Forms within the receptacle (50c). But, in addition to this dualistic scheme,
we now have self-moving divine souls who order and move the physical
cosmos – they maintain the motion and organization of the universe by the
agency of *nous*. The divine souls are in fact incarnate in the physical cosmos: the Demiurge placed the World-Soul in the World-Body, through its
entire extent, attaching the two at the center (36d–e); and each individual
star has its own divine soul which causes it to revolve in a circle.[93] Divine
souls are not, of course, imprisoned in bodies or in any sense limited by
them – they have a separate ontological existence. But they do inhabit the
physical cosmos and govern its motions. This conception of the universe
alters the way that we view and value the physical realm, since we can
now see "visible gods" in the cosmos. And it also offers us a model for
practical as well as intellectual activities, since we humans can – like divine
souls – bring order out of the chaos of bodily elements, making of ourselves
a (micro-)cosmos.

Of course Plato has not abandoned the idea that the contemplation of
metaphysical realities is the highest epistemic activity. But, in the *Timaeus*,
astronomy and the contemplation of the heavens plays an important role
in the philosophic life. By viewing "the harmonies and revolutions of the
universe," we must "assimilate the part [of us] which thinks to the object
of thought" (90d). This suggestion that we must "assimilate" our *nous* to
the motions in the heavens clearly indicates that the contemplation of the
heavens is part of the philosophical activity of making ourselves divine.
No doubt we become fully divine by "seeing" the Forms, but the activity
of theorizing the heavens – which involves both visual and mathematical
apprehension – plays a significant role in the development of the faculty of
nous.

PHILIP OF OPUS' *EPINOMIS*: THEORIZING
THE HEAVENLY BODIES

The *Epinomis* was written as a sort of coda to Plato's *Laws*, and features the
same dramatic context and characters. At the beginning of the *Epinomis*,
the Athenian Stranger says that they have completed their discussion of

[93] Note that, at *Laws* 898e–899a, Plato raises the question whether the divine souls inhabit the star
bodies (as we inhabit our bodies) or push them from without. The text does not offer an answer to
this question.

laws and legal matters and must now define what a man should learn if he is to be truly wise (973a–b). This connection between the *Laws* and the *Epinomis* has led some scholars to identify Plato as its author; but it is now generally agreed that this dialogue was written by Philip of Opus, a fourth-century astronomer who was a member of Plato's Academy.[94] Ancient sources indicate that Philip wrote on a wide range of subjects, including texts on astronomy, optics, mathematics, meteorology, and ethics.[95] But he was best known as an astronomer and mathematician.

Philip sets forth a novel claim: that astronomy, or the *theoria* of the heavens, is the highest form of wisdom. The *Epinomis* invites the reader to follow this way of life and learning. The protreptic rhetoric resembles that of Plato, but it defends a very different conception of *theoria*. According to this text, when a person beholds the stars tracing their courses in heaven,

At first this happy man feels awe, and then he conceives an eros for learning as much as is possible for mortal nature, believing that in this way he will spend his life in the happiest way and that he will go, when he dies, to regions that are fitting for virtue. And, having been truly and really initiated (μεμυημένος ἀληθῶς τε καὶ ὄντως) and achieving perfect unity, he will partake of a wisdom that is unitary and will continue for the rest of time to be a *theoros* of the most beautiful things, so far as sight will allow (τὸν ἐπίλοιπον χρόνον θεωρὸς τῶν καλλίστων γενόμενος, ὅσα κατ᾽ ὄψιν, διατελεῖ). (986c–d)

Note that the feelings of awe and wonder precede the acquisition of knowledge – the mere vision of the heavens produces a religious response that will be given a rational grounding by the subsequent study of philosophy and mathematics. In this passage, Philip follows Plato in comparing philosophic *theoria* to the initiation at the Mystery festival with its "vision" of the sacred revelation. Strangely, however, he suggests in the last line that the philosophic *theoros* will theorize the heavens with his eyes even after death – that the astronomical contemplation of the heavens will continue in the afterlife.[96]

---

[94] For arguments that Plato was not the author of the *Epinomis*, see Heidel [1896]/1976, 72–3, Cherniss 1950, 1953, 371–5, Einarson 1958, and (in copious detail) Tarán 1975; cf. Taylor 1921, 1929b, Des Places 1931, 1942, 1952, 1956, Dicks 1970, 141–50. I agree with Tarán, who offers a detailed discussion of the scholarship and arguments on this issue. Note that Diogenes Laertius reports that Philip of Opus "revised" or "transcribed" (μετέγραψεν) the text of the *Laws*, which was still on wax tablets when Plato died (III.37). It is unclear whether μεταγράφειν in this passage means to "transcribe" a completed text onto papyrus, or to "revise" and therefore finish a work which was not yet complete.

[95] On the ancient source material dealing with Philip's life and works, see Tarán 1975, 115–39.

[96] But note that he states at 992b that "when the wisest man dies, if he still exists, he will not partake of the many sensations then as he does now, having alone partaken of a single lot and having grown from many into one." This may be his more considered position.

Philip repeatedly emphasizes that the wise man must spend his time contemplating the heavens: "for if one advances to the right *theoria* of this thing, whether one calls it the cosmos or Olympus or Heaven . . . one must follow where it adorns itself and turns the stars in all their courses . . ." (977b). The philosophic *theoros* watches a spectacle that is compared to a chorus of dancers (a regular feature of religious festivals in Greece): the stars "are the fairest things to see, dancing the fairest and most magnificent of all dances" (χορείαν πάντων χορῶν καλλίστην καὶ μεγαλοπρεπεστάτην χορεύοντα, 982e).[97] In these passages, Philip describes the visual *theoria* of the heavens. But he makes it clear elsewhere that this kind of *theoria* is accompanied and, indeed, made possible by expertise in the mathematical sciences: the wise man is "he who has studied seven out of the eight orbits, each traveling through its own circuit – a phenomenon that no ordinary nature would easily be able to theorize" (θεωρῆσαι, 990a–b). Only the mathematical study of astronomy will enable a person to acquire this knowledge (a study which requires a full education in arithmetic, geometry, and stereometry; 990b–991b). *Theoria*, then, includes both visual and intellectual activities – activities that are equally necessary and mutually reinforcing.

Like Plato, Philip argues for the ontological dualism between body and soul. Although he does not explicitly identify the soul as self-moving motion, he clearly endorses this idea.[98] According to Philip, soul moves and shapes the world of body: good and divine souls order the heavens and work "towards the good," whereas lesser souls gravitate towards earth and its disorder (988d–e). In short, "those creatures which are earthly move in disorder, whereas those which are made of fire [i.e. the stars] move in a perfectly orderly fashion" (982a). Philip also echoes Plato in his identification of the stars as "visible gods" (θεοὺς . . . τοὺς ὁρατούς).[99] As in Plato, divine souls move the star-bodies. But Philip dispenses with the theory of Forms, and this makes for a very different scheme.

Philip is struggling to articulate a new conception of *theoria* in Platonic language. Consider, for example, his account of the heavenly bodies:

Either we must glorify these things as actual gods, or suppose them to be images of the gods such as *agalmata* (θεῶν εἰκόνας ὡς ἀγάλματα), which the gods themselves have made . . . and we must suppose them to be one of these things or the other, and if we class them as the latter, we must honor them above all *agalmata*. (983e–984b)

---

97 Plato uses this same image at *Timaeus* 42c.
98 On dualism: 981b–c, 983b–c, 983c–e, 988d–e; on soul as self-moving and/or creative agent: 981b–c, 982a, 983b–e.
99 *Epinomis* 984d; see also 984c, 982a, 991b.

In the *Timaeus*, Plato argued that the heavenly bodies (and the cosmos as as whole) are both gods and *agalmata*. They are gods because they are divine souls in perfect bodies, and they are *agalmata* because they embody and enact an "image" of the Forms. Though the Forms exist on a higher ontological plane – they are the most perfect and divine beings – it is still the case that the heavenly bodies and the cosmos itself are gods (since they are governed by divine *nous*). Philip, by contrast, has no higher reality than the cosmos and its visible gods; he thus has a very different conception of the *agalmata* in the heavens.[100]

Philip does not take a stand, here or elsewhere, on the question whether the heavenly bodies are "themselves gods" or, rather, are *agalmata*. What makes him hesitate, I think, is his belief that soul is ontologically distinct from and superior to body: to say that anything with a body is itself a god seems to fly in the face of this basic dualistic postulate. Strictly speaking, the soul is the "most *truly* divine entity in the universe" (981b). But the divine souls with their star-bodies are nonetheless "visible gods." "Whom do I magnify with the name of god?", asks Philip: "heaven" (977a). Philip seems to want it both ways (and is therefore not logically consistent): the beings we see in the heavens are indeed visible gods, but their bodies may be "sacred images" rather than divine entities. As he goes on to say, if the stars are "sacred images" rather than gods proper,

Never will *agalmata* be seen that are more beautiful and common to all mankind, having been established and dedicated (ἱδρυμένα) in such exceptional places, being exceptional in purity and in holiness and in their whole manner of life. (984a)

Here, the physical heavens become a sort of temple in which the stars are the *agalmata* of the incorporeal souls of the gods. In this passage, the philosophic *theoros* now sees *agalmata* in the very temple of the heavens.[101] Here, Philip cleaves closely to the traditional practice of theorizing sacred images in religious sanctuaries and temples.

The *Epinomis*, like the *Timaeus*, claims that the gods gave man the faculty of vision in order that they might see the heavens. In contemplating the heavens, says Philip, humans learned the art of number:

The first thing god implanted in us was the capability to comprehend what is shown to us; and then he proceeded to show us and still shows us [the heavens]. Among the things god shows us, what more beautiful thing can a person see than the world

---

[100] I agree with Tarán (1975, 332 and *passim*) that Philip does not allude to or espouse a theory of ideal numbers or idea-numbers in the *Epinomis*. The mathematical sciences and the study of "number" serve the higher purpose of theorizing the heavens.

[101] As Tarán observes (1975, 88), this is "the earliest instance in extant Greek literature of the notion of the cosmos as a temple of the gods, a notion destined to have a lasting influence on subsequent thought."

184 Spectacles of Truth in Classical Greek Philosophy

of day? And, later, he beholds the night with his vision, and he sees another sight before him. And so the heaven never stops revolving these very objects for many nights and many days, and never ceases to teach men one and two . . . (978c–d)

The art of number is a great gift, for it enables us to study astronomy and contemplate divine beings. Of course the discipline of astronomy is a highly technical, mathematical enterprise, and thus people must study arithmetic, geometry, and stereometry as preparatory disciplines (990c–991b). The *telos* of this education, however, is the contemplation of "the most beautiful and divine nature of visible things" (τὴν τῶν ὁρατῶν καλλίστην τε καὶ θειοτάτην φύσιν, 991b; see also 977b). Here and elsewhere, Philip identifies astronomy as the highest form of wisdom, and equates it with philosophical study.[102] As in Plato's *Timaeus*, the faculty of vision plays a vital role in the theoretical enterprise, since the knowledge of the heavens and its revolutions is the highest form of wisdom. The visual contemplation of the heavens, then, is an essential part of philosophic wisdom. But it is *nous* which apprehends the divine souls and their motions; in fact, only the invisible, incorporeal soul is fully "knowable" (νοητῷ, 981c).[103]

Let us turn now to the connection between *theoria* and *praxis*. At the opening of the text, Philip raises the central question of the dialogue: what is the nature of wisdom (*sophia*), and how do we acquire it (976d)? Philip begins by claiming that true wisdom must have an essential practical and political component: "when a man acquires wisdom, he will be neither a *banausos* nor a fool, but will be a wise and good citizen, ruling and being ruled justly in his city, and also be orderly and well tuned" (976d). He returns to this issue later in the text, when he asserts that "there is no greater part of virtue, for mortals, than piety" (*eusebeia*, 989a–b). This is a novel claim, not found in Plato. As we have seen, Plato emphasizes in the *Phaedrus*, *Timaeus*, and *Laws* that the soul feels awe and reverence when it encounters the "divine" Forms or the astral gods. These feelings play a vital role in human behavior, but can hardly be identified as the highest form of virtue. Plato goes further in the *Laws*, which explicitly says that

---

[102] Philip does not mention dialectic in the *Epinomis*, though he does make several references to the elenctic refutation of false claims (974c, 974d–976e, 991c). He also appears to make a brief gesture towards the method of collection and division at 991c, but he says that this is a method for "testing" ideas (see Tarán 1975, 342). As Festugière (1949, 215) rightly points out, astronomical theorizing is completely compatible with the *theoria* of the Forms (as we have seen in Plato); but he wrongly suggests that Philip was advocating the latter as well as the former.

[103] As Tarán shows (1975, 92 n. 418), Philip often uses φρόνησις and νοῦς interchangably (as Plato sometimes does). I disagree with Tarán's claim (1975, 58–60) that Philip "identifies" the invisible motions of divine souls with the visible movements of the stars (though he does, at times, blur the distinction between them) and hence fails to distinguish between *nous* and visual perception. In fact, Philip explicitly articulates a dualistic opposition between body and soul (981b–c, 983b–c, 983c–e, 988d–e); the claim that soul alone is apprehensible by *nous* should not be explained away.

the knowledge of the nature of the cosmos and its divine governance instils piety (967d–968a). In this text, Plato says that all the citizens in the good city must learn the "prelude" to the laws against impiety (which takes up all of *Laws* x); indeed he identifies this prelude as the cornerstone of the entire lawcode (887b–c).[104] This indicates that piety – the recognition of and reverence for the divine souls that govern the cosmos – provides the fundamental grounding for good and lawful behavior in the polis.[105] But Plato does not suggest in the *Laws* that piety is the highest of the virtues. This is Philip's innovation.

What science, Philip asks, teaches and develops the virtue of piety? "It is a rather strange thing to hear, and it is not what inexperienced people would think – I say that it is astronomy . . . and that it is necessary for the wisest man to be an astronomer" (990a). The *theoria* of the heavens and cosmos, in short, leads directly to piety. The man with a complete understanding of the intelligible structure of the universe and of the divine souls which govern its motions will know, when he looks at the heavens, that he is seeing "visible gods." And the encounter with these gods – which is both physical and intellectual – automatically produces piety. As Philip claims, "if a person should see the divine and the mortal elements in the generated world" – that is, if he could see the whole cosmos – "he will learn piety and number" (τὸ θεοσεβὲς γνωρισθήσεται καὶ ὁ ἀριθμός, 977e–978a). The alliance between the mathematical science of astronomy and the virtue of piety could not be stronger. Here, Philip advances a new and rather outlandish conception of the relation of *theoria* to *praxis*.[106] The mathematical and ontological "truths" about the cosmos, which are obtained through a combination of visual and noetic *theoria*, lead to an encounter with divinity and thus to the virtue of piety. The philosophic *theoros*, then, moves directly from a scientific "is" to an "ought" that is generated by piety and religious reverence. Philip does not tell us how piety is related to the other virtues, or why it makes one a good citizen and ruler (presumably he believes that it will produce and safeguard lawful behavior, though this is hardly an adequate answer to the question). But he does make it quite clear that the contemplation of the "visible gods" in the heavens leads the philosopher to develop the "virtue" of piety (which, in turn, will directly affect his practical behavior). This is a quite new contribution to the fourth-century debate about *theoria* and *praxis*.

[104] On the "preludes" in the *Laws*, see Nightingale 1993; cf. Bobonich 1991.
[105] As the Athenian says, "no one who believes in gods as the law directs ever willingly commits an unholy act or lets any lawless word pass his lips" (885b).
[106] See Einarson 1936, 281, who argues that Philip "skillfully" combines his new theoretical wisdom with the old Platonic *sophia* concerned with virtue. But Philip's identification of piety as the highest form of virtue is not Platonic.

We must remember that the *Epinomis* was designed to be read in the context of Plato's *Laws* – a context that is fundamentally political. Though the *Epinomis* says much more about astronomy than it does about politics, Philip explicitly claims that the wise man will be a good citizen who will rule justly in the city, and not be "a *banausos* or a fool" (976d). Here, Philip uses the rhetoric of *banausia* to distinguish the theoretical philosophers – who, he claims, will make up the ruling class in the good city – from all other members of the state.[107] He tells us more about this elite ruling class near the end of the dialogue, where he says that the theoretical philosophers, when they have "received due rearing and education, will be able to restrain the masses – their inferiors – in the most correct way by means of their thoughts, their deeds, and their discourse concerning the gods . . ." (989c). At this point, Philip seems to have forgotten that in the *Laws* it is the lawcode that provides this restraint; the philosophers who make up the "Nocturnal Council" are not above the law and are therefore not philosophic rulers in the strict sense (like those in the *Republic* and *Statesman*). Be that as it may, Philip makes it quite clear that astronomical *theoria* has an essential practical and, ideally, political aspect. Indeed he never conceives of "true wisdom" as solely contemplative: theoretical wisdom is both contemplative and practical, with piety providing the link between the two.

In this chapter, I have examined the emergence of a form of *theoria* that is based on the visual apprehension of a god or the sacred image of a god. This apprehension is not of course merely visual: the sense-data must be interpreted in the correct way for the theorist to successfully "see" the divine. Neither Plato nor Philip describe this activity in a technical way, but the overall picture is reasonably clear. In this kind of theorizing, the philosopher contemplates the order, harmony, and beauty in the physical world. Because beauty and orderly motion are directly linked to divinity, the visual perception of such wondrous phenomena leads to the intellectual grasp of a divine being. To be sure, the *theoros* can only fully perceive this when he has mastered mathematics and philosophy. But, as these texts indicate, the vision of the *agalmata* of divinity and, indeed, the visible gods in the heavens can produce reverence even in the philosophical beginner. And reverence will play an important role in the philosopher's actions.

---

[107] As I suggested in chapter 3, Plato transformed the rhetoric of *banausia* in his middle dialogues such that all non-theoretical philosophers, including ordinary aristocrats, were categorized as *banausoi*. Philip's use of this rhetoric is more traditional than Plato's.

CHAPTER 5

"Useless" knowledge: Aristotle's rethinking of theoria

It is entirely correct and completely in order to say, "You can't do anything with philosophy." The only mistake is to believe that with this, the judgment concerning philosophy is at an end. For a little epilogue arises in the form of a counter-question: even if *we* can't do anything with it, may not philosophy in the end do something *with us?*

Heidegger, *Introduction to Metaphysics*

If one looks at the history of knowledge, it is plain that at the beginning men tried to know because they had to do so in order to live . . . The desire for intellectual or cognitive understanding had no meaning except as a means for obtaining greater security as to the issues of action. Moreover, even when after the coming of leisure some men were enabled to adopt knowing as their special calling or profession, *merely* theoretical certainty continues to have no meaning.

Dewey, *The Quest for Certainty*

Aristotle's conception of *theoria* represents a distinct departure from his predecessors.[1] Aristotle explicitly refers to traditional *theoria* in discussing philosophic contemplation, but he uses only some of its standard features. In particular, he retains the idea that *theoria* involves detachment from practical affairs and "seeing" something divine and true. But he dispenses with the notion of a round-trip journey abroad. As we will see, he compares the philosopher to a *theoros* who goes to a festival simply for the sake of seeing the spectacle. He makes no mention of the theorist's return trip, or his report to the city. Rather, the act of spectating is the final goal or *telos* of this activity – nothing is produced or generated "beyond"

---

[1] There is a great deal of scholarly literature on Aristotle's conception of *theoria*. See, e.g., Kapp 1938, Snell 1951, Stigen 1961, Bien 1968, Gauthier and Jolif 1970, *passim*, Defournay 1972, Gigon 1973, Eriksen 1976, Adkins 1978, Hardie 1980, ch. 16 and *passim*, M. White 1980, A. Rorty 1980, Moline 1983, Parker 1984, Cooper [1987]/1999, Lear 1988, 116–40, 293–319, Broadie 1991, ch. 7, Reeve 1992, 139–59.

that goal.[2] In fact, Aristotle does not use the metaphor of the journey of *theoria* at all. He identifies philosophic theorizing solely with the spectatorial activity in traditional *theoria*: Aristotelian theorizing is simply a matter of intellectual "vision" and is not nested in or connected to practical projects. This kind of *theoria*, then, is private rather than civic, and is in no way "useful" in the practical or political sphere. Indeed, in its highest instantiation, the Aristotelian *theoros* apprehends god or divine *nous*, thus engaging in a sacralized form of "seeing" that has no connection to the mundane realm.

In abandoning the notion of a journey to enlightenment, Aristotle also rids himself of the narrative mode in which this was conveyed: there is no myth or drama depicting a philosophic protagonist journeying towards the light. Even in his popularizing *Protrepticus*, Aristotle does not offer a dramatic or existential account of the activity of theorizing. He deploys a good deal of rhetoric, but does not narrate a "story" of the philosopher and his intellectual quests. Aristotle identifies *theoria* as the activity that characterizes the wisest man and the happiest life. But he does not represent the theorist as a whole person practicing an "art of living." Rejecting the narrative mode, Aristotle uses a combination of philosophical analysis and rhetoric in his attempts to define and defend *theoria*. He adopts this approach, in part, because he is forging a more technical account of *theoria* than his predecessors. But he also does this because Plato's myths and metaphors do not fit his conception of philosophic *theoria*. Aristotle develops a new theory of the soul and its theoretical activities, and he presents it in a different mode of discourse.

Aristotle is famous for his rejection of Plato's negative view of the human and terrestrial world – for "saving the phenomena" from the clutches of his teacher. For Aristotle, the human world is not a region of darkness and ignorance from which the philosopher must escape to achieve enlightenment. Whereas Plato inveighed against traditional social and political practices, Aristotle is more complacent about human affairs. He does of course have very strong views about social and political institutions, and clearly prefers aristocratic government and its values; indeed he regularly criticizes lower-class and "banausic" workers (who had a share in ruling the Athenian democracy), favoring the ideals of the aristocratic gentleman who does not work for a living. But, unlike Plato, Aristotle does not attack the ruling elite or claim that all nonphilosophers are mired in ignorance and

---

[2] The achievement of wisdom and *eudaimonia* are essential features of the activity of *theoria*, and are not conceived as a product of theorizing.

vice. He clearly elevates the theoretical over the political life, but argues that the latter kind of life is nonetheless valuable and happy (if conducted properly in its own sphere).

In spite of this more genial assessment of the human world, however, Aristotle conceives of *theoria* as an activity that is radically cut off from social life.[3] Indeed, Aristotle goes further than both Plato and Philip in claiming that *theoria* is a contemplative activity that has no "results" in the practical or political sphere. For Aristotle, *theoria* involves the actualization of *nous*, which is the divine part of man; it is the pure noetic activity that gods engage in, and is only done "for its own sake." Whereas Plato and Philip conceived of *theoria* as comprising both contemplation and action – both spectating and performing – Aristotle confines it to the activity of contemplation. This detachment of *theoria* from *praxis* is a momentous move that effectively situates the wise man even further from practical and political affairs than Plato and Philip did. To be sure, Aristotle's theorist must engage in virtuous *praxis* insofar as he is a human being; but his theoretical activities, in themselves, will have no practical results and are even said to be "impeded" by practical and political exigencies (*NE* x.7, 1178b3–5).

Plato, as we have seen, did not distinguish between practical reasoning (which grasps particulars) and theoretical reasoning (which apprehends essences).[4] Rather, he suggests that the rational faculty does the "seeing" in both the physical and metaphysical realms: a single faculty performs both contemplative and practical reasoning. Plato never explains how the rational faculty – which is, after all, akin to the Forms rather than the material world – grasps the shadowy particulars in the physical and social world. But he makes it quite clear that reason can and does use its contemplative knowledge in practical action and affairs.

Aristotle offers a more technical analysis of these philosophical issues. But he still turns to traditional *theoria* in his conceptualization of theoretical philosophy. This move first appears in the *Protrepticus* – a popularizing "exoteric" work which is preserved in substantial fragments. This text is more rhetorical and fulsome than the treatises, but it presents many ideas

---

[3] Note that I am discussing Aristotle's technical conception of *theoria* (designated by the noun θεωρία, and identified as a noetic activity with distinct features and objects). Aristotle often uses the verb *theorein* to signify the act of "observing" and "examining" in the broad sense; the verb therefore has a much wider and less technical sense than the noun. We should not assume, then, that the isolated use of the verb *theorein* refers to philosophic *theoria* in the strict sense. For discussions of the terminology of *theoria* and *theorein*, see Guthrie 1981, 396–8, and Lear 1988, 121.

[4] He does speak of *doxa* in *Republic* v as presiding over the earthly sphere of change and flux, but he does not identify this as an intellectual or practical virtue.

found in the later works. In this chapter, I will begin by examining Aristotle's use of traditional *theoria* in the *Protrepticus* in his attempt to define and legitimize philosophic theorizing. In this text, Aristotle develops the claim that *theoria* is a "useless" (*achreston*) activity that is an end in itself. This argument anticipates the treatises, where Aristotle defines *theoria* in opposition to "useful" and "necessary" pursuits which aim at external ends. Clearly, "useless" activities, as Aristotle conceives them, are in no way worthless or trivial; on the contrary, they are supremely important and fine. The English word "useless" has negative connotations that are completely at odds with Aristotle's use of *achreston* (and *ou chresimon*) in these and other passages. For the lack of a better alternative, I will translate these terms as "useless" with the qualification that this does not mean "worthless" or "unimportant." The "useless" activity of *theoria*, in fact, is eminently important and valuable, since it actualizes the best part of man and offers the highest degree of happiness.[5]

After examining the *Protrepticus*, I will turn to Aristotle's discussions of *theoria* and theoretical "science" in the *Nicomachean Ethics* and *Metaphysics*. In these texts, Aristotle sets forth his most detailed analyses of theoretical activity. He draws a distinction between theoretical, practical, and technical reasoning, identifying *theoria* as a noetic activity that is chosen only for its own sake. He offers a number of technical arguments for this position, defining *theoria* in opposition to practical and productive pursuits. *Theoria*, he claims, is a radically free and disinterested activity that has nothing to do with (or in) the human world. I want to investigate Aristotle's claim that *theoria* is not "useful" or goal-oriented but rather a final end, chosen only for its own sake. According to Aristotle, the fact that *theoria* is useless and nonproductive is part of what identifies it as supremely fine. Productive activities – and those who labor as producers – are inferior precisely because they "serve" something (or someone) beyond themselves.

I will conclude by analyzing Aristotle's account of "liberal education" in the *Politics* VIII. In this book, Aristotle sets forth an educational system designed for the elite youths in the "good" city. As I argue, this education has a theoretical orientation, even though it does not train students to be philosophical theorists. In this text, Aristotle proposes that the best young men should be trained in the activity of observing and judging artistic spectacles in a liberal and discerning fashion. Although this activity is not philosophical, Aristotle defines it in the very terms that he uses

---

[5] One might argue that theoretical pursuits are "useful" for the happy life, but this terminology is not Aristotelian: Aristotle uses the word "useful" for activities that are not pursued for their own sakes or for the sake of happiness alone.

to characterize *theoria*: the liberal activity of artistic spectating is "useless," "unnecessary," "leisured," and "free." By engaging in this "noble" activity in his leisure time, the educated man can approach (though never fully achieve) the freedom and happiness of the philosophic theorist. This educational system reflects and reinforces the supreme status of *theoria* as well as the aristocratic value system that defines its superiority.

As I have suggested, Aristotle uses rhetoric as well as philosophic analysis in all his discussions of *theoria*. In particular, he deploys traditional aristocratic rhetoric to make the claim that *theoria* is the only activity that is truly free, leisured, and noble. Unlike Plato, Aristotle almost never uses the "rhetoric of estrangement." Rather, he develops a "rhetoric of disinterest" – a discourse that portrays certain activities as superior to productive and practical endeavors that serve a separate end. By identifying *theoria* as a nonutilitarian ("useless") activity done only "for its own sake," Aristotle sets forth an idea that has had a profound effect on Western thinking about "pure" intellectual activities and the "liberal" education. As I argue, Aristotle uses aristocratic rhetoric to convey the idea that *theoria* (and certain other "liberal" pursuits) are superior precisely because they are "useless" and disinterested. An examination of this rhetoric will help us to understand Aristotle's philosophy in the cultural context of fourth-century Greece.

THE RHETORIC OF "USELESSNESS": *PROTREPTICUS*

As its title indicates, the *Protrepticus* was a popular work designed to attract people to the life of philosophy.[6] This text presents numerous interpretative difficulties, since most of the fragments derive from Iamblichus' *Protrepticus*, which contains a mix of Aristotelian and non-Aristotelian material. Given the difficulty of determining precisely which passages in Iamblichus' treatise came from Aristotle's *Protrepticus*, it is not surprising that scholars have widely divergent ideas about this text. Consider the following two positions, which offer a good sense of the spectrum of scholarly arguments. On the one hand, Jaeger argues that Aristotle wrote the *Protrepticus* in an early "Platonic" period, when he still subscribed to Plato's theory of Forms;

---

[6] I will use Düring's text of the *Protrepticus* (1961, including his numeration of the fragments), which has been honed by later studies but is still unsurpassed. He follows Bywater (1869) and, after him, Jaeger (1923, ch. 4) in treating Iamblichus' Λόγος προτρεπτικὸς ἐπὶ φιλοσοφίαν as consisting of verbatim excerpts from Aristotle's text. For a contrarian position, see Rabinowitz 1957, who argues that we cannot accept any fragments as genuine which do not mention Aristotle's name as well as the title of the *Protrepticus*. For a brief discussion of the attempts to reconstruct the *Protrepticus*, see Chroust 1973, ch. 7. Düring (1961, 9–36) and Rabinowitz (1957, *passim*) survey the scholarship on this text.

its conception of *theoria* therefore differs from that of the extant treatises, which were (for the most part) written when Aristotle had moved beyond Plato to develop his mature philosophy.[7] Düring, by contrast, argues that the text is completely Aristotelian, claiming that "there is no substantial difference of method or in the general theory of morals between the *Protrepticus* and the three ethical treatises."[8]

I want to examine the most prominent arguments and rhetorical strategies that Aristotle uses to define "theoretical" philosophy in the *Protrepticus*. Aristotle sets forth a number of quite new ideas about *theoria* in this text, and begins to develop a line of argument that is only fully worked out in the treatises. As Barnes observes, the fragments of this early work "prove neither that Aristotle was a Platonist nor that he was not a Platonist."[9] In my view, they depart from Plato in substantial ways, but stop short of the mature Aristotelian position.[10]

Since modern scholars rarely discuss or analyze this text – in spite of its great popularity in antiquity – I will take the liberty of including some rather long quotes in this section.[11] Let us consider first fragment B44, which draws an explicit analogy between traditional *theoria* and philosophic contemplation:

> Wisdom is not useful or advantageous (μὴ χρησίμη . . . μηδ' ὠφέλιμος), for we call it not advantageous but good, and it should be chosen not for the sake of any other thing, but for itself. For just as we go to the Olympian festival for the sake of the spectacle (θέας), even if nothing more should come of it – for the *theoria* (θεωρία) itself is more precious than great wealth; and just as we go to theorize (θεωροῦμεν) at the Festival of Dionysus not so that we will gain anything from the actors (indeed we pay to see them) . . . so too the *theoria* (θεωρία) of the universe must be honored above all things that are considered to be useful (χρησίμων).

Here, Aristotle compares the activity of philosophic contemplation with that of the theoric spectator at the Olympian and Dionysian festivals. Clearly, Aristotle refers here to the private form of *theoria* at religious festivals. In this kind of *theoria*, as we have seen, an individual attends a festival on his own, simply to see the sights and spectacles; he is not sent by the city, and is not required to return and report on his findings. Although this

---

[7] Jaeger [1923]/1948.

[8] Düring 1961, 278. Düring (1960 and 1961, *passim*) offers a number of excellent criticisms of Jaeger's position. See also Gadamer 1928 and (very differently) S. Mansion 1960.

[9] Barnes 1995a, 18.

[10] This does not mean that I endorse a developmentalist approach to Aristotle's entire *oeuvre* but merely that I accept the consensus that the *Protrepticus* was an early work.

[11] Düring (1961, 13, 32–5) discusses the influence of the *Protrepticus* on Aristotle's contemporaries and successors.

model is familiar from Plato and other fourth-century writers, Aristotle introduces some brand new ideas. First, he makes no mention of the journey to the sanctuary or to the return home: the focus is entirely on the activity of spectating.[12] Second, he claims that viewing the spectacle is an end in itself, and that there is absolutely nothing "useful" or "advantageous" in this activity; this is in stark contrast to his predecessors, who explicitly argued that *theoria* is "useful." Third, he addresses the question of why and how one engages in *theoria*: the wise man does not aim at or produce anything beyond the activity of spectating and does not theorize "for the sake of any other thing."

As I suggested in the Introduction, Aristotle and other fourth-century philosophers retrojected the activity of *theoria* back onto the ancients, thus claiming for it a venerable pedigree. In the *Protrepticus*, Aristotle cites as evidence for his own position the "fact" that Pythagoras and Anaxagoras privileged the activity of "theorizing" the heavens over all other pursuits:

For what end (οὗ χάριν) did nature and god bring us into being? Pythagoras, when asked this question, said, "to behold (θεάσασθαι) the heaven"; and he also claimed that he was a *theoros* (θεωρόν) of nature and for this reason he had come into being. And when someone asked Anaxagoras for what end (τίνος ἂν ἕνεκα) he would choose to exist and live, he said "for the sake of beholding (θεάσασθαι) the heaven and the stars and the moon and sun," since all other things were worth nothing... According to this argument, Pythagoras rightly said that every man was put together by god in order to acquire knowledge and to theorize (θεωρῆσαι). Whether the cosmos is the object of this knowledge or some other nature, we must inquire later; but this is sufficient as a beginning. (B18–20)

Here, even as Aristotle ascribes the activity of *theoria* to the ancients, he gestures towards his own more mature position: whereas these early thinkers were (he claims) practicing some form of astronomical contemplation, the true objects of *theoria* may be quite different. In particular, these objects will be metaphysical rather than physical.

Using language that anticipates his technical treatises, Aristotle claims in the *Protrepticus* that the "end" (*telos*) and function (*ergon*) of human life is the activity of "theorizing":

To engage in the activity of *phronesis* and *theoria* (τὸ φρονεῖν ἄρα καὶ τὸ θεωρεῖν) is the *ergon* of the soul, and this is the most choiceworthy thing for men just as the capacity to see with the eyes [is choiceworthy]; for one would choose to have sight even if nothing other than sight itself were to result from it. (B70)

---

[12] As we have seen, Plato makes use of the traveling metaphor in all of his "*theoria*" texts except the *Timaeus*.

Here, Aristotle uses the analogy of sight in his effort to conceptualize philosophical *theoria*. He develops this point in more detail elsewhere, arguing that "thoughts (αἱ νοήσεις) are the activities (ἐνέργειαι) of *nous*, and these involve the vision of intelligible things (ὁράσεις οὖσαι νοητῶν), just as seeing visible things is the activity of sight" (B24).

To those familiar with Aristotle's treatises, one of the most striking features of the *Protrepticus* is that it identifies *phronesis* with *nous* and *theoria*.[13] For example, Aristotle defines the philosopher as "the man who engages in *phronesis* and *theoria* (ὁ φρονῶν καὶ θεωρῶν) according to the most exact science" (ἐπιστήμην, B85; so also B91). In contrast with the *Nicomachean Ethics*, which separates *phronesis* from *nous* and *epistemē* (and, by association, from *theoria*), Aristotle argues in the *Protrepticus* that *phronesis* is a theoretical science:

> If *phronesis* is to be productive (ποιητική), it will always produce results different from itself; for example the art of building produces a house but is not a part of the house. But *phronesis* is part of the *aretē* of the soul and of happiness. For we say that happiness either comes from *phronesis* or is it. *Phronesis*, then, cannot be a productive knowledge. For the end must be better than that which comes to attain it. But nothing is better than *phronesis* . . . Therefore we must say that it is a theoretical science (θεωρητικήν . . . ἐπιστήμην), since it is impossible for *poiesis* to be its end (ἐπείπερ ἀδύνατον ποίησιν εἶναι τὸ τέλος). (B68–9)

Here, Aristotle defines "theoretical" *phronesis* in opposition to the productive arts and sciences; it does not produce results "other than itself" and is, for this reason, the true *telos* of human striving.

The argument that theoretical wisdom is not productive leads to one of the central claims of the text: that *theoria* must be chosen for its own sake and is not "useful" or "necessary." As Aristotle states:

> To seek from every kind of knowledge that some other thing come into being [from it] and that it must be useful (χρησίμην) is the act of someone who is completely ignorant of how great the distance is between things that are noble and and those that are necessary (τὰ ἀγαθὰ καὶ τὰ ἀναγκαῖα); for the difference is vast. Those things that are loved for the sake of some other thing (which one cannot live without) should be called "necessities" (ἀναγκαῖα) and secondary causes, but those that are loved for themselves, even if no other thing results (ἀποβαίνῃ) from them, should be called goods in the strict sense . . . It is completely ridiculous, then, to seek from everything a benefit beyond the thing itself (ὠφέλειαν ἑτέραν

---

[13] Exceptions to this general rule are fragments B27 and B29, where Aristotle separates pure *theoria* from practical reasoning which, confusingly, he calls "*phronesis*" (note that Rose does not include these two fragments in his edition, whereas Düring does). Aristotle also appears to distinguish *theoria* from moral virtue and practical reasoning in B42, B43, and B68.

παρ' αὐτὸ τὸ πρᾶγμα) and to ask "how is this profitable (ὄφελος) for us?" And "how is this useful" (χρήσιμον)? (B42)

Aristotle proceeds to illustrate this point with a fascinating little thought experiment:

> We would see the truth of my point if someone should carry us to the Islands of the Blessed. In that place there is no use (χρεία) of anything, and no profit (ὄφελος) from anything. There remain only thinking and theorizing (τὸ διανοεῖσθαι καὶ θεωρεῖν), which even now we say is the free life (ἐλεύθερόν φαμεν βίον) . . . For just as we receive the rewards of justice in Hades, we receive those of *phronesis* in the Islands of the Blessed. (B43)

Here, Aristotle indicates that pure theorizing is completely separate from practical activities, and even suggests that souls who possess practical virtue go to a different place in the afterlife than those who have perfected their theoretical capacities. This distinction between "useful" skills and activities and those that are not useful or necessary is central to Aristotle's reconception of *theoria*. *Theoria*, in short, is "useless knowledge." Indeed its uselessness is part of what identifies it as supremely free and fine.

Note that Aristotle also claims in this passage that the pure theorizer lives "the free life," since he is released from "useful" activities (both practical and productive). Here, Aristotle articulates a distinctly aristocratic notion of freedom, which is conveyed in politically charged rhetoric:

> Of thoughts, those are free (ἐλεύθεραι) which are chosen for themselves, but those that bring knowledge for the sake of other things are like slaves (δούλαις δ' ἐοικυῖαι). That which is chosen for itself is superior to that chosen for something else, just as that which is free is superior to that which is not free.[14] (B25)

All activities dealing with the "necessities" of life, Aristotle suggests, are slavish and servile. One may be tempted to believe that Aristotle uses this aristocratic rhetoric because this popularizing text is directed towards the cultured elite. But Aristotle uses this same rhetoric and terminology in his discussions of *theoria* in the treatises; as we will see, this kind of discourse plays an important role in his conception of theoretical activity.

What, then, are the objects of the theoretical gaze? In the *Protrepticus*, Aristotle answers this question only in the most general terms. We have seen that he calls into question the idea that *theoria* is astronomical. But he never specifies the precise object of philosophical theorizing. For example,

---

[14] Düring puts daggers around the word ἀπερείδουσαι; he conjectures that the proper word was ἀπεργάζουσαι or ἀποδιδοῦσαι. This crux does not interfere with the overall sense of the passage, which is quite clear.

Aristotle suggests that the philosophic theorist "looks to nature and the divine" (πρὸς τὴν φύσιν βλέπων ζῇ καὶ πρὸς τὸ θεῖον, B50) and "theorizes the nature and truth of realities" (τὴν δὲ τῶν ὄντων φύσιν καὶ τὴν ἀλήθειαν . . . θεωρεῖν, B44; B65). More specifically, he seeks knowledge of "the causes and the elements" (τῶν αἰτίων καὶ τῶν στοιχείων) and understanding of "the first principles" (τὰ πρῶτα, B35). Some scholars claim that these passages refer to Plato's Forms or (alternatively) to Aristotle's own theory of causes and first principles. But these passages are extremely vague, and it seems likely that Aristotle chose to avoid a technical discussion of the objects of *theoria* in a popularizing text.[15]

We come, now, to a problem in the text. For, having argued in a number of fragments that *theoria* and *phronesis* are not "useful" or "productive" but pursued only as ends in themselves, Aristotle occasionally makes the claim that theoretical reason *is* useful and beneficial in practical and productive activities. He smooths over the problem by saying that *theoria* should be chosen as an end in itself – i.e. as an activity that is completely free, nonutilitarian and unproductive – but that it can also serve as the basis for practical activities and is thus "useful" after all. This "both . . . and" argument is readily seen in fragment B41:

> To think wisely (τὸ φρονεῖν) and to come to know is in itself desirable for men (for it is not possible to live a human life without these activities), and useful (χρήσιμον) too for practical life. For unless something is accomplished after we have formed an opinion about it and acted wisely, it does not accrue to us as good.

It is worth noting that the fragments which attest to the "usefulness" of *theoria* echo the language and ideas of Plato. Consider, for example, Aristotle's use of the Platonic analogy of the doctor and trainer: "that theoretical *phronesis* is supremely useful (ὠφελείας τὰς μεγίστας) for human life can be seen from the arts and skills. For all intelligent doctors and trainers say that those who are to be good doctors or trainers must have a general knowledge of nature" (B46).[16] Aristotle also appropriates the Platonic conception of *mimesis* to make the claim that the philosopher uses theoretical knowledge in the practical sphere:

> In the other arts and crafts men do not take their tools and their most accurate reasonings from first principles (τῶνπρώτων); . . . rather, they take them at second or third hand or at a distant remove, and base their reasonings on experience. Only

---

[15] As he says, cagily, in fragment B36: "whether it be fire or air or number or some other natures that are the causes and first principles (αἰτίαι καὶ πρῶται), if we are ignorant of them we can't have knowledge of anything else."

[16] I discuss Plato's use of the medical analogy in Nightingale 1999a.

the philosopher enacts a *mimesis* of objects that are exact; for he is a spectator (θεατής) of things that are exact, and not of *mimemata* . . . An imitation (μίμημα) of what is not divine and stable (θείου καὶ βεβαίου) in its nature cannot be immortal and stable (ἀθάνατον καὶ βέβαιον). Clearly, stable laws and good and right actions belong to the philosopher alone among craftsmen. (B48–9)

Here, Aristotle suggests that the theoretical philosopher gazes at "exact," "immortal," and "stable" things, and then "imitates" them by producing good laws and actions. This clearly reflects Platonic language and ideas.

Having previously defined theoretical wisdom in opposition to all productive activities, then, Aristotle now indicates that the philosophical theorist is a craftsman who performs "demiourgic" tasks in the practical sphere. As he claims, "this knowledge is theoretical (θεωρητικὴ ἥδε ἡ ἐπιστήμη), but it enables us to fashion (δημιουργεῖν) all things in accordance with it" (B51). As we saw in chapters 3 and 4, Plato regularly uses the language of *"demiourgia"* in discussing the translation of *theoria* into *praxis*. In Aristotle, this language comes as a surprise, since he has been at pains to define *theoria* as essentially non-productive. When he writes the treatises, Aristotle will retain the argument that *theoria* is non-productive (and non-practical), but will drop the idea that it can also be useful (and serve as the basis for "producing" virtuous actions). In the *Protrepticus*, however, Aristotle argues that theoretical knowledge is *both* separate from (and superior to) practical and productive activities, *and* useful as a basis for action and various kinds of production. In my view, Aristotle's account of *theoria* in the *Protrepticus* is not fully consistent, since he still retained some key Platonic positions even as he began to articulate his own ideas.[17] This tension in the *Protrepticus* reveals the difficulty that theoretical philosophers in the Academy and Lyceum were facing in conceptualizing *"theoria"* and its relation to *praxis*.

DETACHMENT AND DISINTEREST

In most of his discussions of *theoria*, Plato depicted the activity of "seeing" truth as one phase in the theoric journey: the philosophic soul goes to the realm of reality, contemplates the Forms, and returns home to implement his theoretical knowledge in practical and political life. The "seeing" part of the journey is marked as a separate and distinct phase – when the soul is in the receptive state of contemplation – but it nonetheless forms part of a

---

[17] Alternatively, however, one may claim that the text is not really inconsistent, since the fact that the theorist engages in *theoria* in a nonutilitarian fashion is compatible with the claim that theoretical knowledge can produce useful results in other scientific and technical endeavors (as Tony Long has suggested to me).

continuum. For it leads inevitably to the return "home," and provides the basis for all action. Aristotle, by contrast, completely separates theoretical contemplation from all practical endeavors, treating it as an isolated activity that is an end in itself. Of course the Aristotelian theorist must use his practical reason to organize his life around the activity of contemplation, but *theoria* itself is completely detached from *praxis* and does not provide the basis for action. Aristotle severs the connection that Plato forged between *theoria* and *praxis*, and thus has no use for the metaphor of a journey in which contemplating and acting are conceived as a continuum.

Aristotle abandoned the metaphor of the journey because it presented the wrong conception of *theoria*. What, precisely, did Aristotle object to in the Platonic scheme? First of all, he rejected Plato's claim that theoretical knowledge is practical and productive; and he also criticized Plato for his failure to distinguish between practical and technical reasoning. As we have seen, Plato draws a very general distinction between "unworldly" contemplative activities and the "worldly" activities of action and production, but he does not place *praxis* and *technē* in separate categories. In fact, he often uses the "craft analogy" as a way of exploring moral reasoning; at times, he seems almost to conflate practical and technical activities, using metaphors from the crafts in his descriptions of virtuous action.[18] To be sure, Plato sometimes criticizes the craft analogy on the grounds that virtue (unlike *technē*) is not a value-neutral activity, but he does not develop this idea in a systematic way.[19] In short, Plato never distinguished a faculty of moral reasoning distinct from *technē* and *theoria*.

Plato does of course discuss the category of *technē* in many dialogues. In particular, he develops the idea that there are *technai* which are not productive: in the *Charmides*, Critias points out that *technai* such as mathematics do not produce anything (165c). In the *Euthydemus* and, even more explicitly, in the *Sophist*, Plato makes a distinction between "productive" and "acquisitive" *technai*, the latter of which are exemplified by the mathematical sciences (and hunting in general).[20] In the *Statesman* (258b–260b), Plato divides "*technē gnostikē* (which is "bereft of any *praxis*, and only

---

[18] Roochnik 1996; see also Nehamas 1999b on the performative/practical aspects of *mimesis*.

[19] Irwin (1977, 174 and *passim*) argues that, in the middle dialogues, Plato criticizes the craft analogy because it "misrepresents the proper status of virtue by making it worthwhile only for its consequences." Cf. Vlastos 1978 and 1991, 6–11 and ch. 8. Roochnik (1996) claims that Plato never believed in the analogy between *technē* and virtue, even in the early dialogues.

[20] *Euthydemus* 288d–290d, *Sophist* 218e–219e. In the *Euthydemus* Socrates also mentions the "user's" art, but this is not practical (the dialecticians "use" what the mathematicians have acquired); as Roochnik (1996, 274) observes, "use in this context does not carry a practical connotation, but refers to a sort of meta-mathematical analysis."

supplies knowledge") from *technē praktikē*" (which is in fact productive).[21]
Thus, Plato does separate the intellectual, "acquisitive" *technai* from the
"productive" *technai*. But it is not clear how the activity of contemplation
fits into this scheme. As we saw in chapter 3, contemplating the Forms is
conceived as a receptive act of "seeing" rather than an acquisitive activity;
and it only becomes productive after the theorist returns from his con-
templations and enters the practical world. The contemplative activity of
theoria, then, appears to be neither acquisitive nor productive – indeed,
it is not identified as a *technē* at all. Yet Plato claims that the knowledge
achieved in contemplation forms the basis of action in the practical and
technical sphere. Unfortunately, he never analyzes the distinction between
contemplation and action – or the necessary link between them – and thus
raises more questions than he answers.

Aristotle attempts to do what Plato did not: he offers a technical discussion of *theoria* and analyzes theoretical activity in relation to other forms of
reasoning. In the *Protrepticus*, Aristotle defines *theoria* in opposition to production or productivity. In the treatises, he draws a technical distinction
between *theoria*, *praxis*, and *poiesis/technē* (production). These categories
have become so commonplace in Western thinking that it has become
almost impossible to think them away. But we must keep in mind that they
were not articulated by Aristotle's predecessors – including Plato – and thus
represent a new conceptual turn. Aristotle departed from Plato, first of all,
because he conceived of practical reasoning as separate from technical or
theoretical reasoning. In addition, Aristotle rejected the theory of Forms,
claiming that the Form of the Good, even if it did exist, would be of no
use for *praxis*, which deals with particulars (*NE* 1.6, esp. 1096b–1097a).
Practical reasoning responds to the shifting and particularized world of
human affairs. Virtuous behavior is generated by a stochastic intelligence
that grasps the particulars as well as the general principles – indeed, according to Aristotle, the apprehension of the particulars is the most important
part of practical reasoning (*NE* vi.7, 1141b14–22).

From Aristotle's point of view, Plato's conception of virtuous *praxis*
involved the technical application of universal truths to the practical sphere:
the person first apprehends the Forms and then uses them as a model for
action. This is not responsive to the complexity and messiness of practical
life, in which no single model can encompass the ever-shifting and evolving
realm of particulars.[22] Aristotle brilliantly articulated what Plato glimpsed

[21] See also the *Philebus* 58b–e, which distinguishes between *technai* that are precise (which use or are
based on mathematics) and those that are not precise.
[22] See Nussbaum 1986, chs. 10–12, Dunne 1993, chs. 8–10.

but did not successfully formulate: that practical reasoning is not a "craft" or *technē*, but a completely separate mode of intelligence. *Phronesis* is a mode of reasoning distinct from both *theoria* and *praxis*. Aristotle's construction of this new distinction was a major conceptual achievement. But Aristotle created some new problems of his own. In particular, by severing the link between *theoria* and *praxis*, Aristotle seems to indicate that the contemplative theorist need not be a virtuous person. And even if the theorist is an ethically good person, this is not a result of the practice of *theoria per se*. For *theoria* operates in a sphere that has no connection to ethical and political life. *Qua* theorist, the person is not answerable to the social community.

PHRONESIS AND TECHNĒ: NICOMACHEAN ETHICS VI

Let us look first at book VI of the *Nicomachean Ethics*, where Aristotle distinguishes between *epistemē, nous, technē,* and *phronesis*. Much of the discussion in book VI focuses on *phronesis* or practical reasoning, which Aristotle distinguishes from theoretical and technical activities. He separates it from *nous* and *epistemē* by reference to their differing objects: *phronesis* deals with objects that vary (i.e. things in the realm of becoming and chance), whereas the objects of *epistemē* and *nous* are unvarying and eternal, and they exist of necessity.[23] But *phronesis* still needs to be separated from *technē*, since both kinds of knowledge have as their object the class of things that vary.

How does Aristotle distinguish between "making" and "doing"? *Technē* (making), he claims, has both rational and productive aspects – it is a "capacity accompanied by reasoning" (ἕξις μετὰ λόγου) which is productive (ποιητική): it has a goal or end (*telos*) that "differs from the act of making."[24] How, then, does *phronesis* differ from *technē*? Like *technē*, *phronesis* is a "capacity accompanied by reasoning" (1140b4–5) and it too deals with objects that vary. But *phronesis* is a capacity that is *praktikē* rather than *poietikē*. The key point of difference is that *phronesis* does not have an end beyond itself: for "doing well is itself the end" (b7).[25] Unlike technical

---

[23] Though *nous* apprehends first principles and *epistemē* does not. See also *Posterior Analytics* 1.6 (75a.18–37), 1.8, 1.30, 1.31; *Met.* VI 2.

[24] *NE* VI.4, 1140a10, VI.5, 1140b6–7. *Technē*, moreover, is a *poiesis* or making in which the maker is the efficient cause that brings something into existence; in other words, the source or *archē* is in the maker rather than the product made.

[25] Aristotle says in VI.12, 1144a6–9 that *phronesis* does "produce" something in that it "gives us good aim" (*skopos*) and brings about good actions. *Phronesis*, then, can only be said to be productive insofar as it makes the person engage in action – this is quite different from producing a separate product in the world. As we will see, Aristotle will alter this position in *NE* x.7, where he claims that moral virtue does "produce" external results.

reasoning, which has an end other than itself (*technē* being the means to this other end), practical reasoning is an end in itself.

This distinction between productive and practical reasoning is related to the distinction drawn in the *Physics* and *Metaphysics* between *kinesis* (motion) and *energeia* (actualization).[26] As Aristotle explains in the *Metaphysics* (IX.6, 1048b18–36), a *kinesis* is a process within a set limit (*peras*) that moves toward an end; it exists only as long as the limit has not been reached and the end does not yet exist (it is *atelēs*). An *energeia*, by contrast, has no unreached limit – its end, or complete condition, already exists in it at any moment of its duration (it is an "entelechy"). Aristotle gives as examples of *kinesis* losing weight, learning, walking, and building. Examples of *energeiai* are seeing and thinking (for "at the same time one is seeing and has seen, is thinking and has thought," 1048b23–24). All *kineseis* initiated by humans, then, are means and not ends, and are therefore not actualizations in the strict sense, since they are incomplete and the end is not present in the action.[27] In a *kinesis*, "something comes into being" (γίγνεταί τι) as a result of the action; an *energeia*, by contrast, is complete at all times and "nothing comes into being" (οὐθὲν γίγνεται) beyond the activity itself (1050a24–8).

Aristotle clarifies the distinction between *kinesis* and *energeia* later in book IX:

> In some cases the ultimate point is the exercise of the faculty, e.g., in the case of sight it is seeing, and nothing comes into being beyond this which is distinct from sight; but in other cases something comes into being, e.g., from the art of building a house comes into being, which is distinct from the act of building. (IX.8, 1050a23–7)

A *kinesis*, unlike an *energeia*, has a *telos* that is separate from the activity itself, and its actualization resides in this *telos*:

> In cases where something comes into being (τι . . . τὸ γιγνόμενον) beyond the use of the faculty, the actualization is in the thing produced (τῷ ποιουμένῳ), e.g. the actualization of building is in the house, that of weaving in the thing woven, and so on, and in general the movement is in the thing moved. But where there is no other product (ἔργον) beyond the actualization, in these cases the actualization is in the agents, e.g., seeing resides in the seer, theorizing in the theorizer. (1050a30–6)

---

[26] See also *NE* X.3–4, where Aristotle discusses *energeiai* and *kinesis* in the course of his analysis of pleasure. For discussions of Aristotle's distinction between *energeia* and *kinesis*, see Kenny, 1963, ch. 8 and Ackrill 1965; cf. M. White 1980.

[27] Aristotle says in *Physics* III.1 that "*kinesis* seems to be a kind of *energeia*, but imperfect" (201b31). There is, then, a sense in which a *kinesis* is an actualization, but only insofar as it is an actualization of an imperfect potentiality. See, e.g., Ross [1936]/1955 ad loc. 1.201a9–b15, and Ackrill 1965, 138–40.

Note that, in this passage, Aristotle shifts from the language of "coming into being" to that of something "being produced." This reveals that Aristotle closely associates *kinesis* with making and production. Though *technē* is only one subset of *kinesis*, it is noteworthy that Aristotle slides into the language of production in this technical definition of *kinesis*.

Returning to the *Nicomachean Ethics* VI, we can place *technē*, as a productive activity that has an end other than the activity itself, in the category of *kineseis*. *Phronesis*, by contrast, is its own end and does not produce anything beyond itself: it is thus an *energeia*. Note that the distinction between a *kinesis* and an *energeia* is, at least in principle, value-neutral. In principle, the identification of *technē* as a *kinesis* simply tells us something about the nature of technical activity, i.e. that it is a process that moves towards an end beyond the activity itself. But the distinction between *kinesis* and *energeia* nonetheless has a place in Aristotle's hierarchical system of values. For he ranks *technē* as inferior to *energeiai* such as *phronesis* and *theoria* precisely because it is a *kinesis* and a means to another *telos*. Just as actuality is better than potentiality, and the *telos* of an action is better than the process that achieves it, so also *phronesis* and *theoria* (as *energeiai*) are better than *technē* (as a *kinesis*).[28]

The key point of opposition between *phronesis* and *technē*, then, is productivity. As we will see, productive activities are often denigrated in Aristotle. Indeed, production is associated with a variety of less-than-admirable human pursuits. Aristotle does of course value some forms of productivity over others, but he generally views production as inferior because it is utilitarian and unleisured – it is a form of labor associated with lower-class and "banausic" people who work for a living. Productive activity, moreover, deals with things that are merely serviceable for sustaining human life – things that are "useful and necessary" rather than "noble." I will discuss Aristotle's aristocratic disdain for productive activity later on. But we should be aware of these ideological associations from the outset, since they directly impact upon his conception of *theoria*.

PHRONESIS AND NOUS: NICOMACHEAN ETHICS VI

In the *Nicomachean Ethics*, *nous* is the faculty of reasoning that operates in the activity of *theoria*. In book VI, Aristotle groups *nous* with *epistemē* and

---

[28] On the claim that actuality is "better and more valuable" than potentiality, and the question of the metaphysical implications of the normative element of a teleological explanation (and hence of the relation between is-statements and ought-statements), see Cooper 1982, Kahn 1987; cf. Balme 1987b, Gotthelf 1987 and 1989.

sophia, which are different forms of intellectual virtue. *Epistemē* deals with objects that do not vary, are eternal, exist of necessity, and do not come into being or perish (VI.3, 1139b18–24). But only *nous* grasps the "first principles" (*ta prota*), which *epistemē* uses in demonstration and argument but does not apprehend (VI.6.2, 1141a2–8).[29] Since *nous* and *epistemē* deal with objects that are eternal and unvarying and which cannot be affected or changed by human endeavor, they are not practical or productive. In *NE* VI, *nous* is said to "stand in opposition" (ἀντίκειται) to *phronesis*; for, as Aristotle explains, "*nous* apprehends definitions, of which no account can be given, whereas *phronesis* deals with the ultimate particular, which is not apprehended by knowledge but by perception" (VI.8, 1142a25–7).

In *NE* VI, Aristotle makes it clear that theoretical activity has no practical results or effects. For "thought by itself moves nothing"; only thoughts which are "practical" and "for the sake of something" can motivate action (VI.2, 1138a35–6). We can infer that non-practical thoughts have no motive power of their own, and thus that theoretical knowledge does not "move anything" or serve as the basis for action or production.[30] As Aristotle goes on to argue, wisdom (*sophia*) "does not theorize at all about the means to human happiness, for it is not concerned with anything that comes into being" (1143b19–20). Correlatively, *phronesis* does not make use of *theoria* but rather organizes other activities for its sake: "*phronesis* does not stand in authority (*kuria*) over *sophia*, or over the better part of us, just as the medical art does not stand in authority over health. For *phronesis* does not use (χρῆται) it [*sophia*], but provides for its coming into being; hence it issues orders for its sake but not to it."[31]

Aristotle illustrates the radical separation of practical and theoretical reasoning in the following (quite rhetorical) passage:

Wisdom (*sophia*) comprises the *epistemē* and *nous* of things that are the most honorable by nature. This is why people say that men such as Anaxagoras and Thales are *sophoi* but not *phronimoi* when they see them displaying their ignorance of things that are advantageous to themselves; they say that these men possess a knowledge that is rare, marvelous, difficult, and divine, but that it is useless (*achresta*), because they are not seeking things that are good for human beings. *Phronesis*, by contrast, is concerned with human affairs, and with things that are

---

[29] The combination of *nous* and *epistemē* is called *sophia* and identified as the highest form of knowledge.

[30] Note that Aristotle says in VI.12 (1144a2–6) that theoretical wisdom does, in a certain sense, have a result: it "produces happiness, not in the way that the art of medicine produces health but in the way that healthiness is the cause of health. For it is a part of virtue as a whole, and it makes a man happy by his possession and exercise of it." This is in keeping with I.7, 1097b2–5, but at odds with the claim in book X that *theoria* is coextensive with or identical to happiness and thus doesn't produce it.

[31] *NE* VI.13, 1145a6–9; cf. *Eudemian Ethics* VIII.3, 1249b.

the objects of deliberation. For we say that the ability to deliberate well is the most characteristic activity of *phronesis*, but nobody deliberates about things that cannot vary or about things that have no practical goal. (vi.7, 1141b2–12)

Aristotle draws this contrast between the *sophos* and the *phronimos* to illustrate the differences between theoretical and practical activities. Although Aristotle credits some unnamed "people" with this view, he clearly agrees with their basic position. To be sure, he may be exaggerating the claim that the theoretical *sophos* completely ignores his own interests and is thus entirely impractical (since Aristotle's theoretical philosopher does need *phronesis* to live well as a human being and to organize his life around the practice of *theoria*). But the passage suggests that the supremely wise man lives a very different kind of life than the man who has perfected his practical capacities: the first is the *sophos* and the second is the *phronimos*.

As I suggested in the Introduction, when Aristotle portrays Thales and Anaxagoras as impractical theorizers, he joins other fourth-century thinkers who cast certain earlier thinkers as contemplative philosophers who were "ignorant" of human affairs.[32] Plato paints a picture of the impractical philosopher in the "Digression" in the *Theaetetus*, where Socrates draws a stark contrast between the philosopher and the politician and their disparate ways of life.[33] Here, Socrates reports the story that Thales fell into a well while gazing at the stars because he didn't see what was at his feet (174a–b). In this tale, Thales is stargazing rather than engaging in metaphysical *theoria*, but Socrates explicitly identifies him with other contemplative philosophers.[34] This passage represents, for the first and only time in Plato, a philosopher who is completely ignorant of human affairs: he doesn't know his neighbors, doesn't notice what he is doing, and "scarcely knows whether he is a man or some other kind of creature" (174b).[35] Socrates describes him as experiencing complete *aporia* in the human world, since "only his body lives and sleeps in the city" while his mind wings its way up into the heavens (173e–174a). Whether or not Plato advocated this conception

---

[32] In fact, as earlier sources attest, Thales was quite involved in practical and political endeavors. There is no evidence for an impractical, contemplative Thales until the fourth century.

[33] The *Theaetetus* is an aporetic dialogue that does not deal with *theoria*, and I have therefore not analyzed it in this book. Only in the rhetorical "digression" do we find any sign of intellectual "seeing," and even here the metaphor is not pressed (173c–177c).

[34] Note that Socrates does not identify the philosopher in this passage as a "theorist" (by using the language of *theoria* or referring to the theory of Forms). As I argued in the Introduction, in the *Theaetetus* Thales is not a practitioner of Platonic *theoria*, but a sort of generic contemplative.

[35] Even the otherwordly *Phaedo* does not suggest that the philosopher, while on earth, is or should be impractical and ignorant of human affairs. I discuss this passage in more detail in the Introduction.

of the philosopher, the fact that he mentions it at all reminds us that fourth-century thinkers were exploring the idea of a radically contemplative philosopher, and that this formed part of the debate about the nature and value of *theoria*.

In *NE* VI, Aristotle portrays Thales and Anaxagoras as theoretical philosophers who turn away from ethical and practical affairs. Aristotle's contemplative philosopher, however, is even more impractical than the one described in Plato's *Theaetetus*. For Aristotle's *sophoi* aim at theoretical knowledge that has no bearing on *praxis*, whereas the ultimate goal of the philosopher in the *Theaetetus* is the virtue of justice:

The god is in no way unjust, but is as just as it is possible to be, and there is nothing more similar to god than the man who becomes as just as possible . . . For the knowledge of this is wisdom and virtue in the true sense, and the ignorance of it is manifest folly and viciousness. All other things that appear to be cleverness and wisdom – whether their sphere is politics or the other arts – are vulgar or banausic (βάναυσοι). (176c–d)

Here, Socrates suggests that the philosopher's wisdom consists in justice. This is a bit hard to square with the claim that the philosopher doesn't know his neighbors, ignores political affairs, and focuses exclusively on universals.[36] Nonetheless, Socrates asserts that since the god is "as just as it is possible to be," the god-like philosopher must be completely just. Thus, even when drawing an extreme picture of the impractical contemplative, Plato claims that his unworldly wisdom will make him just. He therefore stops short of separating theoretical from practical wisdom and assigning them to two different kinds of life.

Like Plato, Aristotle contrasts the philosopher and the politician, and sees them as living different kinds of lives. In fact, as he claims in *NE* I, there are three kinds of life – the life of pleasure, of politics, and of theoretical contemplation (1.5.1–3; note that, in book X, Aristotle says that *phronesis* is best and most fully enacted in politics and war). But Aristotle goes beyond Plato in separating theoretical and practical wisdom and assigning them to different kinds of virtuous men. To be sure, Aristotle affirms Plato's claim that the contemplative philosopher likens himself to god, but he has a completely different conception of the gods and their activities. As he says in *NE* X, the activity of the gods is exclusively contemplative: the gods do not engage in practical affairs and could never make or produce anything

---

[36] As Socrates says, the philosopher doesn't ask questions about "my injustice towards you and yours towards me" but rather about the nature of justice and injustice (175b–c).

(x.8.7). Aristotle thus opposes Plato's claim that the gods are perfectly rational, ethically virtuous, and also creative and demiourgic. In addition, while Plato denounced all nonphilosophical politicians, comparing them to servile *banausoi*, Aristotle grants the *phronimos* who engages in politics the second happiest life (reserving the rhetoric of *banausia* for the category of production and those whose work is productive). In *NE* vi, then, Aristotle diverges from the Platonic model in key ways, and he also moves beyond the position he articulated in the *Protrepticus*, which tended to identify *phronesis* and *nous*.

BASIC FEATURES OF *NOUS*: *NICOMACHEAN ETHICS* X

In *NE* vi, Aristotle says that *phronesis* and "political science" are not the highest forms of wisdom, since they deal with the human realm; theoretical wisdom is superior, since its objects are divine (vi.7, 1141a18–22). In book x.7–9, he sets forth a detailed account of *theoria* and a powerful defense of the theoretical life. This section of the *Nicomachean Ethics* has generated a huge amount of scholarly controversy, which still continues today.[37] In brief, book x identifies *theoria* as the exclusive ingredient of the happy life, whereas the earlier books seemed to indicate that happiness also includes moral virtue (as well as the externals that make the practice of moral virtue possible).[38] This raises the question whether the text offers a consistent account of human happiness. Fortunately, I do not need to enter this debate, since I am not interpreting the *NE* as a whole or attempting to determine Aristotle's final position on the subject of *eudaimonia*. I will thus draw on the scholarship on this issue only to the extent that it pertains to my argument.

The faculty identified with *theoria* in *NE* x is that of *nous*.[39] *Nous* is the highest and most divine part of man: whereas practical virtue is the activity of the "composite" of body and soul, *nous* is pure thinking which is "separate" or "separable" (κεχωρισμένη) from the "composite" (x.8, 1178a22). How are we to understand the claim that *nous* is "separable"? Does *nous* operate in a completely metaphysical sphere? Let us look briefly at Aristotle's discussion of *nous* in the *De Anima* iii.4. Here, Aristotle claims

[37] For discussions of the relation of *NE* x to the earlier books, see Hardie 1980, Ackrill 1973b and 1980, Cooper 1975 and [1987]/1999 (which retracts his former position), Keyt 1978, Whiting 1986, Heinaman 1988 and 1996, Kraut 1989, Broadie 1991, Reeve 1992.

[38] See also *Eudemian Ethics* viii.3,1249b, where Aristotle suggests that all choices in life should promote "the contemplation (*theoria*) of god."

[39] In the *Metaphysics* and *De Partibus Animalium* (which I examine in the Epilogue), theoretical activity sometimes appears to include *epistemē* as well as *nous*.

that, in itself, *nous* is a kind of potential; lacking a particular nature of its own, it is a featureless receptacle that becomes the form of its object in the act of thinking.[40] When it contemplates a form, "*nous* is constituted for the time being by the essence which that form is."[41] In *NE* x, of course, Aristotle is referring to actualized *nous*, which has become identical with its object in the activity of theorizing. What, then, of Aristotle's claim that the activity and excellence of *nous* is "separate"? Does Aristotle believe that this faculty of human beings has some sort of separable existence from the composite of body and soul? In the *De Anima*, he says that *nous* is not "mixed" with the body and does not in fact exist until it thinks (III.4, 429a). In a famously obscure passage, Aristotle divides "active" from "passive" *nous*, claiming that only the former is "separable and impassive and unmixed" (χωριστὸς καὶ ἀπαθὴς καὶ ἀμιγής). As he goes on to say, "when it is separated, [*nous*] is itself alone and nothing more, and this alone is immortal and everlasting" (whereas "passive" *nous* is perishable).[42] Is Aristotle working with this conception of "active *nous*" in the *NE* x? We cannot answer this question with certainty, though the use of the terminology of "separation" in both these texts is suggestive.[43] Whether or not it refers to "active *nous*," the *NE* x does appear to indicate that *nous* does not depend on the "composite" – i.e. the living body – for its actualization (a claim which is at odds with Aristotle's theory of hylomorphism).[44]

In *NE* x Aristotle claims that the activity of *nous* is the actualization of the best and most divine part of man.[45] As he asserts:

A man should not obey those who urge that, as a human, he should think human thoughts and, as a mortal, he should think the thoughts of a mortal, but rather, to the extent possible, he should be immortal (ἀθανατίζειν) and strive in every way to live in accordance with the highest thing in him. (x.7, 1177b31–4)

---

[40] 429a15; cf. 414a10, 424a18, 425b23, 429a24.   [41] De Filippo 1994, 407.

[42] *De Anima* III.5, 430a (cf. III.4, 429b, where Aristotle says that *nous* is χωριστός). This obscure passage is the subject of endless debate and cannot be interpreted conclusively: see, e.g., Hicks [1907]/1988, lviii–lxix, Ross [1924]/1981, cxliii–cxlix, Hardie 1980, 347–55, Kahn 1981, Lear 1988, 135–41, Kosman 1992, Brentano 1992 (who includes a helpful review of ancient, medieval, and modern interpretations), and Reeve 2000, 160–82.

[43] Cooper (1975, 162, 174–8) and Kenny (1978, 180) claim that the *NE* is using the conception of the ontologically separate *nous* which is articulated in the *De Anima* (Kahn 1992 argues along similar lines; cf. Whiting 1986). Broadie (1991, 436–7n. 56) argues that, even if *nous* can be active in a way that is not ontologically dependent on the body or non-rational soul (and thus purely theoretical), it can also be practical "when it finds itself in charge of a psycho-physical complex."

[44] According to Aristotle, the human mind learns via experience and sensory perception, and it depends on the body for its functioning. But, in the activity of contemplation, theoretical *nous* appears to operate independently of the body: Aristotle's account of noetic theorizing thus deviates from his hylomorphism.

[45] I will discuss Aristotle's conception of the noetic activity of god below.

In fact, Aristotle claims that *nous* – which is "divine in comparison with the human" – should be considered our true self, since it is the dominant and best part of man (1177b30–1, 1178a2–4). This rather paradoxical conception of human identity conflicts with the ideas articulated in the first nine books of the treatise. Nonetheless, *NE* x clearly defines *theoria* as a pure noetic activity in which the human being becomes its true self by identifying with its divine objects.

In *NE* x.7–8, Aristotle identifies *theoria* as an activity or *energeia* in the technical sense set forth in the ninth book of the *Metaphysics* (IX.6–8). In fact, in that book Aristotle uses sight and *theoria* as his primary examples of *energeia* (in contrast with *kinesis*). In an *energeia*, as we have seen, "nothing comes into being" beyond the activity itself, and the actualization resides in the subject of the activity rather than in a product; as Aristotle puts it, "the actualization of seeing resides in the person who sees and that of *theoria* resides in the person who theorizes" (IX.8, 1050a35–6). Note that "learning" (*mathesis*) is a *kinesis* rather than an *energeia*, presumably because it is a process that moves towards the external goal of knowing something (1048b29–30). Aristotle makes a similar distinction between learning and knowing in *NE* x, where he says that *theoria* is the most pleasurable of all activities because "knowing is a more pleasant pastime than seeking knowledge" (x.6, 1177a26–7).[46]

In the *Metaphysics*, Aristotle yokes together seeing and theorizing as *energeiai*, and he also says that knowledge is a kind of seeing.[47] Insofar as it is an *energeia* akin to that of sight, *theoria* can be identified as a pure noetic "seeing" of unchanging, eternal, and divine objects. It is not the process of learning and moving towards the goal of knowledge – this, after all, is a *kinesis* – but rather the full actualization of thought thinking the appropriate objects. As Rorty observes,

Theoria is the self-contained activity par excellence. Not only is it done for its own sake, but it is complete in its very exercise: there is no unfolding of stages, no development of consequences from premises. It is fully and perfectly achieved in the very act. When he contemplates the divine, or the fixed stars, the contemplator

---

[46] See also *De Anima* II.5 417a31–2, where Aristotle says that, in learning, there is a "qualitative alteration" in the soul of the learner. But, as he goes on to say, in the case of actualizing one's potential for thinking, that which thinks is not being altered (II.5). There are numerous discussions of the question of how the *energeia* of theorizing is related to the kinetic process of learning, i.e., of whether *theoria* is completely non-developmental: see, e.g., Gauthier and Jolif (1970, vol. II 852–5), who claim that *theorein* should be translated as "regarder" and defined in opposition to "appréhender" and "savoir" (see also Ackrill 1965, 140–1, Hardie 1980, 344–5); cf. Eriksen 1976, 83, A Rorty 1980, M. White 1980.
[47] See, e.g., *Met.* I.1, 980a26–7; XIII.10, 1087a19–20.

is no more interested in explaining them – no more interested in constructing the science of theology or astronomy – than he is in achieving nobility or serenity.[48]

By definition, then, *theoria* is not productive or practical, since nothing comes into being beyond the activity of theorizing itself. This means that Aristotle cannot argue (as Plato and Philip did) that *theoria* is the most exalted activity both in itself and because of the benefits it brings in the practical and technical sphere. In his effort to valorize *theoria* as a pure noetic "seeing" that produces no results and has no end beyond itself, Aristotle must use arguments quite different from those of his predecessors.

THEORIA VS. PRAXIS: NICOMACHEAN ETHICS X

In *NE* x.7, Aristotle argues that if happiness is "activity in accordance with the highest virtue," this will be the virtue of the "best part of us." This, he now claims, is the activity of *theoria*, which is supreme because *nous* is the "highest element in us, and the objects of *theoria* are the supreme objects of knowledge" (1177a20–1). Aristotle has no more to say about the objects of theoretical knowledge in this book, presumably because he has already discussed them in book VI.[49] In the discussion of *theoria* in book x, Aristotle defines it in terms of the activity itself rather than its objects. In particular, he argues that *theoria* is the highest form of activity because it is the most "continuous" and the most "pleasurable." And he also says that it is the most "divine" insofar as *nous* is the divine part of man (1177b30–1178a2). The most important claims, however, are made when Aristotle develops the contrast between theoretical and practical activities (which both builds on and alters the account of *nous* and *phronesis* in book VI). In *NE* x, Aristotle defines *theoria*, in large part, by way of a contrast with practical life and activities.

Aristotle commences this important argument at x.7 (1097a27). He first argues that *theoria* is the most "self-sufficient" and "leisured" of all activities. This terminology, as we have seen, has powerful ideological associations. In particular, self-sufficiency and leisure are the primary markers of the aristocratic class (for aristocrats did not have to work for a living or labor to serve others). In fact, aristocrats in this period attempted to distinguish themselves from the upwardly mobile by laying claim to "true" freedom,

---

[48] A. Rorty 1980, 378–9; cf. Cooper (1975, 174), who identifies *theoria* with *sophia*, i.e. the combination of *nous* and *epistemē*, rather than *nous per se*.
[49] I will return to the question of the objects of theoretical knowledge when I discuss the *Metaphysics*.

which was associated with leisure rather than with practical activities and pursuits.[50] As Burger rightly observes, "[*theoria's*] victory over the practical life, as a ranking of leisure and freedom over business and necessity, is expressed in categories that belong to a political class structure."[51] Although Aristotle does not explicitly mention class or status in *NE* x, the terms and categories that he is using directly reflect aristocratic values.

Let us look more closely at Aristotle's elevation of *theoria* over *praxis*. First of all, he argues that the man who engages in *theoria* is "self-sufficient" because he can engage in *theoria* by himself, without other people or external props (although the theorizer does require the necessaries of life in order to subsist as a human being). When an individual engages in practical virtue, by contrast, he needs other people – to be just, he needs people in order to practice justice, and to be temperate and brave he also requires externals. This means that his activities are not self-sufficient. Practical activity, in short, is not fully free, since it is dependent on a variety of external goods and factors.

In addition, Aristotle claims, *theoria* is the only activity that is truly "leisured." It is here that we find the most decisive argument in book x:

[The activity of *theoria*] seems to be the only one which is loved for its own sake (αὐτὴ μόνη δι' αὑτὴν ἀγαπᾶσθαι); for nothing comes into being from it (οὐδὲν γὰρ ἀπ' αὐτῆς γίνεται) beyond the activity of theorizing, whereas from practical activities we make for ourselves a byproduct, be it larger or smaller, beyond the action itself (ἀπὸ δὲ τῶν πρακτικῶν ἢ πλεῖον ἢ ἔλαττον περιποιούμεθα παρὰ τὴν πρᾶξιν). And happiness seems to involve leisure, since we are unleisured for the sake of being leisured, and we wage war for the sake of peace. Now the activity of the practical virtues (τῶν . . . πρακτικῶν ἀρετῶν . . . ἡ ἐνέργεια) is exercised in politics and in war. But the actions that concern these things seem to be unleisured – those of war in fact entirely so . . . But the activity of the political man is also unleisured, since it makes for itself a byproduct (περιποιουμένη) beyond the mere activity of engaging in politics – be it positions of power and honor or at least the happiness of the man himself and the citizens, as being something distinct from the political activity. (*NE* x.7, 1177b1–15)

The language in this passage requires careful scrutiny. The phrase "nothing comes into being from the activity" is familiar both from Aristotle's definition of the distinction between *energeia* and *kinesis* (in *Met.* ix.6–8) as well as from his separation of *phronesis* and *technē* (in *NE* vi). As we saw in our analysis of *NE* vi, *phronesis* is an *energeia* that has no *telos* beyond itself, whereas *technē* is a *kinesis* that produces a *telos* beyond the activity itself. In book vi, it was productivity – i.e. the making of an external work or *telos* – that served to distinguish *technē* from *praxis*. How, then, should we interpret Aristotle's claim in book x that in practical activities we "make for ourselves a byproduct" (περιποιούμεϑα) beyond the action itself?

Scholars have long noted the discrepancy between the account of practical activity in book x and that in book vi. But they have focused on the fact that, in book x, people engaging in practical activities are said to be "aiming at" ends external to themselves: what is at issue, as it seems, is the intention or aim of the agent, who appears to be deliberately striving for something other than (or, in addition to) "acting well in itself." Aristotle does indeed say that practical reasoning "aims at" external ends in *NE* x, but that is not what he is saying in this passage. Only in the subsequent section (at 1177b16–20) does he bring up the notion of "aiming at" an end. There, Aristotle claims that even the noblest practical activities – those dealing with politics and war – "are unleisured and *aim at* some external end" (τέλους τινὸς ἐφίενται), and are not "chosen for themselves" (δι' αὐτὰς αἱρεταί εἰσιν). The activity of *nous*, by contrast, "*aims at* no end beyond itself" (παρ' αὐτὴν οὐδενὸς ἐφίεσϑαι, 1177b16–20). In this passage, Aristotle introduces the notion of "aiming at" a given end, conveyed by the verb ἐφίεσϑαι. But the verb that he used in the previous passage (quoted above) was περιποιεῖσϑαι, which deals with *poiesis* or productivity rather than "aiming at" an end. Περιποιεῖσϑαι centers on productivity, whereas ἐφίεσϑαι deals with choice, intention, and aim.[52]

The verb περιποιεῖν means, in the active, "to make to remain over and above"; in the middle it takes on a reflexive sense, which can be literally translated as "to make for oneself something that remains over and above" (it thus can have the sense of "acquire" or "gain"). Given that Aristotle used the word *poiesis* in his articulation of the technical distinction between *technē* and *phronesis* in book vi, we should take seriously the verbal form of *poiesis* in book x. Most translators completely ignore the notion of *poiesis* or productivity conveyed by περιποιεῖσϑαι, choosing to identify or assimilate this verb with ἐφίεσϑαι. Ross, for example, translates the two uses of περιποιεῖσϑαι as (1) "from practical pursuits we *look to secure some advantage,* greater or smaller, beyond the action itself"; and (2) "the activity of the politicians is also unleisured, and *aims at securing* something beyond the mere participation in politics – positions of authority and honor . . ." He then goes on to translate both instances of ἐφίεσϑαι in the next section

---

[52] This notion of "productivity" need not imply manufacturing something in the most literal sense. Rather, the point is that practical activity brings about a sort of change in the external world, be it large or small.

as "*aim at*," thus conflating περιποιεῖσθαι with ἐφίεσθαι.[53] Irwin translates the two instances of περιποιεῖσθαι as (1) "from the virtues concerned with action we *try* to a greater or lesser extent *to gain* something beyond the action itself"; (2) "beyond political activities themselves, the actions [of politicians] *seek* positions of power and honours . . ." He then translates both uses of ἐφίεσθαι as "*aim at*." Here, "trying to gain" gives way to "seeking," which is very close to "aiming at."[54] Finally, Rackham translates the two instances of περιποιεῖσθαι as (1) "from practical pursuits we *look to secure some advantage*, greater or smaller, beyond the action itself"; and (2) "the activity of the politician is also unleisured, and *aims at securing* something beyond the mere participation in politics – positions of authority and honor . . ." In translating the two instances of ἐφίεσθαι, he says that "political actions are '*directed to*' some further end, whereas *theoria* '*aims at*' no end beyond itself."[55] He thus uses the phrase "aims at" for both περιποιεῖσθαι and ἐφίεσθαι (though his translations are not consistent).

In all of these translations, the notion of productivity or *poiesis* inherent in *peripoieisthai* is completely eclipsed by the idea of "aiming at" or "aiming to secure" something. Of course, *peripoieisthai* can convey the sense that the agent "gains" something, and we can infer that he wants or aims to gain it. Thus the above translations offer acceptable renderings of the Greek, but do not take into account the technical sense of *poiesis* in Aristotle – i.e. the making or producing of a *telos* that is separate from the activity itself. This differs from the question of *motivation* – of whether to aim at something as an end in itself or, alternatively, as a means to another end. A productive or ποιητική action is, by definition, a *kinesis* or motion that creates an external product; but the notion of "aiming at" something focuses on the quite different issue of motivation and choice.

In the first passage (quoted in full above), I suggest, Aristotle is saying that "in practical activities we make for ourselves a byproduct (περιποιούμεθα) beyond the action itself."[56] In using this language, he identifies making and productivity – producing a byproduct – as a crucial marker of practical activities as opposed to theoretical ones. Thus the very thing that distinguished practical from technical reasoning in *NE* vi – productivity – is identified as a feature of practical activity in book x. Ethical action, as it turns out, makes or produces a change in the world, be it large or small, beyond the mere enactment of moral virtue. Since ethical virtue is carried out in the

---

[53] Ross's translation is found in Ackrill 1987, 470.

[54] Irwin 1985, 285–6.   [55] Rackham 1934, 615–17.

[56] Cf. ix.8, 1168b27, where Aristotle suggests that, when a man acts virtuously, he "creates goodness in himself" (τὸ καλὸν ἑαυτῷ περιποιοῖτο): this differs from book x, which indicates that the practical agent brings about a change in the world that is *distinct from the activity itself.*

physical and social world, something inevitably "comes into being" from its enactment. There is, in short, an aspect or element of ethical action that is productive or, at the very least, associated with productivity. This aspect of ethical activity brings things into being that are distinct from the activity itself – it introduces some sort of change in the external world. Note that this is the case even if one's motives are good, i.e. if one chooses or "aims at" virtuous action for itself: for even if a person chooses a virtuous action as an end in itself, the action will still produce some sort of effect or byproduct in the world. *To this extent*, the "ethical activity" deriving from the practical virtues intersects with "productive activity."

It is only after claiming that practical activities include a productive element that Aristotle brings up the notion of aim and intention. As we have seen, in this latter passage he claims that virtuous practical activities performed in politics and war "are unleisured and aim at some external end (τέλους τινὸς ἐφίενται) and are not chosen for themselves" (οὐ δι' αὑτὰς αἱρεταί εἰσιν), whereas the activity of *nous* "aims at no end beyond itself" (παρ' αὑτὴν οὐδενὸς ἐφίεσθαι, 1177b16–20). This does not apply to all cases of *praxis*, since the passage deals only with actions in the public sphere and does not necessarily characterize every instance of practical activity. As Aristotle says later in book x, a person can exercise moral virtue in private life as well as in politics (1179a6–8). Aristotle does not, then, claim that *all* practical activities are chosen for the sake of an external end (and are never chosen for themselves). Rather, he believes that *praxis* can be chosen either for its own sake or for the sake of external ends.

One could argue, of course, that *theoria* differs from practical activity in that it can be chosen *only* as an end in itself and never for the sake of an end distinct from the activity. But, even if one accepts this latter distinction, the basic criterion of choosing something as an end in itself vs. choosing it as a means to a higher end (which is the criterion that Aristotle uses in this passage in book x) will not serve to distinguish theoretical from practical activity in every case (since practical activity can be chosen as an end in itself). It is only the identification of practical activity as *possessing a productive element* (which theoretical activity lacks) that generates a cate-gorical distinction between *theoria* and *praxis*. For, by definition, *theoria* is never productive and cannot produce a byproduct or change in the external world.

If this is on target, then the distinction that Aristotle draws in the *Nicomachean Ethics* between technical, practical, and theoretical activi-ties is not as clear and consistent as it might at first appear. For the very thing that marks off technical from moral reasoning in *NE* vi – produc-tivity – serves as the crucial marker of the difference between practical and theoretical activity in *NE* x. In *NE* vi, in short, Aristotle *contrasts* the activities of practical virtue with productive ones, whereas in book x he is, in certain ways, *assimilating* them. I am not suggesting that Aristotle's use of the word *peripoieisthai* in book x serves to collapse the distinction between *technē* and *phronesis*. Although practical activities do, as book x suggests, have a productive element, they are nonetheless based on a different form of reasoning than *technē*; the enactment of moral virtue is not a craft or science that proceeds according to technical rules. My point is that Aristotle's claim that practical activities "make for themselves a byproduct" does important conceptual work in book x. While the suggestion that practical activities possess an element of productivity (along with their many other defining features) is not consistent with the discussion of *phronesis* in book vi, it nonetheless tells us something important about moral and practical action: that, regardless of one's motives, practical activities bring something into being, be it large or small, in the social and/or physical world.

Aristotle explicitly says that practical reasoning is enacted in the social and physical realm. As he claims, the activity of moral virtue involves "intercourse with our fellow humans" (1178a10–13). It is thus carried out by the "composite" of body and soul in the social and physical world. As Aristotle argues:

> The liberal man will need wealth in order to perform liberal actions, and the just man will need it in order to pay his debts (since mere intentions are invisible [*adeloi*], and even unjust men pretend that they wish to act justly). And the courageous man will need strength if he is to perform any brave actions, and the temperate man will need opportunities for intemperance. For how can he or any other man be visibly (*delos*) virtuous? It is debated whether the choice or the performance of the action is the most important feature of virtue, since it depends on both. Clearly, the perfection of virtue will consist in both. (1178a28–b1)

Here, moral virtue is identified (and perfected) by its "visible" performance in the physical world – it is identified, in short, by its results, not simply by the aim or intention of the agent. Whereas *nous* operates "separately" from the body, practical virtue is performed by the "composite" of body and soul (1178a20–1). In short, Aristotle's contemplative man, *qua* theorist, is a disembodied spectator; he does not (and, indeed, cannot) put his *theoria* to practical use in the social and physical world but rather engages in the divine activity of theoretical contemplation.[57]

---

57 The existence of a practical form of *nous* (which Aristotle seems to refer to at 1139b4–5), is debatable: A. Rorty (1980) argues in favor of this position; but cf. Cooper 1975, 162, 174–8, and Kenny 1978, esp. 180. Whether or not one accepts this position, theoretical reasoning is a separate noetic activity with a completely different orientation.

Aristotle confirms this point by reference to the activity of the gods. As he states:

> We believe that the gods, most of all, are blessed and happy. But what sorts of actions can we attribute to them? Just actions? Wouldn't they appear ridiculous if they were entering into contracts, restoring deposits, and doing other such things? And, as for brave actions, would they withstand terrors and run risks because this is noble? Could they perform liberal actions? To whom will they give gifts? It would be absurd if they had a currency of some kind! And what would their temperate actions be? It would be demeaning to praise them for not having base desires. If we go through the virtues, we will see that all forms of virtuous action are petty and unworthy of the gods. (1178b8–18)

After drawing this ludicrous picture of gods as moral agents – thus contesting Plato's conception of divinity – Aristotle concludes that their sole activity is that of theorizing: "in the case of a living being, if moral action is eliminated, and still more productive activity, what will remain except *theoria*? Thus the activity of god, which is supreme in blessedness, would be that of *theoria*" (1178b21–2).

Obviously, a human being cannot theorize continuously, as the gods do. He will have to attend to his physical wellbeing and (if he is to be a good man) conduct himself virtuously in the social and political world. According to Aristotle, one does not need to be a rich man or a ruler in order to perform good deeds; in fact, "men living a private form of life" are no less capable of acting virtuously than powerful men who engage in politics (1179a42–8). Here, Aristotle seems to indicate that the theoretical philosopher will abstain from politics, but still cultivate (at least some of) the practical virtues. As we have seen, the life of the public man relies on a wide range of external conditions and resources (indeed, his activities are dependent on the entire social and political arena). The theorizer, by contrast, "needs none of these externals to engage in his activity; in fact, these things are generally a hindrance to *theoria*" (ἐμπόδιά ἐστι πρός γε τὴν θεωρίαν, 1178b3–5; cf. 1177a28–34). This is a very important claim: the suggestion that external affairs and exigencies can actually obstruct the activity of theorizing is a pointed reminder of the fundamental opposition between the theoretical and the practical life. For this indicates that the theorizer and the man of action not only engage in different activities but lead lives that have conflicting orientations.[58] As Aristotle claims, the theorizer who aims at complete happiness must engage in *theoria* for "the

---

[58] *NE* x.8, 1178b3–5; cf. vi.7, 1141b5–14. Note also Aristotle's discussion of the three kinds of life – the life of pleasure, the political life, and the theoretical life – in book 1.5.

entire span of his life" (1177b25). The theoretical philosopher will thus live as a private man and use his practical reasoning to organize his life around the activity of *theoria*. To be sure, he will need to exhibit moral virtue in order to live well as a "composite" human being. But his life, as a whole, will be directed towards *theoria*.

THEORIA FOR ITS OWN SAKE: *NICOMACHEAN ETHICS* X

According to Aristotle, *theoria* is an *energeia* chosen only for its own sake and never for the sake of an end beyond the activity itself. In the first book of the *Nicomachean Ethics*, Aristotle discusses the difference between instrumental activities and those that are ends in themselves. In 1.7, Aristotle claims that "a thing which is pursued (διωκτόν) as an end in itself is more final than one which is pursued as a means to something else, and a thing which is never chosen (αἱρετόν) as a means to anything else is more final than things which are chosen both for themselves and as means to other things" (1097a30–4). In introducing the notion of "pursuit" and "choice," Aristotle ushers us into the realm of motivation. As he claims, there are some things which one can choose both as ends in themselves and for the sake of other ends. It is *phronesis* or practical reason that determines whether, in a given situation, one should pursue something as an end in itself or as a means to another end. For *phronesis* presides over all choices, and it determines in what way a given activity should be pursued.

In this passage, Aristotle does not refer to the technical distinction between *kinesis* and *energeia*, but it clearly subtends the discussion. Note that the issue of the choiceworthiness of an activity differs from the technical and (in its basic formulation) value-neutral distinction between a *kinesis* and an *energeia*. By using the term *telos* in the discussions of both physics and ethics, however, Aristotle seems to link the technical notion of a *kinesis* with the moral notion of choosing something as a means to a more choiceworthy end. Correlatively, an *energeia*, as an end in itself, is sometimes identified as morally valuable and choiceworthy.[59] But the mere

---

[59] As Ackrill (1965, 137–8) rightly argues, Aristotle does not "draw the distinction between *energeiai* and *kineseis* with the aid of a psychological or evaluative criterion, that is, in terms of human desires as they are or as they ought to be." Thus the fact that the *kinesis* of housebuilding is directed towards the production of a house (as its *telos*) "is not put forward as a fact about the motivation of builders, but as a fact about the concept of house-building (a fact that can be expressed by the formula 'it is not true that at the same time one builds a house and has built it')." But Aristotle often tends to slide (without argument) from the "is" to the "ought." Thus a *kinesis* is an activity whose defining structure is that it has an end or *telos* beyond itself: according to Aristotle, it should (or must) be

fact that an activity is an *energeia* (in the technical sense) does not, by itself, mean that it is invariably chosen only for its own sake. For an *energeia* can be an activity that is nested within other, larger human projects. For example, seeing is an *energeia* which we would choose to have even if it were not nested in the affairs of life. But we do not, in every case, choose the activity of seeing just to gape and gaze. Most of the time, we use the *energeia* of vision to help us in our practical and physical lives. Thus, the fact that something is an *energeia* does not prevent it from being chosen and used as a means to other ends. Again, it is *phronesis* which will decide, in a given case, how to pursue something. I may choose to use my eyes for the simple purpose of perceiving objects. But I may also choose to use my eyes to search for an image that will serve in an advertisement for a Sports Utility Vehicle.

As I would urge, seeing *qua* seeing is an *energeia* that is complete at all times, and this activity is separate from the actions which are done in response to what one sees; but this *energeia* can also be part of another project in which *phronesis* chooses to see something in order to achieve a goal beyond the act of seeing. The question of how and why we choose to engage in an *energeia* at a given moment is a matter of motivation and practical reasoning rather than an issue that is determined by the mere fact that it is an *energeia*. A single *energeia*, then, can be chosen for different reasons and for disparate goals. There is only one case, in fact, where an *energeia* can be chosen *only* as an end in itself: namely, if the *energeia* is the final end or *telos* of all human pursuits and thus could *never* be chosen for the sake of other ends.

Theoria, as Aristotle suggests in *NE* x, is not one among many *energeiai* but an activity that is intrinsically choiceworthy and nonutilitarian. *Theoria*, in short, can *only* be chosen as an end in itself. Rorty offers an interesting explanation of this claim:

Two people can be doing the same things – discussing philosophy, passing legislation, writing poetry, or kneading dough – that is, they may be performing virtually the same physical motions and saying virtually the same things but be performing different actions. One person may be performing it as a self-contained activity that is intrinsically valuable, the other as a process structured and motivated by external goals.[60]

---

chosen for the sake of this *telos* because an end is valued more highly than the process that leads to it and is therefore intrinsically better and more choiceworthy. Likewise, an *energeia* is an activity that is complete at all times and serves as its own *telos*; it therefore must be *chosen* for itself since it is an end in itself and superior to things that are the means to this *telos*.

[60] A. Rorty 1980, 380.

The same is true of philosophy, she adds, since it can be done "with different intentions by different practictioners" – e.g. for the sake of fame, for the pleasure of intellectual combat, or as a mode of poetry or politics.[61] This is because philosophy is a process of learning rather than the full actualization of thinking. *Theoria*, by contrast, "has to be done for its own sake if it is to be done at all."[62] But if one can engage in philosophy for disparate reasons and with different motivations, why can't one do the same with *theoria*? According to Rorty, philosophy can be treated as either an *energeia* or a *kinesis* (a "motion towards a goal"), but the activity of *theoria* can never be a *kinesis*, and therefore cannot be (as she puts it) "motivated by external goals." But why can't an activity that is not a "*motion* towards a goal" be *motivated* by external factors? To borrow an example from Plato, one may choose (like Leontius) to look at corpses: the seeing is an *energeia* but the activity is motivated by the person's sick desires. *Theoria*, then, may not be as inherently disinterested as Aristotle suggests (though it can certainly be chosen and practiced as a nonutilitarian activity).

THEORIA AND HAPPINESS: *NICOMACHEAN ETHICS* X

In *NE* x, Aristotle claims that *theoria* is identical to or coextensive with happiness. As we have seen, Aristotle says in *NE* I.7 that there are some things which can only be pursued as means to other ends, some which can be pursued both as means and as ends in themselves, and some which can only be pursued as ends in themselves. In this passage, Aristotle singles out happiness (*eudaimonia*) as that which is pursued *only* for its own sake, and claims that "honor, pleasure, thinking (*nous*), and all of virtue" are chosen for their own sakes but also as a means to happiness (1179a34–b6). It seems reasonable, within the framework of a eudaimonistic theory, to identify the "final end" as happiness and to rank noetic activity with other desirables as something that can be chosen both for its own sake and for the sake of happiness. But Aristotle changes ground in book x, where he argues that *theoria*, which is the activity of *nous*, "is the only activity that is loved only for its own sake," thus elevating it above the other activities and pursuits that he listed in book I. Indeed, in book x he appears to make theoretical activity coextensive with happiness, thus identifying *theoria* and happiness as the "final end." If *theoria* is indeed identical to or coextensive

---

[61] As she argues, a person who is pursuing philosophy as an end in itself will not for that reason "find more truths than the intellectual prize-fighter" (A. Rorty 1980, 381).

[62] A. Rorty 1980, 386.

with happiness, one could only choose theoretical activity for its own sake and never for another end.

In *NE* x.8, Aristotle appears to identify happiness and contemplation: "complete happiness is a contemplative activity" (ἡ δὲ τελεία εὐδαιμονία . . . θεωρητική τις ἐστὶν ἐνέργεια).[63] This statement is, I think, extremely problematic, for it is hard to see how contemplation can be an activity of the same type as happiness. What sort of an activity is contemplation? Note that, in discussing "activities," Aristotle sometimes uses the word *energeia* in a non-technical sense, to designate any activity which one may choose (or refuse) to engage in;[64] at other times, he uses it in the technical sense of an "actuality" (in contrast with *kinesis*).[65] *Theoria*, I believe, is an "activity" in both of these senses, whereas happiness is an "activity" only in the second, technical sense. Unfortunately, Aristotle almost completely ignores the fact that *theoria* (unlike happiness) is an activity in the first sense – like other human activities, it is something one chooses and arranges to do.

If one views *theoria* as a distinct activity among the many activities and actions that make up a human life (i.e. an activity in the first sense), then its difference from happiness is easy to see. First, one cannot demarcate the happiness of a life in the same way one demarcates the activity of *theoria*: theoretical activity, for humans, occurs at periodic intervals. Second, and even more important, happiness is not in our control in the same way that contemplation is. We choose to spend the afternoon theorizing (assuming that we have the requisite expertise), or we choose to take a walk instead of theorizing. In fact, as Broadie observes, *theoria* is ". . . wholly dependent, under human conditions, on the good will of practical virtue for being realized."[66] Clearly, *theoria* is an activity which must be arranged for and chosen as part of a human life. We simply do not choose happiness in this way. Indeed, according to Aristotle, happiness is not a matter of choice at all – by nature, humans have this as their final end. Since we always aim at happiness no matter what we else we are doing, happiness cannot be put in the category of activities or ends that are the objects of choice. As Aristotle says in book III, "we wish to be happy . . . but it would not be fitting to say that we choose to be happy; for, in general, choice is concerned with things that are in our control" (*NE* III.2, IIIIb28–30). *Theoria*, by contrast,

---

[63] 1178b7–8; see also 1177a16–18, 1178b32.

[64] E.g. at *NE* x.5, 1175b24–7: "since *energeiai* differ in being fine or base – some are choiceworthy, others to be avoided, and yet others are neutral – the same is true of their pleasures; for each *energeia* has a pleasure of its own."

[65] E.g. *Metaphysics* IX.6, *NE* x.3–4.   [66] Broadie 1991, 389.

is something that is in our control – it is an activity that a human being must choose to do or not do. Unlike happiness, *theoria* must be *made* a priority – it must be chosen over other alternatives.

In spite of its many unique qualities, then, *theoria* resembles other human activities in important ways. Once we locate the activity of *theoria* within a human life, we can raise the question whether it is in fact intrinsically nonutilitarian. Consider for a moment the analogy with music. Obviously, *theoria* resembles musical activity insofar as it must be arranged for and chosen by an individual (i.e. both are activities in the non-technical sense). In Aristotle's discussion of education in *Politics* VIII, he claims that the activity of music can be chosen for right or wrong reasons and pursued in right and wrong ways.[67] Can the same be said about *theoria*? According to the *Politics*, the worst approach to musical activity is to perform it in a professional context (i.e. to make a living by this activity). Can *theoria* be located in a utilitarian or professional context? Isn't it possible for a single individual to engage regularly in contemplation and, at the same time, to practice theoretical activity in a professional context? Is there some reason why the theorizer can never be occupied as a sophist? If not, then we cannot say that *theoria* is intrinsically nonutilitarian but rather that it becomes "useless" by virtue of being pursued as such. In short, it would be the *choice* to engage in theorizing in a nonutilitarian way that would make the activity useless. *Theoria* would be nonutilitarian only if it were chosen for the right reasons and in the right way.

One might argue that the activities of the sophist *qua* professional are completely separate from his activity *qua* theorizer. But it is difficult to deny that the activity of *theoria* would be extremely serviceable to the sophist, since his reflection on theoretical knowledge will help him to present it to an audience. Kraut suggests, in fact, that *theoria* "occurs not only when one silently reflects, but also when one lectures or writes about a certain subject, when one reads a book, when one listens to a book being read, or when one hears someone presenting a lecture."[68] If this is true, then the activity of *theoria* can be going on at the same time that the sophist is teaching. We come back, then, to the question of the motives of the sophist. It is of course possible for a sophist to earn his living in order to theorize, and not the reverse – *theoria* would still be his final end. But the professional musician could make the same claim, and yet Aristotle insists that the activity of music in a professional context is, by definition, illiberal and banausic. In addition, while some sophists may charge money simply

---

[67] I will discuss this point in detail below.   [68] Kraut 1989, 73.

to fund their theoretical activities, others may aim at money or some form of power as the final end of *theoria*. These sophists, then, would be engaging in *theoria* in the wrong way, since they put it to useful ends rather than pursuing it as an end in itself.

But is the analogy with music sound? Is there something about the activity of *theoria* that makes it impossible to pursue in the wrong way? One could argue that the theorizer, during the time that he theorizes, is completely absorbed in the activity and cannot be either using or thinking of using the thoughts he is having. In addition, the objects of contemplation are, by definition, divine, unchanging, and eternal (*NE* vi.1, 1139a6–8, b18–24; vi.7, 1141b2–8). Indeed, Aristotle distinguishes practical from theoretical reasoning in *NE* vi by asserting that the former deals with things that are "expedient," "good for humans," and "good for the individual himself," whereas the latter is "superhuman" and unconcerned with "what is good for human beings" (1141b2–12; cf. 1140a25–8, 1140b4–6, 1141b29–30, 1142b31–3). Clearly, theoretical activity is unique, and differs from musical activity in fundamental ways.

I do not wish to deny the uniqueness of the activity of *theoria*. But, regardless of the intellectual state of the individual at the time he theorizes (or of the nature of the objects that he contemplates), we must still ask *how a person fits this activity into his life as a whole*. Why can't the activity of *theoria* be chosen for disparate reasons and with different motivations? Why can't it be located within a project which brings the theorizer money, honor, or some kind of power? Clearly, Aristotle wanted to argue that *theoria* is intrinsically nonutilitarian and nonproductive. But, for this to be the case, there would have to be something in the nature of *theoria* and/or the objects of theoretical thought that invariably and necessarily affects the individual in such a way that he could never choose to theorize for the wrong reasons.[69] In other words, theoretical activity would have to have a determinate and invariable effect on the person's practical reasoning. It is not enough to say that the theorizer *should* opt to engage in this activity for the right reasons. He must necessarily do so, and this must be a direct result of the activity of contemplation. Otherwise, it would always be possible for a person to engage in *theoria* for the utilitarian purposes – to make theorizing useful instead of useless in the practical sphere.

---

[69] Alternatively, one could argue that only perfectly virtuous people are able to engage in *theoria*, and thus that they would never use it for the wrong reasons. But, even in this case, the uselessness of *theoria* would not inhere in the activity but would depend on the perfected practical virtues of the theorizers.

Aristotle does suggest that *theoria* affects practical reasoning insofar as it serves as a final end. But this is just the point: an individual must use his practical reason to *choose* contemplation over other activities. And it is always possible that a gifted theorizer may not have perfected all the practical virtues and that he will therefore approach his theoretical activities in a fashion which is not completely disinterested. It would seem, then, that it is the context in which a person pursues the activity of *theoria* that determines whether it is useful or useless. And this context is, like the activity of contemplation itself, organized and chosen by the individual *qua* practical reasoner. *Theoria*, in sum, is not intrinsically nonutilitarian and nonproductive. Rather, the choice and the value system of the individual practitioner must determine its orientation.

Let me emphasize that Aristotle himself would have disagreed with this argument. He clearly wanted to say that *theoria* is intrinsically nonutilitarian and nonproductive – it is not just one activity among many but rather the final end of all activities (like happiness). Aristotle could have argued that *theoria*, like the practical virtues, is a good that can be desired for its own sake and also for the sake of other things (this, after all, is the category in which he places "*nous* and every virtue" in book I, 1097b1–5). But he preferred to argue that *theoria* is intrinsically nonutilitarian – that it can never be chosen for the sake of something else.

Here is what is at stake: if *theoria* has no bearing on virtuous *praxis*, then the theoretical philosopher does not have to be an exceptionally good person (and, correlatively, he need not practice *theoria* in order to engage in virtuous action). In fact, even if the theoretical philosopher does practice some virtues to live well overall, he will organize his life around the pursuit of a noetic activity that is neither practical nor political. As a private *theoros*, Aristotle's philosopher is not obliged to report back to people on his findings or to justify his activity in practical terms. In fact, *qua* theorist, he does not interact in the social or political world. Theoretical wisdom, in short, is essentially amoral.

FROM *TECHNĒ* TO *THEORIA*: *METAPHYSICS* I.1

Metaphysics I.1–2 offers a detailed discussion and defense of theoretical activity. I want to look closely at this argument and the terminology that Aristotle uses in presenting his case. As we will see, this discussion examines the distinction between *technē* and *theoria*, and brings to the fore the connection between theoretical activity and the aristocratic notions of freedom, leisure, and autonomy (which were articulated but not fully developed in the *Nicomachean Ethics*). Indeed the aristocratic rhetoric is far more pronounced in *Met.* 1.1–2 than it was in *NE* x, and thus calls for a more detailed examination.

Aristotle's discussion in these chapters centers on the distinction between three kinds of knowledge: first, that based on experience (*empeiria*), which is not really knowledge but know-how; second, technical knowledge (which has several divisions); and third, theoretical knowledge. As I will suggest, there is a close correlation between *theoria* and *technē* in *Met.* 1, though Aristotle must purge the latter of all its productive elements in order to make this connection. We will therefore need to examine Aristotle's discussion of *technē* in order to understand the activity of *theoria*.

Aristotle begins by drawing a distinction between the know-how of the man who proceeds by experience and the knowledge of the man who possesses *technē*. Whereas experience involves an understanding of particular cases, *technē* is based on a knowledge of the universal. This latter knowledge is derived from the accumulated data concerning similar particulars gained by experience, which a person can gather from various sources and use to grasp the universal (1.1, 981a5–7). It is of course possible that the same person who has the experiences can discover the universal, but Aristotle speaks as if the man of experience is different from the man of *technē*. According to Aristotle, the man of experience is much more successful when it comes to practical application (πρὸς . . . τὸ πράττειν) than the man who has *technē* and *logos* but lacks experience (981a12–24). But the technician – even if he lacks experience – is nonetheless the wiser man:

We consider that knowledge (τὸ εἰδέναι) and understanding (τὸ ἐπαΐειν) belong to *technē* rather than experience (ἐμπειρίας), and we believe that craftsmen (τεχνίτας) are wiser than men of experience . . . And the reason for this is that the former know the cause (τὴν αἰτίαν ἴσασιν), whereas the latter do not. For men of experience know that the thing is so, but not why it is so. But the craftsmen know the "why" and the cause. (981a24–30)

The craftsman, then, is distinguished from the man of experience by virtue of his knowledge of the universals and of the causes. Though the man of experience deals more successfully with particular situations, the man of *technē* is said to be wiser: knowledge completely trumps action. Note that Aristotle calls the man of *technē* in this passage the *technitēs*, which I have translated as "craftsman." When translating the *technē* words and compounds in this passage (which are numerous), I have opted to use the term "craft" for the sake of consistency (or else I use technician/technical, etc.).

Having elevated the *technitēs* over the man of experience, Aristotle draws an important distinction within the category of the craftsman. The craftsman who works with his hands, he claims, does not in fact possess knowledge (as the previous passage indicated); only the "master-craftsman" (*architektōn*) is wise:

> Hence we believe that the the the master-craftsmen (ἀρχιτέκτονας) in each field are more honorable and that they know more and are wiser than the craftsmen who work with their hands (χειροτεχνῶν) [hereafter, "handi-craftsmen"], because they know the causes of the things that are being made. Handi-craftsmen, like certain inanimate objects, make things, but they make them without knowing what they are making, just as fire burns; but inanimate things do each thing by some natural quality, whereas the handi-craftsmen do them by habit [δι᾽ ἔθος]. Thus the master-craftsmen are wiser, not by virtue of doing things, but by their possession of a rational account and their knowledge of the causes. (1.1, 981a30–b6)

This is an extraordinary piece of rhetoric. First, Aristotle ranks the *technitēs* above the man of experience because he has knowledge of the causes, but now he says that only the *architektōn* has this wisdom, whereas the *cheirotechnēs* does not! Indeed, he compares the latter to a "soulless" or inanimate object that simply produces things without any thought at all – as mechanically and automatically as fire burns. Aristotle also says that the handi-craftsmen work "by habit": here, he assimilates them to the man of experience (for how does the man who proceeds by "experience" differ from the one who works by "habit," especially when both lack a knowledge of the causes?). Only the master-craftsman knows the causes – he is wise "not by virtue of doing things" but because of his knowledge alone.[70]

Clearly, the handi-craftsman engages in productive, manual labor, whereas the master-craftsman is an intellectual laborer (so to speak). To be sure, Aristotle identifies both as craftsmen – as men of *technē* or technicians (*cheirotechnēs*; *architektōn*). But the latter is an "archi"-technician: he is an architect of a sort rather than a productive craftsman or a man who makes things. Lest we think that the master-craftsman has transcended *technē* and engages in *epistemē* or theoretical reasoning, we must note that Aristotle explicitly refers in this passage to the distinction he drew in the *NE* vi between *technē* and *epistemē*.[71] We may infer that, since the master-craftsman is a *technitēs*, he deals only with the sublunary realm, in which things "vary" and "come into being." He will have to understand the formal and material causes of the particular things that he engineers, and the

---

[70] Cf. *Politics* VII.3, 1325b21–3: "in the case of actions done for the sake of external goals we say that the master-craftsmen (*architektonas*), who make use of thoughts, are the most active of all."

[71] *Met.* 981b25–7; he refers here to the argument at *NE* vi.3–7 (1139b14–1141b8).

universals that apply to the particulars.[72] His knowledge should not, then, be identified as *epistemē*, which deals only with objects that are imperishable, eternal, and exist by necessity.

In dividing *technē* into two classes, Aristotle creates some conceptual confusion. Is the handi-craftsman (*cheirotechnēs*) merely a man of experience? Then why call him a "craftsman" at all, and why distinguish him from the man who relies on experience? Aristotle does not address this question, and persists in referring to both the *cheirotechnēs* and the *architektōn* as "craftsmen" (men possessing *technē*). Note that the distinction between these two kinds of craftsmen reflects a distinction in the conception of *technē* itself. As Aristotle says in *Metaphysics* VII:

Things are generated by *technē* whose form (*eidos*) is contained in the soul [of the craftsman]. By "form" I mean the essence of each thing and the primary substance (τὸ τί ἦν εἶναι ἑκάστου καὶ τὴν πρώτην οὐσίαν) . . . Therefore health comes from health, and a house from a house . . . In [technical] generation and activity, part of the process is called thinking (ἡ νόησις), and part called making (ἡ ποίησις) – that which proceeds from the first principle and the form (ἀπὸ τῆς ἀρχῆς καὶ τοῦ εἴδους) is the thinking, and that which proceeds from the final step of the thinking (ἀπὸ τοῦ τελευταίου τῆς νοήσεως) is the making.[73] (1032a32–b17)

Here, Aristotle identifies two quite distinct activities in the realm of *technē* – one that involves "thinking" and deals with "the first principle and the form" and one which involves "making" and begins at the end or "final step" of the thinking process. The "making" activity begins where the "thinking" leaves off. These two activities, as it seems, are categorically different and may not even overlap. As Dunne observes, the architectonic *technē* "resides in a knowledge and thinking which are aloof not only from experience but also, it seems, from the very process of making itself."[74]

---

[72] His technical knowledge deals with substances that are sensible and perishable (as opposed to those that are sensible and imperishable and those that are neither sensible nor perishable). For this threefold classification of substances, see, e.g., *Metaphysics* XII.1, 1069a30–b2. See also *Met.* XII.9, 1074b38–1075a3, where Aristotle says: "in the productive sciences, if we leave out the matter, the object of knowledge is the substance and essence [of the particular thing that is being produced], but in the theoretical sciences the object is the *logos* and the thinking" (*noesis*).

[73] As Hintikka observes (1973, 106), the most striking feature of Aristotle's theory of change, one of the principal spheres of which is *technē* (*phusis* or nature being the other) is that "the change always has as its beginning an actual instantiation of the same 'form' as the outcome, existing potentially during the change. This actual individual may be a member of the same species as the outcome ('man begets man') but it may also be the form realized in the mind of a conscious producer of the outcome according to a plan. In all cases, however, there will have to be such an antecedently existing form which initiates the *kinesis*: the mover or agent will always be the vehicle of a form . . . which, when it acts, will be the source and the cause of the change . . . From this it follows that whenever it is true to say that a certain universal ('form') exists potentially, there must have been an earlier exemplification of the same universal actually existing."

[74] Dunne 1993, 284.

Given this schematic division between "noetic" *technē* and "poetic" or productive *technē*, one can better understand Aristotle's distinction between the two different technicians in book I: the master-craftsman does the "thinking" and the handi-craftsman does the "making." This distinction effectively denies that the handi-craftsman understands the causes of the things he is making (his knowledge is reduced to routine know-how), while also removing the master-craftsman from lowly productive activities.

The rhetoric and argumentation that Aristotle uses here clearly denigrates productive labor and laborers. It thus reflects (and reinforces) the traditional ideology of the aristocracy, whose claim to superiority was in part based on the fact that they did not have to work for a living (and thus were "truly" free). Aristotle takes this even further in the next passage, when he introduces the distinction between "useful" forms of wisdom (which deal with the "necessities") and those associated with leisure and freedom (which do not aim at utility):

> The first person to invent any *technē* that went beyond common perception was admired by men, not only because some of his inventions were useful (χρήσιμον), but also because he was wise and superior to others. And as more *technai* were discovered, some of them relating to the necessities (τἀναγκαῖα), and others to cultivated pastimes, the latter were always considered wiser than the former, because their sciences (ἐπιστήμας) did not aim at utility (χρῆσιν). Hence when all of the useful things were furnished, those sciences (τῶν ἐπιστημῶν) that do not deal with pleasure or the necessities (τἀναγκαῖα) were invented, and this first occurred in places where men had leisure. Thus mathematics first arose in Egypt because the class of priests had lives of leisure.[75] (I.1, 981b13–23)

Here, Aristotle demotes the *technai* that are "necessary" and "useful" for practical life and elevates activities that are nonutilitarian and leisured. Using the discourse of aristocratic rhetoric, Aristotle explicitly opposes theoretical activity to *technai* that are "necessary" for human life: *theoria* is "superior" precisely because it is not "necessary or useful."

This same aristocratic rhetoric – together with the hierarchical value system that subtends it – is found in many other Aristotelian texts (as we will see, it positively pervades the *Politics*). Recall, for example, Aristotle's claim in the *Protrepticus* that the person who demands that knowledge be "useful" (χρησίμην) does not understand the "vast" difference between "the good and the necessary" (τὰ ἀγαθὰ καὶ τὰ ἀναγκαῖα). As Aristotle goes on to say: "it is ridiculous to seek from everything a benefit beyond

---

[75] Note that, in this passage, the words *technai* and *epistemai* are used (as it seems) interchangeably; the fact that Aristotle switches from "*epistemê*" to "*technê*" in the last line shows that he is not using either word in the technical senses articulated in *NE* VI (see also 981b8–9, where Aristotle says that "*technê* rather than experience is *epistemê*").

the thing itself (ὠφέλειαν ἐτέραν παρ᾽ αὐτὸ τὸ πρᾶγμα) and to ask "how is this profitable (ὄφελος) for us?" And "how is this useful (χρήσιμον)?" (Β 42). In this passage, Aristotle denigrates "useful" and productive skills and elevates knowledge that is pursued only for its own sake. As we have seen, Aristotle offers a similar argument in *NE* x.7–8 (and VI.7, 1142b2–14): *theoria* is a "self-sufficient" and "leisured" activity that is superior to productive and utilitarian activities because it is pursued as an end in itself. In identifying *theoria* as an elite activity marked by leisure, self-sufficiency, and freedom, Aristotle taps into an aristocratic ideology that defines the *kalos k'agathos* in opposition to men who work for a living.

Let us look, finally, at the passage that concludes the argument in *Metaphysics* I.I:

> . . . all men believe that wisdom is concerned with the primary causes and first principles (πρῶτα αἴτια καὶ τὰς ἀρχάς), so that the man of experience is wiser than those who possess any sort of perception; the craftsman (τεχνίτης) is wiser than those who rely on experience; the master-craftsman is wiser than the craftsman who works with his hands (χειροτέχνου δὲ ἀρχιτέκτων); and the theoretical sciences have more wisdom than the productive ones (αἱ δὲ θεωρητικαὶ τῶν ποιητικῶν). (1.1, 981b28–982a1)

In this passage, Aristotle summarizes the argument in chapter 1, and caps it with the final claim that "theoretical" sciences are superior "productive" ones: here, Aristotle moves from *technē* to *theoria*. Thus, as his argument comes to a close, Aristotle says that "theoretical sciences have more wisdom than productive ones," turning away from *technē* as he hones his definition of *theoria*.[76]

THE REJECTION OF UTILITY: *METAPHYSICS* I.2

In chapter 2, Aristotle introduces the distinction between "choosing" an activity as an end in itself or for the sake of some other end.[77] He begins this argument as follows:

---

[76] Note that the master-craftsman (who possesses technical knowledge but does not, himself, produce anything) forms a sort of bridge between the handi-craftsman (the producer) and the theoretician (the anti-producer). This narrative links *technē* to *theoria* even as it draws a categorical distinction between them. Aristotle uses technical reasoning as an analogue for theoretical reasoning because *technē* was, in this period, a recognized form of knowledge that was demonstrable and teachable. Since *theoria* was just beginning to be developed and defined as a separate mode of wisdom, its legitimacy and status were still in question. Aristotle therefore turned to *technē* in his effort to define and legitimize theoretical activity, since this was the available model for "expert" knowledge. Ultimately, however, he had to separate *theoria* from *technē*, since the latter is associated with productivity.

[77] Which is related, but by no means identical, to the distinction between theoretical and productive activities.

Of the sciences, that which is chosen for itself and for the sake of knowledge (αὑτῆς ἕνεκεν καὶ τοῦ εἰδέναι χάριν αἱρετήν) is more truly wisdom than that which is chosen for the sake of the things that result from it (τῶν ἀποβαινόντων ἕνεκεν); and that which is primary and authoritative (ἀρχικωτέραν) is more truly wisdom than that which is subservient (ὑπηρετούσης). (1.2, 982a14–18)

Here, the nature of a given skill or mode of knowledge is directly linked to the manner in which it is chosen and hence to a specific motivation on the part of the chooser. By definition, true wisdom is chosen for itself, whereas inferior modes of understanding are chosen for the sake of the things that result from them. As Aristotle argues, the objects of theoretical knowledge are the most knowable and the most primary, and thus men will choose this kind of knowledge only for its own sake (982a30–b1).

Theoretical philosophy begins in wonder, Aristotle goes on to claim, and did not arise in response to practical needs or goals. In this famous passage, Aristotle recurs to the distinction between "useful" productive activities and "useless" theoretical activities (i.e. useless in the practical sphere):

That [theoretical] science is not productive (οὐ ποιητική) is clear from the case of those who first practiced philosophy. It is through wonder that men originally began, and still begin, to philosophize, wondering at first about obvious perplexities, and then . . . experiencing perplexity about greater matters . . . Now the man who is perplexed and wonders thinks himself ignorant, . . . therefore if the [early philosophers] philosophized in order to escape ignorance, it is clear that they pursued knowledge for the sake of knowing, and *not for the sake of anything useful* (οὐ χρήσεώς τινος ἕνεκεν). And the actual course of events bears witness to this; for speculation of this kind began to be pursued with a view to recreation and pastime when almost all of the necessaries were already supplied. It is clear, then, that we pursue this not for any extrinsic *use* (χρείαν), but just as *we call a man free who exists for himself and not for the sake of another* (ὥσπερ ἄνθρωπος, φαμέν, ἐλεύθερος ὁ αὑτοῦ ἕνεκα καὶ μὴ ἄλλου ὤν), so also we say that *[philosophy] is the only free science, since it alone exists for itself* (οὕτω καὶ αὑτὴν ὡς μόνην οὖσαν ἐλευθέραν τῶν ἐπιστημῶν· μόνη γὰρ αὕτη αὑτῆς ἕνεκέν ἐστιν). (*Met.* 1.2, 982b11–27)

Here, Aristotle makes an assertion that has no basis in fact: that the perplexities of the early philosophers were confined to intellectual and logical puzzles rather than to social and political problems. According to Aristotle, these men were not aiming at any sort of utility; indeed, the problem of procuring the things that are necessary and useful for life was more or less solved by the time these men started to philosophize. Of course there are numerous practical and productive problems that don't deal with the necessities of life, and it is difficult to see why the philosophers would have avoided all such problems. In Aristotle's revisionist history, the early philosophers were motivated merely by a sort of intellectual deficit: they were ignorant about the cosmos and its causal structures, and fled from this ignorance as something uncomfortable and unendurable. In other words, because the early thinkers pursued philosophy in order to escape ignorance, they could not have been pursuing it for any sort of useful end.[78]

Aristotle's claim that philosophy began in wonder is often quoted but rarely interpreted in its context. In particular, scholars have tended to ignore the fact that the passage as a whole is fueled by powerful aristocratic rhetoric. Philosophy, Aristotle states, is the only "free" science and is thus analogous to the "free" man who "exists for himself and not for the sake of another." All other sciences and skills, we may infer, are less-than-free and, indeed, "servile." This picks up on the argument set forth in *Met.* 1.2, which asserts that the mode of knowledge "which is primary and authoritative (ἀρχικωτέραν) is more truly wisdom than that which is subservient (ὑπηρετούσης); for it is not right for the wise man to receive orders, but rather to give them, nor is it right for him to obey another man, but the man who is less wise should obey him" (982a16–19). In both of these passages, Aristotle describes theoretical wisdom in terms taken from the realm of social class and status. Just as the free man "exists for himself and not for others" – presumably because he never works for anyone but rather stands in authority over them – so also *theoria* is "free" and, indeed, "authoritative" (*archikē*) over all others skills and sciences. In Greek aristocratic ideology, the superior man is defined by the possession of wealth, leisure, and power. In the *Metaphysics*, these features of the aristocratic class are applied to the quite different realm of classes of knowledge.

This argument produces a conceptual problem: for the same knowledge that is defined as "useless" and nonproductive is also said to "command" others and (as it seems) exert power in the external world. Is Aristotle suggesting that theoretical knowledge can in fact be used in the practical sphere (and thus that *theoria* is the basis for practical activity and virtuous action)? This seems extremely unlikely, since it calls into question his repeated claims that *theoria* is neither practical nor productive. In my view, this inconsistency can be explained by the fact that the aristocratic rhetoric which Aristotle uses here is pulling him in different directions. Aristotle needs a way to mark and define the superiority of the activity of *theoria* over all other pursuits, but cannot use the argument that *theoria* has beneficial results in the political and practical world. He thus turns to the notions

---

[78] Even if Aristotle were right in suggesting that these individuals were attempting to escape ignorance, this hardly entails that they were not aiming at useful ends.

of leisure and freedom, which are traditional markers of aristocratic superiority. But the aristocratically "good" man is defined both by his freedom from work and by his possession of power. In using the markers of aristocratic superiority to demonstrate the superiority of *theoria*, Aristotle ends up suggesting that theoretical activities are not only free and leisured, but play some sort of commanding role in the world.

We should not, however, take these rhetorical claims at face value. For they can hardly be taken to outweigh Aristotle's repeated assertions that *theoria* is not useful, necessary, or advantageous – that it is chosen only as an "end in itself." Aristotle's suggestion that theoretical activity "rules" over underlings simply means that it has primacy over other activities and sciences, which should be geared towards this higher *telos*. As Aristotle asserts in the *NE* VI, *"phronesis* is not in authority (κυρία) over *sophia*, or over the better part of us, just as the medical art is not in authority over health. For *phronesis* does not use (χρῆται) it [*sophia*], but provides for its coming into being; hence it issues orders for its sake but not to it" (VI.13, 1145a6–9).[79]

THEORIA AND ARISTOCRATIC "FREEDOM"

Theoria, then, is valued because it is an end in itself and is useless in the practical sphere. But isn't the notion of valuing something on the grounds that it is nonutilitarian and useless a bit paradoxical? Richard Kraut raises this question in his discussion of *NE* x.6–8; as he observes, Aristotle's insistence on the instrumental value of the practical virtues ". . . might be used *in favor of* ethical activity: whatever its intrinsic worth, its overall value is increased by the fact that it leads to other goods." Correlatively, "the unproductiveness of contemplation might be viewed *as one of its disadvantages*: although it is desirable in itself, that is all that can be said in its favor."[80] In response to this dilemma, Kraut argues that Aristotle's suggestion that contemplation is useless and nonproductive ". . . does not commit [him] to the insane idea that lack of instrumental value is by itself a good-making characteristic, or a reason for action."[81] On the basis of the fact that there is nothing "good-making" about useless activities, Kraut concludes that

---

[79] Or, as he puts it in the *Protrepticus*, "those thoughts are free (ἐλεύθεραι) which are chosen for themselves, but those that bring knowledge for the sake of other things are like slaves (δούλαις δ' ἐοικυῖαι); that which is chosen for itself is superior to that chosen for something else, just as that which is free is superior to that which is not free" (B25). Here, Aristotle explicitly asserts the link between freedom and superiority.

[80] Kraut 1989, 193 (my italics).   [81] Kraut 1989, 194.

Aristotle's claim that contemplation is useless and nonproductive simply serves to show that it is the ultimate end. We do not opt for contemplation *because it is useless* but rather because it is intrinsically choiceworthy. Its uselessness, in sum, has nothing to do with its instrinsic value.

While I would agree that the notion that uselessness is a "good-making" characteristic is rather shocking, I nonetheless believe that Aristotle valued useless activities far more than Kraut supposes. One should emphasize that the notion of "useless" knowledge is not found in Greek literature or philosophy previous to Aristotle. There is no evidence that Greeks in the archaic or classical periods valued useless over useful knowledge. Indeed, the Greeks demanded from their sages that they benefit society; the sage was defined precisely by his possession of useful knowledge that had evaded the average man.[82] In the latter half of the fifth century, in fact, as sophists and philosophers began to lay claim to new kinds of wisdom, intellectuals (such as Socrates) were repudiated because their alleged wisdom was not considered useful or beneficial. In the fourth century, moreover, we find numerous references to attacks on sophists and philosophers on the grounds of uselessness. As these references attest, the public demanded that intellectuals be useful and beneficial to family and city; if they did not prove useful, they were denounced as fraudulent.

A few examples from fourth-century texts will help to bring this point into sharper focus. In *Republic* vi, Plato responds at great length to the charge that philosophers are "useless to their cities" (487d, cf. 488e–489a, 489d, 490d). He argues (strenuously) that the true philosopher is eminently useful, and that his apparent uselessness should be blamed on the ignorant people "who do not know how to put him to use" (489b). Plato recurs to the question of the usefulness of philosophic pursuits in book vii (525b–531c). In a discussion of the studies that precede dialectic in the philosophic education, Socrates argues that the art of calculation "is useful in many ways (πολλαχῇ χρήσιμον) . . . provided that it is pursued for the sake of knowledge and not for commerce" (525d).[83] In fact, when Glaucon claims that astronomy is useful for agriculture, navigation, and the military arts, Socrates responds: "apparently you fear that the multitude may think you are proposing useless studies" (ἄχρηστα μαϑήματα, 527d).

---

[82] For an insightful discussion of the nature and activities of the archaic sage, see Martin 1993.

[83] In this passage, Plato anticipates Aristotle when he says that practitioners of geometry "speak as if they were doing something and aiming towards action, saying that they are 'squaring' and 'applying' and 'adding' and the like; but the study as a whole is carried out for the sake of understanding" (*Rep.* vii, 527a–b). But, for Plato, knowledge and understanding are the basis of (and a prerequisite for) ethical action, whereas Aristotle completely segregates theoretical and practical reasoning.

The very opposite is the case, Socrates argues, since the right employment of astronomy will "make the intelligence which is natural to the soul be useful instead of useless" (χρήσιμον . . . ἐξ ἀχρήστου, 530b–c). Finally, Socrates claims that, while philosophical studies aim, first and foremost, at the apprehension of the Forms, they are also useful for a wide range of practical and political projects. The "multitude" that considers theoretical philosophers useless is thus confronted and refuted.

Isocrates' *Antidosis* offers further evidence of the public denunciation of intellectuals who pursued abstruse and "useless" forms of knowledge (such as dialectic, astronomy, and geometry). In this speech, Isocrates reports that "many people" accuse these intellectuals of "empty talk and hair split-ting, since none of these things is useful (χρήσιμον) either in private or in public life" (261–2). He goes on to agree that these studies are useless (μηδὲν χρησίμην . . . τὴν παιδείαν ταύτην, 263), and even argues that the name "philosopher" should not be given to intellectuals "who ignore the things that are necessary" (τοὺς δὲ τῶν μὲν ἀναγκαίων ἀμελοῦντας, 284–5).[84] This title should only be given to men "who learn and practice the studies which will enable them to manage wisely their private households and the commonwealth of the city, since it is for the sake of these things that one should work, philosophize, and act" (285). Championing a prag-matic, anti-theoretical mode of wisdom explicitly designated as "useful" and "necessary," Isocrates exalts his own education precisely by reference to its relevance for practical and political life.[85]

The Greeks, then, considered wisdom inherently useful and identified pretenders by reference to their uselessness. Indeed, it was precisely in response to such attacks that intellectuals such as Plato, Isocrates, and Xenophon (e.g. *Cynegeticus* XIII.1–9, *Memorabilia* II.7, IV.7) explictly argued that philosophic knowledge is exceptionally useful. So far as one can tell from extant texts, it was Aristotle who first responded to such attacks by insisting that, yes, the best and highest form of philosophy *is* useless and this is part of what makes it supremely valuable.[86]

But what would have motivated such a response? The value that Aristotle places on uselessness, I suggest, is explained by his conception of freedom.

---

[84] This claim recalls Protagoras' discussion of wisdom in Plato's *Protagoras* 318e.

[85] Einarson (1936, 272–8) argues that Aristotle's *Protrepticus* was a direct response to Isocrates' argu-ments in the *Antidosis*; the fact that both authors use the same terminology of "useful/useless," "necessary/unnecessary" is indeed striking (see also Eucken 1983 for a more detailed discussion of Isocrates' response to the positions adopted in the Academy and the Lyceum).

[86] This argument was part of the polemic among members of the Academy (post-Plato) and the Lyceum over the question whether "true" philosophy is practical or theoretical (as I suggested in the Introduction; see also Jaeger [1923]/1948, Appendix II).

As we have seen, Aristotle claims in *Metaphysics* I that we pursue philosophy "not for any external use (χρείαν), but just as a man is free who exists for himself and not for the sake of another (ὥσπερ ἄνθρωπος, φαμέν, ἐλεύθερος ὁ αὑτοῦ ἕνεκα καὶ μὴ ἄλλου ὤν), so also [philosophy] is the only free science, since it alone exists for itself" (1.2, 982b24–7). In this passage, one can see how Aristotle's peculiar admiration for the useless affects his conception of philosophy and its history. For the useless is explicitly associated with the free. As Aristotle says in the last line, the perfectly free individual is an analogue for the perfectly free activity: since a man is called free if he "exists for himself and not for another," an activity must be called free if it "exists for its own sake." The fact that an individual or an activity does not aim at utility, then, is one of the principal markers of his/its freedom. As Aristotle says in the *Politics*, "to seek utility everywhere is completely inappropriate for great-souled and free men" (VIII.3, 1338b2–4). The free man will choose "useless" activities precisely because this evinces his freedom.

It is worth examining this notion of freedom as "existing for oneself and not for another," since it will help to shed light on Aristotle's attachment to the useless.[87] The *Politics* explicates this idea in a number of passages. In book III, Aristotle asserts that the people who "exist for others" are slaves, wage-earners, and *banausoi*. In fact, the latter two classes, which consist of freemen and not slaves, are assimilated to slaves simply because they work for others. Thus Aristotle suggests that *banausoi* and wage-earners differ from slaves only insofar as the former "do service for people in common," whereas slaves "do service for one individual master" (III.5, 1278a11–13). Both groups provide "the necessaries" and this "service" is for the sake of others. Aristotle carries this argument to its logical extreme at III.4 (1277a37–b1): "we say that there are several kinds of slave, for their employments are several; one category of slave is the manual laborer; these are, as the name indicates, men who make a living by the use of their hands, and the banausic artisan belongs in this class." In this passage, Aristotle claims that *banausoi* and other laborers – who are, technically speaking, freeborn – are in fact a kind of slave. These freeborn men are not really free, since their occupations render them subservient to others.

What kind of person, then, does not "exist for another"? What characterizes the free man? Consider the passage at *Politics* III.4 (1277a33–b11), where Aristotle claims that the free man is characterized by the exercise of

---

[87] For a useful analysis of the complexities of Aristotle's notion of freedom and the free man, see Muller 1993.

"political rulership" (τὴν πολιτκὴν ἀρχήν 1277b9), in which men of the elite class govern and are governed by men of the same class. This individual is free and not subservient since he shares the possession of political power with his peers and is not ruled by inferior men. In short, he does not "exist for others" in spite of the fact that he is subject to the political rule of his associates.[88] But even this person must be on his guard, since the wrong kinds of activities can diminish his freedom. As Aristotle goes on to say, the good man must never occupy himself with the tasks carried out by slaves, wage-earners, and *banausoi* "except if he does this on occasion for his own sake alone, for then it will not turn out that one becomes a master and another a slave" (III.4, 1277b3–7). Here, Aristotle suggests that if a man engages in work that is done for others rather than for himself, he puts himself in the position of a slave. His claim to true freedom is thus attenuated.

As the above passages attest, the free man is characterized by the fact that he possesses political power as well as by his avoidance of activities and occupations that are servile or "done for the sake of others." One should note, however, that a more complicated notion of freedom is set forth in book VII, in the passage where Aristotle compares the political to the contemplative life.[89] He begins this discussion by reporting that some advocates of the contemplative life "look down on political rule, since they believe that the *life of a free man* (τὸν τοῦ ἐλευθέρου βίον) is different from that of the man who engages in politics" (VII.3, 1325a18–20). Aristotle rejects this claim by suggesting that, while the rule of a master over a slave may not be especially dignified, the exercise of "political rule" – rule over free men rather than slaves – is in fact both free and noble.

Thus far, then, Aristotle corroborates his earlier claim that the free man is defined by his participation in "political rule." But he qualifies this claim when he turns around and defends the contemplatives against their political antagonists. Those advocating the political life against the contemplative, Aristotle reports, argue that the political man is better off because "it is impossible for the man who is not actively engaged to do well, and doing well is the same thing as happiness" (VII.3; 1325a21–3). Aristotle proceeds to attack this argument by insisting that the contemplative life is in fact more fully active than the political life:

---

[88] Although the virtue of the good man *qua* subject is not the same as the virtue of the good man *qua* ruler, "the virtue of the citizen consists in understanding the rule over free men from both positions [i.e. from the position of the ruled and of the ruler]" (III.4, 1277b13–16). Clearly, the good man is not made servile by submitting to the rule of free men.

[89] For an interesting analysis of this vexed passage, see Nichols 1992, 128–36.

The active life is not necessarily active in relation to others (πρὸς ἑτέρους), as some people think, and those kinds of thought that occur for the sake of the things that result from the activity are not the only ones that are active, but much more so are the speculations and thoughts (θεωρίας καὶ διανοήσεις) which are ends in themselves and which are pursued for their own sake. (VII.3, 1325b16–21)

Here, Aristotle indicates that the political life is "active in relation to others" and oriented towards results beyond the activity itself, whereas the contemplative life is active only in relation to itself. In this passage, then, the political life emerges as less free because it is "active in relation to others." Only contemplation is fully free, since it is never done for others. As in the *Nicomachean Ethics*, Aristotle argues that, in comparison with contemplative activity, political activity produces results beyond itself and is to this extent "active in relation to others."

As I would suggest, Aristotle identifies two different kinds of free man in the *Politics* – a man who is a member of the elite ruling class (and does not engage in menial or banausic occupations), and a man whose life is directed towards an activity which is completely useless and nonproductive and never done for the sake of anyone or anything beyond itself. The latter individual, of course, possesses a fuller and more radical mode of freedom than the former, but both men are called "free." Only by engaging in theoretical activity can a person achieve this radical and complete form of freedom.

In sum, the uselessness and nonproductiveness of an activity are important measures of its freedom. Aristotle values "uselessness" insofar as it is an indicator of freedom. Whether or not we claim that uselessness is, in itself, a "good-making characteristic,"[90] we can safely identify it as an essential characteristic of freedom. And freedom surely is a good-making characteristic in Aristotle's view, even if the freedom of a person or an activity isn't the only source of his/its value.

THE SCOPE AND OBJECTS OF THEORETICAL PHILOSOPHY

I want to complete my examination of *theoria* in the *Metaphysics* by looking at the range and objects of theoretical knowledge. Aristotle addressed this

---

[90] Recall the claim in *Met.* I.1 that "when more arts were discovered, some oriented towards the necessaries and some towards pastime, the inventors of the latter were always considered wiser because their branches of knowledge did not aim at utility" (διὰ τὸ μὴ πρὸς χρῆσιν εἶναι, I.1, 981b17–20). Here, the (alleged) fact that certain thinkers did not aim at utility is taken to be the reason why they were called wise. Although Aristotle does not say that the uselessness of the intellectual activities is what makes them good, he does indicate that the pursuit of "useless knowledge" on the part of these thinkers made them wiser and thus (we infer) better men.

question in the *NE* VI, where he said that *nous* deals with things which are unvarying, eternal, and exist by necessity, and that it has as its objects the highest and most divine things in the universe. In the *NE*, Aristotle identified *nous*, and not *epistemē*, as the faculty of theoretical reasoning: *theoria* is the actualization of *nous*, i.e. the knowledge of "first principles"; it is also the essence and sole activity of god. The *Metaphysics* discusses the objects of *theoria* in a number of places; though its account is not fully consistent, it offers vital information about Aristotle's conception of theoretical philosophy.

On the one hand, the *Metaphysics* appears to identify theoretical philosophy with theology.[91] For example, Aristotle says in book I that the object of the highest philosophy is the "theoretical knowledge of the first principles and causes" ([ἐπιστήμην] τῶν πρώτων ἀρχῶν καὶ αἰτιῶν εἶναι θεωρητικήν) – knowledge that is "divine" (982b9–10, 983a6–11). (This chimes with *NE* VI and X, which argued that *theoria* is the actualization of *nous*, which grasps "first principles"). We identify that knowledge as divine, he claims, "if it is most of all the possession of god, or if it is concerned with divine objects." Theoretical knowledge fulfills both of these conditions:

For all believe that god is one of the causes and a kind of principle (τῶν αἰτιῶν . . . εἶναι καὶ ἀρχή τις), and that god is the sole or chief possessor of this kind of knowledge. Thus, although all other sciences are more necessary (ἀναγκαιότεραι) than this one, none is more excellent. (1.2, 983a6–11)

The study of "*first* principles and causes," then, is the study of god. Here, Aristotle appears to identify first philosophy with theology, which studies divine objects or gods. He offers a full discussion of this subject in *Metaphysics* XII, as well as in the last two books of the *Physics*. As he claims, theology deals with first movers – substances that are unmoving, incorporeal, partless, and indivisible; these divine beings are final causes and, as the ultimate objects of desire, perfectly good.

In these passages, then, Aristotle identifies the theoretical study of "first principles and causes" as theology. In book VI, however, Aristotle makes a rather different claim, linking "first philosophy" and theology to the study of being *qua* being:

If there is no other substance beyond those formed by nature, then natural science will be the first science; but if there is a substance that is immovable, the science which studies this must be prior and it must be first philosophy (φιλοσοφία πρώτη), and universal because it is primary. And it will be its task to theorize (θεωρῆσαι) being *qua* being – both what it is and the attributes which belong to it *qua* being. (VI.1, 1026a27–32)

---

91 Thus giving it a limited place within the field of metaphysical philosophy.

The implicit logic of this passage is as follows: "There is a substance that is immovable; the study of this substance is theology; the immovable substance is primary, and thus theology is primary; since it is primary, it is universal; thus it theorizes being *qua* being." Aristotle offers another argument linking the *theoria* of first principles and causes to the study of being *qua* being in book IV:

> Since we are seeking the first principles and the highest causes, clearly these must belong to something by virtue of its own nature. And if our predecessors, who sought the elements of existing things, were seeking these same principles, then these elements must be the elements of being not accidentally but *qua* being. Hence it is of being *qua* being that we must grasp the first causes. (IV.I, 1003a26–31)

Here, Aristotle suggests that the knowledge of "first principles and the highest causes" – which has previously been identified with theological knowledge – is that of the "first causes" of being *qua* being.[92]

Aristotle wants to limit theoretical activity to theology while also broadening the scope of theology to include the study of being *qua* being. But, as Barnes has rightly argued, his arguments are inconsistent; among other things, there is no reason to think that "the study of beings *qua* being will study the *causes* of beings *qua* being."[93] Aristotle does not succeed in his attempts to identify the knowledge of "first principles and causes" with that of being *qua* being or with that of theology: "there is no one science which they all describe."[94]

In *Metaphysics* VI, Aristotle offers a different account of theoretical activity, which gives it a somewhat broader range:

> Physics deals with things which are separable (i.e. exist separately) but not immovable, and some branches of mathematics deal with things which are immovable, but perhaps not separable, but present in matter, while first philosophy deals with things which are both separable and immovable . . . Hence there are three theoretical philosophies (φιλοσοφίαι θεωρητικαί): mathematics, physics, and theology. (*Met.* VI.I,1026a13–18)

Here, Aristotle identifies theology as "first philosophy," thus preserving its superior status, but argues that theoretical activity also deals with mathematics and physics. As he explains, mathematics and physics have their

---

[92] See also *Met.* XII.I: "substance is the subject of our inquiry; for the principles and causes we are seeking are the principles and causes of substances" (1069a18). But the study of first causes can hardly be the same as the study of substances.

[93] Barnes 1995b, 106–8.

[94] Barnes 1995b, 108; see also Ross [1924]/1981, vol. I, lxxvii–lxxxii and *passim*, A. Mansion 1958, Owen 1960 and 1965, Hardie 1980, 336–44, Reeve 2000, ch. 9.

own "principles and elements and causes," but these disciplines proceed by singling out some being or class and focusing on it, and they do not deal with being pure and simple or being *qua* being.[95] Moreover, they do not give an account of the substance or essence or existence of their objects – these are matters for first philosophy – but they assume these things as hypotheses. Mathematics and physics are theoretical sciences, however, because they study "causes and principles" (vi.1, 1025b4–18).[96] Thus, whereas Aristotle previously identified theoretical activity with that of *nous*, which grasps the *first* principles and causes, he now suggests that *theoria* involves both *nous* and *epistemē* (according to the definitions of *epistemē* and *nous* in the *NE* vi), encompassing the knowledge of *all* principles and causes.

I do not intend to resolve this contradiction. Let me simply point out that Aristotle tends to associate *theoria* with supreme knowledge of the highest things, and inclines to identify it with theology. We have seen that Aristotle says in the first book that the highest form of wisdom is divine both because it contemplates divine causes and principles and because god possesses this knowledge (1.2). The latter condition recalls Aristotle's claim in *NE* x that the sole activity of the gods is that of *theoria*.

Aristotle makes this same point in *Metaphysics* xii.6, where he discusses the gods (unmoved movers) in some detail. This book begins by distinguishing between substances that are (1) sensible, moving, and perishable; (2) sensible, moving, and eternal; and (3) insensible and unmoving and eternal. The substances in the first two categories are "natural," whereas the third is unmoving and eternal (xii.6, 1071b3–5). In *Met.* xii.6–9, Aristotle deals with the third category, i.e. that of the gods.[97] After arguing that the gods are unmoved movers and the "first principle" upon which the universe and all of nature depend, Aristotle proceeds to explain the notion of god as the eternal actualization of thinking.[98] He begins by explaining the nature and operation of *nous*:

Nous thinks itself by virtue of participating in the object of thought (κατὰ μετάλ-ηψιν τοῦ νοητοῦ). For it becomes the object of thought by the act of apprehension and thinking, so that *nous* and the object of thought are the same. For that which

[95] See also the discussion of *theoria* in the biological sphere in *De Partibus Animalium* i.5. I will analyze this in the Epilogue.

[96] Ross ([1949]/1966, 234 n.1) suggests that physics is theoretical insofar as it studies "the non-contingent element in contingent events." Cf. Gauthier and Jolif 1970, 853, Hardie 1980, 338–40.

[97] For an excellent discussion of *Metaphysics* xii, see Frede's Introduction in Frede and Charles 2000.

[98] On *Met.* xii.7 and xii.9, see De Filippo 1994, 1995, Reeve 2000, ch. 8, Laks 2000, Brunschwig 2000. Ross ([1924]/1981, cxxx–cliv) offers a more general discussion of Aristotle's theology.

is receptive (δεκτικόν) of the object of thought and of the essence (οὐσία) is *nous*. And it is actualized (ἐνεργεῖ) when it possesses this object. Therefore it seems that actuality rather than potentiality is the divine possession of *nous*, and the activity of *theoria* is what is most pleasant and best. (XII.7, 1072b19–24)

As in the *NE* x, Aristotle identifies *theoria* with the activity of *nous*. But he goes further than the *NE* in claiming that *nous*, when actualized, becomes identical with its object. He makes a similar claim later in book XII:

In the theoretical (θεωρητικῶν) sciences, the formula or the act of thinking is the object; therefore since the thinking and the object of thought (τοῦ νοουμένου καὶ τοῦ νοῦ) do not differ in the case of things that contain no matter, they will be identical, and thinking will be one with the object of thought. (XII.9, 1075a2–5)

Aristotle makes this same point in the *De Anima*: "in the case of things which lack matter, the thinking (τὸ νοοῦν) and the object of thought (τὸ νοούμενον) are the same thing; for theoretical (θεωρητική) knowledge is the same thing as its object" (III.4, 430a3–5).[99]

What does Aristotle mean when he says that "thought thinks itself by virtue of participating in the object of thought"? Although this complex question is beyond the scope of this investigation, a few general observations are in order. Consider, first, Aristotle's conception of physical sensation, which provides an analogue for theoretical apprehension. As Aristotle argues in the *De Anima*, that which is capable of perception (*to aisthetikon*) is potentially what the object of the sense (*to aistheton*) is in actuality (418a3–4); the perceiver is acted upon by the object of perception, so as to become what that object is in actuality (417a6–20). In short, the sense (*aisthesis*) or the sense-organ (*aistheterion*) receives sensible forms without their matter and thus becomes identical with the form of its object (424a–425b, 435a).[100] This is a bit difficult to understand in the case of the senses. And it is even more difficult in the case of divine *nous*.

Divine thinking differs from human *nous* in several important ways. As pure actuality, its essence cannot possess any potentiality (as human *nous* does), nor can it think of things lower than and inferior to itself.[101] As Aristotle argues, "it thinks that which is most divine and most honorable, and

---

[99] For some useful discussions of this idea, see Hardie 1980, 348–55, Lear 1988, 123–35, 293–309, Kahn 1992, 372–5, De Filippo 1994, 1995, and Reeve 2000, ch. 7

[100] Of course the actualization of the sense and the actualization of its object are not one and the same, since their being is different. On Aristotle's theory of perception, see Sorabji 1974 and 1992, Kosman 1975, Silverman 1989, Burnyeat 1992, Nussbaum and Putnam 1992, Everson 1997, Reeve 2000, 149–60 (cf. Rosen 1988, ch. 7, who argues that Aristotle conceived of seeing as a form of touching).

[101] A difference Aristotle expresses by identifying god's thinking as a *noesis* (*Met.* XII.9 1074b21–7 and 1074b28–34; see e.g., De Filippo 1995, 556–9, Brunschwig 2000).

it does not change; for the change would be for the worse, and this would already involve some sort of motion" (1074b25–7). However, if the object of god's thought were superior to the act of thinking, then thinking would not be the supreme good.[102] In a notoriously difficult passage, Aristotle concludes that god's mind "thinks itself, and its thinking is a thinking of thinking" (ἡ νόησις νοήσεως νόησις, 1074b33–5).[103]

Since my analysis focuses on the human theorizer, the nature of divine *nous* is beyond the scope of this argument. For my purposes, what matters is the identification of the theorist's *nous* with its object in the activity of *theoria*. When the theorist's *nous* is actualized in the activity of *theoria*, it engages in an activity akin to that of god. As Aristotle puts it,

> . . . *theoria* is the most pleasurable and best activity. If, then, the happiness which god enjoys always is that which we enjoy sometimes, it is wonderful. And if it is greater, then it is even more wonderful. (*Met.* xii.7, 1072b24–6)

Here, Aristotle suggests that the human theorist experiences for short periods of time the active contemplation that god enjoys all the time.[104] In addition, when the human theorizer contemplates the "first principles and causes," he thereby contemplates god. The most advanced human theorist, then, theorizes divine thinking. By engaging in this highest form of *theoria*, the human mind assimilates itself to god: since the possession of the faculty of *nous* makes humans (potentially) akin to god, the actualization of this faculty marks the fullest flourishing of human nature.

FROM THEORIST TO CULTURAL CRITIC: *POLITICS* VIII

In the *Nicomachean Ethics* and *Metaphysics*, Aristotle claims that theoretical activity is the most "free" and "leisured" of all human pursuits. In the *Politics*,

---

[102] Note the attack on this idea in the practically oriented *Magna Moralia* ii.15 (1212b37–1213a7): "There is an argument about god that runs as follows: Since god possesses all good things and is self-sufficient, what will he do? For he will not be sleeping. In fact, he will contemplate something; for this is the finest and most suitable activity for god. What, then, will he contemplate? For if he contemplates some other thing, he will contemplate something better than himself. But it is absurd that anything should be better than god. He will therefore contemplate himself. But this is absurd. For if a man makes himself the object of investigation, we censure him for being insensate. A god who contemplates himself, then, will be an absurdity."

[103] Most interpreters argue that Aristotle claims that god is a thinking that thinks itself as its object – it thinks *of* thinking. De Filippo challenges this view, arguing that the genitive here is subjective rather than objective: god is the *noesis* belonging to *noesis* (the essence of which is pure actuality) rather than that belonging to *nous* (the essence of which is potentiality).

[104] See Ross [1924]/1981, vol. ii.381. As Ross observes, "for ἡ θεωρία as the actuality, opposed to ἐπιστήμη, the potentiality of knowledge, cf. ix.6 1048a34, 1050a12–14, *Phys.* 255a34, *De An.* 412a, 417a29, *G.A.* 735a, *NE* 1146b31–5."

Aristotle takes this same set of markers – and uses the same language and rhetoric – to identify the "liberal" education of the ruling class in the good city. Aristotle thus defines the "liberal" education and activities of this elite group in terms very similar to those used for the contemplative activity of philosophers. To be sure, the education outlined in the *Politics* is designed to produce rulers and not philosophers. In this text, I will argue, Aristotle transfers the ideals and goals of the activity of *theoria* to the lesser activity of observing and judging artistic spectacles in a cultured, educated fashion.

In chapter 3, I discussed the aristocratic rhetoric of *banausia* which the philosophers used in their definitions of "true" wisdom. As numerous passages attest, aristocratic thinkers of the fourth century argued that *banausoi* are servile, vulgar, and not truly free. These claims provide the context for a second kind of discussion which employs the language of *banausia*. This focuses on the "banausic" or "illiberal" *arts*, which are defined in opposition to "liberal" ("free") arts and activities. Here, the word "illiberal" (*aneleutherios*) does not refer to the occupations of slaves but rather to the slav*ish* and servile occupations of free men of the working class. It is for this reason that the "illiberal" arts are regularly identified as "banausic" arts – i.e. as the *technai* of low-class but freeborn artisans. A "liberal" education, by contrast, will produce virtuous and free men fit to govern a good city.[105]

Needless to say, fourth-century aristocrats were not generally serving as the sole and rightful rulers of their cities (many were living in democracies). But the very fact that these elites did not have an exclusive claim to political power in this period made it all the more important that they find a sure way to distinguish themselves from their inferiors (especially the upwardly mobile.)[106] The possession of a "liberal" education served this purpose, since it identified and separated the elite by recourse to criteria other than wealth or political power. As Raaflaub has shown, the rhetoric of "liberal" and "illiberal" arts and activities was part of a larger ideology constructed by aristocrats hostile to democracy.[107]

The notion of the "banausic" or "illiberal arts," then, is based on an aristocratic ideology that seeks to mark off "true" elites from "vulgar" rivals by casting the latter as servile and uneducated. We have already seen Aristotle's aristocratic disdain for banausic artisans in *Metaphysics* I, where he suggested that banausic activity is fundamentally non-rational, since artisans need no

---

[105] See Nightingale 2001 for a detailed discussion of Plato's and Aristotle's conceptions of the "liberal" education.
[106] See, e.g., Aristotle *NE* II.7, 1107b16–20, IV.2, 1122a28–33, and especially IV.2, 1123a18–27 (on these and related passages, see Von Reden 1995a, 85 and Nightingale 1996b, 32–3).
[107] Raaflaub 1983, 534 (see also Too 1998, 86–9).

more *logos* than an inanimate object such as fire needs to burn. A similar devaluation of the expertise of artisans emerges in the *Magna Moralia* (II.7, 1205a): "some aspects of nature are base, such as maggots and dungbeetles and all such despised animals, but nature is not for this reason to be counted as base; likewise there are base kinds of knowledge, such as the *banausic* ones, but knowledge is not for this reason base."[108] In this period, then, we find a rhetoric and ideology in which the "truly free" individual was contrasted with men who were free in a merely legal and civic sense. The free or "liberal" man, in short, is leisured, educated, and independent, whereas the "banausic" or "illiberal" individual is servile, wage-earning, and uneducated.

Aristotle's discussion of the "liberal" education occupies all of *Politics* VIII.[109] As I will suggest, this book contains two different accounts of the liberal education – accounts which endorse two quite disparate goals. The first account defines the liberal education as a necessary and useful tool for producing virtuous citizens who will participate in the government of the "good" city. As Aristotle claims at the opening of book VIII, one should adapt an educational system to the city's constitution. Better ethical characters produce and uphold a better constitution; in the good polis, then, there must be "a common education and training in matters that concern the city." (VIII.1, 1337a14–16, 1337a26–7). Later in book VIII, Aristotle claims that music is the cornerstone of a liberal education: musical training is productive of virtue since it affects the quality of a person's character (VIII.5, 1339a21–4). Music, says Aristotle, contains "imitations of character," both good and bad: "melodies" and "rhythms" can produce psychic "motions" that are either "vulgar" or "liberal" (VIII.5, 1340b9–10). Proper training in the right kind of music, then, will produce men who are truly virtuous and free rather than vulgar and banausic.[110]

Taken by itself, the notion that education should produce men who can display virtue in ethical and political action is straightforward enough. Indeed, this reflects traditional Greek notions of education. But this is not the only conception of education that Aristotle endorses in the *Politics*. For, paradoxically, Aristotle will also argue that the liberal education must train the young to engage in activities that are in no way useful or practical.

---

[108] This text, if not written by Aristotle, directly reflects Aristotelian ideas and values.

[109] It is possible that book VIII as we have it is not complete; I will confine myself to the material that is extant and refrain from speculating about what might have been left out. There is also a debate about the philosophical coherence of the *Politics* as a whole; in particular, scholars have argued that there are inconsistencies between books IV–VI and the other books (well summarized by Rowe 1977). Since I am not dealing with books IV–VI, this debate is not pertinent to my argument.

[110] I analyze Aristotle's conception of *banausia* in detail in Nightingale 1996b, 29–34 and *passim*. See also Lévy 1979 and Rössler 1981, 226–31 on *banausia* in Aristotle's *Politics*.

This latter account of the liberal education commences in the second chapter of book VIII, where Aristotle distinguishes the liberal from the illiberal and banausic arts:[III]

> It is clear that one must teach those of the useful arts (τῶν χρησίμων) which are absolutely necessary; but it is obvious that not all things should be taught, since liberal activities must be distinguished from illiberal (διῃρημένων τῶν τε ἐλευθερίων ἔργων καὶ τῶν ἀνελευθερίων). The students must learn those useful arts (ὅσα τῶν χρησίμων) which will not make the person who participates in them banausic (βάναυσον). One must consider an activity and also an art or science banausic (βάναυσον) if it renders the body or the soul or the mind of a free man unable to perform the tasks and activities of virtue. Hence we call "banausic" all such arts as damage the body, as well as the wage-earning occupations; for these make the mind unleisured and petty (ἄσχολον γὰρ ποιοῦσι τὴν διάνοιαν καὶ ταπεινήν). (*Pol.* VIII.2, 1337b4–15)

It might seem that training in a craft or any sort of wage-earning occupation defines the banausic education. But the situation is not this simple. For Aristotle goes on to say that to apply oneself to liberal studies too assiduously can actually render a person banausic rather than liberal (VIII.2, 1337b15–17). The liberal arts, in short, can be pursued in the wrong way, with deleterious effects. And just as "liberal" activities can be practiced in the wrong way, thus making a person illiberal, the illiberal arts can be pursued in a liberal way. As Aristotle says in book VII, "hence even free men in their youth can engage in many activities considered menial, since in relation to what is fine and not fine activities do not differ so much in themselves as they do in their ends and objects" (VII.4, 1333a7–11). As these passages reveal, while any *person* who is working for a wage is, by definition, illiberal, the *activity* or *art* in which he engages may or may not be illiberal.

With this backdrop in place, Aristotle proceeds to outline the liberal education, placing special emphasis on training in music. The curriculum has four areas – reading and writing, drawing, gymnastics, and music – each of which has a different orientation. Aristotle suggests that "writing and drawing are useful for life and very serviceable, and gymnastics contribute to courage" (VIII.3, 1337b25–7). But what, he asks, is the purpose of music? Nowadays, he observes, people pursue music for the sake of pleasure, but "those who originally included it in education did so because nature herself seeks to be able not only to engage rightly in unleisured activities, but also to be at leisure in the proper fashion" (1337b28–32). If it is to be a truly liberal art, music must be pursued for its own sake, as a serious leisure activity. As Aristotle concludes, "it is clear that one must learn and be educated in

---

[III] Since the first account is adumbrated in VIII.1, the second account actually interrupts the discussion of the first.

some things with a view to the leisure in the pastime, and that these studies and disciplines are ends in themselves (ἑαυτῶν . . . χάριν), whereas those oriented towards unleisured activities are studied as necessary and as means to other things (ὡς ἀναγκαίας καὶ χάριν ἄλλων)" (VIII.3, 1338a9–13).

Aristotle now insists that music actually meets these requirements:

> Our predecessors included music in education not as something necessary (ἀναγκαῖον) – for there is nothing necessary about it – nor as useful (χρήσι-μον), as writing is useful for business and for household management and for learning and for many political activities . . . Musical education does not aim at health or strength, as gymnastics does (for we see neither of these things produced by music). It remains, then, that music is oriented towards the time spent in leisure. (VIII.3, 1338a13–22)

Music, then, is an activity that is neither "necessary" nor "useful." Note that this nonutilitarian pursuit of music is taken to prove the existence of a larger class of "useless" pursuits. If music is neither necessary nor useful, Aristotle claims, there must be other such activities:

> Clearly, there exists a form of education in which we train the young not because it is useful or necessary (οὐχ ὡς χρησίμην . . . οὐδ' ὡς ἀναγκαίαν) but because it is free and noble (ὡς ἐλευθέριον καὶ καλήν). Whether there is one such subject or several, and what these are and how they are to be pursued, must be discussed later. But now we have made this much progress, because we have some evidence from the education which the ancients instituted. For the point is proved by music. (VIII.3, 1338a30–7)

Clearly, Aristotle gestures here towards philosophic contemplation, which is completely "useless" and nonproductive.

In the *Metaphysics* and the *Nicomachean Ethics*, as we have seen, Aristotle articulates the idea of nonutilitarian or "useless" activities carried out "for their own sake." In the *Politics* VIII, which deals with the liberal education of aristocrats, Aristotle applies this same terminology to a quite different kind of activity. For the educational system in the *Politics* is geared towards musical/cultural activities rather than philosophy; this education is not designed to produce philosophers. Nonetheless, Aristotle's insistence in the *Politics* that "war is for the sake of peace, unleisure for the sake of leisure, and the necessary and useful for the sake of the fine" (VII.14, 1333a35–6) makes it clear that political activities, which by definition are not leisured, do not serve as the final goal for the citizens in the good city. As in the *NE* x, Aristotle privileges leisure over business and politics. In the *Politics*, this is the ultimate goal of the educational system: the good city, as Aristotle says, must educate its young "with an eye to leisure."[112] The educational system, in short, must reflect and communicate the notion that leisure is an end which is higher than political *praxis*. One should remember that the liberal education is designed to produce truly "free" men; in Aristotle's view, men are freer when they are at leisure than when they are engaged in practical and political activities. For this reason, Aristotle claims that the liberal education must train men not only to be good citizens and rulers – good, in short, when they are not at leisure – but also to make a good employment of leisure.

What, then, are the proper leisure activities? Aristotle addresses this question in book VII, where he divides the virtues into three categories: (1) virtues oriented only towards unleisure; (2) virtues oriented only towards leisure; and (3) virtues oriented towards both leisure and unleisure. The specific virtues are categorized as follows: "courage and endurance are oriented towards unleisure, philosophy towards leisure, and temperance and justice towards both" (VII.15, 1334a22–5). Unfortunately, Aristotle does not explicate the principles according to which he makes this threefold division, but he does offer some clues. Note, first of all, that he treats "philosophy" as a mode of virtuous activity; this activity is exclusively oriented towards leisure. Second, and even more important, Aristotle describes the virtues in category 3 – those oriented towards both leisure and unleisure – as being "*useful* for leisure and pastime" (χρήσιμοι . . . πρὸς τὴν σχολὴν καὶ διαγ-ωγήν, 1334a16–17), but he makes no such claim for the virtues in category 2. We may infer, then, that not all virtues which are "oriented towards" leisure are necessarily "useful" for leisure – that some virtues, in short, are appropriate for leisure not by dint of being useful. Clearly, philosophy must be one such virtue. Both in its broadest sense – as intellectual cultivation in general – and in its technical Aristotelian sense (as the activity of the theoretical intellect), philosophy is not "useful" for leisure or for anything else. The practical virtues, by contrast, are necessary for leisure, but they are not the ultimate leisure activity.

TEACHING A TASTE FOR THE "USELESS"

The arguments in *Politics* VIII concerning the "useless" and "unnecessary" nature of music create problems for the interpreter. In particular, they

[112] *Politics* VII.14, 1333a41–b5, 1334a9–10. See Yack (1991, 23), who argues that "although the polis is prior to the individual, according to Aristotle, it still exists for the sake of the good life led by individuals; individuals do not exist for the sake of the perfection of the polis."

appear to contradict Aristotle's assertions elsewhere in book VIII that education is necessary and useful for creating virtuous citizens to govern the good city. As Carnes Lord observes,

> . . . [Aristotle] is so anxious to show that musical education is in no way "necessary" or "useful" that he will not even describe it as being "for the sake of" *diagogē* [pastime]: the education in music must be understood as being "for its own sake" (1338a9–12ff.). Since music is said not to be useful even with a view to "political actions" (1339a15–17), and since it can hardly be denied that virtue is useful with a view to a great many political actions, one is forced to wonder whether Aristotle's two accounts are finally even compatible.[113]

Lord correctly suggests that Aristotle's two accounts of education are disparate if not contradictory. But his solution to the apparent contradiction is, I believe, erroneous. For he simply rejects the argument that music is a useless and unnecessary pursuit, suggesting that this view belongs to "the ancients" and not to Aristotle.[114] By dealing off the argument in this way, Lord can thus conclude that Aristotle's musical training simply aims to produce a virtuous character. The students do not practice it "for its own sake" but rather for the sake of practical virtue which, in turn, serves the end of politics.[115] But, as the text clearly indicates, Aristotle *agrees* with the ancients who treated music as a serious activity pursued for its own sake. As we have seen, the notion of an activity pursued "for its own sake" is of vital importance for Aristotle; it should not be simply dealt off to the ancients.

Lord suggests, then, that we must choose between the two kinds of education discussed in the *Politics*. Either the liberal education is designed to produce civic virtue and practical/political activity or it aims to promote activities that are completely "useless" and nonproductive. Lord identifies the former as the true Aristotelian view, and completely discounts the latter. Nichols argues along similar lines, claiming that "musical activity gives way to political activity" as the boys grow into men; as she claims, "music is a central element in education because it fosters the moral and intellectual virtue (character and judgment) that make possible political participation . . ."[116] Like Lord, Nichols posits as the "end" of education virtuous actions in political affairs. The suggestion that the students must

---

[113] Lord 1982, 76; Too 1998, 87–90 offers a persuasive critique of Lord's interpretation.

[114] Lord 1982, 77.   [115] Lord 1982, 103.

[116] Nichols 1992, 162. According to Nichols (1992, 160), Aristotle equates "pastime" (*diagogē*) with "prudence" (*phronesis*); the musical activities which "contribute to pastime," she infers, must necessarily "contribute to prudence."

engage in music as a nonutilitarian leisure activity and an end in itself is thus completely eclipsed.[117]

Aristotle sets forth two quite different notions of education in *Politics* VIII. I believe that we should take them both seriously in spite of the discrepancy between them. In fact, the discrepancy is itself very revealing. For it shows that Aristotle was wrestling with two different ideologies of education – a traditional one that inculcates ethical virtue via musical activities and a new programme designed to make students "spectators" and "judges" of the good and the fine.[118] The former mode of education aims at the development of practical and political actions, the latter at nonutilitarian activities pursued in periods of leisure.

These two conceptions of liberal education in the *Politics* are grounded in the two different notions of freedom that I discussed above. As I have suggested, Aristotle identifies two kinds of freedom in the *Politics*: first, a man is free if he governs the city as a member of the elite ruling class (and avoids all menial and banausic pursuits); second, a man is free if he engages in activities that are completely "useless" and nonproductive and never done for the sake of some further end. The latter, of course, is a fuller and more radical freedom than the former, but both are acknowledged as types of "freedom."

Which of these two kinds of freedom is the goal of the "liberal" education? The answer, I believe, is both. Aristotle wants his educational system to produce the free men who will rule and act virtuously in civic affairs, but he also wants these men to experience the more radical freedom that accompanies activities that are "not for the sake of" anything or anyone. Aristotle's educational system therefore aims to foster the practical virtues necessary for the unleisured activities of politics, but it also trains youths to engage in noble leisure activities, which are defined in opposition to political and productive pursuits. According to Aristotle, only in leisure activities can the citizens experience a freedom that goes beyond that achieved in

---

[117] Solmsen 1968b takes seriously the claim that "leisure" is the goal of education. He rightly observes that leisure (*scholē*) is conceptualized in opposition to political and civic activities in traditional Greek thinking; Aristotle, he claims, advances a radical idea in making "leisure" the very *telos* of the lives of the citizens. Solmsen argues that, although music does make men "better citizens," Aristotle's educational programme is in fact geared towards "the *private* happiness of the citizens" (p. 27). Unfortunately, he never explains what is meant by the "private happiness" of the citizens and how this squares with their practical and political activities. See also Demont (1993a).

[118] Note that the latter programme is not simply designed to teach aesthetics – for Aristotle, good artistic judgment is both aesthetic and ethical. This educational programme, in short, teaches a form of wisdom which is both artistic and social – a wisdom that is, itself, a marker of social class and status. See Ford's excellent discussion of these issues in 2002, ch. 12 (see also Halliwell 2002, 176 and *passim*).

practical and political activity. This radical freedom is, of course, more fully attained by contemplatives, but the average citizen can, in his leisure hours, certainly get a taste of – and develop a taste for – such freedom. By learning to value this kind of freedom and to engage in the "useless" activities that define it, the citizens can at least approach the highest form of human happiness. In adopting this educational system, the city as a whole will be possessed of the right values and priorities, even if only a few men can "be at leisure" in the best and fullest sense (i.e. as theoretical philosophers).

A closer look at the arguments in *Politics* VIII will bring this into better focus. At VIII.4 (1339a), Aristotle raises the question whether music should be used in education (1) "for the sake of amusement and relaxation," (2) "in order to create a good character," or (3) "as contributing to the activity of pastime (*diagogē*) and wisdom."[119] In order to understand Aristotle's argument here, we need to clarify the conception of "pastime" (which has a broad range of connotations). As Lord suggests:

When Aristotle speaks of "the leisure associated with pastime" [1338a21–2], he does so . . . precisely in order to distinguish the leisure that is associated with political activities from leisure in the proper sense of the term – the leisured "pastime" that constitutes the end of the best life or the true source of happiness for the best regime.[120]

In short, *diagogē* or "pastime" is connected with cultivated pursuits such as music and philosophy, which require leisure and freedom from practical and political activities.[121]

Which of these three goals, then, is the proper aim of education? Aristotle argues that "amusement" cannot be the primary aim of education. In addition, he claims, "it is not fitting to assign pastime (*diagogē*) to boys and youths, since that which is an end (*telos*) is not suitable for that which is imperfect (*atelei*)." In other words, because youths are "imperfect" (in the sense of immature), they cannot participate in activities in a manner that is fully perfect and end-like.[122] At this point, then, it looks as though Aristotle will adopt the second goal – the cultivation of character – as the exclusive aim of his educational system. But he goes on to say that music is in fact

---

[119] (1) "amusement and relaxation": παιδιᾶς ἕνεκα καὶ ἀναπαύσεως; (2) "creating a good character": τὸ ἦθος ποιόν τι ποιεῖν; (3) "contributing to pastime and wisdom": πρὸς διαγωγήν τι συμβάλλεται καὶ πρὸς φρόνησιν (VIII.4, 1339a16–17, 24–6).

[120] Lord 1982, 56–7.

[121] See Kraut 1997, 178: "making music is a way of exercising the virtue of wisdom, and this role is to be distinguished from the contribution it makes to the ethical virtues."

[122] Kraut 1997, 188–9.

directed towards all three of the goals (VIII.5, 1339b). First of all, music does give pleasure, which can play a role in education so long as it is not taken to be the primary goal. Even more importantly, he says, proper training in music contributes to the formation of a good character (1340a). After Aristotle argues for this point (in some detail), we expect him to turn to category three – that of leisure and "pastime." But, at this point, he appears to change the subject, raising the question whether the students should participate in singing and playing instruments or whether they should simply watch others perform music (VIII.6, 1340b). He discusses this issue for the rest of the treatise, and never explicitly addresses the contribution that music makes to "pastime and wisdom."

As I would urge, he does in fact deal with the subject of "pastime" indirectly in this final passage. Since "pastime" is associated with leisure rather than political or practical affairs, an education geared towards pastime must teach students activities that are appropriate for leisure. Aristotle addresses this very issue when he says that the purpose of teaching youths to sing and play music is to make them good "judges" when they reach adulthood:

Since it is necessary to take part in these activities [i.e. singing and playing instruments] for the sake of judging (κρίνειν), people must, when they are young, learn to [sing and play instruments]. When they grow older, they should be released from these activities, but be able to judge things (κρίνειν) that are fine and to rejoice in them properly on account of the education they had in their youth.[123]

Aristotle makes it quite clear that the young should not learn to play instruments in order to become professional musicians; this, in fact, would render them banausic (VIII.6, 1341a9–11). Rather, one performs music in youth in order to be a good spectator and judge as an adult. As Aristotle argues, if men do not participate in musical performances when they are young, "it is difficult if not impossible to become good judges" (*kritas . . . spoudaious*, 1340b25). This chimes with Aristotle's earlier claim that "pastime" should not be assigned to the young, since "that which is an end (*telos*) is not suitable for that which is imperfect (*atelei*)." Since the young are not ready to participate in activities that are fully end-like, they must be prepared and educated to do this later on in life. In short, young people must learn music so that they can use their leisure in the proper fashion when they grow up. They practice and master music as youths for the purpose of being good judges and spectators when they become adults (in periods of leisure). They

---

[123] τοῦ κρίνειν χάριν . . . τὰ καλὰ κρίνειν . . . (VIII.6, 1340b35–9). Ford (2002, ch. 12) discusses Aristotle's notion of the *kritikos* and the mode of judgment that he exercises.

cannot be at leisure in a full way as students, but they can be educated in this kind of pursuit.

It might seem that the capacity to "judge the things that are fine" is geared towards *praxis*, since the recognition of what is good is an important element in virtuous action. But that is not what Aristotle says in this passage. Rather, he claims that judging the fine and the noble is an end in itself. In short, he does not aim to make the students good agents and actors (i.e. good at doing fine actions) but rather to turn them into good spectators. As he claims, education in music can and should prepare students for leisure activities. To engage oneself as a good spectator and judge is an activity suitable for leisure – one does this for its own sake rather than to produce some action or event beyond itself. This kind of activity is not, then, a matter of practical reasoning, which involves the application of universals to particulars.[124] As spectators, Aristotle's citizens have no need to deliberate or to choose a specific course of action; in viewing and listening to musical performances, they can focus on the good and the fine as universals. Since practical and political actions are suspended during artistic spectacles, the viewers need only engage in the activity of contemplating what is beautiful and good.[125] Aristotle makes a similar point earlier in the *Politics* VIII, in a discussion of drawing: though drawing may be useful for purchasing furniture and implements, a student should study it not for these reasons but "because it makes him a contemplator (*theoretikon*) of the beauty of bodies.[126] Correlatively, the viewer of a musical spectacle can be a "contemplator" (*theoretikos*) of the beauty of events and characters and actions, as well as of artistic forms and structures. I do not mean to suggest that Aristotle's educational programme teaches aesthetic judgment in isolation from ethical values. Rather, as Ford suggests, it aims at "a hybrid skill, combining technical expertise with a broader vision of social harmony" – a form of wisdom that is at once aesthetic and social.[127] The education in "leisure and pastime," then, fosters the exercise of good (aristocratic) taste rather than practical reasoning *per se*.

---

[124] As Aristotle says in the *NE*, in the case of practical reasoning the understanding of the particulars is perhaps even more important than the grasp of universals (VI.7.6–7, 1141b).

[125] Cf. Depew (1991), who argues that the education in the *Politics* is aimed at *phronesis*, which has both intellectual and practical components. Depew claims that the educational system aims in part at training the intellect; but he emphasizes the intellectual aspects of practical reasoning, whereas I argue that Aristotle aims to educate the youths (among other things) in an activity that is akin to *theoria*.

[126] ὅτι ποιεῖ θεωρητικὸν τοῦ περὶ τὰ σώματα κάλλους (VIII.3, 1338b1–2).

[127] Ford 2002, 272 (see also Halliwell 2002, chs. 5–6).

Let us recall that, in the *Protrepticus*, Aristotle draws a direct parallel between the spectator (*theoros*) at the Olympian or Dionysian festivals and the philosophic contemplator of the universe. As he argues, the activities of both of the spectator and the contemplator are not useful or productive but rather ends in themselves. Being a spectator at a musical performance, provided that one has the capacity to judge "the things that are fine," is an activity analogous to philosophic contemplation. Since the majority of the citizens in Aristotle's good city will not become philosophers, they must spend their leisure time watching and judging musical performances in the correct fashion: they must develop an eye for beauty and excellence (both aesthetic and social). In this way, they engage in an activity that resembles *theoria* (in certain ways) even though its objects are not divine, eternal, or incorporeal.

It is perhaps no surprise that Aristotle does not offer a perfectly coherent account of this kind of education, since the conception of a "liberal" education was just beginning to be articulated in this period. Like Plato's educational system in the *Republic*, Aristotle's system is designed to produce a mix of practical and contemplative virtues (and the disparate kinds of freedom that accompany these different virtues). But Plato sets forth an educational system for philosophers which aims at the contemplation of the Forms and the enactment of true virtue in the practical sphere. Aristotle, by contrast, sets forth an education that does not produce philosophers. In addition to fostering civic virtue, his "liberal" education aims at the leisured activity of spectating, which is a nonutilitarian activity that cultivates artistic judgment and taste for its own sake. The "liberally" educated man is not a philosophic theorist but a *kritēs* – a judge and spectator of artistic representations. Here, Aristotle introduces a new kind of elite: the cultural critic.[128]

Aristotle's definition and defense of theoretical activity has had a massive impact on Western thinking. The very terms and categories we use to conceptualize different forms of knowledge derive from Aristotle. In addition, the rhetoric which valorizes disinterested and nonutilitarian pursuits and disciplines has pervaded Western discussions of education and knowledge.[129] Yet the interpreter of Aristotle is left to question whether

---

[128] As Too (1998, 90) rightly argues, "the good judge must be a good literary critic precisely because being able to discern the appropriate forms of culture for society and its citizens is one of the bases of good society."

[129] Ironically, even Heidegger (who set out to overthrow the entire metaphysical tradition) claims that wisdom is "useless" and disinterested.

theoretical activity is really as disinterested and nonutilitarian as he claims. Certainly Aristotle's own *defense* of *theoria* is far from disinterested: the self-proclaimed superiority of theoretical activity makes a clear bid for cultural capital. This becomes especially clear when Aristotle uses the same terminology and discourse that he applied to *theoria* to describe the leisure activities of "liberal" elites in the good city.

As I have suggested, Aristotle deploys traditional aristocratic rhetoric in texts as disparate as the *Protrepticus*, the *Nicomachean Ethics*, the *Metaphysics*, and the *Politics*. In part, Aristotle uses this rhetoric to distinguish the "true" elites from wealthy and powerful individuals from the non-aristocratic class (as well as from all other low-class people). But he also deploys this rhetoric to identify a group of individuals – the theoretical philosophers – who are nobler and freer than the *aristoi* in the ruling elite (a claim that would have puzzled the aristocrats of his day). Aristotle joins Plato in claiming that *theoria* is the most elite and free activity, thus demoting other contenders. But, in contrast to Plato, Aristotle honors the virtuous members of the elite ruling class, and accords them the second happiest life: they, too, are noble and free, but in a lesser degree than the philosophers. Finally, Aristotle sets forth an educational system that will train elites to engage in non-philosophical activities which mimic, in certain ways, the activity of *theoria*, thus making them cultured, liberal, and virtuous men (as well as arbiters of taste). We are very far, indeed, from the demotic performances of Socrates.

Epilogue: "Broken knowledge"?
Theoria *and wonder*

It is true that the contemplation of the creatures of God hath for its
end . . . knowledge, but as to the nature of God, no knowledge, but
wonder; which is nothing but knowledge broken off, or losing itself.

Francis Bacon

For the clarity we are aiming at is indeed *complete* clarity. But this
simply means that the philosophical problems should *completely* disappear. The real discovery is the one that makes me able to stop doing
philosophy when I want to – the one that gives philosophy peace.

Wittgenstein

Wonder is the foundation of all philosophy, inquiry its progress, ignorance its end. I'll go further: there is a certain strong and generous
ignorance that concedes nothing to knowledge in honor and courage,
an ignorance that requires no less knowledge to conceive it than does
knowledge.

Montaigne

Wonder plays an essential role in the pursuit and practice of *theoria*, yet it is
rarely analyzed in the scholarly literature. As Aristotle stated so memorably
in the *Metaphysics*:

It is through wonder (θαυμάζειν) that men originally began, and still begin, to
philosophize, wondering at first about obvious perplexities, and then . . . experiencing perplexity (διαπορήσαντες) about greater matters . . . Now the man who is
perplexed and wonders (ἀπορῶν καί θαυμάζων) thinks himself ignorant . . . therefore, if it was to escape (φεύγειν) ignorance that men practiced philosophy, it is
clear that they pursued knowledge for the sake of knowing, and not for the sake
of anything useful. (982b)

Here, Aristotle inaugurates what will prove to be a long tradition of linking
philosophy to wonder. The Greek word for "wonder" is, in the verbal
form, θαυμάζειν and, as a noun, θαῦμα. In this passage, Aristotle yokes
wonder together with perplexity: to wonder is to experience *aporia*, to
be "perplexed" or, more literally, "without a path." But the Aristotelian

253

philosopher does find the path that leads him from *aporia* to certainty. As Aristotle indicates, the philosopher "escapes" from perplexity and ignorance when he acquires knowledge or, to put it in his words, when he "theorizes the cause" (τεθηωρηκόσι τὴν αἰτίαν, 983a14–15).

To "theorize" or "see" the cause of something perplexing is to move from a state of wonder to a state of certainty. Philosophy, then, begins in wonder and ends in *theoria*. As Aristotle asserts, the philosopher begins by wondering why certain perplexing things are as they are; but when he attains theoretical knowledge, he ceases to wonder (since he now has the answers) and "he would be surprised if things were *not* as they are."[1] Aristotle makes a similar point in the *Nicomachean Ethics*, where he distinguishes the *possession* of knowledge from its pursuit (x.7, 1177a25–7). As Hardie observes, the Aristotelian philosopher "desires to know the answer and not just to occupy himself in looking for it. It is not like fox-hunting in which some hunstman may even prefer not to kill a fox."[2] Interestingly, the noetic faculty has the capacity to receive even divine objects without being astounded or overwhelmed: as Aristotle says in the *De Anima*, even when *nous* theorizes something that is "vehemently" or "exceedingly intelligible" (*sphodra noeton*), it is not overwhelmed or blunted (as the senses are in the case of intensely strong sensations; iii.4, 429a31–b3). Theorizing divine essences, then, does not produce wonder or astonishment.

This conception of wonder and its relation to philosophy was accepted as almost a truism in Western thinking up through the eighteenth century.[3] Consider, for example, Albertus Magnus:

All men who have practiced philosophy, both now and in the past, were not moved to philosophize by anything except wonder . . . Now the man who is puzzled and wonders apparently does not know. Hence wonder is the movement of the man who does not know on his way to finding out, so that he may know the cause of that thing at which he wonders.[4]

---

[1] "All begin by wondering that things should be as they are (e.g. with regard to marionettes, or the solstices, or the incommensurability of the diagonal of a square). Because it seems wonderful (θαυμαστόν) to everyone who has not yet theorized/contemplated (τεθεωρηκόσι) the cause that a thing should not be measurable by the smallest unit. But we must end with the contrary and better view . . . for a geometrician would wonder at nothing so much as if the diagonal were to become measurable" (*Met.* 983a).

[2] Hardie 1980, 345.

[3] For some discussions of wonder in the medieval and modern periods, see Daston and Park 1998, Bynum 2001, ch. 1 and *passim*. For some philosophic studies of wonder, see Rosen 1957, 1959, and Heidegger, [1937–8]/1994.

[4] *Nam omnes homines, qui et nunc in hoc nostro tempore et primum ante nostra tempora philosophati sunt, non sunt moti ad philosophandum nisi per admirationem . . . Qui autem dubitat et admiratur, ignorare videtur; est enim admiratio motus ignorantis procedentis ad inquirendum, ut sciat causam eius de quo miratur* (*Metaphysica* 1.2.6, in *Opera Omnia* , ed. Geyer, vol. xvi/1, p. 23).

Similarly, Descartes says in *The Passions of the Soul* that wonder is the "attention to unusual and extraordinary objects" which is beneficial insofar as it leads to knowledge.[5] Descartes adds, however, that it is possible to wonder too much and thus to "pervert the use of reason." We must, he says, try to "free ourselves" from wonder as much as possible by achieving knowledge and certainty. Otherwise, we may end in the state that Descartes calls "blind curiosity," which characterizes "men who seek out things that are rare solely to wonder at them and not for the purpose of knowing them." Here, Descartes explicitly identifies wonder as curiosity, and claims that knowledge brings wonder to an end. Francis Bacon argues along the same lines when he calls wonder "broken knowledge" (or "knowledge broken off"); this condition, he claims, must be repaired by the achievement of certainty.[6] Finally, consider Adam Smith, who borrows directly from Aristotle: "wonder, not any expectation of advantage from discoveries, is the first principle which prompts mankind to the study of Philosophy . . . and [philosophers] pursue this study for its own sake, as an original pleasure or good in itself, without regarding its tendency to procure them the means of many other pleasures."[7] Smith's philosophers, like Aristotle's, journey from a state of wonder to the experience of certainty: "if we can answer the questions," he says, "our wonder is entirely at an end."[8]

Of course, this conception of wonder and *theoria* has also had its detractors. Nietzsche, for example, deconstructs this idea in the *Gay Science*:

What do they want when they want "knowledge"? Nothing more than this: Something strange is to be reduced to something *familiar*. And we philosophers – have we really meant *more* than this when we have spoken of knowledge? What is familiar means what we are used to so that we no longer marvel at it, our everyday, some rule in which we are stuck, anything at all in which we feel at home. Look, isn't our need for knowledge precisely this need for the familiar, the will to uncover under everything strange, unusual, and questionable something that no longer disturbs us? Is it not the *instinct of fear* that bids us to know? And is the jubilation of those who attain knowledge not the jubilation over the restoration of a sense of security?[9]

---

[5] Descartes, "The Passions of the Soul" part 2, LXX–LVIII (in Haldane and Ross 1978, 362–6).

[6] Bacon articulates this notion in "Advancement of Learning" (Spedding et al. 1863, 96), and in "Valerius Terminus or the Interpretation of Nature" (*ibid.* p. 29).

[7] Smith, "The History of Astronomy" (Whiteman and Ross 1982, 50–1). See also Hume (*Essays: Moral, Political, and Literary*), who said that "from law arises security, from security curiosity, and from curiosity knowledge" (Green and Grose 1889, 1 p.180).

[8] Smith, "History of Astronomy" (Whiteman and Ross 1982, 51). As Griswold argues (1999a, 336–44, 361–76), Smith's philosophers, unlike Aristotle's, construct rather than discover the causal links between phenomena (which enables them to move from wonder to certainty).

[9] Nietzsche, *The Gay Science* v, 355 (trans. Kaufmann).

Heidegger takes this a step further, articulating a new conception of wonder in direct opposition to the Aristotelian tradition:

In wonder, what is most usual of all and in all, i.e. everything, becomes the most unusual . . . While wonder must venture out into the most extreme unusualness of everything, it is at the same time cast back wholly on itself, knowing that it is incapable of penetrating the unusualness by way of explanation, since that would precisely be to destroy it.[10]

The Aristotelian path from wonder to certainty, from *aporia* to *theoria* is, I think, clear enough. Let me turn now to a different conception of wonder – Platonic wonder – which occurs at the end, rather than the beginning, of the philosophic quest. This kind of wonder has its roots in the very earliest Greek texts.[11] In Homer and archaic literature, *thaumazein* and its cognates are very rarely used in the sense of puzzlement, perplexity, or curiosity.[12] In fact, *thauma* is never confined to merely cognitive experiences: archaic wonder is both cognitive and affective, intellectual and emotional, ranging from the feelings of reverence and awe to admiration and amazement. In this period, wonder is closely connected with the faculty of vision (hence the frequent occurrence of the formulaic phrase *thauma idesthai* – "a wonder to look upon" – in archaic poetry). One quite complex form of archaic wonder is characterized by the feeling of reverence for something that is perceived as both divine and yet also kindred to the human viewer. Here, a person "looks with wonder" at something that is both similar and different, kindred and strange.

An example of this kind of wonder occurs in the famous scene near the end of the *Iliad* where the aged Priam visits his enemy Achilles to offer gifts for the ransoming of his dead son Hector (a scene which is, itself, truly wondrous). When Priam first arrives, Achilles and his companions "look with wonder" at him and, though they know who he is, pronounce him to be "godlike" (θεοειδέα).[13] Priam then appeals to Achilles as a grieving father, entreating him to be mindful of his own father in his sorrowful old age (xxiv.486–506). Amazingly, as these two enemies look at each other, each is "reminded" of his own beloved kin – Achilles sees his own father in

---

[10] Heidegger *The Basic Questions of Philosophy* (trans. Rojcewicz and Schuwer 1994, 144).

[11] Prier (1989, esp. 84–97) has listed and, in some cases, analyzed the different uses of *thauma* and its cognates in archaic literature (as well as a number of related words that signify "wonder" in this period). Prier does not discuss the form of wonder that I am analyzing here, though he does identify the passages in which it is found in his list of *thauma* examples.

[12] Prier 1989, 93–4.

[13] The Greek word for "wonder" here is *thambos*, which is used (as a noun and a verb) three times in three lines (*Iliad* xxiv.482–4). As Prier (1989, 87–97) has shown, *thambos* is very closely related to *thauma* (the words are often used as synonyms).

Priam, and Priam sees his son in Achilles. This experience causes both men to weep, Achilles for his absent father Peleus and Priam for his dead son Hector (XXIV.509–12). When the scene comes to an end, the two men are still gazing at each other in wonderment: "And Dardanian Priam looked with wonder (ϑαύμαζ') at Achilles/ . . . for he was like the gods to behold face-to-face./ And Achilles looked with wonder (ϑαύμαζεν) at Dardanian Priam/ as he gazed upon his visage" (XXIV.629–32). Here, both Priam and Achilles perceive each other as "godlike" and yet each sees the other as kindred. It is the combination of the perceptions of kinship and difference that creates this complex form of wonder. Each knows that the other is a human being and, in fact, an enemy. Yet each sees in the other both the superhuman strangeness of divinity and the familiarity of his nearest kin. The very same object "resembles" divinity at the same time as it "reminds" the viewer of his own son or father. This simultaneous experience of strangeness and kinship produces a unique kind of wonder. This is a wonder that persists from beginning to end – it does not cease when the perceiver has achieved certainty or solved a puzzle. It is more like awe or reverence than perplexity or curiosity. But it is a reverence that does not bow down before the alien presence and power of god. This kind of wonder looks upon what is godlike and alien and finds some sense of kinship with it.[14]

As we have seen, in Aristotle philosophy begins in wonder; when the philosopher is able to "see" or "theorize" the causes, the wonder comes to an end. Plato articulated a similar idea in the *Theaetetus*, claiming that wonder and perplexity are the origins of philosophy (Aristotle was no doubt following Plato when he said that philosophy begins in wonder).[15] In this text, Plato identifies wonder with *aporia*. But in the dialogues that deal with *theoria*, he develops a quite different conception of wonder. These dialogues suggest that the philosophic journey ends – or, better, culminates – in wonder (since, strictly speaking, philosophy never comes to an end). For the activity of contemplation – which is the goal of philosophy – is characterized by the experience of wonder. Platonic *theoria* is not simply a cognitive activity; it has erotic and affective components that take it

---

[14] Another good example of this kind of wonder occurs when Odysseus sees his father Laertes returning home from the bath, when Athena has made him appear taller and stronger: Odysseus "wonders" at him "when he saw him face-to-face, looking like the immortal gods" (ϑαύμαζε . . . ὡς ἴδεν ἀθανάτοισι ϑεοῖς ἐναλίγκιον ἄντην, *Odyssey* XXIV.370–1).

[15] Plato briefly articulates the notion of wonder as perplexity or curiosity in the *Theaetetus* 155c–d. There is no single passage in which he sets forth the operations of wonder-as-reverence; this can be understood by examining the passages in the dialogues that deal with *theoria* or the soul's encounter with the Forms (or, as in the *Timaeus*, with the perception of the noetic activity of the gods as evidenced in the circular motion of the heavenly bodies).

beyond a merely intellectual form of "seeing." *Theoria* leads the philosopher into a state of knowledge, but it also leaves him with a profound sense of wonder.

Consider the following passages from the conversation of Diotima and Socrates in the *Symposium*, which precede the description of the vision of the Form of Beauty:

(1) DIOTIMA: Socrates, why is it that, if in fact all men love the same things at all times, we don't say that all men are in love but that some men are in love and others not.
SOCRATES: I am wondering (θαυμάζω) myself.
DIOTIMA: Do not wonder (ἀλλὰ μὴ θαύμαζ')! For, separating off one form of love, we call it love, applying to this the name of the whole. . . .

(205a–b)

(2) SOCRATES: It is for this reason – knowing that I need a teacher, as I said just now – that I have come to you. Come, tell me the cause of these things as well as the other things that pertain to love.
DIOTIMA: If you believe that love by nature longs for that which we have repeatedly agreed on, you must cease to wonder (μὴ θαύμαζε).

(207c–d)

(3) DIOTIMA: Do not wonder (μὴ οὖν θαύμαζε) if all things naturally value their own offspring. Since it is for the sake of immortality that this eagerness and this love occurs in every creature.
SOCRATES: And, hearing this argument, I wondered (ἐθαύμασα) and said, "well, most wise Diotima, is this really the truth of the matter?". . .
DIOTIMA: Be certain of it, Socrates. Consider, if you will, the desire for honor among men – you would wonder (θαυμάζοις ἂν) at their irrationality if you didn't keep in mind what I have said. . . .

(208b–c)

In these passages, Diotima indicates that Socrates need not tarry in a state of perplexity, since she can provide the correct answers to his questions. Plato's repeated use of the word θαυμάζειν, and the contrast he sets up between Socrates' wonder and Diotima's certainty (lack of wonder), alerts the reader to the importance of this theme. At the end of their discussion, Diotima offers a brief description of the end of the philosophic journey, which culminates in the vision of the Form of Beauty. At this point, we expect that the apprehension of the truth will banish all wonder.

But in fact there is a new wonder to come, a wonder that is quite distinct from perplexity: "When [the philosopher] views beautiful things, one after another in the correct way, he will suddenly see, at the end, a wondrous (θαυμαστόν) vision, beautiful in nature, which is the final object of all his previous toils" (210e). Here, the activity of beholding the Form of Beauty – which is the activity of *theoria* – is described as a "wondrous" vision of "divine beauty" (τὸ θεῖον καλόν, 211e). This experience of wonder – what I call "Platonic wonder" – *accompanies* the vision of the Form. It includes awe, reverence, and astonishment, and is therefore quite different from the perplexed form of wonder.

It should come as no surprise that seeing divine beings would evoke wonder – this is the natural response to the sight of the superhuman. But the Platonic philosopher does not simply see something divine and awesomely different from himself: he also sees something that is intimately related to him. For, as Plato claims in a number of dialogues, the rational part of the human soul is divine in nature and "akin" to the Forms.[16] In fact, Plato regularly uses the language of kinship and family ties to describe the relation of human reason to the Forms. There are, of course, essential differences between the mind and the Forms (the soul, unlike the Forms, is a living, changing being). Nevertheless, in spite of these differences, reason and the Forms are said to be kindred (συγγενής). Indeed, it is precisely because reason has this kinship with the Forms that it can apprehend and associate with them at all. This does not mean that the Forms are commonplace and familiar. Rather, the Forms are, at the same time, superhumanly strange and yet akin to the human viewer.

In Platonic *theoria*, the philosopher achieves a vision of the Forms and experiences a wonder or reverence that does not abate. Plato articulates this point differently in different texts. In the *Republic*, he indicates that the philosopher who beholds the Forms will "wonder" at them and, because he feels this wonder, will endeavor to "imitate" them by making himself good and divine (500c–d).[17] Here, the philosopher's wonder at what is divine and different leads him to assimilate himself to – and find kinship with – this higher reality. Plato recurs to this notion of kinship in the *Timaeus*, where he discusses the contemplation or *theoria* of the stars, which are moved in perfect circles by the divine reason of god. In this text, Plato says that the vision of the heavenly bodies is in fact the origin of philosophy (46e–47b). The faculty of vision and, in turn, the capacity to philosophize was given to human beings, he says, "in order that we might behold the revolutions of

---

[16] For references to the "kinship" of the rational part of the soul to the Forms or to the "intelligible" realm, see *Phaedo* 79d, *Republic* 490b, 585c, 611e, *Phaedrus* 246d–e, *Timaeus* 47b–e, 90a, 90c–d, and *Laws* 897c (the word that Plato generally uses to express kinship is *sungeneia* and its cognates, but there are in fact many different terms and locutions that articulate this idea).

[17] The Greek word for "wonder" in this passage is *agasthai* which, as Prier (1989, 78–81) rightly indicates, is very closely allied to *thaumazein*; the two words are often used as synonyms.

divine reason in the heavens and use them to aid the revolutions of reason that are in us, since these things are akin to each other" (ξυγγενεῖς ἐκείναις οὔσας, 47b–c). Here, Plato explicitly asserts the kinship between human and divine reason. It is this kinship, in fact, which allows us to imitate the gods. But the passage goes on to say that divine reason is "impeturbable" and "unerring" whereas human reason is "prone to wander" (47c). Our human reason is thus akin to that of the gods and yet greatly inferior to it – for human reason "errs" and "wanders," acting (as it were) like a planet among the fixed stars.[18] Here again we find the philosophic theorist discovering both a kinship with and a distance from the divine.

In the *Phaedrus*, Plato sets forth a detailed account of the soul's experience of wonder when it encounters the divine Forms. The central speech in this dialogue describes a man who falls in love with a beautiful boy and the confrontation with the Form of Beauty that this love affair brings about. Socrates describes the pathology of this torrid event in minute detail. When the lover gazes upon the beauty of his beloved, he suddenly remembers that he has seen true beauty somewhere before. In fact, he has seen the Form of Beauty in an early period of his psychic history, before he became incarnate on earth. The trauma of incarnation, however, has driven this experience almost clean out of his mind. It is only the encounter with the beautiful beloved that brings the vision back. When he begins to recollect that preincarnate vision of Beauty, the lover is knocked off his feet (250a).[19] Henceforth the sight of physical beauty evokes powerful feelings of wonder and reverence: the lover begins to revere his beloved as a near-divine

---

[18] The Greek word for "erring" (more literally, "wandering") comes from the verb "*planan*" (to wander) whence comes our English word for the planets. The Greeks believed that, unlike the fixed stars, the planets were "wandering" stars that did not move in fixed orbits. In the fourth century BCE, Eudoxus argued (using a model of heavenly motion consisting of numerous nested circular orbits revolving around different centers) that the planets do not in fact wander but move in circular paths like the fixed stars. Plato adopted a similar position towards the end of his life (see esp. *Timaeus* and *Laws* x); in his view, the heavens are governed by divine souls and contain no true planets (since all stars move in circular or spiral orbits). It is thus only human souls who "wander" like planets.

[19] To Plato's description of the fear/awe and wonder of the philosopher, compare Heidegger's claim at the close of *The Fundamental Concepts of Metaphysics*: the human is a being that "EXISTS, i.e., ex-sists, is an exiting from itself in the essence of its being, yet without abandoning itself. Man is that inability to remain and is yet unable to leave his place. In projecting, the *Da-sein* in him constantly throws him into possibilities and thereby keeps him subjected to what is actual . . . Man is *enraptured* in this transition and therefore essentially 'absent' . . . Transposed into the possible, he must constantly be mistaken concerning what is actual. And only because he is thus mistaken and transposed can he become seized by terror. *And only where there is the perilousness of being seized by terror do we find the bliss of astonishment* – being torn away in that wakeful manner that is the breath of all philosophizing, and that which the greats among the philosophers called '*enthousiasmos*' . . ." (my italics).

being who instantiates the Form of Beauty on earth (251a–254a).[20] What drives the lover here is not intellectual curiosity or puzzlement but rather a desire for true beauty as well as a deep and abiding reverence for its sacred presence. We are often told that Plato despises and denigrates the physical world: in the *Phaedrus*, however, the experience of metaphysical beauty leads the philosopher to revere the embodiment of beauty and to tend to the beloved person who possesses this beautiful body. In addition, the vision of the Forms inspires the philosophic lover to make himself more divine by practicing philosophy and living a virtuous life on earth (252d–253c).

Socrates' speech in the *Phaedrus* returns, again and again, to the reverence and awe that the philosopher experiences at the sight of beauty. This kind of reverence is not unthinking or dogmatic piety. Rather, it is a feeling of wonderment that accompanies the activity of reason as it engages in *theoria*. The philosopher looks with wonder at the superhuman reality of the Forms, which are distant, awesome, and divine; but this same wonder leads the philosopher to assimilate himself to the divine – to find the kinship with divinity that is his birthright. The philosopher is not, then, debased or annihilated by his encounter with divine reality. Rather, he recognizes and reveres a distant yet familiar truth (248b–c, 251b).

This kind of wonder accompanies, rather than precedes, *theoria*. As I have suggested, we do not find this conception of wonder in Aristotle's discussions of theorizing divine essences: the theorist does not experience wonder when he engages in "first philosophy."[21] Interestingly, however, Aristotle does claim that wonder attends the theoretical investigation of animals. In the *Metaphysics*, Aristotle identifies "theology" – the *theoria* of divine, incorporeal, and unchanging beings – as the highest and the "first" form of theoretical philosophy, but he also says that one can theorize in the realms of mathematics and physics.[22] In the *Part of Animals*,

---

[20] The most common words for "reverence" in this passage are *sebesthai* and *aideisthai* (250e, 251a, 252a, 254e), but Plato also uses *deima* (251a) and its cognate *deidō* (254c, 254e) and *thambos* (254c). As Prier shows (1989, 87–91, 107), *thambos* and *sebas* are closely related to *thauma*. I discuss the lover's reverence of the beloved in detail in chapter 4.

[21] In *Met.* xii.7 (1072b24–6), Aristotle says that "if god always enjoys happiness such as we sometimes enjoy [i.e. while theorizing], then it is wonderful (*thaumaston*); and if he experiences more happiness, it is even more wonderful." This is of course quite different from saying that god or humans experience wonder while theorizing.

[22] In the *Metaphysics* vi (1026a13–18), for example, Aristotle states that there are three branches of "theoretical philosophy" (φιλοσοφίαι θεωρητικαί): mathematics, physics, and theology. See also *Metaphysics* iv.3, 1005b1–2, where Aristotle says that physics is "a kind of wisdom but not the first kind."

he discusses *theoria* in one branch of physics – that of biology.[23] This treatise examines the material, formal, and especially the final causes of the organisms of animals. Its analysis of causes resembles that of the *Physics*, though it deals exclusively with the sublunary realm and does not discuss divine beings.[24] In this text, Aristotle offers a powerful protreptic for the practice of *theoria* in the biological realm (1.5, 644b–645a). Surprisingly, he indicates that this kind of theoretical activity includes the experience of wonder. As we will see, the wonder that Aristotle refers to here is aesthetic rather than reverential, though it does have some similarities to Platonic wonder.

Aristotle begins this passage by separating natural entities which "are generated and perish" from those that are "eternal" and "divine." Although we experience far greater pleasure in coming to know divine substances than we do in the study of animals, we can obtain more and better information about the latter because they are "nearer to us and more akin to our nature" (διὰ τὸ πλησιαίτερα ἡμῶν εἶναι καὶ τῆς φύσεως οἰκειότερα, 645a). This passage is quite striking: whereas Aristotle says elsewhere that our noetic faculty resembles that of the gods, and that we should identify this faculty as our true "self" (*NE* 1178a6–7), he claims here that we are more "akin" to animals than to divine beings. Clearly, he is referring to humans as embodied beings who dwell in the earthly realm. These two claims are not necessarily inconsistent: *qua* beings with *nous*, we resemble the gods, and *qua* composite beings, we have a kinship with animals. But it does raise the question of who we really are, and how our god-like self fits with our animal self. Aristotle never answers this question satisfactorily, and this has led many interpreters to privilege one of these accounts over the other. I join those scholars who take both accounts seriously. When discussing our kinship with the gods, Aristotle uses arguments and rhetoric that locate the human in the metaphysical, noetic sphere and identifies him as a "thinking" being separate from the composite. But when Aristotle turns to the sublunar, biological realm, he brings humans back to earth, locating them in the realm of animals.

Aristotle clearly believed that people might object to the study of animals, since he strenuously defends it with a number of rhetorical arguments. He commences as follows: "if there is anyone who believes that the theoretical investigation of the other animals is an unworthy pursuit, he will have

---

[23] For some useful studies of Aristotle's biological treatises, see Pellegrin 1986, the essays in Gotthelf and Lennox 1987, Lloyd 1996.

[24] Balme 1987a and 1987b, and Furth 1987 explore the connection between Aristotle's studies of animals and the conceptions of substance offered in the metaphysical works.

to hold this same opinion about the investigation of himself." As he goes on to argue, the structure and operations of the human body – which include the flesh, bones, blood, and organs – are no different than those of animals; even when we study the human body, if we view any of its parts in isolation from the whole, we would find them quite disgusting. We do not, however, treat the study of the human body as lowly or uninteresting, and we should adopt the same view about animals (645a). The proper approach to the investigation of the body – whether human or animal – is to study the structure as a whole, considering in particular the material, formal, and final causes that operate in each case. Insofar as the philosopher understands these causes, he engages in the activity of *theoria*. Biological theorizing, however, does not deal with objects that are divine, and therefore lacks the theological orientation of "first philosophy." Philosophical study in the biological sphere focuses our attention on the earthly world that is "nearer to us" (645a).

As Aristotle goes on to say, he has already treated the subject of "divine beings" elsewhere and will now turn his attention to the nature of animals. He emphatically proclaims that he will not leave out any animals, even those that are lowly and unlovely. For, as he argues, "even in the case of animals that displease the senses, nevertheless when viewed theoretically (κατὰ τὴν θεωρίαν) the nature which fashioned these things (ἡ δημιουργήσασα φύσις) furnishes incredible pleasures to the man who can discern the causes (τὰς αἰτίας γνωρίζειν) and who is philosophical by nature" (645a). By apprehending causal structures and properties with the eyes of *theoria* (so to speak), that which is ugly to the physical eye becomes beautiful and pleasing to the mind.

Having established that some things are visibly ugly and yet theoretically beautiful, Aristotle now turns to beautiful artworks to elucidate the *theoria* of animals: "it would be absurd and strange if we rejoice when theorizing (θεωροῦντες) artistic representations of [animals] – because then we are contemplating the art which fashioned them (τὴν δημιουργήσασαν τέχνην συνθεωροῦμεν), such as that of painting or sculpture – but do not rejoice all the more in the contemplation (θεωρία) of those things constructed by nature, when we are able to see the causes" (τὰς αἰτίας καθορᾶν, 645a). Here, Aristotle uses the example of the traditional *theoria* of artistic representations to illustrate the philosophic *theoria* of the animal world. Both kinds of *theoria* involve the "viewing" of a technical design – i.e. the *technē* that has formed the artistic or natural object. In this passage, Aristotle draws a direct parallel between "demiourgic" nature and "demiourgic" art, and thus encourages us to view the animal world as the design of nature-as-craftsman (though "nature" does not, of course, operate via intentions and purposes).

Thus far, Aristotle has indicated that the *theoria* of animals affords a pleasure akin to the aesthetic pleasure deriving from the contemplation of artistic representations. Aristotle now moves to wonder: "therefore we should not behave like children and recoil from the investigation of the lowliest animals, for there is something *thaumaston* in all natural things" (ἐν πᾶσι γὰρ τοῖς φυσικοῖς ἔνεστί τι θαυμαστόν). There is, in short, something "wondrous" or "to be wondered at" in all animals and natural forms. Clearly, Aristotle does not use the word "*thaumaston*" here in the sense of "puzzling" or "perplexity-inducing": whatever the natural philosopher's experience of wonder is, it is not the *aporia* that precedes *theoria* (as in *Metaphysics* 1), but rather a disposition that accompanies *theoria*. What, then, does Aristotle mean when he says that there is something *thaumaston* in all natural things? He glosses this claim as follows:

Heraclitus (it is reported) responded to some strangers who, though eager to meet him, stopped when they saw him warming himself at the stove. He told them to take heart and come in, for (as he said) there are gods even here. In like manner, we ought not be ashamed to enter into the investigation of animals, since in all of them there is something natural and beautiful (ὡς ἐν ἅπασιν ὄντος τινὸς φυσικοῦ καὶ καλοῦ. (645a)

This passage is rather complicated. First of all, the vignette about Heraclitus suggests that what appears to be a humble and lowly scene – a kitchen with its stove – is inhabited by divinity and, for this reason, "wondrous." We may be tempted to infer that Aristotle is saying that in the "lowly" parts of the natural world there is also something divine and therefore wondrous. But Aristotle does not believe that the sublunary sphere (including earth and its inhabitants) is divine or inhabited by divinity – indeed, he has said quite explicitly in the passage that precedes this that he will not discuss divine or eternal beings in this treatise. Note that when Aristotle turns to explain the moral of the story, he says that there is something "*beautiful* and *natural* in all animals" rather than saying that there is something divine in them. In the story of Heraclitus, in short, the visitors are told that they should not hesitate to enter, since what appears lowly is in fact divine; in Aristotle's gloss on the story, the readers are told that they should not hesitate to investigate animals, since what appears lowly is in fact "natural and beautiful."

The theorist's "wonder" at the animals he theorizes, then, is aesthetic rather than reverential. It is for this reason that Aristotle compares the *theoria* of animals to that of artistic representations. The example he uses here may seem to emphasize purely visual "seeing," but artistic spectating is never simply visual. When one views a painting or a drama in terms of its technical design, one "sees" how the artwork has been constructed, how its parts fit together, operate, and make up a whole. This same sort of technical "viewing" operates in the *theoria* of animals: though their bodies and parts may be ugly to the eye, they are beautiful in their design and systematic organization. Aristotle reiterates this point when he says that "in the works of nature purpose and not accident is predominant; and the purpose or end for the sake of which things are put together or generated has its place among what is beautiful" (645a). He then adds that the theorist does not focus primarily on the matter (περὶ τῆς ὕλης) that makes up animal bodies but rather on the "form as a whole" (τῆς ὅλης μορφῆς). In this passage, Aristotle emphasizes that the final and formal causes are the true objects of the inquiry, and that these causal structures (unlike the material bodies *per se*) are beautiful to those who can truly grasp them.

The biological theorist sees the animal world as "wondrous," then, not because he admires the physical beauty of animals – much of Aristotle's treatise in fact deals with internal organs and systems – but because he marvels at the beauty and intricacy of their design and causal structures. Although Aristotle seems to be borrowing Plato's discourse of wonder in writing this protreptic to biological study, he depicts the experience of wonder in terms of beauty rather than divinity (indeed we watch him make this substitution in his gloss on the Heraclitus story). Plato does, of course, speak of the Forms as "beautiful," but for him the divine, the good, and the beautiful necessarily go together: he sacralizes beauty and aestheticizes the sacred. Platonic wonder, then, has a theological orientation that is lacking in Aristotle's discussion of wonder. In the *Parts of Animals*, Aristotle separates the aesthetic from the sacred and thereby conceives of a form of philosophic wonder that differs from Plato's: an aesthetic marveling that accompanies the theoretical understanding of the form and design of animals.

While Plato's theological notion of wonder informed the Western religious tradition, Aristotle's aestheticized mode of wonder branched into subsequent theories of aesthetics, including discourses on the sublime. Longinus, for example, states in his treatise *On the Sublime*:

Nature has distinguished man as a creature of no mean or ignoble quality. As if she were inviting us to some great festival, she has called us into life, into the whole universe, there to be spectators of all that she has made and eager competitors for honor. And she breathed into us a passion for what is greater and more divine than ourselves. Thus the entire cosmos does not match the scope of human contemplation (θεωρίας) and thought, but our ideas often pass beyond the boundaries by which we are circumscribed . . . We do not wonder (θαυμάζομεν) at the small streams, though they are clear and useful (χρήσιμα) . . . What is useful and necessary (τὸ χρειῶδες ἢ καὶ ἀναγκαῖον) is easy to come by; it is always the surprising that wins our wonder (θαυμαστόν).[25]

In this foundational text on the sublime, Longinus echoes the rhetoric that Aristotle used in his discussions of *theoria* and aesthetic wonder. Longinus describes the cultured man as a spectator at a festival who eschews what is "useful and necessary" and looks with wonder on the vast spectacle of nature. Although Longinus does refer to divinity in this passage, this is a rhetorical move designed to emphasize the elevation of the person who takes in sublime spectacles and texts. In fact, Longinus' treatise focuses on aesthetics rather than ethics or theology.[26] This famous discourse, moreover, informed the later tradition of theorizing about the sublime and the beautiful – to cite but one example, consider Kant's conception of aesthetic perception as a purely disinterested and nonutilitarian activity (and the apprehension of beauty and sublimity as "purposiveness without a purpose").[27]

The ancient conceptions of *theoria* and wonder, I suggest, can be taken in yet other directions. In particular, some key elements of Greek *theoria* may have a positive role to play in the study and practice of ecology. We live in a society which positively exalts utility and production – a world overtaken by science, technology, and the manipulation of nature. As Weber claimed, this is an age of disenchantment (*Entzauberung*) – an age in which reason, rejecting religion in favor of science, renounces its claim to offer meaning and human self-definition. Of course we cannot renounce the findings of science (nor would we wish to); returning to anti-scientific religious views is hardly a fruitful response to modern disenchantment. But, in confronting the new "religion" of science, we can develop more ecological and less anthropocentric approaches to nature. In particular, we can cultivate the activity of engaging contemplatively with the natural world – an activity that rejects the passion to control nature and resists the imperatives of utility.

[25] Longinus, *On the Sublime* 35.2–5.
[26] Note that most of Longinus' text focuses on sublime texts rather than the sublimity of the natural world.
[27] Nehamas (2000a and 2000b) offers a powerful argument for the necessary detachment of the aesthetic experience of beauty from ethical or utilitarian goals (cf. Scarry 1999).

Borrowing – and also deviating – from Plato, we can develop a "reverential understanding" of the natural world.[28] And we can also build on Aristotle's conception of the "uselessness" of *theoria* in our efforts to become ecological *theoroi*. As we have seen, Aristotle's characterization of theoretical activity as useless and nonproductive is, at least in part, rooted in aristocratic ideology. I find this aspect of Aristotle's philosophy troubling, but am nonetheless attracted by his conception of an activity that is contemplative rather than productive or pragmatic.[29] This sort of activity need not be the prerogative of wealthy or elite individuals: any human being can study and observe the natural world in a nonutilitarian fashion.[30]

The Greek thinkers posited a kinship between the theorizer and the divine objects of contemplation: in the activity of *theoria*, the philosopher both experiences and understands the "natural" affinity between human and divine beings. The philosophic *theoros* does not gaze from a distance upon alien entities; rather, he draws near to – and, in some cases, identifies with – the beings he beholds. In like manner, the ecological *theoros* will discover his kinship with and dependency on the beings that he studies: he will not gaze upon nature from the outside but rather find commonality with the other beings in the ecosystem. In cultivating this sort of contemplative engagement, the eco-theorist will develop a sense of identity that is defined in relation to a broad range of earthly beings (both human and nonhuman).

Let us not, then, simply dismiss the ancient theories of "theory." In the wake of the Enlightenment, many thinkers have opted to replace Aristotelian perplexity with the hermeneutics of suspicion, to abandon theoretical certainty for constructivism or deconstruction. And many, too, have relinquished Platonic wonder by rejecting religious belief and a reverence for the sacred. We may be able to live without certainty. But can we really do without wonder? Nietzsche addressed this question when he discussed the opposition between a "world in which we were at home up to now with our reverences, which perhaps made it possible for us to *endure* life, and another world that consists of us." According to Nietzsche, the Europeans of his era were confronted with these two options: a world where people live with reverence and a world in which religion and reverence are abolished and everything "consists of us." On the one hand, he says, people

---

[28] See Woodruff 2001, whose recent book reconceptualizes reverence as a secular and civic disposition.

[29] This does not mean that contemplative activities should eclipse practical and ethical actions; rather, it should form part of a whole life which includes all of these activities.

[30] I am not suggesting that anyone can be a professional ecologist without a technical education. But, if we are to preserve the health of our planet, ecology cannot simply be left to academics and professionals. The activity of ecological observation and study is one that we are all equipped to engage in, at least as amateurs.

who practice reverence are nihilistic, since they debase life by prostrating themselves before an other-worldly god. But to adopt the other position – to inhabit a "world that consists of us" – also leads to nihilism. For, as Nietzsche argues, when humans abandon religion and become the sole masters of an empty universe, they find the self-aggrandizing ideology of humanism unsustainable and soon lapse into pessimism and self-loathing.[31] We end up, then, in an all-too-human world that is empty and unendurable.

Plato articulates the experience of wonder in theological terms – since the objects of *theoria* are superhuman and divine beings. But this kind of wonder can also be conceived in ecological terms. We can look with wonder at the nonhuman beings in the natural world, finding a kinship with many of the life forms in the world around us. Aristotle in fact explicitly invites us to theorize animals in the *Parts of Animals*, since they are "nearer to us and more akin to our nature." In its root sense, the word ecology means "having an understanding (*logos*) of the world as an *oikos* or 'household'." Ecologically conceived, the world does not simply "consist of us" nor is it completely inhospitable and alien to humans: it is, rather, a household made up of many interdependent members. The natural world is the home in which we dwell rather than an "environment" adjacent to human homes and communities. The understanding of nature as a household is at the heart of the more radical ecological philosophies. Challenging anthropocentric arguments and ideologies, the "eco-theorist" will study and contemplate the natural world with wonder and reverence rather than treating it as mere material for human use. This need not take the form of unthinking piety or naïve nature worship. Rather, ecological *theoria* can be conceived as an activity in which rigorous inquiry is accompanied by reverence and restraint. This kind of *theoria*, of course, will differ in important ways from the theoretical activities of the Greeks. But it has its roots in the same sense of wonder.

---

[31] F. Nietzsche, *The Gay Science* v, 346 (trans. Kaufmann).

References

Ackrill, J. L. 1965. "Aristotle's Distinction between *Energeia* and *Kinesis*," in R. Bambrough, ed., *New Essays on Plato and Aristotle* (New York: Humanities Press), 121–41.

1973a. *Aristotle's Ethics* (London: Faber).

1973b. "*Anamnesis* in the *Phaedo*: Remarks on 73c–75c," in *Exegesis and Argument* (*Phronesis* supplementary vol. 1), 175–95.

1980. "Aristotle on Eudaimonia," in A. Rorty, ed., *Essays on Aristotle's Ethics* (Berkeley: University of California Press), 15–33.

ed. 1987. *A New Aristotle Reader* (Princeton: Princeton University Press).

Adam, J. 1902. *The Republic of Plato*, vol. II. (Cambridge: Cambridge University Press 1902).

Adkins, W. D. H. 1978. "*Theoria* Versus *Praxis* in the *Nicomachean Ethics* and the *Republic*," *Classical Philology* 73: 297–313.

Alcock, S. and R. Osborne, edd. 1994. *Placing the Gods: Santuaries and Sacred Space in Ancient Greece* (Oxford: Clarendon Press).

Allen, R. E., ed. 1965. *Studies in Plato's Metaphysics* (New York: The Humanities Press).

1971. "Participation and Predication in Plato's Middle Dialogues," in Vlastos 1971b, ch. 8.

Annas, J. 1981. *An Introduction to Plato's Republic* (Oxford: Clarendon Press).

1982a. "Plato's Myths of Judgement," *Phronesis* 27: 119–43.

1982b. "Plato on the Triviality of Literature," in J. Moravcsik and P. Temko, edd., *Plato on Beauty, Wisdom and the Arts* (New Jersey: Rowman and Littlefield), 1–23.

1985. "Self-Knowledge in Early Plato," in O'Meara 1985, 111–38.

1993. *The Morality of Happiness* (New York: Oxford University Press).

1999. *Platonic Ethics, Old and New* (Ithaca: Cornell University Press).

2002. "What are Plato's 'Middle' Dialogues in the Middle Of?," in Annas and Rowe 2002, 1–24.

Annas, J. and C. Rowe, edd. 2002. *New Perspectives on Plato, Modern and Ancient* (Cambridge, Mass. Harvard University Press).

Anton, J. P., ed. 1980. *Science and the Sciences in Plato* (New York: Eidos).

Arendt, H. [1971]/1978. *The Life of the Mind* (repr. San Diego: Harcourt, Inc.).

Ashbaugh, A. F. 1988. *Plato's Theory of Explanation: A Study of the Cosmological Account in the Timaeus* (Albany: State University of New York Press).

Aubenque, P. 1963. *La Prudence chez Aristote* (Paris: Presses Universitaires de France).

Austin, M. M. and P. Vidal-Naquet. 1977. *Economic and Social History of Ancient Greece: An Introduction*, trans. and revised by M. M. Austin (Berkeley: University of California Press).

Bakhtin, M. 1981. *The Dialogic Imagination*, trans. C. Emerson and M. Holquist, ed. M. Holquist (Austin: University of Texas Press).

1986. *Speech Genres and Other Late Essays*, trans. V. W. McGee, edd. C. Emerson and M. Holquist (Austin: University of Texas Press).

Balme, D. M., tr. and comm. 1972. Aristotle's *De Partibus Animalium I and De Generatione Animalium I* (Oxford: Clarendon Press).

1987a. "The Place of Biology in Aristotle's Philosophy," in Gotthelf and Lennox 1987, 9–20.

1987b. "Teleology and Necessity," in Gotthelf and Lennox 1987, 275–85.

Barnes, J. 1969. "Aristotle's Theory of Demonstration," *Phronesis* 14: 123–52.

1981. *Aristotle* (Oxford: Oxford University Press).

1983. "Aphorism and Argument," in Robb 1983a, 91–109.

ed. 1995a. *The Cambridge Companion to Aristotle* (Cambridge: Cambridge University Press).

1995b. "Life and Work," in Barnes 1995a, 1–26.

1995c. "Metaphysics," in Barnes 1995a, 66–108.

Barnes, J., M. Schofield, and R. Sorabji, edd. 1975. *Articles on Aristotle I* (London: Duckworth).

Bartch, S. forthcoming. *The Mirror of the Self: Sexuality, Self-Knowledge, and the Gaze in the Early Roman Empire* (Chicago: University of Chicago Press).

Bartlett, R. C. and S. D. Collins, edd. 1999. *Action and Contemplation: Studies in the Moral and Political Thought of Aristotle* (Albany: SUNY Press).

Beare, J. I. 1906. *Greek Theories of Elementary Cognition from Alcmaeon to Aristotle* (Oxford: Clarendon Press).

Belfiore, E. 1983. "Plato's Greatest Accusation against Poetry," in F. Pelletier and J. King-Farlow, edd., *New Essays on Plato* (*Canadian Journal of Philosophy* suppl. vol. IX), (Ontario), 39–62.

1984. "A Theory of Imitation in Plato's *Republic*," *Transactions of the American Philological Association* 114: 121–46.

Benardete, S. 1978. "On Wisdom and Philosophy: The First Two Chapters of Aristotle's *Metaphysics* A," *Review of Metaphysics* 32: 205–15.

Bergren, A. 1992. "Architecture Gender Philosophy," in R. Hexter and D. Selden, edd., *Innovations of Antiquity* (New York: Routledge), 253–310.

Berti, E. ed. 1981. *Aristotle on Science* (Padua: Editrice Antenore).

Bien, G. 1968. "Das Theorie-Praxis-Problem und die politische Philosophie bei Platon und Aristoteles," *Das Philosophische Jahrbuch* 76: 265–315.

Bill, C. P. 1901. "Notes on the Greek ϴεωρός and ϴεωρία," *Transactions of the American Philological Association* 32: 196–204.

Blondell, R. 2002. *The Play of Character in Plato's Dialogues* (Cambridge: Cambridge University Press).

Bluck, R. S. 1965. "Logos and Forms in Plato: A Reply to Professor Cross," in Allen 1965, 33–41.

Blumenberg, H. [1957]/1993. "Light as a Metaphor for Truth," in Levin 1993a, 30–62.

1987. *The Genesis of the Copernican World*, trans. R. Wallace (Cambridge: MIT Press).

Bobonich, C. 1991. "Persuasion, Compulsion, and Freedom in Plato's *Laws*," *Classical Quarterly* 41: 365–88.

Boedeker, D. and K. Raaflaub. 1998. *Empire and the Arts in Fifth-Century Athens* (Cambridge: Harvard University Press).

Boegehold, A. L. and A. C. Scafuro. 1994. *Athenian Identity and Civic Ideology* (Baltimore: Johns Hopkins University Press).

Boesch, P. 1908. ΘΕΩΡΟΣ. *Untersuchung zur Epangelie griechischer Feste* (Berlin: Mayer and Müller).

Bourdieu, P. 1988. *Homo Academicus*, trans. P. Collier (Stanford: Stanford University Press).

Bowman, G. 1985. "Anthropology of Pilgrimage," in M. Jha, ed., *Dimensions of Pilgrimage: An Anthropological Appraisal* (New Delhi), 1–9.

Brague, R. 1985. "The Body of the Speech: A New Hypothesis on the Compositional Structure of Timaeus' Monologue," in O'Meara 1985, 53–83.

1999. *La Sagesse du monde: histoire de l'expérience humaine de l'universe* (Paris: Fayard).

Branham, B., ed. 2002. *Bakhtin and the Classics* (Evanston, Ill.: Northwestern University Press).

Branham, R. B. and M.-O. Goulet-Cazé, edd. 1996. *The Cynics: The Cynic Movement in Antiquity and its Legacy* (Berkeley: University of California Press).

Brennan, T. and M. Jay. 1996. *Vision in Context: Historical and Contemporary Perspectives on Sight* (New York: Routledge).

Brentano, F. 1992. "*Nous Poiētikos*: Survey of Earlier Interpretation," in Nussbaum and Rorty 1992, 313–42.

Brisson, L. 1974. *Le Même et l'autre dans la structure ontologique du* Timeé *de Platon* (Paris: Klincksieck).

1982. *Platon, les mots et les mythes: Comment et pourquoi Platon nomma le mythe?* (Paris: P. Maspero).

Brisson, L. and F. W. Meyerstein. 1995. *Inventing the Universe: Plato's Timaeus, the Big Bang, and the Problem of Scientific Knowledge* (Albany: State University of New York Press).

Broadie, S. 1991. *Ethics with Aristotle.* (New York: Oxford University Press).

1998. "Interpreting Aristotle's Directions," in Gentzler 1998, 291–306.

1999a. "Rational Theology," in Long 1999a, ch. 10.

2001. "Theodicy and Pseudo-History in the *Timaeus*," *Oxford Studies in Ancient Philosophy* 21: 1–28.

Brumbaugh, R. S. 1989. *Platonic Studies of Greek Philosophy: Form, Arts, Gadgets, and Hemlock* (Albany: State University of New York Press).

Brunschwig, J. 2000. "*Metaphysics* Λ 9: A Short-Lived Thought Experiment?" in Frede and Charles 2000, 275–306.

Buchanan, J. J. 1962. Theorika: *A Study of Monetary Distributions to the Athenian Citizenry during the Fifth and Fourth Centuries BC* (Glückstadt: J. J. Augustin).

Buck, C. 1953. "ΘΕШΡΟΣ," in G. Mylonas and D. Raymond, edd., *Studies Presented to David Moore Robinson*, vol. II (St. Louis: Washington University Press) 443–4.

Burford, A. 1972. *Craftsmen in Greek and Roman Society* (Ithaca: Cornell University Press).

——— 1993. *Land and Labor in the Greek World* (Baltimore: Johns Hopkins University Press).

Burger, R. 1984. *The Phaedo: A Platonic Labyrinth* (New Haven: Yale University Press).

——— 1995. "Aristotle's 'Exclusive' Account of Happiness: Contemplative Wisdom as a Guise of the Political Philosopher," in May Sim, ed., *The Crossroads of Norm and Nature. Essays on Aristotle's Ethics and Metaphysics* (Lanham, Maryland: Rowman and Littlefield), 79–98.

Burke, E. M. 1992. "The Economy of Athens in the Classical Era: Some Adjustments to the Primitivist Model," *Transactions of the American Philological Association* 122: 199–226.

Burkert, W. 1960. "Plato oder Pythagoras? Zum Ursprung des Wortes 'Philosophie'," *Hermes* 88: 159–77.

——— 1972. *Lore and Science in Ancient Pythagoreanism*, trans. E. L. Minar (Cambridge, Mass.: Harvard University Press).

——— 1985. *Greek Religion*, trans. J. Raffan (Cambridge, Mass.: Harvard University Press).

——— 1987. *Ancient Mystery Cults* (Cambridge, Mass.: Harvard University Press).

Burnet, J. 1911. *Plato's Phaedo* (Oxford: Clarendon Press).

——— [1914]/1953. *Greek Philosophy: Thales to Plato* (repr. London: Macmillan and Co. Ltd.).

——— [1924]/1979. *Plato: Euthyphro, Apology of Socrates, Crito* (Oxford: Clarendon Press).

Burnet, J. 1930. *Early Greek Philosophy* 4th ed. (London: A. & C. Black Ltd.).

Burnyeat, M. 1976. "Plato on the Grammar of Perceiving," *Classical Quarterly* 26: 29–51.

——— 1981. "Aristotle on Understanding Knowledge," in Berti 1981, 97–139.

——— 1987. "Platonism and Mathematics: A Prelude to Discussion," in A. Graeser, ed., *Mathematics and Metaphysics in Aristotle* (Bern: P. Haupt).

——— 1992. "Is an Aristotelian Philosophy of Mind still Credible? A Draft," in Nussbaum and Rorty 1992, 15–26.

——— 1999. "Utopia and Fantasy: The Practicability of Plato's Ideally Just City," in Fine 1999, 297–308.

Bynum, C. 2001. *Metamorphosis and Identity* (New York: Zone Books).

Bywater, I. 1869. "On a Lost Dialogue of Aristotle," *Journal of Philosophy* 2: 55–69.

Calvino, I. [1963]/1985. *Mr. Palomar*, trans. W. Weaver (San Diego: Harcourt, Brace, and Co.); Originally published as *Palomar* (Torino: Giulio Einaudi Editore, 1983).

Campbell, M. B. 1988. *The Witness and the Other World: Exotic European Travel Writing, 400–1600* (Ithaca: Cornell University Press).

Carson, A. 1986. *Eros the Bittersweet. An Essay* (Princeton: Princeton University Press).

Carter, L. B. 1986. *The Quiet Athenian.* (Oxford: Clarendon Press).

Cartledge, P. 1985. "The Greek Religious Festivals," in Easterling and Muir 1985, 98–127.

    1998. *Democritus* (London: Phoenix).

Cartledge, P., P. Millet, and S. von Reden. 1998. *Kosmos: Essays on Order, Conflict and Community in Classical Athens* (Cambridge: Cambridge University Press).

Cherniss, H. F. 1944. *Aristotle's Criticism of Plato and the Academy I* (Baltimore: Johns Hopkins University Press).

    1950. Review of Festugière, *La Révélation d'Hermès Trismégiste. II. Le Dieu cosmique. Gnomon* 22: 204–16.

    1953. Review of G. Müller, *Nomoi. Gnomon* 25: 367–79.

    [1954]/1977. "The Sources of Evil According to Plato," *PAPS* 98 (1954), repr. in Cherniss 1977, 253–60.

    [1957]/1965. "The Relation of the *Timaeus* to Plato's Later Dialogues," *American Journal of Philology* 78 , repr. in Allen 1965, 339–78.

    1965, "The Philosophical Economy of the Theory of Ideas," *American Journal of Philology* 57 (1936), 445–56, repr. in Allen 1965, 1–12.

    1977. *Selected Papers*, ed. L. Tarán (Leiden: E. J. Brill).

Christ, M. R. 1990. "Liturgy Avoidance and *Antidosis* in Classical Athens," *Transactions of the American Philological Association* 120: 147–69.

Chroust, A.-H. 1973. *Aristotle*, vol. II, *Observations on Some of Aristotle's Lost Works* (Notre Dame: University of Notre Dame Press).

Clarke, K. 1999. *Between Geography and History* (Oxford: Clarendon Press).

Clay, D. 1985. "The Art of Glaukos (Plato *Phaedo* 108d4–9)," *American Journal of Philology* 106: 230–6.

    1988. "Reading the *Republic*," in Griswold 1988/2002, 19–33.

    1992a. "The World of Hesiod," *Ramus* 21: 131–55.

    1992b. "Plato's First Words," in T. Cole and F. Dunn, edd., *Beginnings in Greek Literature* (*Yale Classical Studies* 29) (Cambridge: Cambridge University Press), 113–29.

    1994. "The Origins of the Socratic Dialogue," in P. A. Vander Waerdt, ed., *The Socratic Movement* (Ithaca: Cornell University Press), 23–47.

    2000. *Platonic Questions: Dialogues with the Silent Philosopher* (University Park, PA: Pennsylvania University Press).

Clay, D. and A. Purvis. 1999. *Four Island Utopias* (Newburyport, Mass.).

Clifford, J. 1997. *Routes: Travel and Translation in the late Twentieth Century* (Cambridge, MA: Harvard University Press).

Clinton, K. 1993. "The Sanctuary of Demeter and Kore at Eleusis," in Marinatos and Hägg 1993, 110–24.

Cohen, E. E. 1992. *Athenian Economy and Society. A Banking Perspective* (Princeton: Princeton University Press).

Cohen, E. 1992. "Pilgrimage and Tourism: Convergence and Divergence," in Morinis 1992, 47–61.

Cole, T. 1991. *The Origins of Rhetoric in Ancient Greece* (Baltimore: Johns Hopkins University Press).

Coleman, S. and J. Elsner. 1995. *Pilgrimage Past and Present: Sacred Travel and Sacred Space in the World Religions* (London: British Museum Press).

Connor, W. R. [1971]/1992. *The New Politicians of Fifth-Century Athens* (repr. Indianapolis: Hackett).

1987. "Tribes, Festivals, and Processions: Civic Ceremonial and Political Manipulation in Archaic Greece," *Journal of Hellenic Studies* 107: 40–50.

1988. "'Sacred' and 'Secular'," *Ancient Society* 19: 161–88.

1989. "City Dionysia and Athenian Democracy," *Classica et Mediaevalia* 40: 7–32.

1993. "The *Histor* in History," in R. M. Rosen and J. Farrell, edd., *Nomodeiktes. Greek Studies in Honor of Martin Ostwald* (Ann Arbor: University of Michigan Press), 3–15.

1994. "The Problem of Athenian Civic Identity," in Boegehold and Scafuro 1994, 34–44.

Cooke, E. 1999. "The Moral and Intellectual Development of the Philosopher in Plato's *Republic*," *Ancient Philosophy* 19: 37–44.

Cooper, J. M. 1975. *Reason and Human Good in Aristotle* (Harvard: Harvard University Press).

1982. "Aristotle on Natural Teleology," in M. Schofield and M. Nussbaum, edd., *Language and Logos: Studies in Ancient Philosophy presented to G. E. L. Owen* (Cambridge: Cambridge University Press), 197–222.

1987. "Hypothetical Necessity and Natural Teleology," in Gotthelf and Lennox 1987, 243–74.

[1987]/1999. "Contemplation and Happiness: A Reconsideration," *Synthese* 72: 187–216; reprinted in Cooper 1999, ch. 9.

1999. *Reason and Emotion: Essays on Ancient Moral Psychology and Ethical Theory* (Princeton: Princeton University Press).

Couprie, D. R., R. Hahn, and G. Naddaf. 2003. *Anaximander in Context: New Studies in the Origins of Greek Philosophy* (Albany: State University of New York Press).

Cornford, F. M. [1937]/1952. *Plato's Cosmology* (repr. London: Routledge and Kegal Paul).

1965. "Mathematics and Dialectic in the *Republic*," in Allen 1965, 61–95.

Crary, J. 1999. *Techniques of the Observer* (Cambridge, Mass.: MIT Press).

Crombie, I. M. 1963. *An Examination of Plato's Doctrines* vol. II. (London: Routledge and Kegan Paul).

1964. *Plato: The Midwife's Apprentice* (London: Routledge and Kegan Paul).

Cross, R. C. 1965. "Logos and Forms in Plato," in Allen 1965, 13–31.

Crowther, N. B. 1985. "Male 'Beauty' Contests in Greece: The *Euandria* and *Euexia*," *Antiquité Classique* 54: 285–91.

Cunningham, J. V. 1951. *Woe or Wonder: The Emotional Effect of Shakespearean Tragedy* (Denver: The University of Denver Press).

Damasio, A. R. [1994]/2000. *Descartes' Error: Emotion, Reason, and the Human Brain* (repr. New York: Quill).

Daston, L. and K. Park. 1998. *Wonders and the Order of Nature 1150–1750* (New York: Zone Books).

Davies, J. K. 1981. *Wealth and the Power of Wealth in Classical Athens.* (New York: Arno Press).

Defourny, M. 1972. "Die Kontemplation in der aristotelischen Ethik" in Hager, F. ed., *Ethik und Politik des Aristoteles* (Darmstadt: Wissenshaftliche Buchsgesellshaft), 219–34.

Demont, P. 1993a. "Le Loisir (σχολή) dans la *Politique* d'Aristote," in P. Aubenque, ed., *Aristote Politique: Études sur la Politique d'Aristote* (Paris), 209–30.

1993b. "Die *Epideixis* über die *Techne* im V. und IV. Jh.," in W. Kullmann and J. Althoff, edd., *Vermittlung und Tradierung von Wissen in der griechischen Kultur* (Tübingen: Press Universitaires de France), 181–209.

Demos, R. 1968. "Plato's Doctrine of the Psyche as a Self-Moving Motion," *Journal of the History of Philosophy* 6: 133–45.

Depew, D. J. 1991. "Politics, Music and Contemplation in Aristotle's Ideal State," in D. Keyt and F. D. Miller, Jr. edd., *A Companion to Aristotle's* Politics (Oxford: B. Blackwell), 346–80.

De Filippo, J. G. 1994. "Aristotle's Identification of the Prime Mover as God," *Classical Quarterly* 44: 393–409.

1995. "The 'Thinking of Thinking' in *Metaphysics* Λ.9," *Journal of the History of Philosophy* 33: 543–62.

Derrida, J. 1978. "Violence and Metaphysics: An Essay on the Thought of Emmanuael Levinas," *Writing and Difference* (Chicago: University of Chicago Press).

Des Places, E. 1931. "Sur l'authenticité de l'*Epinomis*," *Revue des Études Grecques* 44: 153–66.

1937. "La Portée religieuse de l'*Epinomis*," *Revue des Études Grecques* 50: 321–8.

1942. "Une Nouvelle défense de l'*Epinomis*," *L'Antiquité Classique* 11: 97–102.

1952. "L'Authenticité des *Lois* et de l'*Epinomis*," *L'Antiquité Classique* 21: 376–83.

ed. 1956. *Epinomis. Platon. Oeuvres Complètes* Tome XII, 2e partie. (Paris: Les Belles Lettres).

Detienne, M. [1981]/1986. *The Creation of Mythology*, trans. M. Cook (Chicago: University of Chicago Press); originally published as *L'Invention de la mythologie* (Paris: Gallimard).

1996. *The Masters of Truth in Ancient Greece*, trans. J. Lloyd (New York: Zone Books).

Detienne, M. and J.-P. Vernant. 1991. *Cunning Intelligence in Greek Culture and Society*, trans. J. Lloyd (Chicago: University of Chicago Press).

Dicks, D. R. 1970. *Early Greek Astronomy to Aristotle* (Ithaca: Cornell University Press).

Diels, H. 1952. *Die Fragmente der Vorsokratiker* 6th ed., revised with editions and index by W. Kranz (Berlin: Weidmannsche Buchhandlung).

Dihle, A. 1962. "Herodot und die Sophistik," *Philologus* 106: 207–20.

Dillon, M. 1997. *Pilgrims and Pilgrimage in Ancient Greece* (London: Routledge).

Dorter, K. 2001. "Philosopher-Rulers: How Contemplation becomes Action," *Ancient Philosophy* 21: 335–56.

Dougherty, C. and L. Kurke. 1993. *Cultural Poetics in Archaic Greece* (Cambridge: Cambridge University Press).

Dover, K., ed. 1980. *Plato: Symposium* (Cambridge: Cambridge University Press).

Dunne, J. 1993. *Back to the Rough Ground: Practical Judgment and the Lure of Technique* (Notre Dame: University of Notre Dame Press).

Düring, I. 1943. *Aristotle's De Partibus Animalium*, critical and literary commentary (Güteborg: Elanders Boktryckeri Aktiebolag).

    1960. "Aristotle on Ultimate Principles from 'Nature and Reality': *Protrepticus* fr. 13," in Düring and Owen 1960, 35–55.

    1961. *Aristotle's Protrepticus* (Göteborg: Almquist and Wiksells).

Düring, I. and G. E. L. Owen, edd. 1960. *Aristotle and Plato in the Mid-Fourth Century* (Göteborg: Almquist and Wiksell).

Durkheim, E. [1912]/1964. *The Elementary Forms of the Religious Life*, trans. J. Swain (London: Allen and Unwin).

Dyson, M. 1974. "Some Problems concerning Knowledge in Plato's *Charmides*," *Phronesis* 19: 102–11.

Eade, J. and M. J. Sallnow. 1991. *Contesting the Sacred: The Anthropology of Christian Pilgrimage* (London: Routledge).

Easterling, H. J. 1967. "Causation in the *Timaeus* and *Laws* X," *Eranos* 65: 25–38.

Easterling, P. E. and J. V. Muir, edd. 1985. *Greek Religion and Society* (Cambridge: Cambridge University Press).

Edmunds, L. and R. W. Wallace., edd. 1997. *Poet, Public, and Performance in Ancient Greece* (Baltimore: Johns Hopkins University Press).

Einarson, B. 1936. "Aristotle's *Protrepticus* and the Structure of the *Epinomis*," *Transactions of the American Philological Association* 67: 261–85.

    1958. "A New Edition of the *Epinomis*: Review Article," *Classical Philology* 53: 91–9.

Elsner, J. 1992. "Pausanias: A Greek Pilgrim in the Roman World," *Past and Present* 135: 3–29.

    1994. "The Viewer and the Vision: The Case of the Sinai Apse," *Art History* 17: 81–102.

    1997. "Hagiographic Geography: Travel and Allegory in the *Life of Apollonius of Tyana*," *Journal of Hellenic Studies* 117: 22–37.

    1998. "Performing Pilgrimage: Walsingham and the Ritual Construction of Irony," in F. Hughes-Freeland, ed., *Ritual, Performance, Media* (London: Routledge), 46–65.

2000. "Between Mimesis and Divine Power: Visuality in the Greco-Roman World," in R. Nelson, ed., *Visuality Before and Beyond the Renaissance* (Cambridge: Cambridge University Press), 45–69.

2001. "Structuring 'Greece': Pausanias' *Periegesis* as a Literary Construct," in S. Alcock, J. Cherry and J. Elsner, edd., *Pausanias: Travel and Memory in Roman Greece* (Oxford: Oxford University Press), 3–20.

forthcoming. "Piety and Passion: Contest and Consensus in the Audiences for Early Christian Pilgrimage," in Elsner and Rutherford forthcoming.

Elsner, J. and I. Rutherford, edd. forthcoming. *Seeing the Gods: Patterns of Pilgrimage in Antiquity* (Oxford: Oxford University Press).

Eriksen, T. B. 1976. *Bios Theoretikos* (Oslo: Lie & Co.).

Euben, P. 1990. *The Tragedy of Political Theory* (Princeton: Princeton University Press).

Eucken, C. 1983. *Isokrates. Seine Positionen in der Auseinandersetzung mit den zeitgenössischen Philosophen.* (Berlin).

Everson, S. 1997. *Aristotle on Perception* (Oxford: Clarendon Press).

Faraguna, M. 1992. *Atene nell'età di Alessandro* (Rome).

Fehling, D. 1989. *Herodotus and his Sources. Citation, Invention, and Narrative Art*, trans. J. G. Howie (Liverpool: Francis Cairns).

Ferrari, G. R. F. 1984. "Orality and Literacy in the Origin of Philosophy," *Ancient Philosophy* 4: 194–205.

1987. *Listening to the Cicadas: A Study of Plato's Phaedrus* (Cambridge: Cambridge University Press).

1989. "Plato and Poetry," in G. Kennedy, ed., *The Cambridge History of Literary Criticism* vol. 1 (Cambridge: Cambridge University Press), 92–148.

Festugière, A.-J. 1947. "L'*Epinomis* et l'introduction des cultes étrangers à Athènes," *Coniectanea Neotestamentica* 11: 66–74.

1948. "La Religion de Platon dans l'*Epinomis*," *Bulletin de la Société Française de Philosophie* 42: 33–48.

1949. *La Révélation d'Hermès Trismégiste. II. Le Dieu Cosmique*, par le R. P. Festugière (Paris: Gatalda).

1950. *Contemplation et Vie Contemplative selon Platon* (Paris: J. Vrin).

Field, G. C. 1930. *Plato and his Contemporaries.* (New York: E. P. Dutton).

Fine, G., ed. 1999. *Plato 2: Ethics, Politics, Religion, and the Soul* (Oxford: Oxford University Press).

Finley, M. I. [Finkelstein] 1935. "Ἔμπορος, ναύκληρος, and κάπηλος: A Prolegomena to the Study of Athenian Trade," *Classical Philology* 30: 320–36.

1952. *Studies in Land and Credit in Ancient Athens, 500–200 BC* (New Brunswick: Rutgers University Press).

1962. "Athenian Demagogues," *Past and Present* 21: 3–24.

1970. "Aristotle and Economic Analysis," *Past and Present* 47: 3–25.

1981. *Economy and Society in Ancient Greece*, edd. B. D. Shaw and R. P. Saller (London: Routledge).

1985. *The Ancient Economy* 2nd ed. (Berkeley: University of California Press).

Flowers, M. A. 1994. *Theopompus of Chios. History and Rhetoric in the Fourth Century BC* (Oxford: Clarendon Press).

Foley, H. 1993. "Tragedy and Politics in Aristophanes' *Acharnians*," in Scodel 1993, 119–38.

1998. "'The Mother of the Argument': *Eros* and the Body in Sappho and Plato's *Phaedrus*," in M. Wyck, ed., *Parchments of Gender: Deciphering the Bodies of Antiquity* (Oxford: Clarendon Press), 39–70.

2000. "The Comic Body in Greek Art and Drama," in B. Cohen, ed., *Not the Classical Ideal: Athens and the Construction of the Other in Greek Art* (Leiden: Brill), 275–311.

2003. *Female Acts in Greek Tragedy* (Princeton: Princeton University Press).

Ford, A. 1993. "The Price of Art in Isocrates: Formalism and the Escape from Politics," in T. Poulakos, ed., *Rethinking the History of Rhetoric* (Boulder: University of Colorado Press), 31–52.

2002. *The Origins of Criticism: Literary Culture and Poetic Theory in Classical Greece* (Princeton: Princeton University Press).

Foster, H., ed. 1988. *Vision and Visuality* (New York: The New Press).

Fowler, R. L. 1996. "Herodotos and his Contemporaries," *Journal of Hellenic Studies* 116: 62–87.

Frede, M. 1992. "Plato's Arguments and the Dialogue Form," *Oxford Studies in Ancient Philosophy* supplementary volume (Oxford: Oxford University Press), 201–20.

Frede, M. and D. Charles, edd. 2000. *Aristotle's Metaphysics Lambda: Symposium Aristotelicum* (Oxford: Clarendon Press).

Friedländer, P. 1958. *Plato: An Introduction*, trans. H. Meyerhoff (New York: Harper and Rowe).

Fritz, K. von. 1936. "Herodotus and the Growth of Historiography," *Transactions of the American Philological Association* 67: 315–40.

Furley, D. J. [1973]/1989. "Notes on Parmenides," repr. in Furley 1989, 27–37.

1987. *The Greek Cosmologists* vol. 1 (Cambridge: Cambridge University Press).

1989. *Cosmic Problems: Essays on Greek and Roman Philosophy of Nature* (Cambridge: Cambridge University Press).

Furley. D. J. and R. E. Allen, edd. 1970. *Studies in Presocratic Philosophy* vol. 1 (London: Routledge and Kegan Paul).

Furth, M. 1987. "Aristotle's Biological Universe: An Overview," in Gotthelf and Lennox 1987, 21–52.

Gabrielsen, V. 1986. "Φανερά and ἀφανὴς οὐσία in Classical Athens," *Classica et Mediaevalia* 37: 99–114.

1987. "The *Antidosis* Procedure in Classical Athens," *Classica et Mediaevalia* 38: 7–38.

Gadamer, H.-G. 1928. "Der aristotelische *Protreptikos* und die entwicklungsgeschichtliche Betrachtung der aristotelischen Ethik," *Hermes* 2: 138–64.

[1960]/1990. *Truth and Method*, 2nd revised ed., trans. J. Weinsheimer and D. Marshall (New York: Crossroads Publishing Corporation). Originally published as *Wahrheit und Methode* (Tübingen).

1980. "Idea and Reality in Plato's *Timaeus*," in his *Dialogue and Dialectic: Eight Hermeneutical Studies on Plato*, trans. P. Smith (New Haven: Yale University Press), 156–93.

Gallop, D. [1975]/1988. *Plato: Phaedo*, trans. with notes (repr. Oxford: Clarendon Press).

Garland, R. 1992. *Introducing New Gods: The Politics of Athenian Religion* (Ithaca: Cornell University Press).

Gauthier, R. A. and J. Y. Jolif. 1970. *L'Éthique à Nicomaque*, 2nd ed., 3 vols. (Louvain and Paris: Publications Universitaires).

Geertz, C. 1973. *The Interpretation of Cultures* (New York: Basic Books).

Gentzler, J., ed. 1998. *Method in Ancient Philosophy* (Oxford: Clarendon Press).

Gernet, L. [1968]/1981. *The Anthropology of Ancient Greece*, trans. J. Hamilton and B. Nagy (Baltimore: Johns Hopkins University Press). First published as *Anthropologie de la Grèce antique* (Paris: F. Maspero).

Gerson, L. P., ed. 1996. *The Cambridge Companion to Plotinus* (Cambridge: Cambridge University Press).

Gigon, O. 1973. "Theorie und Praxis bei Platon und Aristoteles," *Museum Helveticum* 30: 65–87.

Gill, C. 1993. "Plato on Falsehood – not Fiction," in C. Gill and T. P. Wiseman, edd., *Lies and Fiction in the Ancient World* (Exeter: University of Exeter Press), 38–87.

1996. *Personality in Greek Epic, Tragedy, and Philosophy* (Oxford: Clarendon Press).

Gill, M. L. 1971. "Matter and Flux in Plato's *Timaeus*," *Phronesis* 32: 34–53.

Glotz, G. [1926]/1987. *Ancient Greece at Work* (repr. Hildesheim).

Goldhill, S. 1990. "The Great Dionysia and Civic Ideology," in Winkler and Zeitlin 1990, 97–129.

1991. *The Poet's Voice. Essays on Poetics and Greek Literature* (Cambridge: Cambridge University Press).

1994. "Representing Democracy: Women at the Dionysia," in Osborne and Hornblower 1994, 347–70.

1996. "Refracting Classical Vision: Changing Cultures of Viewing," in Brennan and Jay 1996, 15–28.

1997. "The Audience of Athenian Tragedy," in P. E. Easterling, ed., *The Cambridge Companion to Greek Tragedy* (Cambridge: Cambridge University Press), 54–68.

1999a. "Programme Notes," in Goldhill and Osborne 1999, 1–29.

1999b. "Literary History without Literature: Reading Practices in the Ancient World," *Substance* 88: 57–89.

Goldhill, S. and R. Osborne, edd. 1994. *Art and Text in Ancient Greek Culture* (Cambridge: Cambridge University Press).

Goldhill, S. and R. Osborne, edd. 1999. *Performance Culture and Athenian Democracy* (Cambridge: Cambridge University Press).

Goldhill, S. and S. von Reden, 1999. "Plato and the Performance of Dialogue," in Goldhill and Osborne 1999, 257–89.

Goody, J. and I. P. Watt. 1968. *Literacy in Traditional Societies* (Cambridge: Cambridge University Press).

Gotthelf, A. 1987. "Aristotle's Conception of Final Causality," in Gotthelf and Lennox 1987, 204–42.

1989. "The Place of the Good in Aristotle's Natural Theology," *Proceedings of the Boston Area Colloquium in Ancient Philosophy* 4: 113–39.

Gotthelf, A. and J. G. Lennox. 1987. *Philosophical Issues in Aristotle's Biology* (Cambridge: Cambridge University Press).

Gottschalk, H. B. 1980. *Heraclides of Pontus* (Oxford: Clarendon Press).

Gregoric, P. 2001. "The Heraclitus Anecdote: *De Partibus Animalium* I 5.645a17–23," *Ancient Philosophy* 21: 73–85.

Green, T. H. and T. H. Grose, edd. 1889. *David Hume. Essays: Moral, Political and Literary*, 2 vols. (London: Longman's Green).

Griswold, C. L., Jr. 1981. "The Ideas and the Criticism of Poetry in Plato's *Republic*, Book 10," *Journal of the History of Philosophy* 19: 135–50.

[1986]/1996. *Self-Knowledge in Plato's* Phaedrus (New Haven: Yale University Press, reprinted by Penn State University Press).

1988. "Plato's Metaphilosophy: Why Plato Wrote Dialogues," in Griswold [1988]/2002, ch. 9.

ed. [1988]/2002. *Platonic Writings/Platonic Readings* repr., with new Preface and Bibliography (University Park, Pennsylvania: Pennsylvania State University Press).

1999a. *Adam Smith and the Virtues of Enlightenment* (Cambridge: Cambridge University Press).

1999b. "Platonic Liberalism: Self-Perfection as a Foundation of Political Theory," in J. M. Van Ophuijsen, ed., *Plato and Platonism* (Washington, D. C: Catholic University of America Press), 102–34.

2000. "Irony in the Platonic Dialogues," in D. Conway and P. Kerszberg, edd., *The Sovereignty of Construction* (The Netherlands: Rodopi Press), 1–23.

2002. "Plato and the Problem of Chronology" (Commentary on Charles Kahn's "On Platonic Chronology"), in Annas and Rowe 2002, 129–44.

2003. "Longing for the Best: Plato on Reconciliation with Imperfection," *Arion* 11: 101–36.

Guthrie, W. K. C. 1955. "Plato's View on the Nature of the Soul," *Fondation Hardt* 3: 2–22.

1962. *A History of Greek Philosophy*, vol. I. *The Earlier Presocratics and the Pythagoreans* (Cambridge: Cambridge University Press).

1965. *A History of Greek Philosophy*, vol. II. The *Presocratic Tradition from Parmenides to Democritus* (Cambridge: Cambridge University Press).

1971. *Socrates* (Cambridge: Cambridge University Press).

1975. *A History of Greek Philosophy*, vol. IV. *Plato, the Man and His Dialogues: Earlier Period* (Cambridge: Cambridge University Press).

1978. *A History of Greek Philosophy* vol. V. *The Later Plato and the Academy* (Cambridge: Cambridge University Press).

1981. *A History of Greek Philosophy*, vol. VI. *Aristotle* (Cambridge: Cambridge University Press).

Hackforth, R. 1936. "Plato's Theism," *Classical Quarterly* 30: 4–9.

1952. *Plato's Phaedrus* (Cambridge: Cambridge University Press).

[1955]/1972. *Plato's Phaedo* (repr. Cambridge: Cambridge University Press).

Hadot, P. 1983. "Physique et poésie dans le *Timée* de Platon," *Revue de Théologie et de Philosophie* 115: 113–33.

1995. *Philosophy as a Way of Life*, trans. M. Chase (Oxford: Blackwell).

Hahn, R. 1992. "What did Thales Want to be When he Grew up? or, Re-appraising the Roles of Engineering and Technology on the Origin of Early Greek Philosophy/ Science," in B. P. Hendley, ed., *Plato, Time, and Education. Essays in Honor of Robert S. Brumbaugh* (Albany: State University of New York Press), 107–29.

Haldane E. and G. R. T. Ross. trans. 1978. *The Philosophical Work of Descartes*, vol. 1 (Cambridge: Cambridge University Press repr.).

Halliwell, S. 1984. "Plato and Aristotle on the Denial of Tragedy," *Proceedings of the Cambridge Philological Society* n.s. 30: 50–8.

2002. *The Aesthetics of Mimesis: Ancient Texts and Modern Problems* (Princeton: Princeton University Press).

Hankinson, R. J. 1995. "Philosophy of Science," in Barnes 1995a, ch. 4.

Hardie, W. F. R. 1980. *Aristotle's Ethical Theory*. 2nd ed. (Oxford: Clarendon Press).

Hare, R. M. 1965. "Plato and the Mathematicians," in R. Bambrough, ed., *New Essays on Plato and Aristotle* (New York: The Humanities Press), 21–38.

Harley, J. B. and D. Woodward., edd., 1987. *The History of Cartography*, vol. 1 (Chicago: University of Chicago Press).

Harris, W. V. 1989. *Ancient Literacy* (Cambridge, Mass.: Harvard University Press).

Harrison, T. 2000. *Divinity and History: The Religion of Herodotus* (Oxford: Clarendon Press).

Hartog, F. 2001. *Memories of Odysseus: Frontier Tales from Ancient Greece*, trans. J. Lloyd (Chicago: University of Chicago Press).

Hattaway, M. 1978. "Francis Bacon and 'Knowledge Broken': Limits for Scientific Method," *Journal of the History of Ideas* 39: 183–97.

Havelock, E. A. 1963. *Preface to Plato* (Cambridge, Mass.: Belknap Press).

1983a. "The Socratic Problem: Some Second Thoughts," in J. P. Anton and A. Preus, edd., *Essays in Ancient Greek Philosophy*, vol. 11 (Albany), 147–73.

1983b. "The Linguistic Task of the Presocratics," in K. Robb, ed., *Language and Thought in Early Greek Philosophy* (La Salle, Illinois: Hegeler Institute) 7–82.

Heath, T. [1913]/1981. *Aristarchus of Samos: The Ancient Copernicus* (repr. New York: Dover Publications).

Heidegger, M. [1937–8]/1994. *Basic Questions of Philosophy*, trans. R. Rojcewicz and A. Schuwer (Bloomington: Indiana University Press).

[1924–5]/1997. *Plato's Sophist*, trans. R. Rojcewicz and A. Schuwer (Bloomington: Indiana University Press).

[1935]/2000. *An Introduction to Metaphysics*, trans. G. Fried and R. Polt (New Haven: Yale University Press).

Heidel, W. A. [1896]/1976. *Pseudo-Platonica* (New York: Arno Press).

Heinaman, R. 1988. "Eudaimonia and Self-Sufficiency in the *Nicomachean Ethics*," *Phronesis* 33: 31–53.

1996. "Activity and *Praxis* in Aristotle," *Proceedings of the Boston Area Colloquium in Ancient Philosophy* 12: 71–111.

Helms, M. W. 1988. *Ulysses' Sail: An Ethnographic Odyssey of Power, Knowledge and Geographical Distance* (Princeton: Princeton University Press).

Henderson, J. 1990. "The *Dēmos* and Comic Competition," in Winkler and Zeitlin 1990, 271–313.

1991. "Women and the Athenian Dramatic Festivals," *Transactions of the American Philological Association*. 121: 133–47.

Hepburn, R. W. 1984. *"Wonder" and Other Essays* (Edinburgh: Edinburgh University Press).

Herman, G. 1987. *Ritualized Friendship and the Greek City* (Cambridge: Cambridge University Press).

Herter, H. 1957. "Bewegung der Materie bei Platon," *Rheinisches Museum für Philologie* 100: 327–47.

1958. "Gott und die Welt bei Platon (Eine Studie zum Mythos des *Politikos*)," *Bonner Jahrbücher* 158: 106–17.

Hicks, R. D. [1907]/1988. *Aristotle: De Anima* (repr. Salem, New Hampshire: Ayer Company Publishers).

Hintikka, J. 1973. *Time and Necessity: Studies in Aristotle's Theory of Modality* (Oxford: Clarendon Press).

1974. *Knowledge and the Known: Historical Perspectives in Epistemology* (Dordrecht-Holland/Boston USA: D. Reidel).

Hoorn, W. van. 1972. *As Images Unwind. Ancient and Modern Theories of Visual Perception* (Amsterdam: University Press of Amsterdam).

Hoffleit, H. 1937. "An un-Platonic Theory of Evil in Plato," *Americal Journal of Philology* 58: 45–58.

Humphreys, S. C. 1978. *Anthropology and the Greeks* (London: Routledge and Kegan Paul).

1983. *The Family, Women, and Death: Comparative Studies* (London: Routledge and Kegan Paul).

1985. "Social Relations on Stage: Witnesses in Classical Athens," *History and Anthropology* 1: 313–69.

Irwin, T. H. 1977. *Plato's Moral Theory: The Early and Middle Dialogues* (Oxford: Clarendon Press).

1985. *Aristotle: Nicomachean Ethics*, trans. with notes and commentary (Indianapolis: Hackett).

1986. "Coercion and Objectivity in Plato's Dialectic," *Révue Internationale de Philosophie* 40: 49–74.

1995. *Plato's Ethics* (New York: Oxford University Press).

Jaeger, W. 1939–44. *Paideia: The Ideals of Greek Culture*. 3 vols., trans. G. Highet (Oxford: Oxford University Press).

[1923]/1948. *Aristotle: Fundamentals of the History of his Development*, 2nd ed., trans. R. Robinson (Oxford: Clarendon Press), originally published as

Aristoteles, Grundlegung einer Geschichte seiner Entwicklung (Berlin: Weidmannsche Buchhandlung).

Jameson, M. H. 1988. "Sacrifice and Ritual: Greece," in M. Grant and R. Kitzinger, edd., *Civilization of the Ancient Mediterranean: Greece and Rome* II (New York: Scribners), 959–79.

1990. "Private Space in the Greek City," in O. Murray and S. Price, edd., *The Greek City from Homer to Alexander* (Oxford: Clarendon Press), 169–93.

1994. "Theoxenia," in R. Hägg, ed., *Ancient Greek Cult Practice from the Epigraphical Evidence* (Swedish Institute at Athens; ActaAth-80, 13, Stockholm), 35–57.

1997. "Religion and the Athenian Democracy," in I. Morris and K. Raaflaub, edd., *Democracy 2500? Questions and Challenges* (Dubuque, Iowa: Kendall/Hunt Pub. Co.), 171–95.

1999. "The Spectacular and the Obscure in Greek Religion," in Goldhill and Osborne 1999, 321–40.

Jay, M. 1993. *Downcast Eyes: The Denigration of Vision in Twentieth-Century French Thought* (Berkeley: University of California Press).

Jha, M., ed. 1985. *Dimensions of Pilgrimage: An Anthropological Appraisal* (New Delhi: Inter-India Publications).

Joachim, H. H. 1951. *Aristotle: The Nicomachean Ethics*, commentary by Joachim, ed. D. A. Rees (Oxford: Clarendon Press).

Joly, R. 1956. *Le Thème philosophique des genres de vie dans l'antiquité classique* (Brussels: Palais des Académies).

Jonas, H. 1966. "The Nobility of Sight: A Study in the Phenomenology of the Senses," in *The Phenomenon of Life: Toward a Philosophical Biology* (New York: Harper and Rowe), ch. 1.

Jouanna, J. 1984. "Rhétorique et médecine dans la Collection Hippocratique," *Revue des Études Gracques* 97: 26–44.

1988. *Hippocrate. Des vents – De l'art* (Tome V, 1re partie), texte et traduction (Paris: Belles Letters).

1990. *Hippocrate. L'Ancienne médicine* (Tome II, 1re partie), texte et traduction (Paris: Belles Lettres).

[1992]/1999. *Hippocrates*, trans. M. B. DeBevoise (Baltimore: Johns Hopkins University Press). (Translation of *Hippocrate*, Paris: Fayard 1992).

1996. *Hippocrate. Airs, eaux, lieux* (Tome II, 2e partie), texte et traduction (Paris: Belles Letters).

Kahn, C. H. 1979. *The Art and Thought of Heraclitus* (Cambridge: Cambridge University Press).

1981. "The Role of *Nous* in the Cognition of the First Principles in *Posterior Analytics* II 19," in Berti 1981, 385–414.

1983. "Philosophy and the Written Word: Some Thoughts on Heraclitus and the Early Uses of Prose," in Robb 1983a, 110–24.

1987. "The Place of the Prime Mover in Aristotle's Teleology," in A. Gotthelf, ed., *Aristotle on Nature and Living Things: Philosophical and Historical Studies*

Presented to David M. Balme on his Seventieth Birthday (Pittsburgh: Mathesis Publications, Inc.), 183–205.

1992. "Aristotle on Thinking," in Nussbaum and Rorty 1992, 359–79.

1996. *Plato and the Socratic Dialogue: The Philosophical Use of a Literary Form* (Cambridge: Cambridge University Press).

2001. *Pythagoras and the Pythagoreans* (Indianapolis: Hackett).

Kapp, E. 1938. "Theorie und Praxis bei Aristoteles und Platon," *Mnemosyne* 3rd series, vol. vi: 178–191.

Kavoulaki, A. 1999, "Processional Performance of Dialogue," in Goldhill and Osborne 1999, 293–320.

Kenny, A. 1963. *Actions, Emotions and Will* (London: Routledge and Kegan Paul).

1978. *The Aristotelian Ethics* (Oxford: Clarendon Press).

Ker, J. 2000. "Solon's *Theôria* and the End of the City," *Classical Antiquity* 19: 304–29.

Kerferd, G. B. 1981. *The Sophistic Movement* (Cambridge: Cambridge University Press).

Keyt, D. 1978. "Intellectualism in Aristotle," in *Paideia* (Special Aristotle Issue): 138–57.

Kingsley, P. 1995. *Ancient Philosophy, Mystery, and Magic: Empedocles and the Pythagorean Tradition* (Oxford: Clarendon Press).

Kirk, G. S., J. E. Raven, and M. Schofield, edd. 1983. *The Presocratic Philosophers*, 2nd ed. (Cambridge: Cambridge University Press).

Kokolakis, M. 1992. "Intellectual Activity on the Fringes of the Games," in W. Coulson and H. Kyrieleis, edd., *Proceedings of an International Symposium on the Olympic Games* (Athens: Lucy Braggiotti), 153–8.

Koller, H. 1957. "Theōros und Theōria," *Glotta* 36: 273–87.

Konstan, D. 1995. *Greek Comedy and Ideology* (New York: Oxford University Press).

2001. *Pity Transformed* (London: Duckworth).

Kosman, A. 1973. "Understanding, Explanation, and Insight in the *Posterior Analytics*," in E. Lee, A. Mourelatos, and R. Rorty, edd., *Exegesis and Argument: Studies in Greek Philosophy presented to Gregory Vlastos* (*Phronesis* supplementary vol. i), 374–92.

1975. "Perceiving That we Perceive: *On the Soul* iii, 2," *Philosophical Review* 84: 499–519.

1992. "What does the Maker Mind Make?," in Nussbaum and Rorty 1992, 343–58.

Kraut, R. 1989. *Aristotle on the Human Good* (Princeton: Princeton University Press).

1991. "Return to the Cave: *Republic* 519–521," *Proceedings of the Boston Area Colloquium for Ancient Philosophy* 7: 43–62.

1997. *Aristotle: Politics books VII and VIII* (Oxford: Clarendon Press).

Kung, J. 1989. "Mathematics and Virtue in Plato's *Timaeus*," in J. P. Anton and A. Preus, edd., *Essays in Ancient Greek Philosophy* (New York: State University of New York Press), 309–39.

Kurke, L. 1991. *The Traffic in Praise: Pindar and the Poetics of Social Economy* (Ithaca: Cornell University Press).

1993, "The Economy of Kudos," in Dougherty and Kurke 1993, 131–63.

Laird, A. 1999. *Powers of Expresson, Expressions of Power: Speech Presentation and Latin Literature* (Oxford: Oxford University Press).

Laks, A. 2000. "*Metaphysics* Δ 7," in Frede and Charles 2000, 207–43.

Lateiner, D. 1986. "The Empirical Element in the Methods of Early Greek Medical Writers and Herodotus: A Shared Epistemological Response," *Antichthon* 20: 1–20.

1989. *The Historical Method of Herodotus* (Toronto: University of Toronto Press).

Lear, J. 1988. *Aristotle: The Desire to Understand* (Cambridge: Cambridge University Press).

1998a. *Open Minded: Working out the Logic of the Soul* (Cambridge, Mass.: Harvard University Press).

1998b "Eros and Unknowing: The Psychoanalytic Significance of Plato's *Symposium*," in Lear 1998a, ch. 7.

2000. *Happiness, Death, and the Remainder of Life* (Cambridge, Mass.: Harvard University Press).

forthcoming. "The Efficacy of Myth in Plato's *Republic*," *Proceedings of the Boston Area Colloquium in Ancient Philosophy*.

Lee, E. N. 1966. "On the Metaphysics of the Image in Plato's *Timaeus*," *Monist* 50: 341–68.

1976. "Reason and Rotation: Circular Movement as the Model of Mind (*Nous*) in Later Plato," in W. H. Werkmeister, ed., *Facets of Plato's Philosophy* (*Phronesis* supplementary volume II), 70–102.

Lesher, J. H. 1999. "Early Interest in Knowledge," in Long 1999a, ch. 11.

Levin, D. M. 1988. *The Opening of Vision: Nihilism and the Postmodern Situation* (New York: Routledge).

ed. 1993a. *Modernity and the Hegemony of Vision* (Berkeley: University of California Press).

1993b. "Decline and Fall: Ocularcentrism in Heidegger's Reading of the History of Metaphysics," in Levin 1993a, ch. 6.

Lévy, E. 1979. "L'Artisan dans la *Politique* d'Aristote," *Ktema* 4: 31–46.

Lewis, D. M. and R. Stroud. 1979. "Athens Honors King Evagoras of Salamis," *Hesperia* 48: 180–93.

Lilla, M. 2001. *The Reckless Mind: Intellectuals in Politics* (New York: New York Review of Books).

Lindberg, D. 1976. *Theories of Vision from Al-Kindi to Kepler* (Chicago: University of Chicago Press).

Lloyd, A. C. 1969. "Non-Discursive Thought – An Enigma of Greek Philosophy," *Proceedings of the Aristotelian Society* 70: 261–74.

1986. "Non-Propositional Thought in Plotinus," *Phronesis* 31: 258–65.

Lloyd, G. 1993. *Being in Time. Selves and Narrators in Philosophy and Literature* (London: Routledge).

Lloyd, G. E. R. 1966. *Polarity and Analogy: Two Types of Argumentation in Early Greek Thought* (Cambridge: Cambridge University Press).

1979. *Magic, Reason, and Experience: Studies in the Origins and Development of Early Greek Science* (Cambridge: Cambridge University Press).

1987. *The Revolutions of Wisdom: Studies in the Claims and Practice of Ancient Greek Science* (Cambridge: Cambridge University Press).

1990. *Demystifying Mentalities* (Cambridge: Cambridge University Press).

1996. *Aristotelian Explorations* (Cambridge: Cambridge University Press).

Long, A. A. [1988]/1996. "Socrates in Hellenistic Philosophy," *Classical Quarterly* 38: 150–71. Reprinted in Long 1996, 1–34.

1992. "Finding Oneself in Greek Philosophy," *UIT Tijdschrift voor Filosofie* 2: 255–79.

1996. *Stoic Studies* (Cambridge: Cambridge University Press).

1998. "Plato's Apologies and Socrates in the *Theaetetus*," in Gentzler 1998, ch. 5.

ed. 1999a. *The Cambridge Companion to Early Greek Philosophy* (Cambridge: Cambridge University Press).

1999b. "The Scope of Early Greek Philosophy," in Long 1999a, ch. 1.

2000. "Platonic Ethics," *Oxford Studies in Ancient Philosophy* 19: 339–57.

2001. "Ancient Philosophy's Hardest Question: What to Make of Oneself?" *Representations* 74: 19–36.

2002. *Epictetus: A Stoic and Socratic Guide to Life* (Oxford: Clarendon Press).

Longo, O. 1990. "The Theater of the Polis," in Winkler and Zeitlin 1990, 12–19.

Longrigg, J. 1993. *Greek Rational Medicine. Philosophy and Medicine from Alcmaeon to the Alexandrians* (London: Routledge).

Loraux, N. 1989. "Therefore, Socrates is Immortal," in *Fragments for a History of the Human Body* pt. 2, edd. M. Feher, with R. Naddaff and N. Tazi (New York), pp. 12–45.

Lord, C. 1982. *Education and Culture in the Political Thought of Aristotle* (Ithaca: Cornell University Press).

Lynch, J. P. 1972. *Aristotle's School: A Study of a Greek Educational Institution* (Berkeley: University of California Press).

Lyons, J. 1963. *Structural Semantics: An Analysis of Part of the Vocabulary of Plato* (Oxford: Basil Blackwell).

MacDowell, D. M. 1978. *The Law in Classical Athens* (Ithaca: Cornell University Press).

Mansfeld, J. 1990. *Studies in the Historiography of Greek Philosophy* (Assen: Van Gorcum).

Mansion, A. 1958. "Philosophie prèmiere, philosophie seconde et métaphysique chez Aristote,' *Revue Philosophique de Louvain*: 165–221.

Mansion, S. 1960. "Contemplation and Action in Aristotle's *Protrepticus*," in Düring and Owen 1960, 56–75.

Marinatos, N. 1993, "What were Greek Sanctuaries? A Synthesis," in Marinatos and Hägg 1993, 228–33.

Marinatos, N. and R. Hägg, edd. 1993. *Greek Sanctuaries: New Approaches* (London: Routledge).

Marrou, H. I. 1956. *A History of Education in Antiquity*, trans. G. Lamb. (New York: Sheed and Ward).

Martin, A. and O. Primavesi. 1998. *L'Empédocle de Strasbourg* (Berlin: de Gruyter).

Martin, R. 1993. "The Seven Sages as Performers of Wisdom," in C. Dougherty and L. Kurke, edd., *Cultural Poetics in Archaic Greece* (Cambridge: Cambridge University Press), 108–28.

  1996. "The Scythian Accent: Anacharsis and the Cynics," in R. B. Branham and M.-O. Goulet-Cazé, edd., *The Cynics: The Cynic Movement in Antiquity and its Legacy* (Berkeley: University of California Press), 136–55.

Mattéi, J.-F. 1988. "The Theater of Myth in Plato," in Griswold 1988, 66–83.

Matthews, G. B. 1999. *Socratic Perplexity and the Nature of Philosophy* (Oxford: Oxford University Press).

Maurizio, L. 1998. "The Panathenaic Procession: Athens' Participatory Democracy on Display?" in Boedeker and Raaflaub 1998, 297–318.

McCabe, M. M. 1992. "Myth, Allegory and Argument in Plato," in A. Barker and M. Warner, edd., *The Language of the Cave* (*Apeiron* vol. xxv) (Edmonton, Alberta: Academic Printing and Publishing), 47–68.

  1994. *Plato's Individuals* (Princeton: Princeton University Press).

  2000. *Plato and his Predecessors: The Dramatisation of Reason* (New York: Cambridge University Press).

McNeill, W. 1999. *The Glance of the Eye: Heidegger, Aristotle, and the Ends of Theory* (Albany: State University of New York Press).

Meiggs, R. and D. Lewis, edd. 1969. *A Selection of Greek Historical Inscriptions to the End of the Fifth Century BC* (Oxford: Clarendon Press).

Meldrum, M. 1950. "Plato and the "ARXH KAKVH," *Journal of Hellenic Studies* 70: 65–74.

Mikalson, J. D. 1983. *Athenian Popular Religion* (Chapel Hill: University of North Carolina Press).

Miller, M. 1985. "Platonic Provocations: Reflections on the Soul and the Good in the *Republic*," in O'Meara 1985, 163–93.

Millett, P. 1983. "Maritime Loans and the Structure of Credit in Fourth-century Athens," in P. Garnsey, K. Hopkins and C. R. Whittaker, edd., *Trade in the Ancient Economy* (Berkeley: University of California Press), 36–52.

  1990. "Sale, Credit and Exchange in Athenian Law and Society," in P. Cartledge, P. Millet, and S. Todd, edd., *Nomos. Essays in Athenian Law, Politics and Society* (Cambridge: Cambridge University Press), 167–94.

  1991. *Lending and Borrowing in Ancient Athens* (Cambridge: Cambridge University Press).

  1998. "Encounters in the Agora," in Cartledge, Millet, and von Reden 1998, 203–28.

Mitchell, L. G. 1997. *Greeks Bearing Gifts: The Public Use of Private Relationships in the Greek World 435–323 BC* (Cambridge: Cambridge University Press).

Mohr, R. D. 1978. "The Formation of the Cosmos in the *Statesman* Myth," *Phoenix* 32: 250–72.

[1978]/1985. "Plato's Final Thoughts on Evil: *Laws*, 899–905," *Mind* 87: 572–5, repr. in Mohr 1985, 184–8.

1980. "Image, Flux, and Space in Plato's *Timaeus*," *Phoenix* 34: 138–52.

[1981]/1985. "Disorderly Motion in the *Statesman*," *Phoenix* 35 (1981), repr. in Mohr 1985, 141–57.

1985. *The Platonic Cosmology* (Leiden: E. J. Brill).

Moline, J. 1983. "Contemplation and the Human Good," *Nous* 17: 37–53.

Momigliano, A. 1975. *Alien Wisdom: The Limits of Hellenization* (Cambridge: Cambridge University Press).

Monoson, S. S. 2000. *Plato's Democratic Entanglements: Athenian Politics and the Practice of Philosophy* (Princeton: Princeton University Press).

Montiglio, S. 2000. "Wandering Philosophers in Classical Greece," *Journal of Hellenic Studies* 120: 86–105.

Moreau, J. 1939. *L'Âme du monde de Platon aux Stoiciens* (Paris: Société d'Édition "Les Belles Lettres").

Morgan, C. 1990. *Athletes and Oracles* (Cambridge: Cambridge University Press).

1993. "The Origins of Pan-Hellenism," in Marinatos and Hägg 1993, 18–44.

Morgan, K. 1994. "Socrates and Gorgias at Delphi and Olympia: *Phaedrus* 235d6–236b4," *Classical Quarterly* 44: 375–86.

1998. "Designer History: Plato's Atlantis Story and Fourth-century Ideology," *Journal of Hellenic Studies* 118: 101–18.

2000. *Myth and Philosophy from the Presocratics to Plato* (Cambridge: Cambridge University Press).

Morgan, M. 1990. *Platonic Piety: Philosophy and Ritual in Fourth-century Athens* (New Haven: Yale University Press).

Morinis, E. A. 1984. *Pilgrimage in the Hindu Tradition: A Case Study of West Bengal* (Delhi: Oxford University Press).

ed. 1992. *Sacred Journeys: The Anthropology of Pilgrimage* (New York Greenwood Press).

Morrow, G. R. 1948. "Plato and the Law of Nature," in Milton R. Konvitz and Arthur E. Murphy, edd., *Essays in Political Theory presented to George H. Sabine* (Ithaca: Cornell University Press), 17–44.

[1950]/1965. "Necessity and Persuasion in Plato's *Timaeus*," *Philosophical Review* 59, repr. in Allen 1965, 421–37.

1953. "Plato's Concept of Persuasion," *Philosophical Review* 62: 234–50.

1960a. *Plato's Cretan City: A Historical Interpretation of the* Laws (Princeton: Princeton University Press).

1960b. "The Nocturnal Council in Plato's *Laws*," *Archiv für Geschichte der Philosophie* 42: 229–46.

Morson, G. S. 1981. *The Boundaries of Genre. Dostoevsky's Diary of a Writer and the Traditions of Literary Utopia* (Austin: University of Texas Press).

Mossé, C. [1966]/1969. *The Ancient World at Work*, trans. J. Lloyd (New York: Norton). First published as *La Travail en Grèce et à Rome* (Paris: La Decouverte).

Most, G. W. 1992. "New Fragments of Aristotle's *Protrepticus?*" in *Studi su Codici e Papiri Filosofici: Platone, Aristotele, Ierocle* (Firenze: Leo S. Olschki), 189–211.

1999. "The Poetics of Early Greek Philosophy," in Long 1999, ch. 16.

Mourelatos, A. P. D. 1980. "Plato's 'Real Astronomy': *Republic* VII.527d–531d," in Anton 1980, 33–74.

1981. "Astronomy and Kinematics in Plato's Project of Rationalist Explanation," *Studies in the History and Philosophy of Science* 12: 1–21.

Mueller, I. 1980. "Ascending to Problems: Astronomy and Harmonics in *Republic* VII," in Anton 1980, 103–21.

1992. "Mathematical Knowledge and Philosophical Truth," in R. Kraut, ed., *The Cambridge Companion to Plato* (Cambridge: Cambridge University Press), 170–99.

1998. "Platonism and the Study of Nature (*Phaedo* 95eff)," in Gentzler 1998, 67–89.

Muller, R. 1993. "La Logique de la liberté dans la *Politique*," in P. Aubenque, ed., *Aristote Politique: Études sur la Politique d'Aristote* (Paris: Presses Universitaires de France), 185–208.

Mylonas, G. 1961. *Eleusis and the Eleusinian Mysteries* (Princeton: Princeton University Press).

Nagel, T. 1986. *The View from Nowhere* (New York: Oxford University Press).

Nagy, G. 1990. *Pindar's Homer: The Lyric Possession of an Epic Past* (Baltimore: Johns Hopkins University Press).

Nails, D. 1995. *Agora, Academy, and the Conduct of Philosophy* (Dordrecht: Kluwer Academic Publishers).

Nehamas, A. 1985. *Nietzsche: Life as Literature* (Cambridge: Harvard University Press).

1990. "Eristic, Antilogic, Sophistic, Dialectic: Plato's Demarcation of Philosophy from Sophistry," *History of Philosophy Quarterly* 7: 3–16.

1999a. *The Art of Living: Socratic Reflections from Plato to Foucault* (Berkeley: University of California Press).

1999b. *Virtues of Authenticity. Essays on Plato and Socrates* (Princeton: Princeton University Press).

2000a. "The Place of Beauty and the Role of Value in the World of Art," *Critical Quarterly* 42: 1–14.

2000b. "The Return of the Beautiful: Morality, Pleasure, and the Value of Uncertainty," *The Journal of Aesthetics and Art Criticism* 58: 393–403.

Neils, J. 1992. *Goddess and Polis: The Panathenaic Festival in Ancient Athens* (Princeton: Princeton University Press).

Nichols, M. P. 1992. *Citizens and Statesmen. A Study of Aristotle's Politics* (Savage, Maryland: Rowman and Littlefield).

Nicolet, C. 1991. *Space, Geography, and Politics in the Early Roman Empire* (Ann Arbor: University of Michigan Press).

Nietzsche, F. [1887]/1989. *The Genealogy of Morals*, trans. W. Kaufmann (New York: Random House).

[1887]/1974. *The Gay Science*, trans. W. Kaufmann (New York: Random House).

Nightingale, A. W. 1993. "Writing/Reading a Sacred Text: A Literary Interpretation of Plato's *Laws*," *Classical Philology* 88: 279–300.

1995. *Genres in Dialogue: Plato and the Construct of Philosophy* (Cambridge: Cambridge University Press).

1996a. "Plato on the Origins of Evil: The *Statesman* Myth Reconsidered," *Ancient Philosophy* 16: 65–91.

1996b. "Aristotle on the 'Liberal' and 'Illiberal' Arts," *Proceedings of The Boston Area Colloquium in Ancient Philosophy* 12: 29–58, 69–70.

1999a. "Plato's Lawcode in Context: Rule by Written Law in Athens and Magnesia," *Classical Quarterly* 49: 100–22.

1999b. "Historiography and Cosmology in Plato's *Laws*," *Ancient Philosophy* 19: 1–28.

2000. "Sages, Sophists, and Philosophers: Greek Wisdom Literature," in O. Taplin, ed., *Literature in the Greek and Roman Worlds: A New Perspective* (Oxford: Oxford University Press), 156–91.

2001. "Liberal Education in Plato's *Republic* and Aristotle's *Politics*," in Yun Lee Too ed., *Education in Greek and Roman Antiquity* (Leiden: E. J. Brill), 133–73.

2002a. "Towards an Ecological Eschatology: Plato and Bakhtin on Other Worlds and Times," in B. Branham, ed., *Bakhtin and the Classics* (Evanston, Iu.: Northwestern University Press), 220–49.

2002b. "Distant Views: Realistic and Fantastic Mimesis in Plato," in Annas and Rowe 2002, 227–47.

Nussbaum, M. C. 1986. *The Fragility of Goodness: Luck and Ethics in Greek Tragedy and Philosophy* (Princeton: Princeton University Press).

Nussbaum, M. and H. Putnam. 1992. "Changing Aristotle's Mind," in Nussbaum and Rorty 1992, ch. 3.

Nussbaum, M. and A. Rorty, edd. 1992. *Essays on Aristotle's De Anima* (Oxford: Clarendon Press).

Ober, J. 1989. *Mass and Elite in Democratic Athens* (Princeton: Princeton University Press).

1998. *Political Dissent in Democratic Athens* (Princeton: Princeton University Press).

Ober, J. and B. Strauss. 1990. "Drama, Rhetoric, and the Discourse of Athenian Democracy," in Winkler and Zeitlin 1990, 237–70.

O'Meara, D. J., ed. 1985. *Platonic Investigations (Studies in Philosophy and the History of Philosophy* vol. XIII) (Washington, D.C.: Catholic University of America Press).

Ooteghem, J. van 1932. "Démosthène et le *théōrikon*," *Les Études Classiques* 1: 388–407.

Osborne, R. 1991. "Pride and Prejudice, Sense and Subsistence: Exchange and Society in the Greek City," in J. Rich and A. Wallace-Hadrill, edd., *City and Country in the Ancient World* (London: Routledge), 119–45.

1993. "Competitive Festivals and the Polis: A Context for Dramatic Festivals at Athens," in A. H. Sommerstein, S. Halliwell, J. Henderson, and B. Zimmermann, edd., *Tragedy, Comedy and the Polis* (Bari: Levance Editori), 21–38.

1994a. "Archaeology, the Salaminioi, and the Politics of Sacred Space in Archaic Attica," in Alcock and Osborne 1994, 143–60.

1994b. "Looking On – Greek Style. Does the Sculpted Girl Speak to Women Too?" in I. Morris, ed., *Classical Greece: Ancient History and Modern Archaeologies* (Cambridge: Cambridge University Press), 81–96.

Osborne, R. and S. Hornblower, edd. 1994. *Ritual, Finance, Politics: Athenian Democratic Accounts* (Oxford: Clarendon Press).

Ostwald, M. 1992. "Athens as a Cultural Centre," in D. M. Lewis et al., edd., *The Cambridge Ancient History*, vol. v (Cambridge: Cambridge University Press), 306–69.

O'Sullivan, N. 1996. "Written and Spoken in the First Sophistic," in Worthington 1996, 115–27.

O'Sullivan, P. 2000. "Satyr and Image in Aeschylus' *Theoroi*," Classical Quarterly 50: 353–66.

Owen, G. E. L. [1953]/1965 "The Place of the *Timaeus* in Plato's Dialogues," *Classical Quarterly* n. s. 3, repr. in Allen 1965, 313–38.

1960. "Logic and Metaphysics in some Earlier Works of Aristotle," in I. Düring and G. E. L. Owen, edd., *Aristotle and Plato in the Mid-Fourth Century* (Göteborg: Elanders Boktryckeri Aktiebolag), 163–90.

1965. "Aristotle on the Snares of Ontology," in R. Bambrough, ed., *New Essays on Plato and Aristotle* (London: Routledge and Kegan Paul), 69–95.

Parke, H. W. 1977. *Festivals of the Athenians* (Ithaca: Cornell University Press).

Parker, F. 1984. "Contemplation in Aristotle's Ethics," in R. Porrecco, ed., *The Georgetown Symposium on Ethics* (Lanham, MD: University Press of America), 205–12.

Paterson, R. 1986. *Image and Reality in Plato's metaphysics* (Indianapolis: Hacketts).

Pellegrin, P. 1986. *Aristotle's Classification of Animals: Biology and the Conceptual Unity of the Aristotelian Corpus*, trans. A. Preus (Berkeley: University of California Press).

Pelling, C., ed. 1997. *Greek Tragedy and the Historian* (Oxford: Clarendon Press).

Peperzac, A. T. 1997. *Platonic Transformations with and after Hegel, Heidegger, and Levinas* (Lanham: Rowman and Littlefield).

Peponi, A.-E. 2002. "Mixed Pleasures, Blended Discourses: Poetry, Medicine, and the Body in Plato's *Philebus* 46–47c," *Classical Antiquity* 21: 135–60.

forthcoming. "Initiating the Viewer: Deixis and Visual Perception in Alcman's Lyric Drama," *Arethusa* 2004.

Pickard-Cambridge, A. W. 1962. *Dithyramb, Tragedy, and Comedy* 2nd ed., revised by T. B. L. Webster (Oxford: Clarendon Press).

1968. *The Dramatic Festivals of Athens*, 2nd ed., revised by J. Gould and D. M. Lewis (Oxford: Clarendon Press).

Pippin, R. B. 1997. *Idealism as Modernism: Hegelian Variations* (Cambridge: Cambridge University Press).

Podlecki, A. 1990. "Could Women Attend the Theater in Ancient Athens?" *Ancient World* 21: 27–43.

Polanyi, K. 1957. "Aristotle Discovers the Economy," in K. Polanyi, C. M. Arensberg, and H. W. Pearson, edd., *Trade and Market in the Early Empires: Economies in History and Theory* (Glencoe, Ill.: Free Press), 64–94.

Polignac, F. de. 1995. *Cults, Territory, and the Origins of the Greek City-State*, trans. J. Lloyd (Chicago: University of Chicago Press).

Popper, K. R. 1992. "How the Moon Might Shed some of her Light upon the Two Ways of Parmenides," *Classical Quarterly* 42: 12–19.

Prier, R. A. 1989. *Thauma Idesthai: Sight and Appearance in Archaic Greek* (Tallahasee: Florida State University Press).

Raaflaub, K. A. 1983. "Democracy, Oligarchy, and the Concept of the 'Free Citizen' in Late Fifth-century Athens," *Political Theory* 11: 517–44.

Rabinowitz, W. G. 1957. *Aristotle's Protrepticus and the Sources of its Reconstruction* (Berkeley: University of California Press).

Rackham, H. 1934. *Aristotle: The Nicomachean Ethics* (Cambridge, Mass.: Harvard University Press).

Rappe, S. 1996. "Self-Knowledge and Subjectivity in the *Enneads*," in Gerson 1996, 250–74.

Rausch, H. 1982. *Theoria: Von ihrer sakralen zur philosophischen Bedeutung* (Munich: Fink).

Redfield, J. 1985. "Herodotus the Tourist," *Classical Philology* 80: 97–118.

Reeve, C. D. C. 1988. *Philosopher-Kings: The Argument of Plato's Republic* (Princeton: Princeton University Press).

1989. *Socrates in the* Apology (Indianapolis: Hackett).

1992. *Practices of Reason: Aristotle's Nicomachean Ethics* (Oxford: Oxford University Press).

2000. *Subskantial Knowledge: Aristotle's* Metaphysics (Indianapolis: Hackett).

Rehm, R. 1992. *Greek Tragic Theater* (New York: Routledge).

2002. *The Play of Space: Spatial Transformation in Greek Tragedy* (Princeton: Princeton University Press).

Rhodes, P. J. 1972. *The Athenian Boule* (Oxford: Clarendon Press).

Riceour, P. 1984. *Time and Narrative*, 3 vols., trans. K. Mclaughlin and D. Pellauer (Chicago: University of Chicago Press).

Riedweg, C. 1987. *Mysterienterminologie bei Platon, Philo, und Klemens von Alexandria* (Berlin).

Robb, K., ed. 1983a. *Language and Thought in Early Greek Philosophy* (La Salle, Ill.: The Hegeler Institute).

1983b. "Preliterate Ages and the Linguistic Art of Heraclitus," in Robb 1983a, 153–206.

Robins, I. 1995. "Mathematics and the Conversion of the Mind: *Republic* VII 522c1–531e3," *Ancient Philosophy* 15: 359–91.

Robinson, R. 1941. *Plato's Earlier Dialectic* (Ithaca: Cornell University Press).

Robinson, T. M. 1970. *Plato's Psychology* (Toronto: University of Toronto Press).

1984. *Contrasting Arguments. An Edition of the Dissoi Logoi* (repr. Salem, New Hampshire: Cornell University Press).

Romm, J. S. 1992. *The Edges of the Earth in Ancient Thought* (Princeton: Princeton University Press).

Ronchi, V. 1957. *Optics: The Science of Vision*, trans. E. Rosen (New York: Dover Publications).

1975. *The Nature of Light: An Historical Survey*, trans. V. Barocas (London: Heinemann).

Roochnik, D. 1996. *Of Art and Wisdom: Plato's Understanding of Techne* (University Park, PA: Pennsylvania State University Press).

Rorty, A. O. 1980. "The Place of Contemplation in Aristotle's *Nicomachean Ethics*," in A. O. Rorty, ed., *Essays on Aristotle's Ethics* (Berkeley: University of California Press), 377–94.

Rorty, R. 1979. *Philosophy and the Mirror of Nature* (Princeton: Princeton University Press).

Rosen, S. 1957. "Wonder, Anxiety and Eros," *Giornale di Metafisica* 6: 645–56.

1959. "Curiosity, Anxiety, Wonder," *Giornale di Metafisica* 4: 465–74.

1988. *The Quarrel between Philosophy and Poetry: Studies in Ancient Thought* (New York: Routledge).

Ross W. D. [1924]/1981. *Aristotle's Metaphysics*, 2 vols. (repr. Oxford: Clarendon Press).

[1936]/1955. *Aristotle's Physics* (repr. Oxford: Clarendon Press).

[1949]/1966. *Aristotle*, 5th ed. (London: Methuen).

1951. *Plato's Theory of Ideas* (Oxford).

1961. *Aristotle: De Anima* (Oxford).

Rössler, D. 1981. "Handwerker," in E. C. Welskopf, ed., *Untersuchungen ausgewählter altgriechischer sozialer Typenbegriffe (Sociale Typenbegriffe im alten Griechenland und ihr Fortleben in den Sprachen der Welt*, vol. III) (Berlin: Akademie-Verlag), 193–268.

Rostovtzeff, M. 1941. *The Social and Economic History of the Hellenistic World* I (Oxford: Clarendon Press).

Rowe, C. J. 1977. "Aims and Methods in Aristotle's *Politics*," *Classical Quarterly* 27: 159–72.

1986. "The Argument and Structure of Plato's *Phaedrus*," *Proceedings of the Cambridge Philological Society* 32: 106–25.

1987. "Platonic Irony," *Nova Tellus* 7: 83–101.

1991. "Philosophy and Literature: The Arguments of Plato's *Phaedo*," *Boston Area Colloquium in Ancient Philosophy* 7: 159–81.

1993. *Plato: Phaedo* (Cambridge: Cambridge University Press).

1999. "Myth, History, and Dialectic in Plato's *Republic* and *Timaeus-Critias*," in R. Buxton, ed., *From Myth to Reason? Studies in the Development of Greek Thought* (Oxford: Oxford University Press), 263–78.

Rue, R. 1993. "The Philosopher in Flight: The Digression (172c–177c) in the *Theaetetus*," *Oxford Studies in Ancient Philosophy* 10: 71–100.

Ruschenbusch, E. 1979. "Die Einführung des Theorikon," *Zeitschrift für Papyrolgie und Epigraphik* 36: 303–8.

Rutherford, I. 1995. "Theoric Crisis: The Dangers of Pilgrimage in Greek Religion and Society," *Studi e materiali di storia delle religioni* 61: 276–92.

1998. "Theoria as Theatre: The Pigrimage Theme in Greek Drama," in *Papers of the Leeds International Latin Seminar* 10: 131–56.

2000. "*Theoria* and *Darsan*: Pilgrimage and Vision in Greece and India," *Classical Quarterly* 50: 133–46.

2003. "Χορὸς Εἷς Ἐκ Τῆσδε Τῆς Πόλεως: Song-Dance and State Pilgrimage at Athens," in P. Wilson and P. Murray, edd., *Music and the Muses: the Culture of Mousike in the Classical Athenian City* (Oxford: Oxford University Press).

forthcoming. *State Pilgrimage in Antiquity* (Cambridge: Cambridge University Press).

Rutter, N. K. and B. A. Sparkes, edd. 2000. *Word and Image in Ancient Greece* (Edinburgh: Edinburgh University Press).

Saïd, S. 1998. "Tragedy and Politics," in Boedeker and Raaflaub 1998, 275–96.

Sartre, M. 1979. "Aspects économiques et religieux de la frontière dans les cités grecques," *Ktema* 4: 213–24.

Saunders, T. J. 1962. "The Structure of the Soul and the State in Plato's *Laws*," *Eranos* 60: 37–55.

1970. *Plato, the Laws* (Harmondsworth: Penguin Books Ltd.).

1973. "Penology and Eschatology in Plato's *Timaeus* and *Laws*," *Classical Quarterly* 23: 232–44.

Scarry, E. 1999. *On Beauty and Being Just* (Princeton: Princeton University Press).

Schaerer, R. 1939. "Sur l'origine de l'âme et le problème du mal dans le platonisme," *Revue de Théologie et de Philosophie* 27: 62–72.

Schiappa, E. 1991. *Protagoras and Logos. A Study in Greek Philosophy and Rhetoric* (Columbia, South Carolina: University of South Carolina Press).

Schofield, M. 1980. *An Essay on Anaxagoras* (Cambridge: Cambridge University Press).

1999. *Saving the City: Philosopher-Kings and Other Classical Paradigms* (London: Routledge).

Scodel, R., ed. 1993. *Theater and Society in the Classical World* (Ann Arbor: University of Michigan Press).

Scott, D. 1995. *Recollection and Experience: Plato's Theory of Learning and its Successors* (Cambridge: Cambridge University Press).

Sedley, D. 1989. "Teleology and Myth in the *Phaedo*," *Proceedings of the Boston Area Colloquium in Ancient Philosophy* 5: 359–83.

1999a. "The Idea of Godlikeness," in Fine 1999, 309–28.

1999b. "Parmenides and Melissus," in Long 1999a, ch. 6.

Silverman, A. 1989. "Color and Color-Perception in Aristotle's *De Anima*," *Ancient Philosophy* 9: 271–92.

1992. "Timaean Particulars," *Classical Quarterly* 42: 87–111.

Simon, G. 1988. *Le Regard, l'être et l'apparence dans l'Optique de l'Antiquité* (Paris: Seuil).

Skemp, J. B. 1942. *The Theory of Motion in Plato's Later Dialogues* (Cambridge: Cambridge University Press).

1952. *Plato's Statesman* (London: Routledge).

Snell, B. 1951. *Theorie und Praxis im Denken des Abendlandes* (Hamburg: Universität Hamburg).

Solmsen, F. 1936. "The Background of Plato's Theology," *Transactions of the American Philological Association* 67: 208–18.

1942. *Plato's Theology* (Ithaca: Cornell University Press).

[1963]/1968. "Nature as Craftsman in Greek Thought," *Journal of the History of Ideas* 24 (1963), repr. in Solmsen 1968a, 332–55.

1968a. *Kleine Schriften* (Hildesheim: Goerg Olms).

1968b. "Leisure and Play in Aristotle's Ideal State," in Solmsen 1968a, 1–28.

Sommerstein, A. 1997. "The Theatre Audience, the *Demos*, and the *Suppliants* of Aeschylus," in Pelling 1997, 63–79.

Sommerstein, A., S., Halliwell, J. Henderson, and B. Zimmerman, edd., 1993. *Tragedy, Comedy and the Polis* (Bari: Levante).

Sorabji, R. 1974. "Body and Soul in Aristotle," *Philosophy* 49: 63–89.

1982. "Myths About Non-Propositional Thought," in M. Nussbaum and M. Schofield, edd., *Language and Logos: Studies in Ancient Greek Philosophy presented to G. E. L. Owen* (Cambridge: Cambridge University Press), 295–314.

1992. "Intentionality and Physiological Processes: Aristotle's Theory of Sense-Perception," in Nussbaum and Rorty 1992, 195–226.

Sourvinou-Inwood, C. 1990. "What is *Polis* Religion?" in O. Murray and S. Price, edd., *The Greek City from Homer to Alexander* (Oxford: Clarendon Press), 295–322.

1994. "Something to do with Athens: Tragedy and Ritual," in Osborne and Hornblower 1994, 269–90.

Spedding, J. et al. 1863. *The Works of Francis Bacon*, vol. VI (Boston: Taggard and Thompson).

Ste. Croix, G. E. M. de. 1981. *Class Struggle in the Ancient Greek World* (Ithaca: Cornell University Press).

Steiner, D. T. 2001. *Images in Mind: Statues in Archaic and Classical Greek Literature and Thought* (Princeton: Princeton University Press).

Stigen, A. 1961. "On the Alleged Primacy of Sight – With Some Remarks on *Theoria* in Aristotle," *Symbolae Osloenses* 37: 15–44.

Szlezák, T. A. 1999. *Reading Plato*, trans. G. Zanker (London: Routledge).

Taplin, O. 1978. *Greek Tragedy in Action* (Berkeley: University of California Press).

1983. "Tragedy and Trugedy," *Classical Quarterly* 33: 331–3.

1986. "Fifth-century Tragedy and Comedy: A *Synkrisis*," *Journal of Hellenic Studies* 106: 163–74.

1993. *Comic Angels and other Approaches to Greek Drama through Vase Painting* (Oxford: Clarendon Press).

1999. "Spreading the Word through Performance," in Goldhill and Osborne 1999, 33–57.

ed. 2000. *Literature in the Greek and Roman Worlds* (Oxford: Oxford University Press).

Tarán, L. 1965. *Parmenides: a Text with Translation, Commentary and Critical Essays* (Princeton: Princeton University Press).

1971. "The Creation Myth in Plato's *Timaeus*," in J. P. Anton and G. L. Kustas, edd., *Essays in Ancient Greek Philosophy* (Albany: State University of New York Press), 372–407.

1975. *Academica: Plato, Philip of Opus, and the Pseudo-Platonic Epinomis* (Philadelphia: American Philosophical Society).

Tarrant, H. 1996. "Orality and Plato's Narrative Dialogues," in Worthington 1996, 129–47.

Tate, J. 1936. "On Plato's *Laws* x, 889c–d," *Classical Quarterly* 30: 48–54.

Taylor, A. E. 1921. "On the Authenticity of the *Epinomis*," *Logos* 4: 42–55.

1928. *A Commentary on Plato's Timaeus* (Oxford: Clarendon Press).

1929a. *Plato, the Man and his Work* (New York: L. MacVeagh, The Dial Press).

1929b. "Plato and the Authorship of the *Epinomis*," *Proceedings of the British Academy* 15: 235–317.

1934. *The Laws of Plato* (London: Dent and Sons Ltd.).

Thomas, R. 1989. *Oral Tradition and Written Record in Classical Athens* (Cambridge: Cambridge University Press).

1992. *Literacy and Orality in Ancient Greece* (Cambridge: Cambridge University Press).

1994. "Law and Lawgiver in the Athenian Democracy," in R. Osborne and S. Hornblower, edd., *Ritual, Finance, Politics* (Oxford: Clarendon Press), 119–34.

1996. "Written in Stone? Liberty, Equality, Orality and the Codification of Law," in L. Foxhall and A. Lewis, edd., *Greek Law in its Political Setting* (Oxford: Clarendon Press), 9–31.

2000. *Herodotus in Context* (Cambridge: Cambridge University Press).

Thompson, W. E. 1982. "The Athenian Entrepreneur," *L'Antiquité Classique* 51: 53–85.

Thoreau, H. D. 1983. *Walden and Civil Disobedience*, with an intro. by M. Meyer (New York: Penguin Books).

Too, Y. L. 1998. *The Idea of Ancient Literary Criticism* (Oxford: Clarendon Press).

ed. 2001. *Education in Greek and Roman Antiquity* (Leiden: E. J. Brill).

Turner, V. 1974a. "Pilgrimages as Social Processes," in *Dramas, Fields, and Metaphors: Symbolic Action in Human Society* (Ithaca: Cornell University Press).

1974b. "Pilgrimage and Communitas," *Studia Missionalia* 23: 305–27.

Turner, V. and E. Turner. 1978. *Image and Pilgrimage in Christian Culture: Anthropological Perspectives* (New York: Columbia University Press).

Überweg, F. [1871]/1891. *History of Philosophy*, vol. 1, trans. from the 4th German edition by G. S. Morris (New York: Scribner's).

Untersteiner, M. 1954. *The Sophists*, trans. K. Freeman (Oxford: Basil Blackwell).

Usener, S. 1994. *Isokrates, Platon und ihr Publikum: Hörer und Leser von Literatur im 4. Jahrhundert v. Chr.* (Tübingen: Narr).

Vegetti, M. 1999. "Culpability, Responsibility, Cause: Philosophy, Historiography, and Medicine in the Fifth Century," in Long 1999a, ch. 13.

Vernant, J.-P. [1965]/1983. *Myth and Thought Among the Greeks* (London: Routledge and Kegan Paul). First published as *Myth et Pensée chez Les Grecs* (Paris: La Decouverte).

    1989. "Dim Body, Dazzling Body," in *Fragments for a History of the History of the Human Body*, part 1, edd. M. Feher with R. Naddaff and N. Tazi (New York: Zone), 18–47.

    1991. *Mortals and Immortals*, ed. F. Zeitlin (Princeton: Princeton University Press).

Vidal-Naquet, P. [1981]/1986. *The Black Hunter. Forms of Thought and Forms of Society in the Greek World*, trans. A. Szegedy. Masrak (Baltimore: Johns Hopkins University Press). First published as *Le Chasseur noir: Formes de pensée et formes de société dans le monde grec* (Paris: Maspero).

Vlastos, G. [1939]/1965. "The Disorderly Motion in the *Timaeus*," *Classical Quarterly* 33, repr. in Allen 1965, 379–99.

    [1941]/1981. "Slavery in Plato's Thought," *Philosophical Review* 50, repr. in Vlastos 1981a, 147–63.

    1965. "Creation in the *Timaeus*: Is it a Fiction?" in Allen 1965, 401–19.

    1970. "Theology and Philosophy in Early Greek Thought," in Furley and Allen 1970, 92–129.

    1971a. "Reasons and Causes in the *Phaedo*," in Vlastos, ed., *Plato: A Collection of Critical Essays* vol. 1: *Metaphysics and Epistemology* (New York: Anchor Books), ch. 7.

    ed. 1971b. *The Philosophy of Socrates: A Collection of Critical Essays* (New York: Anchor Books).

    1975. *Plato's Universe* (Seattle: University of Washington Press).

    1978. "The Virtuous and the Happy," *Times Literary Supplement* 24, February, 230–3.

    1980. "The Role of Observation in Plato's Conception of Astronomy," in Anton 1980, 1–31.

    1981a. *Platonic Studies*, 2nd ed. (Princeton: Princeton University Press).

    1981b. "Slavery in Plato's Thought," in Vlastos 1981a, 147–63.

    1981c. "Degrees of Reality in Plato," in Vlastos 1981a, 58–75.

    1991. *Socrates, Ironist and Moral Philosopher* (Ithaca: Cornell University Press).

    1994. *Socratic Studies*, ed. M. Burnyeat (Cambridge: Cambridge University Press).

Volpi, F. 1999. "The Rehabilitation of Practical Philosophy and Neo-Aristotelianism," in Bartlett and Collins 1999, ch. 1.

Von Reden, S. 1995a. *Exchange in Ancient Greece* (London: Duckworth).

    1995b. "The Piraeus: A World Apart," *Greece and Rome* 42: 24–7.

Wallace, R. W. 1994. "Private Lives and Public Enemies: Freedom of Thought in Classical Athens," in A. L. Boegehold and A. C. Scafuro, edd., *Athenian Identity and Civic Ideology* (Baltimore: Johns Hopkins University Press), 127–55.

    1997. "Poet, Public, and 'Theatrocracy': Audience Performance in Classical Athens," in L. Edmunds and R. W. Wallace, edd., *Poet, Public, and*

Performance in Ancient Greece (Baltimore: Johns Hopkins University Press), 97–111.

1998. "The Sophists in Athens," in Boedeker and Raaflaub 1998, 203–20.

Wehrli, F. 1944. *Die Schule des Aristoteles*, vol. I *Dikaiarchos* (Basel: Benno Schwabe & Co.).

1953. *Die Schule des Aristoteles* vol. VII, *Herakleides Pontikos* (Basel: Benno Schwabe & Co.).

White, M. 1980. "Aristotle's Concept of Θεωρία and the Ἐνέργεια-Κίνησις Distinction," *Journal of the History of Philosophy* 18: 253–63.

White, N. P. 1976. *Plato on Knowledge and Reality* (Indianapolis: Hackett).

Whitehead, D. 1977. *The Ideology of the Athenian Metic* (Cambridge: Cambridge University Press).

Whiteman, W. P. D. and I. S. Ross, edd. 1982. *Adam Smith: Essays on Philosophical Subjects* (Indianapolis: Liberty Press).

Whiting, J. 1986. "Human Nature and Intellectualism in Aristotle," *Archiv für Geschichte der Philosophie* 68: 70–95.

Williams, B. 1993. *Shame and Necessity* (Berkeley: University of California Press).

1995. *Making Sense of Humanity, and Other Papers* (Cambridge: Cambridge University Press).

Wilson, P. 1997. "Leading the Tragic *Khoros*: Tragic Prestige in the Democratic City," in Pelling 1997, 81–108.

1999. "The *Aulos* in Athens," in Goldhill and Osborne 1999, 58–95.

2000. *The Athenian Institution of the Khoregia: The Chorus, the City, and the Stage* (Cambridge: Cambridge University Press).

Winkler, J. 1990. "The Ephebes Song: *Tragōidia* and *Polis*," in Winkler and Zeitlin 1990, 20–62.

Winkler, J. and F. Zeitlin. 1990. *Nothing to do with Dionysos? Athenian Drama in its Social Context* (Princeton: Princeton University Press).

Wohl, V. 1996. "Εὐσεβείας ἕνεκα καὶ φιλοτιμίας: Hegemony and Democracy at the Panathenaia," *Classica et Mediaevalia* 47: 25–88.

Wolin, S. S. 2001. *Tocqueville between Two Worlds: The Making of a Political and Theoretical Life* (Princeton: Princeton University Press).

Wood, E. M. 1989. *Peasant-Citizen and Slave. The Foundations of Athenian Democracy* (London: Verso).

Woodruff, P. 1982. "What could go Wrong with Inspiration? Why Plato's Poets Fail," in J. Moravcsik and P. Temko, edd., *Plato on Beauty, Wisdom and the Arts* (New Jersey: Rowman and Littlefield), 137–50.

1992. "Plato's Early Theory of Knowledge," in H. Benson, ed., *Essays on the Philosophy of Socrates* (New York: Oxford University Press), 86–106.

2001. *Reverence. Renewing a Forgotten Virtue* (New York: Oxford University Press).

Worthington, I., ed. 1996. *Voice into Text* (Leiden: E. J. Brill).

Yack, B. 1991. "A Reinterpretation of Aristotle's Political Teleology," *History of Political Thought* 12: 15–33.

Yunis, H. 1996. *Taming Democracy: Models of Political Rhetoric in Classical Athens* (Ithaca: Cornell University Press).

Zeitlin, F. 1990a. "Playing the Other: Theater, Theatricality, and the Feminine in Greek Drama," in Winkler and Zeitlin 1990, 63–96.

———. 1990b. "Thebes: Theater of Self and Society in Athenian Drama," in Winkler and Zeitlin 1990, 130–67.

Zeyl, D. 1975. "Plato and Talk of a World of Flux," *Harvard Studies in Classical Philology* 79: 125–48.

Index of passages cited

General index

Penelope's "journey"
The Odyssey, the Telemachy...but what does P. undergo to ready herself for the very real loss of O's non-return?

Undertaking would involve showing similar vocals; type scenes etc. — is P. modeling himself after the Odyss scenes?

[The homeless are in depiction of our societal aporia.

Made in the USA
Lexington, KY
22 November 2013